AN ILLUSTRATED ENCYCLOPEDIA OF
UNIFORMS OF THE GREEK WORLD

AN ILLUSTRATED ENCYCLOPEDIA OF UNIFORMS OF THE GREEK WORLD

A detailed study of the fighting men of Classical Greece and the Ancient World, including Sumerians, Assyrians, Hittites, Egyptians, Mycenaeans, Spartans, Persians and Macedonians

KEVIN F. KILEY
CONSULTANT: PROFESSOR GABRIELE ESPOSITO

LORENZ BOOKS

This edition is published by Lorenz Books
an imprint of Anness Publishing Ltd
info@anness.com
www.annesspublishing.com
© Anness Publishing Ltd 2025

All rights reserved. No part of this publication may be reproduced, stored in a retrieval system, or transmitted in any way or by any means, electronic, mechanical, photocopying, recording or otherwise, without the prior written permission of the copyright holder. A CIP catalogue record for this book is available from the British Library.

Although the information in this book is believed to reflect the latest academic thinking, ancient history is not an exact science and neither the authors nor the publisher can accept any legal responsibility or liability for any errors or omissions that may have been made.

Publisher: Joanna Lorenz
Editorial director: Helen Sudell
Illustrations: Simon Smith and Matthew Vince
Designer: Nigel Partridge
Maps: Richard Thomson
Editorial reader: Charles Phillips
Consultant: Professor Gabriele Esposito
Indexer: Philippa Jevons

This volume is dedicated, as always, to my lovely wife Daisy and to my son, Michael, who has embarked on his own writing career. I am most grateful to the editors, Joanna Lorenz, Helen Sudell and Joanne Rippin, without whose dedicated and professional assistance this book would never have seen the light of day.

Previous page: Alexander the Great and Darius III in the Battle of Gaugamela 331BCE, depicted by Pietro da Cortona in c.1640–50.

With thanks to the picture agencies AKG: 206; Alamy: 2, 10t, 99, 112, 169b; Bridgeman: 14t, 23t, 24, 25, 35, 62, 65, 67t, 69, 70b, 71t, 72t, 77, 78, 89, 91, 93, 102, 108, 110, 113, 114, 115b, 115t, 116b, 116t, 117b, 142, 151, 153, 164, 165, 167b, 168b, 168t, 169t, 171b, 176, 179, 184, 191, 193, 194, 197, 215b, 219b, 243, 244; Dreamstime: 10br; Fotosearch: 12bl, 13tr; Istock: 16t; Museum/Wikicommons: 7t, 9b, 9t, 10bl, 11b, 12t, 12br, 13, 14b, 15b, 15t, 16b, 17b, 17t, 18b, 18t, 19b, 19t, 20b, 20t, 21b, 21t, 22b, 22t, 23b, 27b, 28b, 29b, 29t, 30, 31b, 31tr, 47, 53, 55, 57, 58, 66, 67b, 68, 70t, 71b, 72b, 73, 81, 85, 88, 95, 117t, 118, 119, 129, 139, 166, 167t, 170, 171, 172, 188, 202, 203, 210, 213, 214, 215tl, 215tr, 216b, 216t, 218, 219br, 219t, 236, 249; Shutterstock: 6t, 7b, 8b, 8t, 11t, 27t, 28t, 30b, 31tl, 32, 37, 38, 64, 212, 246

CONTENTS

INTRODUCTION 6
TIMELINE OF THE ANCIENT WORLD 12
THE FERTILE CRESCENT 14
ANCIENT EGYPT 16
ANCIENT GREECE 18
ANCIENT PERSIA 20
ALEXANDER THE GREAT 22

ARMIES OF THE FERTILE CRESCENT 24
A SUCCESSION OF EMPIRES 26
TIMELINE OF THE FERTILE CRESCENT 30
THE SUMERIAN ARMY 32
THE HITTITE ARMY 36
THE BABYLONIAN ARMY 40
THE ASSYRIAN ARMIES 42
ARMS AND ARMOUR 60

ARMIES OF ANCIENT EGYPT 64
THE MIGHT OF ANCIENT EGYPT 66
EGYPT'S NEIGHBOURS AND ENEMIES 70
TIMELINE OF ANCIENT EGYPT 72
WARRIORS OF THE OLD KINGDOM 74
MIDDLE KINGDOM TROOPS 76
THE ARMY OF THE NEW KINGDOM 82
EGYPTIAN WAR CHARIOTS 90
EGYPT'S ENEMIES 96
THE EGYPTIAN NAVY 102
ARMS AND ARMOUR 108

ARMIES OF ANCENT GREECE	**112**
FROM THE MINOANS TO THE CITY-STATE	114
TIMELINE OF ANCIENT GREECE	118
THE MINOANS AND EARLY GREEKS	120
THE MYCENAEANS	122
THE RISE OF THE GREEK PHALANX	132
GREEKS AGAINST PERSIANS, AND THE BATTLE OF MARATHON	134
THE SPARTANS AND THERMOPYLAE	138
ARMIES AND NAVIES, AND THE SIEGE OF SYRACUSE	144
INTERNECINE WARFARE, GREEKS AND THRACIANS	146
IPHICRATES AND THE BATTLE OF LECHAEUM	148
THE THEBAN PHALANX, AND THE BATTLE OF LEUCTRA	150
NEIGHBOURS AND ENEMIES OF GREECE	152
NAVAL POWER AND THE BATTLE OF SALAMIS	158
ARMS AND ARMOUR	162
ARMIES OF THE PERSIAN EMPIRE	**164**
THE RISE AND FALL OF PERSIA	166
TIMELINE OF THE PERSIAN EMPIRE	170
ORGANIZATION OF THE PERSIAN EMPIRE AND ARMY	172
THE PERSIAN COMMAND AND ARMY ELITE	174
THE PERSIAN CAVALRY	182
THE PERSIAN LIGHT INFANTRY	188
GREEK MERCENARIES IN THE SERVICE OF PERSIA	194
NATIONAL CONTINGENTS IN A MULTICULTURAL ARMY	196
THE PERSIAN ARMY AGAINST ALEXANDER AND AFTER	200
THE PERSIAN NAVY	206
ARMS AND ARMOUR	210
ARMIES OF ALEXANDER	**212**
PHILIP II AND THE RISE OF MACEDONIA	214
ALEXANDER AND THE CONQUEST OF PERSIA	216
TIMELINE OF ALEXANDER'S EMPIRE	218
THE MACEDONIAN JUGGERNAUT	220
ELITE TROOPS – CAVALRY AND COMPANIONS	222
TRAINED INFANTRY – HYPASPISTS AND PHALANGITES	228
THE MACEDONIAN PHALANX	230
ALLIES AND ENEMIES – SCYTHIANS, PHRYGIANS AND PARTHIANS	232
BEYOND PERSIA – THE INDIAN ENEMY	234
MACEDONIAN ARMIES AFTER ALEXANDER	236
ARTILLERY AND SIEGE ENGINES	244
ARMS AND ARMOUR	246
GLOSSARY	250
INDEX	251

INTRODUCTION

The history of the ancient peoples of the Middle East encompasses the rise, the rule and the decline and fall of a succession of empire-builders – from the Sumerians and Akkadians in the 23rd century BCE to the Macedonians led by Alexander the Great in the 4th century BCE. In the course of these millennia, great military minds developed the war chariot, and the cavalry charge of mounted soldiers, the fierce and disciplined infantry formations of the Greek and Macedonian phalanx; they invented the siege tower, battering ram, onager catapult and other tools used to gain entry to a heavily fortified city. Fighting men wielded dagger, sword, bow and arrows, hammer, pike, spear and the 5.4–6m (18–20ft) sarissa used by the Macedonians; they and their leaders developed body

▼ *A broad overview of the ancient world covered in the chapters of this volume.*

▲ *Remnants of a Hittite helmet, made from iron. The ear flaps are still present.*

armour, greaves, helmets and a variety of shields to protect themselves. In tactics, clothing, weaponry and other equipment, military men learned from both their allies and their enemies as they searched for the improvements that would give them the edge where it mattered, in battle.

Climate and Terrain

In the ancient period, peoples developed weapons and tactics suited to where they lived and what raw materials or weapon-making technologies were available. Local climate had a significant impact on the development of armour and military clothing. For example, the Ancient Egyptians, living in a generally hot climate, wore military outfits developed from civilian clothing and designed above all to keep their soldiers cool, attempting to protect them from the elements as much as from their enemies.

Terrain was also a major influence on the development of ancient military systems. Where the ground was flat and level, as in desert or steppe, first chariots and then cavalry were developed as the striking arm of the different armies. Where the terrain was uneven, mountainous with little arable land, infantry came forward

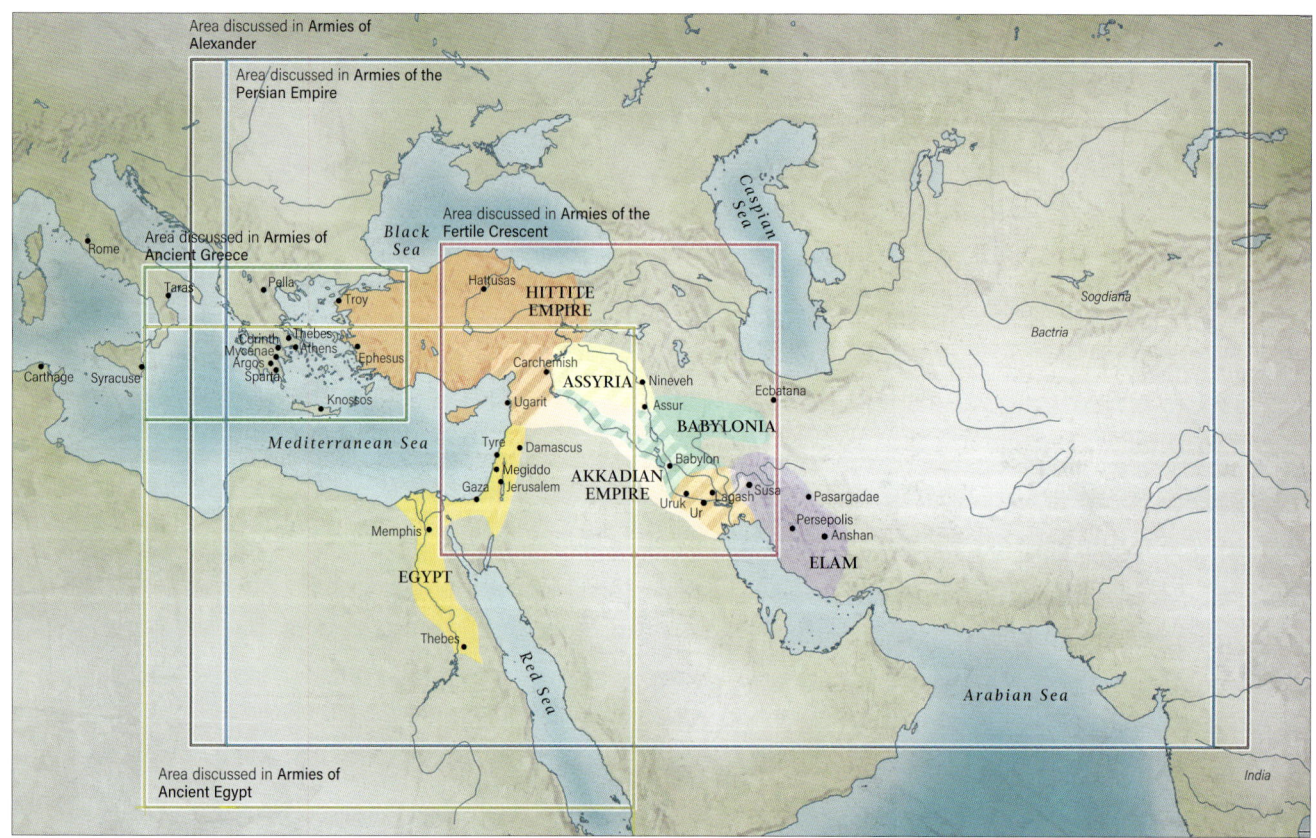

as the primary arm. In the rugged landscape of Ancient Greece, both chariots and cavalry were present and employed when necessary, but were greatly overshadowed by the use of infantry in the form of the well-armed hoplite, so-named after the large, round shield he carried – the hoplon.

Bronze and Iron

The art and science of metallurgy was of major importance to the ancient armies: as metallurgists developed in skill, and discoveries were made in the process of making armour and weapons, more and better arms and armour became available. Two major developments in metallurgy that gave their name to time periods are critical to this study: the discoveries of bronze and of iron. The Bronze Age lasted from approximately 3600 to 600 BCE but those beginning and end dates are general, and not region-specific. For the areas that are broadly included in this study, the Bronze Age lasted 3200–1200 BCE in the Near East, 3200–600 BCE in Europe and 3300–1200 BCE in India. Europe, during this period, was behind both India and the Near East in terms of development. The Iron Age, and the development of steel, began around 1200 BCE in the Near East and India, and 600 years later in Europe. Steel was well known in Sparta in c.650 BCE.

Bronze tools and weapons were less brittle and longer-lasting than the stone ones they replaced. The major difference between bronze and iron is that bronze is an alloy (initially formed from copper and arsenic and later copper and tin) and iron a basic metal. The development of first the bronze alloy (about 90 per cent copper and 10 per cent tin) and then the ability to make steel from iron led to more and better weapons and armour being made. The initial shift from bronze to iron came about because iron was more plentiful than the raw materials for making bronze; but after the development of steel, artisans were able to make weapons and tools that were stronger and kept an edge better than their bronze forerunners.

▲ *The Stele of Vultures, c.2450 BCE shows the Sumerian king, Eannatum, using a sickle-like sword. The sword may be a prototype of the Egyptian khopesh.*

Warriors and Soldiers

At the start of the period covered by this book, around 3000 BCE, army organization and development was very primitive. The term 'army' can be misleading with the early empires and conquerors. Similarly, the name 'soldier' can be inaccurate, especially if used interchangeably with 'warrior'.

The term army can only be applied loosely in the early days of semi-organized warfare, when opposing forces were not much more than armed mobs – groups which, once set in motion, were usually not controlled well or at all by the commander, who would also fight as a warrior. Often, when the chief warrior was killed, his army would fall apart and run; possibly pursued by the victorious army, which would be just as disorganized in victory as their opponents were in defeat.

A warrior is an individual, whether formally trained or not, who fights as an individual in combat. A soldier on the other hand is trained to fight in a group led by a commander – a soldier of greater experience or one appointed by the king or his representatives; the term is applicable to the ancient Greeks, once the phalanx was adopted as a fighting formation that required trained and disciplined infantrymen in its ranks in order to function.

Early Military Clothing

There were no such things as military uniforms in the ancient world, even though a generally similar appearance in arms, equipment and armour did eventually develop. The modern idea of clothing soldiers in a military uniform did not arise until the 16th century CE. In the ancient world soldiers and warriors were largely clothed in a version of what was worn by their native peoples, or the king and chieftains for whom they fought.

The use of common equipments in the armies of Antiquity cannot be interpreted as an anticipation of uniforms that appeared several centuries later. However, the Hellenic practice of painting standardized emblems on shields is a response to the same practical needs that led to the development of military uniforms.

▼ *A rusted Scythian akinakes, the distinctive short sword of the Achaemenid Persian warriors. The knife below would have had an animal-shaped handle.*

◀ *Ramesses II in the Battle of Kadesh, on his chariot, with bow and arrow.*

The War Wagon and the Chariot

Before the development of cavalry as a combat arm, the chariot, both four- and two-wheeled, was developed by several of the ancient empires.

Chariot is a Latin term, meaning 'car'; the chariot was a mobile fighting platform from which javelins or spears could be thrown and bowmen could launch their arrows.

Chariots needed wheels and animals to pull the vehicles. The wheel may have been invented as early as 4000BCE and evidence can be found of wheeled vehicles from Central Europe and the Balkans, as well as in the Caucasus and Mesopotamia – where the Sumerians were probably the first in that area to have the wheel and wheeled vehicles. The Sumerian wheel was solid and not spoked. The first evidence of a combination of a wheel with an axle was probably as early as 3500BCE. By 3000BCE the wheel had spread to the Indus Valley in India and by around 1200BCE the chariot with a spoked wheel could be found to the east, in China, and in the west, in Scandinavia.

The horse was probably domesticated between 4000BCE and 3500BCE on the Eurasian steppes – the large grasslands that exist in the Ukraine and surrounding regions. The first domesticated horse was smaller than the modern horse, which is able to carry a man as well as his equipment; nevertheless, the early horses were capable of carrying goods and equipment and could be harnessed to pull two- and four-wheeled vehicles.

The Sumerians may have been the first to develop the four-wheeled chariot – often referred to by modern authors as a 'war wagon'. These vehicles were pulled by oxen or jackasses and not by horses. The chariot team was possibly protected with sheepskins draped around the front of them. In time, lighter, more mobile, two-wheeled chariots were developed.

Other armies who used the chariot in war included the Philistines, the Sea Peoples (the ship-borne invaders who swept destructively through the Near East in c.1250–1200BCE) and the Mycenaeans of ancient Greece, whose vehicles were usually of two types: the so-called box chariot, where the platform on which driver and crew stood was enclosed; and the rail chariot, where this platform was not enclosed. Early Israelite armies probably also used the chariot. Although not substantiated by other sources or archaeology the Bible states that Joshua and King Solomon used chariots as well as cavalry in the 10th century BCE, as did a later Biblical Israelite king, Ahab, in the following century. Ahab's chariots were possibly based in the city of Jezreel, which may have served as a chariot depot, where they were manufactured and repaired.

Chariots were made of wood with iron or bronze fittings (depending on the era) that were placed on the stress points of the vehicle to strengthen them, just as iron fittings were placed on artillery pieces from the advent of gunpowder artillery to the late 19th century CE. The component parts of the chariot were: the wheels and connecting axle (sometimes called the beam); the body of the chariot (sometimes referred to as the basket),

◀ *Charioteer driving two horses, from the 6th century BCE.*

◀ Alexander the Great was said to have a Homeric delight in battle. A renowned horseman, he would lead the cavalry charge.

where the crew took their places; the harnessing pole; and the double yoke, which was attached to the harnessing pole. The wheels developed from a solid construction to a spoke design, from four to eight spokes. The wheel was wooden, but could be reinforced by an iron tyre that was fitted around the perimeter.

The body of the chariot was either open or closed on the front and sides, but the rear of the body was always open so that the crew could mount the chariot. Sometimes the sides were armoured, but that would retard the speed and manoeuvrability of the chariot and reduce its overall effectiveness. The front and side 'walls' of the chariot were probably just under 1m (3ft) high.

The harnessing pole was either attached to the body or the axle. The double yoke was attached to the front of the harnessing pole and would fit over the shoulders of the horse team. The chariot did not have a suspension system, so the ride for the crew would definitely have been rough and bumpy; the crew had to adjust to the movement to keep their footing and remain in the chariot. An unwary driver or bowman could be tossed from a chariot moving at speed – and the horse team would drive on, oblivious.

A basic harness was used with the horse team. Two small saddle-like devices were attached to the yoke, which again were fitted over the horses' shoulders. Horses had a bridle fitted on their heads and a set of reins ran back to the chariot body and to the driver, who controlled the horse team from the body of the chariot. However, no one thought of having the driver ride one of the horses of the team so he could control them from there; this system, which was later developed in Europe for military horse teams, would have allowed another bowman or a shield bearer to be in the chariot body.

The Power of Cavalry

By the time of Alexander the Great, towards the end of our survey, the chariot was obsolete. Cavalry was then the primary mounted arm. Commanders used these highly trained, often elite units of mounted warriors to deliver swift and concentrated assaults on a particular enemy position, to press home a sudden advantage or to pursue an enemy who had broken rank. Cavalry also served to threaten the enemy's flank or rear, to perform reconnaissance or to shield infantry movements from enemy eyes.

Both the Macedonians and the Persians fielded excellent cavalry in the late 1st millennium BCE. The Persians also still used chariots at this time, but these were proven ineffective against Alexander's infantry. After his campaigns destroyed and conquered the Persian empire, the chariot was no longer employed by any army. With the victorious campaigns of Philip II and Alexander, cavalry became an effective tactical tool that determined the outcome of major pitched battles. The heavy equipment of their cavalrymen enabled them to break the defensive formations of any enemy.

▼ Depicted on a relief at the Assyrian palace of Tiglath-Pileser III, c.728BCE; two of the king's cavalrymen pursue an enemy on a camel, with spears. Their horses are tasselled in typical style.

Development of the Bow

This ancient weapon was used in warfare by different civilizations, probably earlier than recorded history. The bow developed independently in Europe, Asia, the Near East, Africa and North America. The Central and South American civilizations of the Mayans, Aztecs and Incas do not seem to have developed this weapon, just as they did not develop the wheel. The Native North Americans did not develop the wheel, either, but did use the bow.

Bows are constructed and shaped by bowyers, and arrows made by fletchers, both specialist craftsmen who were highly valued in any army. The bow is made simply from a single piece of suitable wood strung with a string, called a bowstring, made of different flexible materials. Arrows launched from the bow are made of various materials, such as reeds and wood, and can be tipped with shaped stone, carved into shape with some type of blade and then fire-hardened, or metal arrowheads, which are the most efficient and deadly.

To launch, or loose, an arrow from a bow, the bow is held straight-armed in front of the body with one hand, and an arrow notched in the middle of the bowstring. The bowman then raises the bow, aims at the target and pulls the arrow and bowstring back with the non-bow grasping hand. The arrow is drawn either to the chest, less accurate, or to the cheek, more

▲ A Scythian Persian archer blowing a trumpet, on a black-figure plate painting ascribed to Psiax, c.520BCE.

accurate, and then loosed. Arrows loosed en masse, on command, by ranks of trained archers, were very impressive and deadly. Bows could be employed at close range, with the bowman aiming directly at his enemy, or at longer range by the simple procedure of elevating the bow.

In the composite bow, animal sinew was bound to the front of the bow and animal horn to the back: when the bow was drawn, the sinew stretched but the horn pieces were pressed together, and both added force to the release and flight of the arrow.

The Greeks and others used a simpler bow, not so powerful or long-ranged as the composite bow used by the Persians, Medes and other peoples from the East, but effective enough within its range. Along with the sling and the javelin, the bow of whatever type was the principal missile weapon of the ancient world, and remained an effective missile weapon until the advent of gunpowder; in fact the bow continued to be used alongside gunpowder weapons for a few centuries after the introduction of the latter on European battlefields in the 14th century CE.

◀ Herodotus wrote the acclaimed Histories, an account of the Greco-Persian wars.

▶ Xenophon was a Greek warrior and historian, writer of Anabasis and books on history and horsemanship.

Ancient History-Writing

The difficulty with any study of ancient peoples – Rome generally excepted – is that much of the available source material was written after, and sometimes long after, the events described. Accounts of the period are coloured by legend; actual events became legends through repeated retellings. Moreover it should also be born in mind that, in a phrase attributed to Churchill and many others, 'history is written by the victors' – those who reported events presented the account to favour their own side.

The best references for our period of interest are the writings of the Greek historians Herodotus (c.484–c.420BCE), Thucydides (c.460–c.404BCE) and Xenophon (c.430–c.350BCE). Herodotus wrote the first narrative history in the ancient world, an account of the wars between the Persians and the Greeks in 499–449BCE; he was celebrated as 'the father of history' by Roman scholar and statesman Cicero. Thucydides then wrote a great History of the Peloponnesian War, the conflict fought between Sparta and Athens in 431–404BCE, while Xenophon in Anabasis ('March Upcountry') famously wrote of the homeward march from Asia Minor of 10,000 Greek mercenaries after their paymaster, the Persian prince Cyrus the Younger, was killed in the Battle of Cunaxa (near Babylon) in 401BCE.

The Scope of this Volume

This is a study of the arms, armour and military clothing of some of the great ancient peoples: the Sumerians, the Hittites, the Assyrians, the Babylonians, the Egyptians, the Greeks, the Persians and the Macedonians. The book focuses on armies, what they wore and how they were armed rather than the political systems, forms of government or cultural and social aspects of the countries covered, nor indeed of the battles and conflicts in detail. Our study covers an immense area, from Eastern Europe through the Balkans to the Near East, into North Africa and eastward into Asia to the Indus River of India. A very large number of peoples – many of them nomads – came into decisive contact with these kingdoms, including Scythians, Phrygians, Hebrews, the Sea Peoples, the Mitanni and the Medes. Ancient Rome, which is covered in detail already in a companion volume, is referred to only when Roman military developments impacted upon the kingdoms and peoples that are under our scrutiny.

▲ *Alexander as the Romans saw him, in a mosaic from Pompeii c.100BCE.*

The principal kingdoms and empires covered in this volume overlap considerably – especially those that existed in the same general area. Sumerians, Babylonians and Assyrians fought over and occupied generally the same territories at different times, at the same time or consecutively as one empire fell and another arose in its place. The Egyptians and Hittites occupied different lands, south and north of the Near East respectively, but they had several encounters at times when they ventured into each others' territories for conquest, or when they fought for supremacy outside their native lands.

Two vast empires, those of the Persians under the Achaemenid dynasty and the Macedonians led by Alexander the Great, arose on opposite sides of the ancient world. They came into deadly contact after the Persians had twice attempted and twice failed to invade Greece; and after the Macedonians had conquered Greece in the aftermath. Alexander took over the Persian empire that Cyrus the Great had built, but then his empire in turn lost its own landholding to internal squabbles and settlements, to be finally overcome by that great behemoth of the ancient world, Rome.

▼ *A painting by Lionel Royer (1852–1926CE) encapsulates the awe Alexander the Great inspired, centuries after his death and to this day. Octavian (to become Augustus Caesar) visited his tomb in Alexandria c.30BCE, and laid a wreath on the mummified body in homage.*

TIMELINE OF THE ANCIENT WORLD 3200BCE–323BCE

This brief timeline demonstrates how different periods, civilizations and empires overlapped. Further detail is offered in the chapter timelines.

c.3500BCE: The Sumerians developed the wheel. The horse is first domesticated on the Eurasian Steppes by nomadic tribes.
3200BCE: The Bronze Age in the Near East begins.
3000BCE: The cuneiform system of writing develops in Sumer. The Minoan civilization begins in Crete.
2925BCE: The 1st Dynasty is established in Egypt.
2700BCE: The Jiroft civilization begins in Persia/Mesopotamia.
2649BCE: The Old Kingdom in Egypt is established.
2550BCE: The construction of the Great Pyramid in Egypt at Giza.
c.2334–2279BCE: Sargon of Akkad in Mesopotamia reigns.
c.2150BCE: The Old Kingdom in Egypt collapses as does the Akkadian empire in Mesopotamia.
2030BCE: The Middle Kingdom in Egypt is established.
2025–1393BCE: The period of the Old Assyrian empire.

▼ *The dark-red columns of the ruined Minoan Palace of Knossos, Crete, Greece, constructed in around 2000BCE.*

▲ *A Sumerian plaque with engraved scene of a votive offering to a king, 2600–2350BCE.*

c.2000BCE: The city of Knossos in the Minoan civilization has developed into a metropolis of 80,000 people.
c.2000BCE: Evidence of the use of horse-drawn chariots is found in burial sites from this period.
1650BCE: The Hittite capital of Hattusa is established by Hattusilis.
1620BCE: The Hittite king Mursilis I conquers Aleppo and Babylon.
1600BCE: The Minoan civilization is completely destroyed on Crete by a natural disaster. Around the same period, the Hittites emerge as a dominant force in the eastern Mediterranean and its empire begins. Mycenaean Greece begins to develop.
1550BCE: The New Kingdom in Egypt is established. Construction on the huge Karnak temple complex at Luxor begins under Amenhotep I and continues under later pharaohs.
1393–1056BCE: The Middle Assyrian empire.
1350BCE: The Mitanni kingdom is destroyed by the Hittite king Suppiluliuma.
1275BCE: The Battle of Kadesh between Egypt and the Hittites, who were joined by the Sea Peoples.
c.1250–1200BCE: Over a period the Sea Peoples invade Egypt and the eastern Mediterranean.
1237BCE: The Hittites are defeated in northern Mesopotamia by the Assyrians.
1209BCE: Even though the Hittite kingdom is in decline, they build an effective navy and win an important naval battle off the coast of Cyprus.
1200BCE: The end of the Bronze Age and the beginning of the Iron Age in the Near East and India.
c.1184BCE: The fall of Troy to the Mycenaeans after a ten-year siege; the city is destroyed in the ensuing sack.
c.1180BCE: The Hittite empire begins to fragment, ending around 1100BCE.
1070BCE: The end of the New Kingdom in Egypt.
c.1000BCE: The Kingdom of Israel emerges as a monarchy under their first kings Saul and then David.
911–612BCE: The New Assyrian empire.
800BCE: City-states begin to emerge in mainland Greece.
753BCE: Rome is founded on the Italian peninsula. Rome would become through wars of conquest against its neighbours the dominant power on the Italian peninsula and its army would develop into the most efficient and deadly in the ancient world.

▼ *Luxor was the ancient city of Thebes in Upper Egypt, with temple complexes covering a vast area, in c.1400BCE.*

▲ *A surviving wall with relief at Persepolis, the palace built by Darius I of Persia in 518BCE.*

745BCE: The Assyrian empire begins to emerge and expand through the aggressive invasion and conquest of neighbouring states.
728BCE: The Median empire is established in Mesopotamia and expands, until it is absorbed into other empires in the same area.
c.700BCE: Homer is thought to have written the *Iliad* and the *Odyssey* in the late 8th or early 7th century BCE, four hundred years after the fall and destruction of Troy.
c.650BCE: Steel is now being used in Sparta.
605BCE: Nebuchadnezzar II defeats Assyria and Egypt at the Battle of Charchemish. He reigns in Babylon until 561BCE.
586BCE: The Babylonians besiege and capture Jerusalem, the capital of Israel, and destroy the Temple built by King Solomon. The Israelites are taken captive and are removed to Babylon.
550BCE: Cyrus the Great founds the Persian empire.
546BCE: Cyrus defeats and overthrows Croesus, the king of Lydia.
539BCE: The Babylonian empire is defeated and overthrown by Cyrus, who then frees the captive Jews.
530BCE: Cyrus the Great dies.
525BCE: Cambyses II, the successor of Cyrus the Great, conquers Egypt.

514–512BCE: A Persian invasion of southern Russia under Darius I, sometimes called the Great, is defeated by the Scythians.
512BCE: Darius takes Thrace, Macedonia and Libya, expanding the Persian empire to its largest extent.
509BCE: Rome overthrows its last king and declares itself a republic.
508BCE: The Greek city-state of Athens establishes the world's first democracy.
499BCE: The Persian Wars begin, between Persia and Greece.
490BCE: The Persians invade Greece and are defeated by the Athenians and their allies at the Battle of Marathon.
480BCE: King Xerxes invades Greece in the second Persian invasion in ten years. The Spartans die to the last man holding back a vast Persian force at the Pass of Thermopylae. A month later the Athenian navy defeats the Persian fleet at sea in the Battle of Salamis.
479BCE: A united Greek army defeats the Persian army at the Battle of Plataea and the second Persian invasion of the region is defeated.
469BCE: The Greek philosopher Socrates is born in Athens.
465BCE: Xerxes is murdered by his own soldiers.
449BCE: The Persian Wars finally end.
447–432BCE: The Athenian empire is at its peak, and the city builds the Parthenon, a temple in honour of Athena, on the Acropolis.
431BCE: The Peloponnesian Wars between Sparta and Athens begin, with other city-states taking sides.
427BCE: The Greek philosopher Plato is born in Athens.
404BCE: The Peloponnesian Wars end, with Sparta victorious over Athens.
401BCE: The Battle of Cunaxa between the Persian kings; 10,000 Greek mercenaries march home.
400BCE: The beginning of the Celtic migrations into southern and western Europe. The Celts probably originated in west-central Europe.
399BCE: Socrates dies of self-poisoning after being convicted of treason.

▲ *The Dorian columns of the Parthenon, in Athens, constructed between 447 and 432BCE.*

384BCE: The Greek philosopher Aristotle is born. He later becomes the tutor of Alexander.
350BCE: The rise of Macedonia and the creation of a formidable Macedonian army by Philip II, father of Alexander the Great.
338BCE: Philip II of Macedon's greatest victory came at Chaeronea, where he gained control of Greece.
336BCE: Philip II is assassinated and Alexander ascends the throne of Macedon.
334BCE: Alexander defeats the Persians at the Battle of Granicus.
331BCE: Alexander defeats the army of Darius III of Persia in the Battle of Gaugamela, a defeat which signals the fall of the Persian empire. Darius is later slain by his own people.
330BCE: Alexander captures and burns Persepolis.
326BCE: Alexander's empire reaches its peak with the defeat of the Indian king Porus at the Battle of the Hydaspes.
323BCE: Alexander dies in Babylon at the age of 33.
322–275BCE: Alexander's empire is divided up and eventually collapses, as the Successors go to war with one another over territory and prestige.
27BCE: Augustus Caesar declares himself the first emperor of Rome.

THE FERTILE CRESCENT

Mesopotamia – the territory between the rivers Tigris and Euphrates, now principally Iraq, Kuwait and part of Syria – is often referred to as 'the cradle of civilization'. From it arose the first organized human society, Sumer, the great empires of Assyria, Babylon and eventually Persia, which had so much influence on the region and endured in one form or another right through to the 7th century CE. The history of the area in this period involves the rise and fall of peoples and empires whose histories were intermittently entangled with one another. The Hittites emerged in Asia Minor and the Assyrians in the Fertile Crescent to conquer and rule and in their turn to fall from power. The story of the Babylonians is intertwined with that of other peoples who conquered them or were absorbed by them.

Beginnings in Sumer

The civilization of Sumer was founded by a people who, judging from archaeological finds, came from or settled in southern Mesopotamia about 4500–4000BCE, although their history only began to be recorded c.2700BCE. The Sumerians, pioneers of one of the earliest forms of writing in human history with the cuneiform script, became a great civilization. In the beginning they were a collection of city-states. As these evolved, they fought one other to gain power and influence.

The Sumerian civilization gradually developed into the Akkadian empire. The founder of this empire, Sargon of Akkad (c.2334–2279BCE) set out on a policy of conquest, expanding his empire at the expense of the neighbouring peoples. With Sargon, the Akkadian empire was at its peak, and as it declined, from c.2100BCE, this collapse opened the way for the emergence of the Hittites, the Assyrians and later what would become the Babylonian empire.

Power of the Warlike Hittites

The rise to ascendency of the Hittites in the region began about 1600BCE. The Hittites were an Indo-European, warlike people who had migrated to and settled in Anatolia probably before 2000BCE, as part of a general Indo-European migration into Europe and the Near East. Aggressive, violent and ruthless, they were greatly feared by their neighbours; they expanded their hard-won empire outwards and waged war for loot and conquest amongst the native peoples with whom they came into contact.

Hittite territory eventually encompassed all of Asia Minor; they pushed down into Syria and fought

▲ *The ruins of the ancient Sumerian city of Kish, apparently first occupied c.3100BCE and located in present-day Iraq. Sargon of Akkad claimed to be the king of Kish.*

▼ *Twelve Hittite gods of the underworld depicted on a rock relief at Hattusa, the capital city of the Hittite empire, today situated in the Çorum Province, Turkey.*

▲ *A scene in embossed bronze, showing Shalmaneser III in a chariot with his Assyrian archers, on the Balawat Gates, dating to 858–824BCE.*

the Ancient Egyptians. They also expanded by conquest into parts of Mesopotamia, which marked the greatest extent of their empire. Their power eventually declined in the face of more sophisticated enemies; the Hittites were defeated over several decades, and their empire gone by c.1100BCE.

Long Rule of the Assyrians

The Assyrian empire or state was one of the most long-lasting of the ancient empires, existing in one form or another from c.2500BCE to 605BCE, when the Chaldeans and their allies revolted and destroyed the Assyrians. At times the Assyrians were a subject people to another empire, but twice the Assyrians were resurgent and re-established themselves as a dominant power in the region. The Assyrian empire went through three phases in its existence: the Old Assyrian empire (2025–1393BCE), the Middle Assyrian empire (1393–1056BCE) and the Neo-Assyrian empire (911–612BCE).

The Assyrians created a sophisticated civilization that extended to their army and military operations. Skilled engineers, they excelled in siege operations and their siege engines – including catapults, battering rams and elaborate siege towers – were among the most effective of the time.

The Assyrians not only dominated their own immediate territory but were an aggressive, expansionist and dangerous neighbour.

Chaldeans and Babylonians

The Assyrian empire degenerated into civil war after 626BCE when the Chaldeans allied themselves with other minority subject peoples within the empire and rebelled against Assyrian rule. The rebels took and sacked the Assyrian capital Nineveh in 612BCE and then won the final battle of the revolt at Carchemish in 605BCE. The Assyrian empire disappeared from recorded history. (The modern city of Mosul is now on the site of Nineveh.)

The first ruler of the new Chaldean dynasty was Nabopolassar, who had led the armed coalition. He died the year after Carchemish, in 605BCE, and was succeeded by his son Nebuchadnezzar II. The new king set out to rebuild the kingdom after the destructive civil war. Babylon itself received Nebuchadnezzar's special attention and he was the ruler that built the spectacular hanging gardens, which became one of the seven wonders of the ancient world. The Babylonian empire of the Chaldean dynasty lasted until 539BCE, when it was assimilated into the new Persian empire under Cyrus the Great. The rule of Persia over the region lasted until Alexander the Great invaded in 334BCE and destroyed the empire established by Cyrus the Great.

▼ *A Phoenician warship (in the Assyrian navy) depicted in bas-relief on the walls of the palace in Nineveh, 700–692BCE. The ship is a bireme, with two levels of oars, and protective shields are secured around the structure. The pointed bow forms a ram.*

ANCIENT EGYPT

The civilization that developed alongside, and relied upon, the River Nile in north-eastern Africa was a shining star in the development of human culture – home, like the Fertile Crescent, to one of the world's earliest literate urban societies. It was also a powerful military force, creator of a vast empire that was at its height in 1450BCE. From the dawn of recorded history until it was conquered by Macedonian general Alexander the Great in the 4th century BCE, Egypt thrived under a succession of native rulers, occasionally interrupted by short periods of foreign rule – an independent state that was a cornerstone of ancient civilization.

Historians identify three main and four supplementary periods that comprise what is now called Ancient Egypt. The three main eras are Old Kingdom (c.2575–c.2130BCE), Middle Kingdom (1938–c.1630BCE) and New Kingdom Egypt (c.1539–1075BCE). The supplementary epochs are the Archaic Period, which preceded the Old Kingdom; the First Intermediate

▼ *The New Kingdom period Tomb of Sennedjem reveals timeless scenes of farming, alongside the all-important river Nile. Sennedjem was named as 'Servant in the Place of Truth'.*

Period (c.2130–1938BCE), which linked the Old and Middle Kingdoms; the Second Intermediate Period (c.1630–c.1539BCE), which connected the Middle and New Kingdoms; and the Third Intermediate Period (1075–664BCE), which was followed by the Late Period (664–332BCE).

The Late Kingdom marked the last era in the history of Ancient Egypt, for after that period of decline, conquest by the Macedonians and then the Romans marked the country's history until the rise of the Eastern Roman empire based in Constantinople

▲ *The Great Sphinx of Giza, carved from limestone. It is thought to have been created c.2500BCE in the Old Kingdom period. The body represents that of a lion and the head is said to depict the 4th-Dynasty pharaoh Khafre.*

(modern Istanbul, Turkey) and the conquest of Egypt by Muslim Arabs in the 7th century CE.

Egypt counts 31 dynasties of rulers, from c.2575BCE to 332BCE. A pharaoh (the ancient Egyptian word for king), an event or a cultural artefact is usually identified by dynasty, one of the historical periods listed above, or both. For example, the first pyramid was built by King Djoser, a pharaoh of the 3rd Dynasty in the Archaic Period; the world-renowned pyramids at Giza (now part of the Egyptian capital Cairo) were raised as monuments to honour pharaohs Khufu, Khafre and Menkaure of the 4th Dynasty in the Old Kingdom; Ramesses II, the great military leader who led the Egyptian army in the celebrated Battle of Kadesh against the Hittites in 1275BCE, was a pharaoh of the 19th Dynasty in the New Kingdom and built extensive monuments including Abu Simbel.

Gift of the Nile

The history of Egypt, as well as the prosperity of the kingdom, centred on the great River Nile and its annual flooding. The world's longest river, the Nile runs for 6,650km (4,132 miles) from the highlands of east Africa to empty into the Mediterranean Sea: in Egypt its two main sections are the Nile Valley and the Nile Delta, called Upper and Lower Egypt respectively in ancient times. The Valley is essentially a limestone canyon, while the Delta is a great flood plain encompassing 11,000 square km (4,250 sq miles).

The great Greek historian Herodotus declared Egypt to be the 'gift of the Nile' – the river's annual flooding gave the ancient Egyptians fertile land to till that made the country a bread basket for not only itself but for the later Romans. The Nile and the fertile land it supported by its flooding is essentially a long, narrow oasis in the desert. In coordination with the annual flood, the Egyptians developed an efficient irrigation system that expanded arable land for agriculture.

A Great Civilization

As is well known, the Egyptians were proficient and expert mathematicians

▼ *King Tutankhamun in his chariot defeating his enemies, as depicted on his tomb casket in the Valley of the Kings, 1357–1349BCE.*

▶ *The Sixth Pylon at Karnak, the temple of Amun built by Thutmose III, whose image is on the right. The multiple carvings depict the peoples conquered by the pharaoh.*

and engineers, and the building of the pyramids and other structures clearly demonstrate their skill in engineering. The design and building of the great pyramids still fascinates archaeologists, especially the crafting of the huge stone blocks that make up the pyramids and the intricacy of design of the monuments' interiors, which incorporate burial chambers, tunnels and passageways.

Further, the Egyptians made advances in the study of medicine and demonstrated skill in the production of glass. Egyptian art has survived to the present day and is a hallmark of their civilization. The Egyptians were great builders of boats for travel and commerce on the Nile, and this skill was later developed militarily: they had an imposing naval presence on the Nile and in the eastern Mediterranean at the height of the empire. The Egyptians were the builders of the first known ships in history. From their earliest designs for the construction of viable river craft, warships were designed.

The Egyptians were bent on conquest and expanding their territory. They were also faced with hostile neighbours who were engaged in expanding empires; warfare was, if not almost constant, undoubtedly viewed as normal for both the leaders and people of Egypt. Egyptian armies ranged from Libya to Nubia, north to Canaan (Palestine) and beyond. Egypt would finally fall to two stronger empires – that of Alexander the Great, who would found the city of Alexandria, and to Rome. The kingdom of the pharaohs would be no more.

ANCIENT GREECE

The Ancient Greeks were a fiercely independent, trade-minded and warlike race. They developed into a maritime people because of their native terrain and its geography in the eastern Mediterranean. Living close to the sea and confronted with a mountainous landscape and a shortage of fertile lands, they looked out across the sea and found a plentiful supply of places to settle and many opportunities for trade.

Greek civilization developed not only on the Greek peninsula, but also on the Mediterranean islands of Cyprus and Crete – and on the Cyclades, a group of around 30 islands in the Aegean Sea off the region of Attica in mainland Greece. The Cyclades, which amount to about one-fifth of the land area of modern Greece, include celebrated islands such as Náxos, Míkonos, Íos and Páros. Ancient Greek settlement on Crete began as early as 7000BCE.

The history of Ancient Greece is generally divided into three periods: the Archaic Period (c.800–500BCE), the Classical Period (500–323BCE) and the Hellenistic Period (323–146BCE). The Archaic Period covers the development and maturity of the Greek city-states and the expulsion of kings from many of those city-states. The Classical Period includes the defeat of two Persian invasions of Greece, the Peloponnesian Wars (431–404BCE) between Athens and an alliance led by Sparta, the rise of the Kingdom of Macedon in the 4th century BCE and the period of the conquests and empire of Macedonian king Alexander the Great, ending with his death. The Hellenistic Period covers the end of Macedonian hegemony in Greece and the rise of the Roman empire. The dominant military powers of the Hellenistic age – which were all defeated by Rome – were Antigonid Macedonia, Seleucid Syria and Ptolemaic Egypt.

Widespread Influence

Resourceful travellers and bold adventurers, the Greeks established colonies outside of their homeland, especially in Anatolia and, later, in Italy and Sicily, where they had a profound influence on the fledgling Roman republic; they even established trading centres as far away as the Crimean peninsula (at the north edge of the Black Sea). Through Rome, the Greeks had a lasting effect on the development of war, arms and armour.

Ancient Greece was the most sophisticated civilization and culture of the ancient world. Its people excelled in literature, engineering and mathematics, and were pioneers in the theatre and poetry. They created the Olympic Games, which were held in honour of the god Zeus every four years at Olympia near the city-state of Elis in the Peloponnese.

▲ *Hoplite warrior on an Attic black-figure vessel from the 5th century BCE.*

◄ *The imposing ruins of the Parthenon today, on the top of the Acropolis above the city of Athens.*

► *Hoplites fighting at close quarters. Each large round shield gave good protection to the man on the left but the bearer's right flank was left exposed. The Spartans excelled at the discipline of training in line.*

Greek City-States

There was little feeling of what we would recognize as nationhood in Greece, for various reasons – not least the mountainous terrain that made travel problematic. The Greek city-states developed independently and had significant differences in government and culture. Athens can lay claim to being the developer of democracy; Sparta was a military state whose warriors were respected for decades if not centuries throughout the ancient world and beyond – but these Hellenic cities were often at war with each other rather than presenting a united front.

Other city-states, such as Thebes and Corinth, were also important during the period, and, if not strong enough on their own, would ally themselves with the main antagonists, Athens and Sparta, in order to survive. The Peloponnesian Wars would find the two main alliances in Greece at each other's throats, and the idea of neutrality during what was for all intents and purposes a Greek civil war, was nearly impossible to achieve. The Greek city-states would eventually fall to Philip of Macedon (with the exception of Sparta), but ultimately the greatest threat to Greece would be Rome.

▲ *From lucrative merchant trade, city-states such as Athens grew into maritime powers, within Greece and against foreign invaders. This 19th-century painting depicts the Athenians returning to Piraeus in triumph after the Battle of Salamis.*

The Greek City-States

There were myriad Greek city-states, not all on mainland Greece. The Greeks established colonies overseas initially because of overpopulation on the Greek mainland, with a shortage of land for the younger sons of families. The Greek colonies ranged from Asia Minor through the Near East to North Africa and as far west as Italy and Sicily. Listed below are the most famous on mainland Greece as well as the most powerful – the ones that influenced Greek culture and its expansion, and which set the standards for military and naval excellence.

Name	Location
Argos	Peloponnese
Athens	Attica
Corinth	Isthmus of Corinth
Delos	Cyclades
Delphi	Mount Parnassus
Dodona	Epirus
Eritrea	Euboea
Laodicea	Arcadia
Megara	Attica
Thebes	Boeotia
Sparta	Peloponnese

ANCIENT PERSIA

Originating as a tribal group, the Persians moved to the forefront of history with the coming to the throne in c.559BCE of Cyrus II, who created the Persian Achaemenid empire. Like the *Madai* (Medes), with whom they are associated, the Persians – originally the *Parsa* – were Indo-Europeans who probably originated from the southern Russian steppes and/or the Caucasus mountains. From that region the Parsa swept into the plateau of Iran sometime before 1000BCE and gave their name 'Persia' to the country and its subsequent empire.

The land in which the Persians settled lies between the Caspian Sea to the north and the Persian Gulf to the south, eastwards of the fertile plain of the rivers Euphrates and Tigris in which the civilizations of Sumer, Babylon and Assyria flowered. One-

third of the Iranian plateau is either desert or mountain and almost all of it lies at more than 1,500ft (450m) above sea level.

Rise and Fall of the Medes

The Medes, like the Parsa, migrated to what became Persia in about 1000BCE. Both the Medes and Persians were originally subject peoples of the Assyrians, but they asserted their independence and overthrew the Assyrian empire. The Median ruler

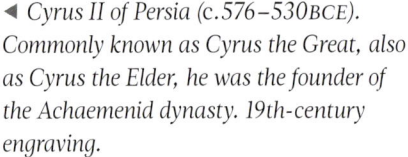

◀ *Cyrus II of Persia (c.576–530BCE). Commonly known as Cyrus the Great, also as Cyrus the Elder, he was the founder of the Achaemenid dynasty. 19th-century engraving.*

Cyaxares allied with the Chaldean King Nabopolassar of Babylon to capture the Assyrian capital, Nineveh, in 612BCE and went on to establish a new empire.

Cyrus rose up against Cyaxares's son Astyages and in 550BCE, after a mass defection of Median troops to his side, took control of the empire. From the start Cyrus demonstrated the qualities of magnanimity and good judgement for which he was to become celebrated: he treated Astyages very well and gave the Medes a prominent position, behind only the Persians themselves, in honour and in battle.

The Medes are usually counted among the Persians, although they did have a definite and separate identity. They were originally composed of six separate tribes, but were absorbed into the Persian empire: they dressed in the Persian manner and were eventually assimilated into the way of life. To the Greeks who fought them, there was no distinction between the Medes and the Persians – they were considered one and the same.

Defeat of Babylon

In 539BC Cyrus invaded and defeated the Babylonians at the Battle of Opis. After achieving a major engineering feat by diverting the River Euphrates, Cyrus and his army entered Babylon and secured the city unopposed. Cyrus declared himself to be the king of Babylon, and both Babylon and Assyria became provinces of Persia, governed by Persian officials. One of the first things Cyrus accomplished was the freeing of the Jews who had been forced to settle in Babylon after they were captured by Nebuchadnezzar II in 586BCE. By

▼ *King Xerxes ordered the building of a pontooon bridge over the Hellespont for the immense Persian army to cross from Asia to Europe in 480BCE. He set up a throne to survey the action. 19th-century painting by Jean-Adrien Guignet.*

▲ *A terracotta griffin from the walls of Darius I's palace in Susa, the administrative capital of the Persian empire.*

a decree of 538 BCE he ended their 'Babylonian captivity' and allowed them to return to Jerusalem and rebuild the Temple there.

The Babylonians revolted against Persian rule in 521 BCE and declared their independence, and a Babylonian, Nidinta-Bel, 'ruled' in Babylon for less than a year under the name Nebuchadnezzar III. However, the Persians then mounted an expedition to recover the city. Babylon again revolted against the Persians in 514 BCE, but this insurrection was put down ruthlessly, and some of the fortifications of the city were razed as an example.

Thwarted by Greece

The Persians were angered by Greek intervention in internal Persian affairs and resolved to punish the Greeks by invading Greece proper in 490 BCE. This invasion was defeated by Athens and allied Greek states at the Battle of Marathon, and the Persian king Darius withdrew back to Persia. His son, Xerxes, was resolved to avenge this humiliating defeat and gathered a huge army and navy and again invaded the Greek mainland in 480 BCE. Crossing the Hellespont, the Persians were first delayed by a determined force of 7,000 Greek hoplites, the core of which, 300 Spartans, held off the Persian army (until they were betrayed and died to a man), which allowed the rest of the Greeks to withdraw. Soon after, the combined Greek fleets, led by the powerful Athenian Navy, decisively defeated the Persians at the naval Battle of Salamis. The Persians, though outnumbering the Greeks, were defeated by a combination of factors, most importantly Greek superiority in naval power, weapons and armour. The following year, the Greeks won the land battles of Plataea and Mycale and the Persians were driven out of Greece.

The Persian empire, under Darius III, would later be defeated and destroyed by Alexander the Great and his Macedonians and Greeks in the next century. A new Persian empire, which is outside the scope of this study, grew from the ashes of this conquest and the wreck of Alexander's empire, and would continually wage war against the Eastern Roman empire until finally defeated by the Eastern Roman Emperor Heraclius. Greatly weakened by constant warfare and defeat, it would then fall to the great onslaught of Muslim Arabs that happened in the 7th century CE.

▶ *The facade of the tomb of Darius I (Darius the Great) carved in a rock near Persepolis, the ancient capital.*

ALEXANDER THE GREAT

Alexander of Macedon was the first great captain in military history. In unrelenting campaigns he briefly made Macedonia into the most extensive empire on earth, conquering Egypt, Asia Minor, the Near East and Persia.

Alexander did not create the army that he led to greatness. This was the achievement of his father, Philip II of Macedon. Philip was an excellent king, a competent soldier and expert organizer. The army that he planned, raised and trained was the best in the ancient world, combining Greek steadiness with a military organization that took into account training, discipline, command and control, logistics and supply. The army was designed for conquest, first of Greece, and then the rest of the known world.

The Rise of Macedonia

The Greeks to the south of Macedonia considered the Macedonians poor cousins, mere 'barbarians' who herded sheep and did their best to farm an inhospitable, mountainous country. Macedonia actually was disadvantaged compared to the rest of Greece in many ways, but that inferiority ended with Philip. Philip's kingship transformed Macedonia into a kingdom that was able to take its place alongside other countries of the period.

Philip himself was an outstanding soldier, a courageous leader and commander who led by example and suffered physically from his wars. He lost an eye, was badly scarred by that loss, and was wounded in the leg and hand – injuries that left him limping and partially crippled. However, despite the handicaps incurred on the battlefield, he defeated a Greek alliance led by Athens and Thebes at the Battle of Chaeronea in 338BCE. Philip then united Greece with Macedonia and formed the League of Corinth; the only city-state that refused to join the new alliance was Sparta. Philip was now the commander of a combined Greek and Macedonian army, but was murdered before he could embark on his goal of conquering Persia.

▲ *A Roman copy of a now-lost portrait of Alexander in bronze by Lysippos, reputedly Alexander's sculptor of preference.*

The Empire of Alexander

Philip's heir and successor Alexander was only twenty years old when his father was murdered. He was not universally acclaimed as the new king of Macedon, but Philip's generals remained loyal to their new king, ensuring that Alexander could ascend the throne with little or no trouble.

What followed was a thirteen-year career of invasion and conquest east and south of Greece and Macedon that would result not only in the destruction of the existing Persian empire, but also in the capture of Asia Minor, the Near East and Egypt. His campaigns were unsurpassed at the time and few of the great captains that followed him would be as successful as he. However, he failed to establish a dynasty to inherit or an administration to govern and maintain his vast military conquests.

The empire of Alexander the Great was the greatest in the ancient world

◀ *In 338BCE Philip II called a Panhellenic Congress at Corinth. In the League of Corinth, Philip was voted as general of the Greek alliance, the de-facto leader of the planned campaign against Persia.*

▶ *This late 18th-century painting by Pierre-Henri de Valenciennes depicts Alexander at the Tomb of Cyrus the Great. Cyrus was the famous founder of the Persian empire which Alexander had just defeated. He discovered the tomb desecrated and in disrepair.*

until the advent of the Romans. After Alexander's death, the empire was divided among his generals. He was never defeated, but his empire crumbled into warring factions soon after his death.

Alexander's Successors

After Alexander's death at the age of 33, the empire rapidly fell apart. Alexander's Successors maintained the excellent Macedonian army, but divided the new empire among themselves. Alexander's empire was permanently split into separate kingdoms that were ruled independently of Macedon.

As Rome grew stronger in the west, the Successors' kingdoms and the subsequent rulers of Macedon fell victim to the Roman Republic's dreams of conquest. Egypt, the Near East, Asia Minor, Greece, Thrace and Macedon itself all became provinces of the Roman empire. However, it took Rome centuries to match the territorial extent that Alexander, his army and subordinate commanders achieved in just thirteen years. Compared to Macedon and its expansion under Alexander, which was akin to a comet streaking across the sky, the conquests of Rome were methodical and plodding. Nonetheless, they lasted far longer – enduring more than 2,000 years due to the excellent infrastructure created from the basic Roman government. Yet from what was basically a backwoods existence, when Philip II became king of Macedonia, leading to a kingdom that ruled the known world, Philip's son Alexander the Great achieved a record of conquest of which future rulers down through the ages could only dream.

▼ *The Alexander or Sidon Sarcophagus (so-called because it depicted him, posthumously, on a tomb found in Sidon) featured scenes from the Battle of Issus in painted bas-relief. Here, Alexander, in a lion-skin headdress, is shown routing the Persian cavalry.*

ARMIES OF THE FERTILE CRESCENT

The development of early warfare in the Middle Eastern area known as the Fertile Crescent clearly demonstrates how the various peoples created armies to not only defend themselves but to defeat and conquer their enemies. This vast period encompasses 2,500 years of empire building and civilization, from the primitive warriors of Sumer through the warlike and savage Hittites to the near-unbeatable Assyrians and the more sophisticated Babylonians. All of these peoples contributed significantly to the evolution of warfare, and the use of ever-more effective weapons and machinery of war from the composite bow to the chariot and fearsome siege engines that could breach the strongest fortress and city walls.

▲ A 16th-century depiction of Babylon, the city-state of ancient Mesopotamia and one of the seven wonders of the ancient world. Painted by Adriaen I van Nieulandt.

◄ Prisoners and booty captured after the siege of the town of Lachish in 701BCE, depicted on a wall relief of the Assyrian king Sennacherib's palace at Nineveh.

A SUCCESSION OF EMPIRES

The late Uruk and the Early Dynastic Period coincided with the beginning of the Bronze Age in the area. Metalworking greatly enhanced the development of weapons for self-defence and for waging war. At around the same time, c.3500BCE, the Sumerians developed the wheel, which brought both military and civilian advantages. The Sumerians of Mesopotamia led the way in devising and using the earliest battle chariots and the development of bronze weapons. By the middle of the 3rd millennium BCE they were fighting with spears, axes and large rectangular shields, wearing simple animal-skin clothing and leather or cloth skullcaps.

In the 2nd millennium BCE the Hittites had a much more sophisticated army, with iron weapons and tactics based on powerful, highly mobile chariots. Neither of these armies knew of or used the bow, but towards the end of the period the Assyrians were feared for their powerful and deadly horse archers. They also employed siege engines and tactics that were far more advanced than any others in the ancient world.

Six Periods of Sumer
1. Ubaid Period: 5300–4100BCE
2. Uruk Period: 4100–2900BCE
3. Early Dynastic Period: 2900–2334BCE
4. Akkadian empire: 2334–2218BCE
5. Gutian Period: 2218–2047BCE
6. Ur Period: 2047–1940BCE

Sumer

The Sumerians were originally tribal merchants who branched outwards from the villages and cities they established in southern Mesopotamia; the Sumerian city of Uruk eventually became the foremost city in Mesopotamia. Ethnically, they were not Semitic in origin, unlike most of their neighbours, and at first they were not particularly warlike. Originally their form of government was theocratic and they were ruled by religious leaders and priests instead of kings; the period of monarchic dynastic rule probably began c.2900BCE.

After the rule of kings began, the Sumerians began to expand at the expense of their Semitic neighbours. As they became more militarily sophisticated, they began to fortify their cities and the older villages in the southern part of Mesopotamia began to disappear; more Sumerians moved to the cities for protection against the equally warlike neighbouring tribes and emerging peoples.

The land in which the Sumerians lived had no natural building materials, no wood from forests, and it was virtually without metal or rock types, so the Sumerians built their cities and fortifications from sun-dried bricks usually made of clay and straw. The Ubaid and Uruk periods are both prehistoric, and evidence that has been found about these two periods is largely archeological in nature. In these centuries, Sumerian city-states came to prominence and power in the region. The Sumerians began to develop a written record by the 27th century BCE, but early written records are few and far between. There is, however, a written record that developed in the late Early Dynastic Period, around 3000 BCE.

Sumer was the first unified empire to emerge in Mesopotamia. Its history and development can be divided into six major periods (see table above). Sumer was the dominating 'power' in the area and the first to field an army that had impact on the period.

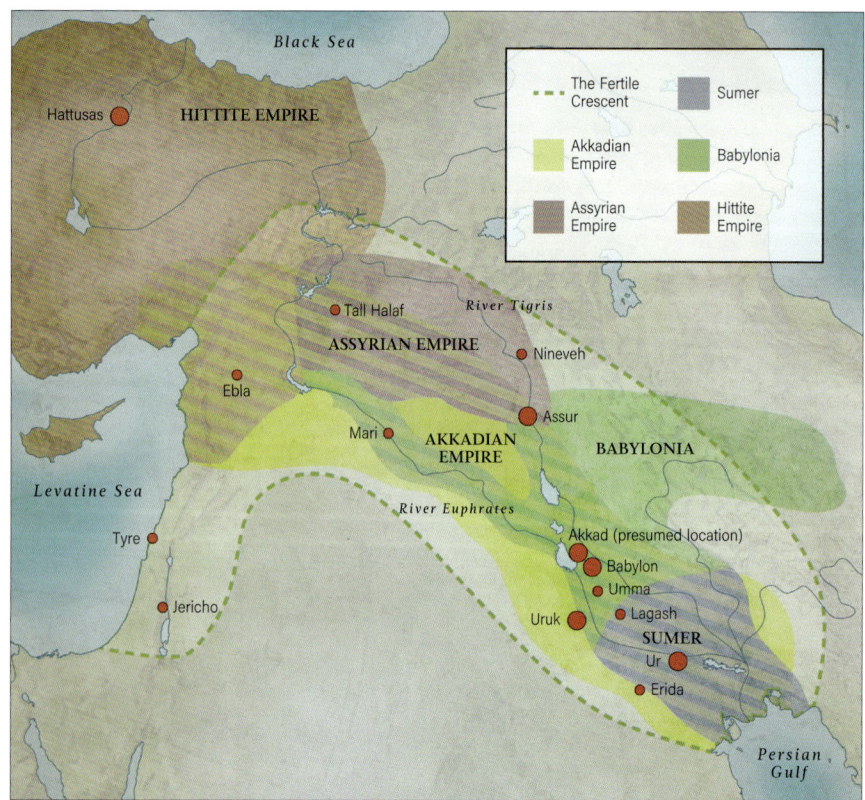

◀ *The Fertile Crescent formed by the Rivers Tigris and Euphrates is known as the 'Cradle of Civilization'; settlement here is believed to be as old as 6,000 years. The major peoples and empires are shown.*

▲ *The partially restored 3rd Sumerian Dynasty ziggurat in the ancient city of Ur, originally built c.2100BCE.*

Akkadia and the Amorites

The Sumerian empire reached its peak during the Early Dynastic Period when it began to face threats from other peoples, and the classical period of the Sumerian empire ended with the rise of the Akkadian empire during the 23rd century BCE. The Akkadians were a restless, nomadic Semitic people who were looking for a better land in which to settle. Under the great Akkadian king, Sargon, the empire expanded east from Mesopotamia to control the Levant along the Mediterranean coast.

Following the decline of the Akkadian empire in c.2100BCE, the Amorites, another Semitic people, gained prominence and continued in power until around 1700BCE. The Amorites were from the area of Syria, to the southwest of Mesopotamia. The Amorites radically changed the region politically and developmentally: the entire area of Mesopotamia was conquered and united under the rule of the Amorite dynasty of Babylon, notably the great Amorite king Hammurabi (reigned c.1792–c.1750BCE). This led to more centralized government in the area and the establishment of a code of laws, the first in history to be written down and known to the entire population. Law in other nations and empires developed from this first system.

The Hittites

The kingdom of the Hittites, known as Hatta, was founded in Asia Minor (the region of Anatolia, now Turkey) at the beginning of the 1600s BCE. The Hittites were an aggressive, warlike race, bent on the conquest of their neighbours. They waged war brutally and were rightly feared by any potential enemies.

They established an empire that was unrivalled in the area – encompassing Mesopotamia, the Levant and Syria and the lands southwards, almost to Egypt – until the rise of the Assyrians. At the time of the Hittites' rise, the competing empires were those of the Ancient Egyptians, Assyrians, Babylonians and Mitanni (in northern Mesopotamia). The Hittites destroyed the Mitanni, who also warred against the Egyptians. These empires accepted the existence, at least for a time, of the others: they exchanged ambassadors and on the surface were civil – while at the same time they plotted covertly against one another.

The first Hittite period of ascendency was from c.1650BCE to c.1400BCE, by which time the empire was greatly weakened internally and, being preyed upon by its enemies, was losing territory to them. The Hittites eventually recovered, however, resumed the expansion of their empire, regained lost territory and even developed a navy with which they had some success.

The Hittite economy depended on control of trade routes across and near their borders, and on their power over the sources of metals found in Anatolia or in conquered territories. The Hittite empire extended from Anatolia eastwards and southwards, and they occupied Syria and Lebanon where they had a common border with Egypt.

The collision of two expanding empires was inevitable, and the Hittites and Egyptians, who were under the leadership and command of Ramesses II, met in a celebrated battle near Kadesh in Syria, in 1275BCE. The

▼ *The Lions' Gate set in the walls of Hattusa, the ancient capital of the Hittite empire.*

▶ *The present-day ruins of the Hanging Gardens of Babylon and Ishtar Gate.*

fighting was bitter and prolonged and the chariot forces of the armies met in a confused melée. The Egyptians were led by the pharaoh himself in his personal chariot, and the battle demonstrated the differences in fighting tactics between the two-man Egyptian chariots and the much-vaunted Hittite three-man chariots. It is thought that the battle was most probably inconclusive, although surviving Egyptian records did claim a great victory for Ramesses. The Hittites were eventually defeated as an empire by 1100BCE; the invasions of the Sea Peoples and the ravages they wrought undoubtedly played a large part in the decline and disappearance of the Hittites.

Babylonia

The term 'Babylonian' is often used to define the peoples who occupied the city of Babylon and the territory surrounding it at different periods. This can lead to historical confusion. Babylon itself was occupied by the Assyrians, the Hittites and the Chaldeans; these and other peoples have been identified as Babylonians both in the period and by historians subsequently. The first true Babylonian king, who conquered and ruled an empire centred on the capital of Babylon, was Hammurabi.

The first years of Hammurabi's rule were generally peaceful, but he later launched wars of conquest to expand and consolidate his rule over Mesopotamia. He strengthened the fortifications of his own city and made alliances with other city-states in the region. Through diplomacy and conquest he expanded the territory he ruled, which brought him into conflict with the Assyrians. His successors were not so able or skilled as he had been and they were not able to maintain the empire, or combat the new threat of the Hittites who took and sacked Babylon in 1531BCE.

The Babylonians built a sophisticated society, made notable achievements in both architecture and law and were also an expanding empire. At times they were defeated and made a subject people, but they also conquered their neighbours – the most famous victory being their conquest of Judah and the taking of the Jews to Babylon in a period of ancient Jewish history known as the Babylonian captivity.

The Babylonians were conquered by the Assyrians, until they revolted and once again formed a Babylonian state under the great king Nebuchadnezzar, who ruled in Babylon from c.605BCE to c.561BCE. Under Nebuchadnezzar Babylon was beautified – through the creation of the celebrated hanging gardens – and fortified, a double wall being built to encircle the city with moats to enhance its defences. As the Euphrates River flowed through the middle of Babylon, effectively dividing the city in two, Nebuchadnezzar built a large stone bridge: this not only linked the two halves of the city, but also enhanced the ability of the army to defend it; in case of a siege or attack, Babylonians were able to shift troops rapidly from one half of the city to the other, depending on the threat.

However, the Medes soon spawned a new power to the east of Babylon. The Persians revolted against the Medes and then, under Cyrus (Cyrus of Persia and then Cyrus the Great), reigning 559–530BCE, created a new Persian empire.

◀ *The fabled Hanging Gardens of Babylon as imagined by the artist Ferdinand Knab in 1886.*

Assyria

The Assyrian empire gained power in the Euphrates Valley and developed into a sophisticated society that waged war with the same ruthless efficiency as the Hittites, but was much more developed militarily in both battle and siege tactics. Until the advent of the superb Macedonian army under Philip II and his son Alexander the Great, the Assyrians undoubtedly possessed the most advanced and modern army in the region, if not in the known world.

The Assyrian homeland was in northern Mesopotamia on the upper Tigris River and began as one of the Akkadian city-states that peopled Mesopotamia. While the early history of the Assyrians is mostly unknown, the Assyrian city of Ashur probably dates from 2600BCE. Originally a subject people of the early Akkadian empire, the Assyrians became an independent kingdom c.2100BCE.

As Assyria developed and expanded, its people excelled not only in the art and science of warfare, but also in architecture, engineering, economics, and agriculture. They were pioneers in the study of mathematics, zoology and botany and in the practice of medicine, and they established a legal system and set up public libraries. Their system of government was also highly sophisticated, run by a well-organized civil service that kept the kingdom on an even keel when the king was away on campaign.

The Assyrian empire rose c.1100BCE in the wake of the chaos brought about by the violent and destructive incursions of the Sea Peoples and they remained a powerful force in the Near East until c.600BCE. They conquered Babylon in 729BCE, then went southwards and occupied Egypt in 661BCE. However, the subject Babylonian people allied themselves with the Medes around 620BCE and in 612BCE they attacked, took and sacked the Assyrian capital of Nineveh.

The Assyrians were excellent soldiers and administrators and fielded a skilled army, experts in pitched battle and in besieging enemy fortresses and cities. They excelled in metalworking and forging, and their skilled corps of engineers designed ingenious siege engines. All Assyrian troops were well-armed and well-armoured, using a very powerful composite bow, and they fielded the most advanced and deadly army in the ancient world at the height of their empire. Their rule of subjected peoples, however, was oppressive, and this finally sounded the death knell of their empire, when captured territories to the east allied themselves with neighbours to overthrow their rulers.

▲ *The walls of Nineveh in the time of Ashurbanipal, on a bas-relief c.640BCE. Nineveh was the brutal king's capital.*

▼ *Based on a sketch by James Fergusson, this is a 19th-century impression of the ancient city of Nineveh, Assyria, on the banks of the River Tigris.*

TIMELINE OF THE FERTILE CRESCENT

The quarter-moon curve of this fertile region is also known as the cradle of civilization, and forms a 'bridge' between Africa and Eurasia. The region is regarded as the birthplace of agriculture, urbanization, writing, trade, science and organized religion.
c.4500–c.4000BCE: Ancestors of Sumerians settle in southern Mesopotamia.
c.3500–3000BCE: Development of the cities of Uruk and Ur.
c.3000BCE: The earliest form of cuneiform writing develops.
c.2900BCE: Dynastic rule by Sumerian kings begins.
c.2700BCE: The first Sumerian written records are produced.
c.2334–c.2279BCE: Sargon of Akkad conquers Sumerian city-states.
c.2100BCE: Akkadian empire collapses.
c.2040BCE: The Ziggurat of Ur is built by King Ur-Nammu.
c.2000BCE: Babylonia begins to emerge as the dominant power in the Fertile Crescent region.
c.2000BCE: Ancestors of the Hittites settle in Anatolia.
1894BCE: The Amorite dynasty assumes power in Babylon.

▼ *The remains of Hattusa, the ancient Hittite capital, in Anatolia in modern-day Turkey.*

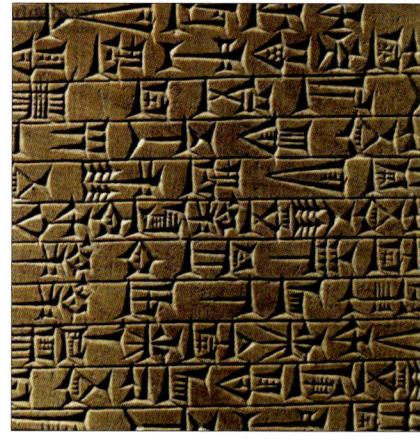

▲ *Detail of Babylonian tablet with writings about the works of King Hammurabi.*

c.1813–1755BCE: The early Assyrian empire emerges.
c.1800–c.1700BCE: The Hittites change from bronze to iron production for tools and weapons.
c.1792–c.1750BCE: Hammurabi rules as King of Babylon.
c.1787BCE: Uruk and Isin are conquered by Hammurabi.
c.1760BCE: Hammurabi writes and publishes the first law code to apply to an entire population.
c.1757BCE: Hammurabi destroys and conquers the Mari.
c.1750BCE: The old Hittite kingdom is founded in Asia Minor.
c.1650–c.1620BCE: Hattusa becomes the Hittite capital under their king Hattusilis I. The Hittites campaign in Anatolia and Syria, some venturing across the Euphrates River.
c.1620–c.1590BCE: Hattusilis is succeeded by his grandson Mursilis, who continues the Hittite conquests, taking Aleppo and Babylon.
c.1595BCE: Babylon is attacked and sacked by the Hittites under King Mursilis. Amorite rule in Babylonia comes to an end.
c.1590–c.1525BCE: The assassination of Mursilis throws the kingdom into chaos and the Hittites are invaded.
c.1595–c.1155BCE: The Kassite dynasty takes over Babylonia.
c.1525–c.1500BCE: King Telipinus takes power and attempts to restore the Hittite kingdom and conquests.
c.1500–c.1400BCE: The kingdom of the Mitanni ejects the Hittites from Syria and northern Mesopotamia.
c.1550BCE to c.1250BCE: Mitannian domination of the Assyrians.
c.1446BCE: A possible date cited by some scholars for the Biblical story of the Israelite exodus from Egypt, led by Moses and Joshua.
1390BCE: The Assyrians become an independent power in Mesopotamia.
c.1370BCE: The beginning and rise of the 'new' Hittite empire in Asia Minor, an expanding empire and aggressive kingdom bent on conquest.
c.1350–c.1322BCE: The Mitanni, at war with both Egypt and the Hittites, are destroyed – being caught between two expanding empires. The Hittites get a strong king in Tudhaliya III, who is succeeded by Suppiluliuma I.
c.1322–c.1295BCE: Mursilis II, son of Suppiluliuma, becomes king and the Hittites are again a regional power.
c.1295–c.1272BCE: Muwatallis II, the son of Mursilis II, becomes king and fights the Egyptians at the Battle of Kadesh in 1275BCE.
c.1272–c.1237BCE: Dynastic problems break out into civil war. Hattusilis emerges as king and concludes a peace with Egypt.

TIMELINE OF THE FERTILE CRESCENT

▲ *The Kurkh monoliths are two Assyrian stelae that contain descriptions of the campaigns of Ashurnasirpal II and his son Shalmaneser III (shown here).*

c.1237–c.1209BCE: The Hittites are defeated by the Assyrians; the decline of their kingdom begins.
c.1250–1076BCE: The dominance of the 'middle' Assyrian empire.
c.1220BCE: Babylon is conquered and ruled by the Assyrians.
c.1200BCE: Collapse of the Hittite kingdom. Ironworking spreads to the eastern Mediterranean.
c.1200–1100BCE: The time and 'rule' of the Judges. The Sea Peoples, especially the Philistines, land and finally settle in Palestine, called Canaan during this period.
1112BCE: The Assyrian ruler, Tiglath-Pileser I restores the power of the Assyrian empire.
c.1076BCE: Assyrian king Tiglath-Pileser I dies.
c.911BCE: Beginning of the late Assyrian empire.
883–859BCE: Assyrian power expands under Ashurnasirpal II, who establishes Nimrud as the new capital.
859–824BCE: The Assyrian empire, now ruled by Shalmaneser III, extends from the Tigris River to the Mediterranean Sea.
c.811–c.746BCE: Assyria is thrown into chaos – known as the 'Period of Weakness'.

c.750BCE: Great engineering projects, such as a system of aqueducts, are built in and around Babylon.
734BCE: The Chaldeans take Babylon.
745–727BCE: Assyrian king Tiglath-Pileser III reigns.
729BCE: The Assyrians return and take Babylon, expelling the Chaldeans.
727–722BCE: Assyrian king Shalmaneser V is in power.
722–705BCE: Assyrian king Sargon II rules.
705–681BCE Assyrian king Sennacherib is in power. Babylon is defeated and Judah and Israel incorporated into the empire. Nineveh is established as the capital.
669–631BCE: Assyrian king Ashurbanipal succeeds Esarhaddon. He is renowned for his brutal campaigns.
612BCE: The kingdom of Chaldea is begun by King Nabopolassar. The Chaldeans and their allies the Medes attack and sack Nineveh.
605BCE: A Chaldean alliance defeats the Assyrians in the Battle of Carchemish.
c.605BCE: Nebuchadnezzar II (later known as Nebuchadnezzar the Great) succeeds to the throne of Babylon upon the death of his father Nabopolassar.
c.586BCE: Nebuchadnezzar takes Jerusalem, deliberately destroying Solomon's Temple and capturing and taking a large part of the population of Judah into exile in Babylon. Portions of Judah's army escape to Egypt and establish military colonies there.
586BCE: Nebuchadnezzar begins the conquest of the Levant, defeating both the Israelites and the Phoenicians.
585–572BCE: The failed siege of Tyre by Nebuchadnezzar.
561BCE: Nebuchadnezzar dies and is succeeded by Nabonidus.
539BCE: Cyrus of Persia (Cyrus the Great) conquers Babylon and returns the exiled Jews to their homeland.
485BCE: Xerxes, King of Persia, takes and destroys Babylon.

▲ *Alabaster bas-relief of Sargon II in the royal palace at Khorsabad, Assyria.*

▼ *Assyrian archers in the army of Sargon II attacking a city, depicted on a bas-relief in the royal palace at Khorsabad, c.710BCE.*

THE SUMERIAN ARMY

Sumerian armies were armed and equipped simply, using edged weapons such as swords and daggers, as well as polearms, but they did not develop the bow. Their warriors wore clothing made of animal hide and cloth – the same as the civilian population. Most wore sheepskin, with the fur outwards. The idea of a military uniform was centuries in the future, so any uniformity of clothing among the Sumerian warriors must have been a matter of choice or necessity, rather than a response to instructions to dress the army in the same manner.

Sumerians went into battle barefoot. Their sheepskin clothing gave some protection in combat, but otherwise – with the exception of the occasional bronze helmet – Sumerian warriors had little or no body armour. Some soldiers covered their heads with a skullcap 'helmet' of cloth or leather and wore a cloak to protect themselves against the cold desert nights and sporadic heavy rains. The helmet, shaped close to the head, probably had a chinstrap, to keep the cap on and offer limited protection for the lower face. Infantrymen carried a spear and a rectangular shield; some infantrymen were armed with a dagger or axe.

An early type of combat chariot, the Sumerian war wagon was a well-balanced, four-wheeled vehicle. The war wagon gave mobility to the Sumerian troops on the battlefield, enabling them to outmanoeuvre the enemy. They made the most of this relative speed of movement to outflank and envelop their enemies or to penetrate enemy lines and operate in the rear.

It would seem the Sumerians had no knowledge of spokes, so the chariot ran on solid wheels. The wagon was constructed with a chest-high barrier at the front to protect the crew, which usually consisted of a driver and a

▲ *The 'war' side of the Standard of Ur, depicting prisoners being brought before the king, with guards and chariot behind him, infantry, and army chariots in battle.*

▼ **SUMERIAN WAR CHARIOT**
This four-wheeled vehicle, pulled by four asses, provided mobility to an army without cavalry. Normally, the crew was two men: one driver and one spearman.

spearman. The wagon was equipped to carry extra spears, suggesting that these weapons might have been thrown from the wagon. A team of asses pulled the vehicle, although some charioteers used oxen instead. The vehicle's sides were lower than the front, which would keep the weight of the wagon down. The back of the wagon was open so that the crew could easily mount or climb down from the vehicle. The ass team was sometimes given colourful trappings: these may have had a unit significance or perhaps an early tribal or city-state designation, but were more probably for decoration. The team's harness was basic; the Sumerians did not use a bit on their animals.

The Standard of Ur

We know what the war wagons looked like and how Sumerian soldiers dressed and equipped themselves in battle in the first half of the 3rd millennium BCE from the scenes of war shown on the Standard of Ur. This incredible artefact, dating to c.2600BCE, was discovered in 1927–28 during excavations led by British archaeologist Sir Leonard Woolley, in the royal cemetery of the city of Ur

▲ **Sumerian Spearman**
A distinction was made between 'line' and 'light' infantry based on the weapons used. This spearman was a 'line' infantryman and in addition to his animal fur 'kilt' he wears a garment that covers his chest and back.

◀ **Sumerian Infantryman**
With the exception of the helmet, infantrymen were not armoured and their clothing was identical to that worn by Sumerian 'civilians'.

▶ **Sumerian Light Infantryman**
This light infantryman is armed with an axe for close combat as well as wearing a reinforced garment over his shoulder and a 'kilt' made of cloth.

(modern Tell el-Muqayyar in Iraq). It consists of a wooden box, which is a frame for mosaics of lapis lazuli, shell and tiny pieces of red limestone, depicting scenes of banqueting on one side and the king leading his army to battle on the other. The combat scenes show some infantrymen wearing cloaks and armed with spears, while others dispatch the enemy with axes, as well as war wagons with solid wheels pulled by four asses riding roughshod over fallen enemies. The war wagons are depicted at three 'speeds': the ass teams walking, cantering and at the gallop. The fact that the war wagons are shown overrunning the enemy demonstrates that the Sumerians definitely used them as an offensive weapon and not merely for transport to the battlefield. The artefact is known as the Standard of Ur because Woolley determined that it was a battle standard carried onto the field of war at the end of a long pole. However, there are other theories about its use, including that it was a musical soundbox.

The Sumerians probably did not carry flags, but they did have battle standards. These were usually images of different animals attached to a pole, which would indicate different units and clearly demonstrate some army organization. The poles might have had coloured designs attached to denote the unit or the commander.

Arms and Equipment

In the period 2500–2000BCE Sumerian warriors began to wear a kilt-like garment of varying pattern and cut, although mostly they continued to use animal skins with the fur side out. As before, they usually fought without footwear and with skullcaps of cloth or leather, but some wore a bronze helmet in the style of the earlier skullcap. This indicates expertise in working with a copper/tin alloy and an ability to advance their weaponry technologically. We know that at this time Sumerian massed infantry fought in a tightly formed grouping with helmets, spears and large rectangular shields. The Stele of Vultures, dating to *c.*2450BCE, commemorates the victory of King Eannatum of the Sumerian city-state of Lagash over a rival power. Seven fragments of the stele have survived. We can see Eannatum leading a tight phalanx of infantrymen into battle. They trample their enemies underfoot – and in the sky above, the vultures that give the stele its name carry the severed heads of enemy warriors.

◀ **SUMERIAN LIGHT INFANTRY**
This infantryman is wearing clothing and headdress of cloth. Being lightly armed and accoutered, he probably was a skirmisher operating in front of the main Sumerian formation or on the flanks of the army.

▶ **SUMERIAN HEAVY INFANTRY**
A frontline infantryman armed with spear and shield as well as helmet. The Sumerians apparently did not wear any combat harness for weapons and accoutrements.

◀ **Sumerian Commander**
This officer's garment covers his whole body, and his more elaborate helmet denotes rank. Like the men he commanded, he does not wear any footgear.

▼ **Sumerian Standard Bearer**
Animal standards were used for recognition on the battlefield and as a rallying point. The unarmoured nature of the bearer indicates that he would need to rely on his comrades for protection in combat.

A second detail shows the king in a war wagon at the head of a force bearing spears at shoulder height.

In addition to the slow-moving heavy infantry depicted on the Stele of Vultures, the Sumerians also deployed a more mobile light infantry whose role was to skirmish in front of the masses of heavy infantry in formation. Light infantrymen were equipped and armed lightly in order to facilitate their movement and mission. Generally they carried no shields and were not armoured; some might have worn the basic helmet while others covered their heads with a portion of their cloak.

As was traditional in ancient armies, Sumerian commanders were better dressed and equipped than the mass of their warriors. This occurred for two reasons: first, because these eminent men had the wealth and resources to finance such equipment and clothing; and second, because the leader needed to be recognized in battle in order to be an effective figurehead in combat. He needed to rally the army quickly if his troops were repulsed. If the commander of these ancient armies was killed or captured, this could settle the battle at a stroke – his army would be put to flight, leaving the field to the victors.

◀ *Fragment from the Stele of Vultures, portraying Sumerian soldiers in a phalanx, being led by Eannatum, c.2450 BCE. The limestone stele would have been 1.8m (5ft 11in) high, and was typical of victory monuments.*

THE HITTITE ARMY

The Hittites were more sophisticated militarily than the Sumerians. They had developed separately from the Sumerians and came from a different ethnic background. Originating from what is now Anatolia, with their capital at Hattusa (near modern Boğazkale in Turkey), they expanded by conquest to the east and south.

The Hittite army fielded a 'universal' infantryman who could be employed for any battlefield task that he was given, either fighting in close formation or in a more open order. The Hittite infantry probably all looked similar no matter what their function or mission, and were armed identically.

Hittite soldiers were usually clean-shaven and wore their hair long, in contrast to other peoples with whom they came into contact. Their appearance disgusted the Egyptians they fought at Kadesh: the Egyptians believed that facial hair and a short haircut were much more masculine in appearance. The different traditions and practices relating to personal appearance and habits derived from the ethnic origin of the different peoples. The Hittites were Indo-Europeans who had migrated from Asia to their homeland in Asia Minor, which suggests that their origins were probably nomadic.

Hittite Weaponry

The Hittites fought with spears, axes and short swords or long daggers. They did not use the bow, at least initially,

◀ **HITTITE INFANTRYMAN**
This infantryman has the same type of iron helmet and figure of eight shield as the spearman, but is armed with an axe and short sword for close combat. He could also carry a spear or javelins.

▶ **HITTITE LIGHT INFANTRYMAN**
Armed with spear and shield, this infantryman is a chariot rider, one of three crewman manning the typical Hittite chariot. His shield is the same as that carried by the prince (see page 38) and he could have been equipped with a helmet when in combat.

THE HITTITE ARMY

▶ **Hittite Heavy Infantry**
This specially armed infantryman could very well be a gate or palace guard. His bronze helmet is distinctive and his clothing appears to be of the same quality as those of the Hittite princes. He was undoubtedly hand-picked for palace duty.

▼ Hittite warriors, shown on an orthostat stele from Kargama (now Ankara, Turkey) c.800BCE.

and this is puzzling because they definitely came into contact with the Egyptians as both enemies and allies. The Egyptians had developed an early model of the composite bow from a very simple V-shaped bow in the Old Kingdom period. Later, when the Hittites did adopt the bow, it was used primarily by the mounted troops of the chariot arm and not by the infantry.

The spear seems to have been the preferred Hittite weapon, and was designed to be thrown like a javelin. It does not appear to have been designed separately for infantry and chariot forces, all troops using a single, all-purpose spear. The Hittites had developed iron-smelting and one reason for their military success was that their hard iron weapons outperformed the softer bronze weapons used by their enemies – notably Egyptians.

Protection in Battle

The Hittites initially either used very basic armour or none at all, with the exception of a round or conical helmet. These were sometimes simple, but at others 'decorated' in the manner of the Sea Peoples in order to appear more terrifying to the enemy. The Hittites fought alongside the Sea Peoples in the famous Battle of Kadesh against Ramesses II of Egypt in 1275BCE. Later, scale and lamellar armour – bronze scales sewn onto a padded undergarment – similar to that used by the Egyptians, was either developed or was borrowed from contact with other peoples, such as the Mitanni.

The Hittites wore more advanced clothing than the Sumerians but usually

▶ **Hittite Spearman**
The regular Hittite infantrymen wore either long robe-like clothing that went to the ankles or a shorter tunic that went to just above the knee. The iron helmet is typical for the period as is the small figure of eight shield.

▶ *A basalt relief from Carchemish, depicting a Hittite chariot and archer in a battle scene.*

▼ **Hittite Noble**
This royal personage is distinguished by his rich clothing and distinctive headdress, which may have been the model for those later worn by Assyrian royalty. He is armed simply with a sword and could very well have been accompanied by a shield bearer.

did not have footwear. However, the question of whether ancient armies really fought barefoot is definitely not a settled matter. While many surviving depictions of Egyptians, Sumerians and Hittites show warriors in battle without sandals or boots, the Egyptians did issue them to their troops, even though they may have only worn them on the march. It appears that in these early armies the use of footwear was minimal.

Hittite Chariots and the Battle of Kadesh

The battle tactics of the Hittites relied on the power of their mobile war chariots. The chariot force was sent in first with the infantry following behind. When the Egyptians commanded by Pharaoh Ramesses II and the Hittites under King Muwatallis met at the Battle of Kadesh in 1275 BCE, there were – according to scholarly estimates – more than 5,000 chariots fighting in a swirling action: the largest chariot battle in military history. In addition to his chariots, King Muwatallis had at his disposal two vast infantry divisions – of 18,000 and 19,000 men respectively.

▶ **Hittite Noble**
The clothing and headdress of this noble are simpler than that of other Hittite royalty pictured; he is probably of lesser rank. Armed with a sword, he carries a simple wooden shield.

The Hittites had probably first employed chariots in the 17th century BCE, and they recorded how they trained their chariot horses in a very early form of 'technical manual', probably in the 15th century BCE. As different peoples developed writing, they also wrote down military practices in the early equivalent of a 'standard operating procedure'. The training of horses for chariot teams and later cavalry units was uniform, and writing the techniques down was an advance that greatly aided the organization and training of armies.

THE HITTITE ARMY

▶ **HITTITE HEAVY INFANTRY**
This specially armed infantryman could very well be a gate or palace guard. His bronze helmet is distinctive and his clothing appears to be of the same quality as those of the Hittite princes. He was undoubtedly hand-picked for palace duty.

▼ *Hittite warriors, shown on an orthostat stele from Kargama (now Ankara, Turkey) c.800BCE.*

and this is puzzling because they definitely came into contact with the Egyptians as both enemies and allies. The Egyptians had developed an early model of the composite bow from a very simple V-shaped bow in the Old Kingdom period. Later, when the Hittites did adopt the bow, it was used primarily by the mounted troops of the chariot arm and not by the infantry.

The spear seems to have been the preferred Hittite weapon, and was designed to be thrown like a javelin. It does not appear to have been designed separately for infantry and chariot forces, all troops using a single, all-purpose spear. The Hittites had developed iron-smelting and one reason for their military success was that their hard iron weapons outperformed the softer bronze weapons used by their enemies – notably Egyptians.

Protection in Battle

The Hittites initially either used very basic armour or none at all, with the exception of a round or conical helmet. These were sometimes simple, but at others 'decorated' in the manner of the Sea Peoples in order to appear more terrifying to the enemy. The Hittites fought alongside the Sea Peoples in

▶ **HITTITE SPEARMAN**
The regular Hittite infantrymen wore either long robe-like clothing that went to the ankles or a shorter tunic that went to just above the knee. The iron helmet is typical for the period as is the small figure of eight shield.

the famous Battle of Kadesh against Ramesses II of Egypt in 1275BCE. Later, scale and lamellar armour – bronze scales sewn onto a padded undergarment – similar to that used by the Egyptians, was either developed or was borrowed from contact with other peoples, such as the Mitanni.

The Hittites wore more advanced clothing than the Sumerians but usually

▶ *A basalt relief from Carchemish, depicting a Hittite chariot and archer in a battle scene.*

▼ **HITTITE NOBLE**
This royal personage is distinguished by his rich clothing and distinctive headdress, which may have been the model for those later worn by Assyrian royalty. He is armed simply with a sword and could very well have been accompanied by a shield bearer.

did not have footwear. However, the question of whether ancient armies really fought barefoot is definitely not a settled matter. While many surviving depictions of Egyptians, Sumerians and Hittites show warriors in battle without sandals or boots, the Egyptians did issue them to their troops, even though they may have only worn them on the march. It appears that in these early armies the use of footwear was minimal.

Hittite Chariots and the Battle of Kadesh

The battle tactics of the Hittites relied on the power of their mobile war chariots. The chariot force was sent in first with the infantry following behind. When the Egyptians commanded by Pharaoh Ramesses II and the Hittites under King Muwatallis met at the Battle of Kadesh in 1275 BCE, there were – according to scholarly estimates – more than 5,000 chariots fighting in a swirling action: the largest chariot battle in military history. In addition to his chariots, King Muwatallis had at his disposal two vast infantry divisions – of 18,000 and 19,000 men respectively.

▶ **HITTITE NOBLE**
The clothing and headdress of this noble are simpler than that of other Hittite royalty pictured; he is probably of lesser rank. Armed with a sword, he carries a simple wooden shield.

The Hittites had probably first employed chariots in the 17th century BCE, and they recorded how they trained their chariot horses in a very early form of 'technical manual', probably in the 15th century BCE. As different peoples developed writing, they also wrote down military practices in the early equivalent of a 'standard operating procedure'. The training of horses for chariot teams and later cavalry units was uniform, and writing the techniques down was an advance that greatly aided the organization and training of armies.

The Hittites designed their chariots differently to the Egyptians, using a six-spoke wheel instead of the Egyptians' eight spokes. They manned their chariots with three crewmen instead of the more common two, and while the Egyptians designed their chariots with the axle at the rear of the chariot, the Hittite axle was situated in the middle of the chariot body; this made for a better-balanced design and explains why the vehicle could carry a third crewman.

The Hittite innovation of the two-wheeled light chariot revolutionized ancient warfare in the Near East. The new chariot, together with the use of domesticated horses instead of oxen or asses on the team, was a game-changer. Domesticated horses were initially not yet large enough for riding, especially with a fully equipped cavalryman as a basic load. They were, however, large and strong enough when used in teams to pull a light chariot and crew.

The three-man crew consisted of a driver, shield bearer and spearman. The driver was unarmed and unarmoured; the spearman wore a dome-shaped bronze helmet and lamellar armour over a short-sleeved tunic, leaving his lower arms, wrists and hands unarmoured for ease of movement. He carried a spear of 2.1–2.4m (7–8ft) length. On the two-horse team, the spearman wore an armoured corselet, as well as a neck and head covering – probably of bronze-studded cloth – for further protection.

What we know about the appearance of Hittite warriors and chariots comes mostly from Ancient Egyptian relief carvings of this period. These suggest that the Hittites originally used a two-man chariot crew but moved to a three-man crew in the later 13th century BCE.

▼ Hittite Chariot and Crew
The three-man Hittite chariot was distinctive, as their opponents used two-man chariots. The fully armoured infantryman might be meant to dismount and fight on foot if necessary.

THE BABYLONIAN ARMY

Like many of their foes, Babylonian troops wore ankle-length robes, sometimes heavily embroidered, or a plain military tunic that came down to mid-thigh or almost to the knee. They often used captured Assyrian body armour and weapons and carried round shields – either flat or conical. The infantry relied on the spear, although soldiers also carried daggers and short swords as a secondary threat. Both infantry and cavalry wore conical helmets. The cavalry used a lance, a longer spear than that used by the infantry, and carried round shields for protection; they also wore a sword, probably on a baldric that was worn over the right shoulder.

The reason Babylonians used similar clothing and equipment to their neighbours is that they developed as an empire alongside other aggressive peoples – Elam to the east, with its capital at Susa (in the Khuzestan region of Iran); Assyria to the north, with its capital at Nineveh (near modern Mosul, Iraq); and the Mitanni to their northwest, with a capital at Harran (near modern Urfa, Turkey). Militarily, there was considerable cross-fertilization of arms, armour, organization, tactics and military engineering. The difference that enabled one empire to become ascendant over others was primarily superior organization and leadership: in the case of Babylonian

◀ **BABYLONIAN CAVALRYMAN**
The Babylonians, also known as Chaldeans, were armed and dressed similarly to their foes. This typically accoutered cavalryman has a spear, scale armour cuirass, iron helmet and irtu, a metal disk worn in the centre of the chest attached to a cross harness.

▶ **BABYLONIAN INFANTRYMAN**
This infantryman is similar in appearance to the cavalryman with the exception of not wearing either a cuirass or an irtu. He has the same type of iron conical helmet along with spear and round shield. He is particularly well-equipped with a type of laced boot.

THE BABYLONIAN ARMY

Hittites. Until the Chaldean dynasty and Nabopolassar, Nebuchadnezzar's father, Babylon was a vassal state of Assyria.

Battle of Carchemish

While still crown prince, Nebuchadnezzar proved his worth as a general and combat commander in leading the Babylonian army to victory at the Battle of Carchemish (May–June 605BCE). He faced a military alliance of Assyrians and Egyptians under Pharaoh Necho II (reigned 609–595BCE). The city of Carchemish in northern Syria was at this time the capital of the Assyrians, who had been forced by Babylonian expansion to move from their capital at Nineveh in 612BCE and from Harran in 608BCE.

Nebuchadnezzar swiftly moved to face his enemies and surprised the Egyptian/Assyrian army in their camp, in a coordinated attack of both infantry and cavalry. He drove the enemy from the field, then crossed the Euphrates and pursued them ruthlessly. According to the Chronicle of Nebuchadnezzar, now preserved in the British Museum, the Egyptians were wiped out. After the campaign was over, he succeeded his father King Nabopolassar (626–605BCE).

Expansion of Empire

Nebuchadnezzar's army had a striking record of success against the Hebrew kingdoms, taking the Hebrew capital Jerusalem twice. On the first occasion, the Babylonians caused little or no damage to the city and left King Solomon's Temple intact: King Jehoiakim of Israel (reigned 608–598BCE) was required to pay tribute to the Babylonians. The Babylonians captured the city for a second time in 587BCE, following a ruthlessly punishing siege. On this occasion, the Temple was destroyed and its treasures carted off to Babylon along with thousands of enslaved Hebrews.

These prisoners of war remained in Babylon with their descendents until they were repatriated to Judah by Cyrus the Great in 539BCE, after he had defeated the Babylonians and established the Persian empire.

▼ BABYLONIAN GUARDSMAN
The dress of this palace guard is of Achaemenid Persian style. It is highly plausible that there was some continuity in the ceremonial costumes worn by Babylonian guardsmen and by the later Persian 'Immortals'. His long robe is formal wear and the absence of a helmet is an indicator of his duty if not his status.

▲ BABYLONIAN ARCHER
This horse archer is very well equipped with the typical iron conical helmet, composite bow and quiver, along with a sword.

King Nebuchadnezzar II (reigned 605–561BCE), it was because he was a highly skilled general, military leader and combat commander.

Babylon had existed as an independent empire under king Hammurabi. After his death in c.1750BCE, the empire had declined and been invaded and overcome by its adversaries, including the Mitanni and

THE ASSYRIAN ARMIES

The Assyrians were among the best soldiers of the ancient period. They were ferocious in attack, resolute and unyielding in defence and – alone among ancient armies until the advent of the Greeks and Macedonians – they had a well-developed engineering arm. Siege engines were superbly designed and constructed, and skilfully deployed.

Assyrian Battle Tactics

There is no surviving Assyrian tactical manual, nor conclusive evidence that there was one. The employment of army tactics was probably based on tradition and experience. The Assyrians preferred attack to defence, and their army was organized with that in mind, especially in reference to their chariot and cavalry arms.

Traditionally the Assyrians employed their infantry in the centre of their battle array and covered their main line with their light infantry. Cavalry was probably posted on the wings to prevent them being outflanked and to take advantage of the mobility of the heavy cavalry and their horse archers. The chariot arm may have been held in reserve to exploit both a breakthrough of the enemy line and to

◀ **Assyrian King**
Ashurnasirpal II is known to have taken part in the sieges that his army undertook, and his dress would mark him as a person of importance to all, both friendly and enemy. He is clothed here in typical 'royal' dress including the headdress, the polo crown of Assyria. He is armed with bow, the usual thin Assyrian sword, and two daggers.

▶ **Assyrian Shield Bearer**
At least two of these would protect the king from enemy missile fire, and one of them would hand the king his arrows as the king would not be carrying his own quiver. The shield bearers would wear typical Assyrian dress along with a sword.

▼ **Light Archer**
Contrary to usual practice, this archer's tunic comes to his knees, not below. Partially armoured, he wears a headband not a helmet.

Leadership and Command
Assyrian commanders led in person in the field and took a full part in the fighting. The chief commander was often the king: he rode out in his chariot at the head of his army, dressed elaborately and distinctively.

His clothing was heavily embroidered and he wore a short-sleeved, robe-like garment, with the skirt reaching down to the ankles. He was heavily armed, with at least two daggers, a long, slender Assyrian sword and a composite bow. He went into battle in the company of a shield bearer: this protection allowed the king to use his bow unfettered by a shield.

pursue in case the enemy was routed. Also, the chariot arm was employed to fight any enemy who had a comparable chariot arm.

It is a logical conclusion that the Assyrians used combined arms tactics – that is they employed two or more arms together to reach a tactical decision. The Assyrian light cavalry was adept at pursuing a broken foe and hunting enemy partisan units, along with the Assyrian light infantry, in swampy or broken terrain.

▶ **Armoured Cavalryman**
This heavy cavalryman is armed with composite bow, a quiver of arrows and a lance. He is basically a heavy horse archer with the addition of a lance. He has upper body armour and conical helmet and he is also well-shod and well-clothed.

Shalmaneser III

In the celebrated Battle of Qarqar (now near Hama in western Syria) in 853BCE, Shalmaneser III took on an alliance of 12 monarchs that included King Ahab of Israel; it was the largest battle then known – a vast Assyrian force numbering 100,000 faced a force of 70,000. The events were commemorated on the Kurkh Stele (see page 31), one of a pair of monoliths discovered in 1861 in Kurkh (now known as Üçtepe Höyük) in Turkey. Judging from the evidence of these and similar triumphal reliefs, Assyrian soldiers fought in pairs in the infantry as well as in the cavalry. Spearmen and archers would typically go into battle in twos, side by side, the spearman using his weapon and shield to keep the enemy at bay while the archer let loose his deadly missiles.

In the Kurkh Stele inscription Shalmaneser boasted that he and his troops killed 14,000 of the enemy: 'I fell upon them like a deadly flood. I laid out their corpses and the plain was filled... I made their blood flow... the plain was too small for all their bodies to be laid out... I seized chariots, cavalry and fine teams of horses...' Such boastful inscriptions should not be taken at face value, however. Although Shalmaneser claimed victory in the battle, it is notable that all the kings in the alliance that had supposedly been defeated continued to reign in the aftermath of the battle and Shalmaneser had to fight further campaigns against these same rulers.

Tiglath-Pileser III

An excellent king as well as general, (reigning 745–727BCE), Tiglath-Pileser III's main reform was to reorganize the Assyrian army. He changed the army from what was essentially a group of conscripts to a standing, professional fighting force that was able to campaign year round instead of merely during 'campaigning season' in the summer. He embarked on a series of campaigns that expanded the empire beyond the borders of what could be considered 'Greater Assyria'. Newly conquered territories were absorbed into the empire and were governed by an Assyrian governor appointed by the king.

In reorganizing his military force (known as the *kisir sharruti* – 'the standing army'), Tiglath-Pileser integrated foreign troops with the native Assyrian professional soldiers. All wore the same clothing and equipment and were armed with the same weapons. All had the appearance of Assyrians, which undoubtedly was an aid to both efficiency and morale. Most of the prisoners-of-

◀ **AUXILIARY ARCHER**
This infantryman is definitely a wartime levy and is very lightly clothed and equipped. As well as bow and arrows, he has also armed himself with a sword for self-defence.

▶ **ARMOURED INFANTRY**
This infantryman is an Assyrian regular, well-armed, well-armoured, and very well-equipped. His conical helmet has ear protection and his Assyrian-style sword is hung on his body with a baldric. His scale armour covers his torso and his shield and spear are well-made, but his spear does not have an iron butt on the wooden shaft.

THE ASSYRIAN ARMIES 45

◀ Light Cavalryman
Well-armed, equipped and clothed, the lack of body armour (with the exception of the helmet) marks this man as a light cavalryman. He is a horse archer, but he is also armed with a lance, and would also have a sword for close combat.

war fighting in his army were placed in the light infantry, while the heavy infantry, charioteers and cavalry remained native Assyrians. The bas-reliefs that depict the royal chariot also show Assyrian warriors driving prisoners and spoils of war in the form of flocks of animals from a city labelled in cuneiform writing as 'Astartu' and thought by historians to be the biblical Ashteroth Karnaim (in northern Transjordan), which would place the campaign as one that took place in 733–732 BCE.

Assyrian Armour
Both infantry and cavalry used spears and/or lances. The cavalry was equipped with bow and lance; how they handled the lance when using the bow remains a puzzle for historians, unless the lance came equipped with a sling at the balance of the piece that could be looped around the upper arm while holding the bow and readying it for fire.

The Assyrian bow was made in one piece, and was used by both infantry and horse archers. The shaping of the composite bow came at its midpoint, where the bowman would hold the bow for firing. As the bow became more advanced, the shape of the bow would become more gradual (the 'U' shape) as contrasted to the sharper, less advanced shape (the 'V' shape). The composite bow was much more powerful than the one-piece wooden bow because the central core of wood was covered during construction with bone and sinew, increasing range and penetrating power although requiring more pulling power than previous simpler bows. Bowmen carried their arrows in a large quiver attached at the waist – or, if the archer was in a chariot, attached to the vehicle. As an army's equipment improved, sometimes the arrow quiver would be carried attached to a baldric over the shoulder, as the sword sometimes was, especially by elite Assyrian formations.

Troops carried daggers and long, thin swords. The swords were attached either to a leather baldric over the shoulder or to a belt around the waist. Shields were round and relatively small, some of them flat, and others concave – rather like a conical hat in appearance. Most Assyrian troops wore a conical iron helmet, which afforded excellent protection from both missiles and edged weapons. The helmets sometimes had iron pieces to protect the ears and side of the head, and others had crests similar to either the Scythians or the Greeks.

▶ ARMOURED RAM
This siege vehicle had a bladed arm suspended by ropes inside the engine. Moved by manpower, it was able to be unassembled and transported and then reassembled in front of the targeted fortress wall. Archers would man the top as support. Animal skins protected the engine from fire.

Seige Warfare

The Assyrians preferred to fight in the open than to pursue siege warfare: even when they were faced with an enemy fortress or city that had to be taken, they would rather take it by assault than by siege. Nevertheless the Assyrians did develop highly effective siege engines, that were second to none in the ancient world. No army before the Romans produced equivalent assault engines.

Large siege towers were built from which bowmen could fire down onto the walls of enemy fortifications, suppressing the enemy's own bowmen. Enemy fortresses or fortified towns that were facing the sea or other body of water would be attacked by Assyrian siege towers that were specially built to be able to float and face those walls. Armoured rams were constructed that worked not just against the gates of the enemy town or fortress but to undermine the enemy's walls where the point of attack was to be made when the walls were breached. The 'ram' portion of the siege vehicle was a moveable arm with a large spade or tool that was used by the siege engine's crew to take the base of the wall apart so that this portion of the wall would collapse, creating a breach through which the Assyrian infantry could attack. The engines were large and wheeled and could be pushed into position. They were covered with animal skins as a protection against fire; some of the troops manning the engines were tasked with putting out any fires caused by enemy missiles. Further, these engines were fortified to protect bowmen and crewmen and allow the Assyrian bowmen to suppress enemy fire from the walls of the fortress.

Assyrian siege procedures were practical and skilful. First, the enemy city or fortress would be surrounded and cut off from outside aid – an attempt to starve the enemy garrison into submission. This would take longer than an assault, but in the long run it was cheaper in terms of

▼ LIGHT RAM
This siege weapon was used to undermine a fortress wall or to knock in a gate which can be the most vulnerable, as well as the best defended, part of a fortress. It was propelled by manpower pushing the poles at the rear.

manpower for the Assyrians. The Assyrian engineers would construct an earthen wall or berm around the fortress and reinforce it with timber if available. A place would then be chosen for the final assault against the fortress and siege operations would then begin in earnest.

The Assyrians built ramps of earth supported by timber and stone that came up to the enemy's walls for use in the assault – as well as to bring the siege engines close to and further up the height of the walls. At all times during active siege operations, Assyrian troops manning the siege engines or performing engineer tasks to facilitate the siege were covered by swarms of bowmen who suppressed the enemy's missile fire.

While the Assyrians preferred not to conduct sieges and made an effort to avoid them, they conducted many noteworthy sieges during their campaigns. They aimed to conduct short sieges, but their engineer arm was capable of conducting formal sieges that required long periods to be successful. The sieges of Jerusalem, Babylon, Arpad (a city in northwestern Syria) and Samaria (modern Sabastiyah, central Palestine) were all more than a year in length. All were successful: after falling to the Assyrian army, they were plundered and looted, their inhabitants abused or put to the sword and many prisoners taken as slaves.

A stone relief panel in the palace of King Tiglath-Pileser III at Kalhu (later called Nimrud, today near the modern village of

▲ *Bas-relief at Nimrud depicting the victorious army of Tiglath-Pileser III laying seige to an enemy town, 730–727BCE.*

Numaniyah, southeast of Mosul, Iraq) shows an Assyrian army besieging a town identified as Upa, thought by historians to be a site in Turkey. While archers provide covering fire, a wheeled platform is pushed up to the walls of the city; at a different spot spearmen carrying shields attempt to scale the walls using ladders. The town's defenders are shown fighting on top of the walls and falling down onto the battlefield, having been wounded by a spearman who had climbed one of the scaling ladders or shot by an arrow loosed by one of the Assyrian bowmen. The platform could have been used as a battering ram and provided a raised position from which archers could fire at the enemy. This may represent different sections of a siege – or else the final assault on a city or fortress when a breach has been made in the walls.

Assyrian siege engines were manhandled into position by soldiers; draft animals were not used within missile range of the fortress walls. Troops would react to commands more readily than animals and casualties were easier to replace.

When the Assyrian army took to the field, they were ruthless in both battle and siege, an attitude readily apparent from the bas-reliefs that have survived. In combat reputation is often a deciding factor. The Assyrians,

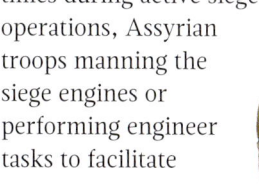

◀ **HEAVY ARCHER**
This bowman wears the usual long Assyrian tunic and the Assyrian conical helmet. His leather jerkin is covered in scale armour and he carries a composite bow, although has no sidearms, unusual for light troops.

respected and feared by their enemies, were very aware of this, and often behaved in ways that would enhance their reputation for ferocity.

Assyrian Cavalry

The Assyrians were not only militarily more advanced than any army that came before them, including the Egyptians, but also the most dangerous. Their cavalry was certainly a major part of their effectiveness, and they used horse archer units with skill and efficiency. The Assyrian cavalry arm was not only a force to be reckoned with on the battlefield, but could also be employed for reconnaissance and shock attacks and on diverse missions such as hunting for rebel forces in marshes and in other types of difficult terrain.

The armoured horse archer of this period was the epitome of the Assyrian cavalryman. The trooper's horse was lightly but effectively protected with a padded caparison that provided a better seat for the rider. Assyrians did not use saddles, instead they made use of a sheepskin saddlecloth that served as a 'seat' for the mounted archer. Sometimes, animal hides such as the skins of leopard and other large cats were used for saddlecloths.

There are period depictions of Assyrian horse archers firing from the gallop with both hands, which suggests that they were highly skilled riders, using their knees to control and direct the horse.

Horse archers fought in pairs,

▶ Armoured Horse Archer
This horse archer is more of a heavy cavalryman, though he is not armed in this instance with a lance as well as a bow. He wears the usual conical helmet but he does wear body armour of scales sewn onto his clothing, as well as being well-shod. His horse is much better caparisoned than that of the light horse archer.

THE ASSYRIAN ARMIES 49

▶ **ARMOURED CAVALRYMAN**
While this horseman does wear body armour and the usual conical helmet, he is actually a light cavalryman as is indicated by his lack of trousers and shoes and by the light trappings of his mount. He is armed with lance and sword.

▶ **LANCER**
This heavy cavalryman is not a horse archer although he is mounted, clothed and equipped in a similar manner. He is armed with lance and sword, as well as an iron-faced conical shield.

employed) was probably around 250–650m (275–700 yards). The bow was slung across the archer's back when not in use and the arrow quiver and/or sheaf was also worn across the back.

The Assyrian army deployed both armoured and unarmoured mounted lancers: the first could be classed as heavy cavalry, while the latter were undoubtedly more similar to light cavalry. The lance was longer than an infantryman's spear: this made it possible for a mounted warrior to reach prone enemies on the battlefield. He also wore a sword or dagger, or probably both. Equipped in one archer holding the reins of both horses, while the other fired successive arrows.

The archer's horse was caparisoned with coloured cloth, which covered most of the horse's body. A deep sky blue tended to be a favourite colour of the Assyrians, according to some modern historians. The bridle and reins were typically decorated in leather and brass.

The archer wore a scale or lamellar shirt, and he wore boots and leg armour that would later be copied by the Persian cavalry of Cyrus the Great. His helmet was typical of the Assyrian army, and was designed to deflect both edged and missile weapons – again, its simple design and construction would be copied and used by other armies up to and through the Middle Ages.

Assyrian horse archers were expert in the use of the powerful composite bow. The range of the Assyrian bow (or bows, as more than one type was this way he was the precursor of the Eastern Roman armoured cataphract, who similarly used both lance and composite bow.

The lance in the hands of a trained cavalryman was a deadly weapon with a longer reach than a sword. It was used by the lancer against infantry with an overhand downward thrust that was highly effective. The heavy lancers were probably employed on the battlefield in cooperation with horse archers. The light lancers were deployed for scouting and screening, and were probably used in conjunction with unarmoured bowmen and light infantry; the idea of 'combined arms' employment by the Assyrians was well developed. The Assyrians also used spearmen and bowmen together, supported by lance-armed horse archers.

Infantry Slingers

Composite bows were not the only missile weapons employed by the Assyrians and other Near Eastern armies; slings were also used. They used a sling made of leather to fire smooth, round stones collected from creeks and riverbeds. The role of slingers was to engage the enemy from a safe position out of range of hand-held weapons such as polearms and edged weapons; they carefully selected missiles for ballistic effect.

These troops were a key part of the army. Well trained, experienced

▶ **Slinger**
Slingers were light infantry, but this example is armoured like any heavy infantryman. He holds his sling, inspecting it for fair wear-and-tear, and that appears to be his only weapon. The leather cross belt would hold the bag or light pack carrying his hand-picked stone ammunition.

◀ **Light Horse Archer**
This horseman is a light cavalryman armed with bow and short sword. His only armour is his iron helmet. The horse is also lightly caparisoned compared to heavy cavalry horses.

slingers were a valuable type of light infantry used to support troops in formation and, when on the defensive, to keep away the enemy short-range missile troops and protect their own troops in defensive positions. Before a clash of regular heavy infantry, the slingers and other light troops would pass to the rear, rally and redeploy as needed.

Slingers were sometimes armed only with a sling, as in many of the Near Eastern armies, but in some cases they were also armed with a sword or dagger for self-defence. They might be armoured in the same fashion as other Assyrian infantry.

Infantry Bowmen

Like their mounted counterparts, foot archers in the infantry were equipped with the excellent composite bow. Some were armoured with a scale armour 'cuirass', as well as a type of scale armour to protect the legs and over this would wear a one-piece tunic that came to the mid-thigh. These infantrymen were also armed with a sword worn at the waist.

Other bowmen wore a long 'skirt' that came to the ankles. On their upper half they had a short-sleeved shirt beneath an armoured vest or cuirass made of scale armour.

▼ ARCHER
This is an example of a levy used to reinforce the Assyrian regular army on campaign. His long robe may be an indicator of a subject people, now employed to fight for their conquerors. He is, however, with the exception of footwear, very well-armed and equipped with the Assyrian conical helmet, bow and quiver, and a sword as a sidearm.

▶ LIGHT ARCHER
This light infantryman wears no armour and so might not be used in line of battle, but as a skirmisher. His colourful clothing and more-than-adequate boots show him to be well-equipped, and he is armed with a sword.

Many wore a conical Assyrian helmet, but some bowmen did not wear a helmet, instead partially protecting the head with a type of bronze headpiece that resembled a headband. They typically wore their hair long and braided; most also had a braided beard although a few, unusually for the Assyrians, were clean-shaven.

Foot archers were also used in two-man teams. One used the bow while the second held a tall wicker shield to protect the archer when firing.

Light Infantry

Assyrian light infantry carried round or rectangular shields and were at least partially armoured. Many wore a helmet with a small horsehair crest, but some light infantry did not wear a helmet. There was an interesting piece of equipment that could be classed as armour: the irtu, a bronze disk worn in the centre of the chest, attached to wide leather cross-belts.

Members of the light infantry were typically equipped with a composite bow, an arrow quiver and the thin, elegant Assyrian sword with belt and baldric. Like other Assyrian troops of the period they wore a thick, broad 'band' around the waist under the waistbelt.

◀ **Spearman**
This infantryman is probably also a levy conscripted for wartime service as he is wearing an older style of helmet, and is armed simply with spear and round shield. His only armour is the irtu, the small bronze disk in the centre of his chest which is attached to a leather harness. He is not equipped with the excellent Assyrian laced boots.

▶ **Light Infantryman**
Another wartime levy, this light infantryman is armed with spear and shield. He is well-clothed, with the usual conical helmet, though without the Assyrian laced boots. His shield is quite modern, being faced with iron and concave in shape.

Differences in Dress

Like other troops at this time, Assyrian infantrymen were not uniform in appearance, armour or purpose, partly because the Assyrians employed Hittites as mercenaries or as auxiliary troops. The Hittite mercenaries and regular Assyrian infantry might have been armed similarly, but shields and armour were different; sometimes infantry would be either lightly armoured or wear no armour at all. Shields could be of different shapes, from a simple round wooden shield to a more elaborate, conically shaped bronze shield.

Differences applied among the cavalry as well as among the infantry. Not all Assyrian horse archers were equipped in the same manner: while armed with the same composite bow as the infantry and usually also with a sword, their clothing and other equipment varied. The reason for

▲ Assyrian spearmen with shields, in a palace bas-relief at Nineveh, 7th century BCE. What is noteworthy about the equipment of the warriors shown is the distinctive 'pointed' shields used by the Assyrians. They were undoubtedly designed to deflect both arrows and blows by hand weapons and polearms.

▼ **ARMOURED SHIELD BEARER**
This infantryman in an older-style helmet with a crest has head-to-foot scale armour and a very large shield. The shield – a hypothetical reconstruction – would cover its bearer from helmet to sandals, and undoubtedly be both heavy and awkward to carry and handle, so would not have been used in close combat.

◀ **MEDIUM INFANTRYMAN**
Well-clothed and armed, the helmet of this infantryman is of a different style than the usual conical helmet. His bronze-faced shield is an outstanding example of the armourer's art and his spear has a counterweight which could also be used as a weapon if necessary.

▼ Royal Chariot
Assyrian splendour for their kings and royalty did not end when the army took the field. This magnificent four-horse heavy chariot is the king's. The four-horse team is matched and well-trained, and the crew is holding the horse team steady.

this could depend where they were recruited, or a preference of their immediate commanders; differences also applied across historical periods.

Two-wheeled Chariots

The two-wheeled chariot pulled by a two-horse team was typical of the Assyrian chariot arm in the period before the adoption of the heavy four-horse team chariot of the later empire. It was solidly constructed, with heavy, eight-spoked wheels that gave it stability in the charge and offset its weight. The two-man team (driver and archer or spearman) was armoured in lamellar and wore the typical Assyrian conical helmet; both were armed with a sword or dagger. The archer's composite bow was deadly in a melée, powerful enough to penetrate the armour of almost any enemy. It could also be fired with effect from a stand-off range before the chariot force was able to close with the enemy.

The horse team was smartly caparisoned. The horses may have been armoured, but could also have been equipped only with a brightly coloured heavy saddlecloth. As with all chariot teams of the period, the horse team was yoked to the pole.

Chariots of Tiglath-Pileser III

The Assyrians built and used a quadriga, a large chariot pulled by four horses abreast and crewed by a driver, an archer and two shield bearers. This magnificent vehicle was not only impressive in size and appearance, but clearly demonstrated the prestige of the king in the field.

King Tiglath-Pileser III, known as 'the Great Reformer', is depicted in this type of chariot in a wall panel at his palace in Kalhu (Nimrud), where the annals of his reign together with carvings depicting his military triumphs are recorded. The chariot is pulled by a team of matched horses

◀ Chariot
The well-built cab had weapon holders and a rear-mounted axle. The eight-spoked heavy wheels were a great improvement over the light Egyptian and Hittite chariots.

wearing body armour in addition to colourful decorations on the panoply on top of the horses' heads as well as throat plumage, later known as 'beards' in European armies of the 19th century. The chariot team is led by two bearded, helmeted footsoldiers.

All of the accoutrements of the chariot and horse team were of the finest quality to set the king apart. He was easily identified in the heat of battle by the grandeur of the vehicle and his distinctive headgear.

One of the men in the royal chariot was a servant who bore aloft a parasol to keep the king out of the sun. There would also be an escort of cavalry to protect the royal personage on campaign and on the battlefield. The royal chariot was armoured, and the driver and umbrella bearer were in good cloth of the king's livery.

Chariots of Ashurbanipal

The war chariot deployed by the army of Assyrian king Ashurbanipal (reigned 668–627BCE) was – like that of King Tiglath-Pileser III – a large, heavily constructed vehicle with a four-man crew consisting of the driver, two shield bearers, one on each side of the compartment, and the spear bearer. The vehicle was huge

▶ *Tiglath-Pileser III in his chariot, on an wall relief at Nimrud, c.730BCE. Above, a cuneiform band details the king's achievements.*

compared to those that preceded it, as can be seen by the size of the solidly built wheels in relation to the chariot itself. It was undoubtedly a terrifying weapon on the battlefield.

The four-horse chariot could only be used on the wide, flat terrain for which it was designed. Its size and the challenge of handling the large horse team made it impossible to manage in other settings; in particular, given the difficulty of controlling a four-horse team, the chariot would have required a relatively large area in which to turn around, making it highly vulnerable to attack. However, when employed against an enemy on an open plain, these large chariots were essentially unstoppable – and a brutally effective weapon of war, especially if equipped with the wheel-mounted sharpened blades that could cut a man in half.

Ashurbanipal was a powerful and effective military leader who crushed uprisings in Egypt early in his reign, and established Assyrian garrisons and appointed surrogate rulers to keep the peace. He was skilled in siege warfare and captured the city of Tyre (now in Lebanon). In 639BCE he celebrated his success in quashing a series of rebellions, including one led by his half-brother Shamash-shum-ukin in Babylonia, and the defeat of the Elamites and the sacking of their capital Susa. He made four captive rulers pull his chariot in triumphal procession.

▼ **Heavy Chariot**
The Assyrian heavy chariot was solidly built with well-constructed heavy wheels able to take punishment over rough terrain and remain in service.

Campaigns of Sargon II

King Sargon II (reigned 722–705BCE) was one of the greatest of Assyrian rulers. Believed to have been the son of one of King Tiglath-Pileser III's concubines, he appears to have seized the throne from his half-brother Shalmaneser V (reigned 727–722BCE) in a coup. Sargon's name is the Hebrew spelling of Assyrian Sharru-kin ('Legitimate King'), and he may have chosen this to consolidate his position by linking his rule to that of the great Sargon of Akkad who ruled c.2300BCE. Sargon II is mentioned in the Bible, in *Isaiah 20:1*, where it is recorded that the Assyrian king dispatched his general to capture the Philistine city of Ashdod (now a city to the south of Tel Aviv in Israel).

▶ **Light Infantryman**
This well-clothed and shod light infantryman is well-armed with spear, shield, and sword. He is armoured with an older-type Assyrian helmet and the irtu in the centre of his chest.

◀ **Guardsman**
This imposing heavy infantryman is the epitome of the regular Assyrian infantry. He wears a leather jerkin covered with scale armour, a conical helmet, and a large metal-covered shield. His spear is especially well-designed and made with an iron butt that could also be used as a weapon in close combat.

A highly successful general, Sargon II led a series of triumphant military campaigns in the years after 720BCE. We know about his attack in 714BCE on the kingdom of Urartu in the Armenian Highlands because he celebrated it in reliefs carved in his palace at Dur-Sharrukin (modern Khorsabad in northern Iraq) and because an account of the campaign survives in the form of a letter reputedly written by the king (but doubtless actually composed by a historian or poet at his court) to the god Ashur. The letter, inscribed on a large clay tablet, was uncovered by archaeologists at the town of Assur in northern Iraq and is now held in the Louvre.

These accounts provide an insight into the practicalities of war in the first millennium BCE: in Urartu Sargon's soldiers had to dismantle their war chariots and carry them across difficult terrain; Sargon is shown in the reliefs being borne aloft in one of the vehicles. The letter to Ashur provides a description of the army cutting its way through difficult forests. Later in the campaign Sargon led the army on a forced march to confront King Rusa I of Urartu and defeated the Urartian army in the most difficult of conditions in a steep, snowbound mountain valley; the highly effective Assyrian spearmen killed all the horses of Rusa's chariots so Rusa had to make a humiliating escape on a mare.

Ruthless Tactics

Sargon then led his army on a campaign of rampage and plunder, tearing down orchards and burning harvests and driving the local people into retreat. He reports that he wiped out 430 villages whose inhabitants had fled in terror to the mountains. At the Urartian royal settlement of Ulhu he drank deep in the enemy king's wine cellars, then marched on to sack the city of Musasir, where he tore down the temple of the Urartian warrior god Haldi and seized five tons of silver and one of gold: this is described at length in the letter to the Assyrian god Ashur. Resistance was minimal: Sargon claims that his army's casualties were only three couriers, two mounted warriors and one charioteer. King Rusa, humiliated, fell upon his sword, and Sargon annexed his territories.

Sargon's kingship also featured campaigns against the Israelites, Babylonians, Chaldeans, Elamites, Syrians and Egyptians, and he was relentless in his pursuit of conquest. He died campaigning against the nomadic Cimmerians and was succeeded by his son Sennacherib. Sennacherib was a gifted administrator and military commander. A revolt along the Mediterranean coast prompted by the Egyptians, and supported by the Israelites,

▼ *Assyrian infantrymen from Sennacherib's army brandishing the heads of their enemies.*

▶ HEAVY CAVALRYMAN
This well-equipped Assyrian horse archer is also armed with spear or lance and sidearms. His helmet is quite modern and his personal equipment includes an armoured or padded 'cuirass'. His horse is also well-equipped, and has a head ornament that might identify his unit.

58 ARMIES OF THE FERTILE CRESCENT

▲ A palace relief at Nineveh shows King Ashurbanipal (reigned 668–c.627BCE) riding at full speed and preparing to fire an arrow: he uses both his hands to manipulate the powerful bow and controls the horse with his thighs and knees.

▼ HORSE ARCHER
While this cavalryman is better clothed and his horse better equipped than other light cavalryman, his lack of armour, with the exception of the conical helmet, indicates he is a light horse archer.

provoked an energetic response: Sennacherib laid waste to the country. He also moved against Jerusalem, but before the issue could be decided he had to withdraw back to Assyria as Babylon had again risen in revolt. This culminated in the bloody and inconclusive battle of Halule (691BCE) against Elamites, Chaldeans and Aramaic tribes. Sennacherib claimed victory, but the Assyrian army was so damaged that it was forced to withdraw and was unable to take the field the next year. However, the Elamites did not continue to support the Chaldeans and the Assyrians besieged Babylon in a long, drawn-out siege that lasted nine months and caused great devastation to the city and surrounding countryside. Sennacherib had beaten the Chaldeans into submission and in the process cowed his other enemies. However, his eldest son was dead and he was murdered himself by two of his other sons in 681BCE. Sennacherib was succeeded by his son Esarhaddon, who continued his father's conquests.

The Army of Sargon

The horse archers that served the Assyrian king Sargon II were armed not only with the strong and accurate composite bow, but with an efficiently designed and constructed lance, complete with a counterweight on the butt, making these cavalrymen some of the most effective the Assyrians ever fielded. These horse archers were employed as light cavalry to support the heavy cavalry and infantry. They typically wore a coloured, embroidered one-piece tunic that would come down to mid-thigh or almost to the knee.

Other equipment worn by Assyrian troops under Sargon included different models of the Assyrian conical helmet and a slender sword, which was attached to a baldric slung over the right shoulder and held in place with a waist belt. The warriors wore long, woollen socks beneath a knee-high, laced-up boot.

Horse furniture was simple, consisting of a saddlecloth or an animal skin. Because he did not use a saddle, the trooper had to find a good 'seat' by sitting a little further back on the horse and using his knees to stay mounted and control the horse when firing the bow while mounted. Decorations such as plumes were used on the bridle and behind the bridle high up on the neck. A leather breast harness provided some protection for the horse from missile weapons and polearms; the harness was also sometimes decorated in the same manner.

Sometimes the Assyrian cavalryman would carry an infantryman double-mounted on his horse. This increased mobility for special missions but was usually used only for short distances and in particular situations. Assyrian cavalry was well-equipped; the horses were usually fitted with simple harness and a multi-coloured crest on their heads. The infantrymen was armed and equipped with the usual infantry spear and round shield. The Assyrian shield was equipped with a long leather strap that allowed the soldiers to sling their shields across their backs.

▲ Light Infantry
This infantryman may or may not be a levy. He is very well-clothed, and is armed with spear and shield, fit for skirmishing, but has no helmet which would put him at a disadvantage in close combat.

▶ Cavalryman Carrying Infantryman
This light cavalryman is giving a light infantryman a lift forward on the march. This would necessarily speed up the march, but care would have to be taken not to wear out the horse, or both soldiers would soon be on foot.

ARMS AND ARMOUR

The development of armour for man and horse is a study in itself. Designs for armour grew up alongside those for weapons; personal armour for fighting men was introduced because of the pressing need to defeat the enemy's weapons with less loss of life than your enemy. Technological developments were also important in the process.

The earliest personal armour consisted of animal skins – as worn by the Sumerians. While light and easy to wear, leather or animal skin clearly gave less protection than armour constructed of metal. Skill in metalworking and progress in the development of metallurgy as a science was needed before practical metal armour could be developed – armour that was protective without immobilizing the wearer.

With the exception of bronze helmets, the Sumerians had little or no armour, although their thick-skinned clothing provided some protection against edged weapons. Hittite armour was usually merely a bronze helmet,

▼ POLEARMS
All of these spears are examples of Assyrian polearms either used at different periods in the empire or by the various troops in the army, regulars as well as levies.

◀ ARMOURED ARCHER
This well-equipped soldier of the regular army is holding his iron conical helmet. Scale armour covers head, torso and thighs. He is armed with a composite bow, quiver and arrows, and the thin Assyrian sword and scabbard are attached to a sturdy belt.

▲ HELMETS
Number 1 is the typical Assyrian conical helmet, numbers 2 and 5 being the same but fitted with cheek pieces. The other helmets (3, 4, 6, and 7) are versions of the same helmet, 3 and 4 being in bronze and 6 and 7 in iron.

▶ Armour

Numbers 1 and 2 are horse armour, either scale armour (1) for the horse's body or padded (2) for the head. Number 3 is a full 'suit' of body armour, which was used by chariot troops and would come down past the knee. Number 4 is torso scale armour for infantry and cavalry. (Note that none cover the forearms.) Number 5 show the metal plates for scale armour that were sewn on the undergarment. Number 6 is the full set of scale armour with the helmet worn over the head armour. Number 7 is the harness and irtu, worn by light infantry.

but some infantry would wear a wide iron belt for protection and some Hittites, especially chariot troops, wore a form of scale or lamellar armour of bronze plates.

Babylonians used armour for both fighting men and horses. Babylonian arms and armour were closely related to those of the Assyrians – because of the close proximity of the two empires, as well as the fact that the Babylonians had been a vassal state to the Assyrians for a lengthy period. While Assyrian light troops were usually not armoured, the use of armour was widespread in the army, either scale or lamellar and worn by both infantry and cavalry.

Even Assyrian horse archers, who would be considered light cavalry, were armoured and there is evidence that Assyrian cavalry also wore some type of protective covering on their legs. Assyrian scale armour covered the chest and upper arms and usually came to the waist, although some Assyrian infantry and archers wore long, armoured split 'skirts' that came down to the ankles.

Horse Armour

As draft animals and later cavalry horses became more common on the battlefield, military men saw that the animals should also be provided with some form of armour protection, dependent on their role. Chariot draft animals as well as heavy cavalry mounts were given armour, at least frontally. Hittite chariot teams used armoured horse blankets – a form of scale armour attached to or sewn on a leather horse blanket.

Assyrian horses were usually caparisoned with colourful saddlecloths for both cavalry and chariot horse teams, probably as a form of identification. Horses wore plumes in a decoration placed behind the ears. Assyrian horse teams were also armoured from time to time with armour similar to that of the Hittites but somewhat more advanced.

Helmets

Head protection evolved from wearing nothing through a cloth cap to a helmet – first of leather and then of bronze or iron, which was a harder metal and offered even better protection. The Hittites, Babylonians and Assyrians wore iron or bronze helmets, usually pointed at the top, the Hittite more rounded than the Assyrian. The Assyrian helmet was much more conical in shape and function, being better able to deflect blows from spears, swords and missile weapons. Some Assyrian helmets were rounded and had a small coloured crest on the top of the helmet. Assyrian helmets sometimes had additional cheek protectors as well as extentions to provide protection for the back of the neck.

Some Assyrian infantry, such as archers and light infantry, did not wear helmets at all or they wore an iron band around their head. Hittite troops also wore what would today be termed 'soft' headgear, made high to help absorb blows, but not exactly a helmet. Both Assyrian and Hittite commanders and princes wore elaborate, somewhat high headgear to denote their status and make them easily recognizable on the battlefield.

Shields

In various shapes and sizes, these were among the earliest forms of self-protection in combat. They were constructed of many types of material: wicker or wood was the most common; wood was also reinforced on the outside with iron or bronze. Shields could be round, rectangular or oval in shape or irregularly shaped with concave cutouts on the sides. They could also be flat, rounded, or disc-shaped and might have pieces cut out of them to a uniform design. All shields, however, would be symmetrical on one or both axes.

Sumerians had rectangular shields made of wood studded with bronze discs. Their shields were of a good size, from the ground to a man's mid-section or waist. The Hittites used round shields, as well as concave shields of wood, faced and strengthened with bronze. Assyrian shields were of carrying shapes including circular and rectangular. High-ranking Assyrians, usually royalty, would have a shield and arrow bearer whether or not they were mounted in a chariot. Assyrian cavalry carried both shield and lance.

It is not clear whether or not the Sumerians, Babylonians or Assyrians used their shields as weapons, as the Greeks and later the Romans would. Shields constructed of wicker would be near-useless in this role and the shape of many of the ancient shields would make them somewhat awkward to use as weapons. It seems logical that these shields were used for defence.

▲ SHIELDS
Numbers 1–5 are a variety of metal-faced round shields, 1, 2, and 5 being bronze, 3 and 4 being iron. The basic construction of them was identical. Number 7 shows the back or inside of the round shield and the apparatus used to hold them. Number 6 is an early wooden shield, and number 8 is a large wooden shield used to protect archers.

Edged Weapons

In addition to the spear, Sumerians carried and used daggers and axes. The

◄ *Assyrian slingers in action, depicted on a stone wall relief in Sennacherib's Palace, Nineveh. Sennacherib, king of Assyria from 704 to 681BCE, led military campaigns against Babylon and Judah.*

Hittites also combined a spear with a short sword. The Assyrians were armed with an assortment of weapons, which included the universal spear, an elegant sword and an excellent bow.

Swords in this period were usually short and were carried alongside other weapons by both infantry and cavalry. They might be wide or thin; the Assyrians favoured a thin sword. The dagger was in use before the sword, and the sword developed from it. Fighting men also used short axes or hatchets: the axe, or more properly the battle–axe, was used with great effect on the battlefield in close combat.

Polearms

The spear was the universal weapon of ancient peoples. It was main arm of the Sumerians. Spears of this period were not uniform in appearance or make and could vary in length from just over the height of an average man to 3m (10ft). They were used for thrusting and stabbing and were often the only weapon an infantryman or cavalryman might be carrying.

Depending on the spear's length, they could also be used as a javelin – that is, a missile weapon. Spears usually had a large iron head and were sometimes counterbalanced at the other end of the shaft with an iron counterweight. Sometimes, the counterweight could be in the shape of an iron or wooden 'ball' and this could also be used as a weapon as a skull cracker.

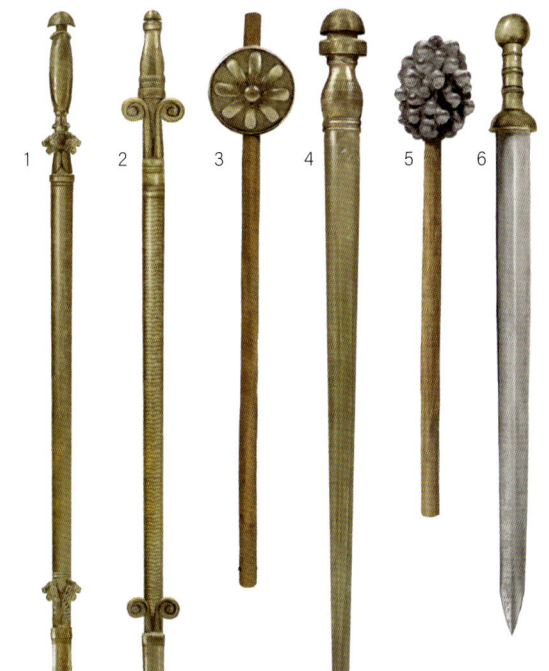

◀ **Swords and Maces**
Numbers 1, 2, and 4 are the typical Assyrian thin swords in scabbards. Numbers 3 and 5 are two types of maces used as a symbol of rank. Number 6 is a more modern sword, still thin, but of a later design and period.

Missile Weapons

In this early period missile weapons were generally of three types: arrow, javelin and slingshot. Archers used in mass could blanket an area to cover attacks on fortresses and on the battlefield. The Assyrian bow was strong, large and powerful and could be used dismounted and mounted.

A skilled thrower of javelins could hurl one accurately to about 9m (30ft). The sling was deadly in the hands of a skilled slinger. He carefully selected the stones he used as his missiles. It was a simple weapon and was used by light infantry. Considerable skill was needed for effective employment of both bowmen and slingers and in the case of the latter, the stone ammunition had to be chosen for shape and size with care to ensure the accurate ballistics of the round.

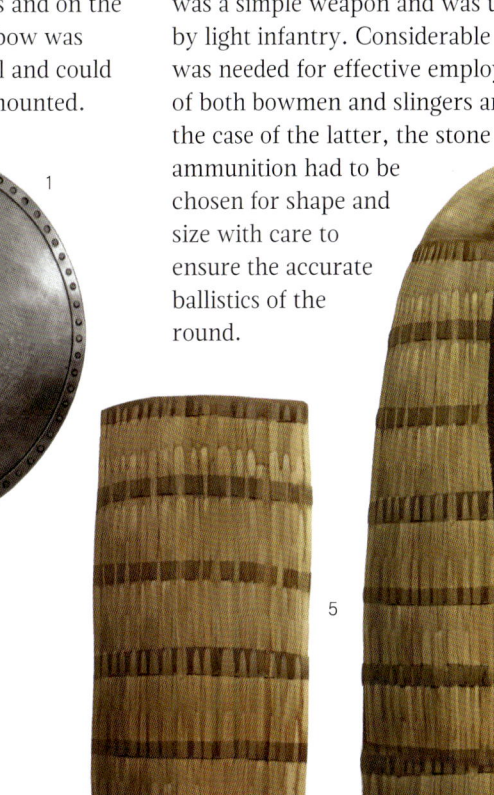

▶ **Bows, Axe and Shields**
Number 1 is an iron-faced round shield. Numbers 2 and 3 are the Assyrian composite bows. Number 4 is the hand-axe, useful for work around camp as well as breaking skulls in combat. Numbers 5 and 6 are large wicker shields used to protect archers by another soldier.

ARMIES OF ANCIENT EGYPT

The Battle of Kadesh between the Egyptian army of Pharaoh Ramesses II (c.1279–c.1213BCE) and the Hittites under King Muwatallis was one of the major encounters of the ancient world. By 1275BCE, when the battle took place, the Egyptian pharaoh was able to lead a disciplined army into battle, comprising four divisions each 5,000-strong – in addition to an auxiliary force. The Egyptian army had developed from the Early Dynastic Period, when it was little more than a militia, into a formidable professional force capable not only of taking the battle to the Hittites in Syria, but also of surviving the invasion of the Sea Peoples who swept into Egypt within a century of Kadesh, in the time of Ramesses III. Crucial to Ramesses III's success was that he could call on naval as well as land forces. The Egyptians defeated the Sea Peoples both on land in Palestine and at sea in the Nile Delta, and in doing so, the Egyptian soldiers and sailors profoundly altered the course of history. The neighbours of Egypt were at different times allies or enemies, and their armies are also studied here.

▲ *Boatmen on the Nile, from the Tomb of Sennefer, in the Valley of the Nobles, Thebes. A mural from the New Kingdom period.*

◄ *Ramesses II fighting the enemy, depicted in the temple of Abu Simbel.*

THE MIGHT OF ANCIENT EGYPT

The earliest period of ancient Egyptian history – the Predynastic Period (c.3100–2925BCE) – was approximately concurrent with the era of the Sumerians and the Akkadian empire. Initially, Upper and Lower Egypt (the two principal parts of the country, the Nile Valley and Nile Delta respectively) were divided: the two countries were not united until close to the start of this pioneering period. This unification is credited to Pharaoh Narmer, as the first ruler of a unified Egypt. This credit used to be given to Menes; however, modern historians generally argue that the name of Menes is honorific, a legendary figure who represents several historical kings.

The Old Kingdom

The period of the Old Kingdom (c.2649–c.2150BCE) established the Egyptians as engineers, artists and developers of an agricultural system based on the flooding of the Nile. The country's capital at this time was Memphis, south of the Nile Delta, on the river's west bank; the site is around 25km (15 miles) south of the modern city of Cairo. Memphis had been established during the Predynastic Period, its foundation another act traditionally ascribed to Menes.

The Old Kingdom period was marked by several agricultural advances and increased production, and the organization of a central criminal justice system (to serve the pharaoh). The pyramids and the Great Sphinx at Giza were constructed. However, the lavish temple culture attendant on the Egyptian religion and the huge and expensive monuments such as the Giza pyramids constructed by the 4th-Dynasty pharaohs Khufu, Khafre and Menkaure put the

▲ *The three pyramids at Giza were built in the 4th Dynasty.*

government into debt, creating major economic problems. The rising power of regional governors undermined the standing of the pharaohs, and central government collapsed, bringing on the First Intermediate Period (c.2150–c.2030BCE). Without central government, the kingdom was thrown into chaos and this was coupled with famines and internal disruption, which at times degenerated into civil war.

In this period regional governors ruled their respective provinces with some autonomy: central government was generally powerless if it existed at all, while the provinces recovered economic prosperity.

The Middle Kingdom

In time, central government again became viable, leading to the establishment of the Middle Kingdom (c.2030–c.1640BCE), which ushered in both a 'cultural reawakening' and improved economic well-being. The divided country was reunited.

The pharaohs of the Middle Kingdom brought back prosperity and civil and military power to Egypt. The country's capital was moved from Memphis to Thebes, which lay astride the river Nile roughly on the site of the modern city of Luxor, 675km

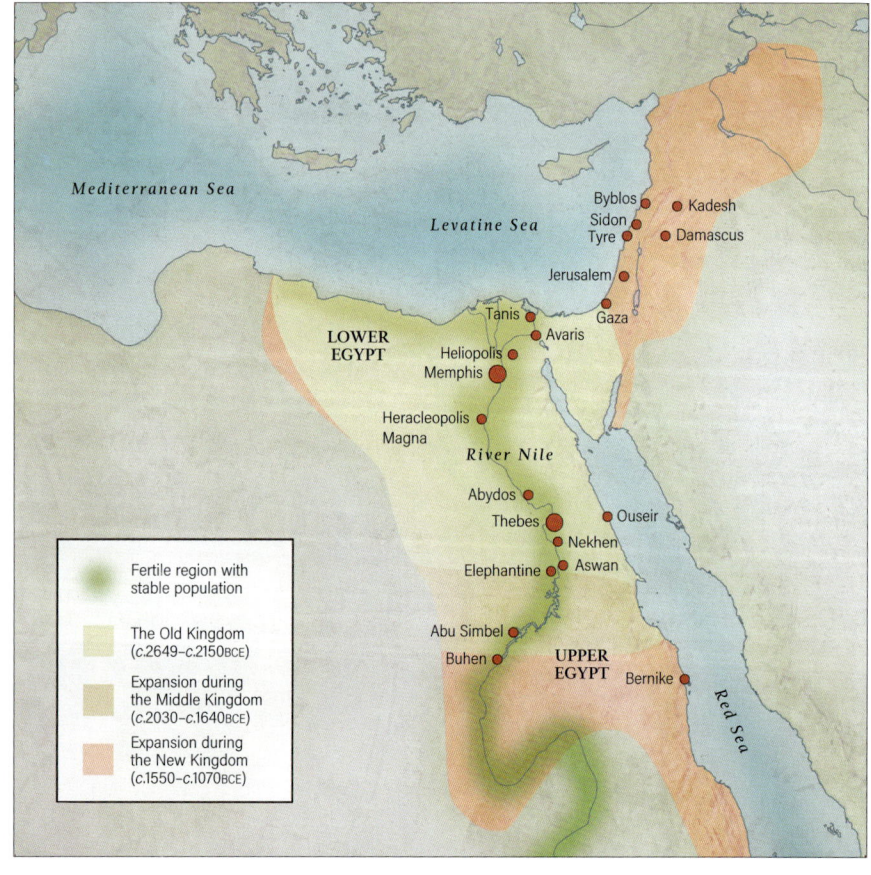

◀ *An overview of Lower and Upper Egypt and the areas taken in the Old, Middle and New Kingdoms.*

THE MIGHT OF ANCIENT EGYPT

▶ *A detail of a painting in the tomb of Userhet, a royal scribe of Amenhotep II in the 18th Dynasty; Userhet hunts gazelles from his chariot.*

(419 miles) south of Cairo. Further advances were made in agriculture and irrigation from the Nile. The Egyptian army was greatly improved and embarked on campaigns that took back territory lost during the decline of the Old Kingdom. The kingdom's defences were substantially strengthened along new and reclaimed borders.

The Rise of the Hyksos

The Hyksos were Semitic settlers from the region of Canaan who established themselves in parts of northern Egypt. Many Caananites were also imported to work in mining and building projects by the last pharaoh of the Middle Kingdom, the 12th-Dynasty ruler Amenemhat III. While initially an asset to the kingdom, these immigrants subsequently proved to be catalysts of another Egyptian decline: as the Hyksos gained in strength, they took control of the important Nile Delta region and seized power. The Egyptian pharaoh was reduced to the position of a vassal ruler in Thebes, and the Hyksos allied themselves with the Nubians from the south of Egypt, trapping the native Egyptians in their own country. Many Semitic immigrants assimiliated, but the Hyksos remained an occupying power.

The Egyptian pharaohs, after carefully building up their military strength, embarked on wars of liberation to defeat first the Nubians to the south and then, eventually, the Hyksos. This long and hard-fought victory led to the creation of the New Kingdom and the establishment of an empire that became increasingly aggressive towards its neighbours.

The New Kingdom

The most prosperous and powerful period in Ancient Egypt was the New Kingdom (c.1550–c.1070BCE). The Egyptians made alliances and diplomatic ties with other powerful empires such as those of Assyria and the Mitanni in northern Mesopotamia, as well as with their former enemies the Canaanites in Palestine. Egyptian territory and the prestige of the empire was greatly increased through far-flung military campaigns, such as those waged in Nubia and Syria by the 18th-Dynasty pharaoh Thutmose I (reigned c.1504–c.1492BCE). His grandson Thutmose III (c.1479–c.1425BCE) brought the empire to the height of its power, defeating the Mitanni, taking control of Syria, and leading the army to victory in the ancient city of Napata (near modern Karima in the Sudan).

Thutmose III campaigned in Palestine and the Levant for twenty years and re-established Egyptian supremacy in the Levant while

▼ *The young king Tutankhamun sits on his throne as his wife, Ankhesenamun, spreads perfumed oil on his collar.*

expanding the Egyptian empire to its greatest extent. His famous victory against the rebellious Canaanites at Megiddo in c.1457BCE was also important because the city controlled the main trade route between Egypt and Mesopotamia. Thutmose III's decisive victory here not only crushed the revolt of the Canaanite vassals and their allies against Egypt, but it also demonstrated the strength of the Egyptian state, and that of its pharaoh, to the other expanding empires in the Levant, Mesopotamia and Anatolia.

The Decline of Empire

Ramesses II 'the Great' acceded to the Egyptian throne in c.1279BCE. He was not only an able ruler, but also excelled as a military commander. While he continued to build temples and monuments, he also conducted military campaigns against the Hittites, fighting the celebrated battle of Kadesh in c.1275BCE. Ramesses finally agreed a peace treaty with the Hittites in c.1258BCE, the first achieved with that expanding empire. A threat from the Assyrians caused Egypt to retreat from the area, however, and then the onslaught of the Sea Peoples, which ruined the equilibrium of the area, began yet another slow decline of Egypt. In c.1070BCE the last Ramesses, the XI, died. Egypt was later invaded by larger, more powerful and more aggressive empires; while it still existed, this was more as a vassal state than an independent and powerful kingdom. The Golden Age was over.

Egyptian Engineering

Possibly before all their other achievements, the ability of the ancient Egyptians as engineers has to be recognized. With no modern tools or machines they built colossal monuments, great temples, and burial buildings to honour their dead leaders. These feats of engineering spanned the entire lifetime of the Egyptian empire and many have lasted through the ages to the present day. Among the greatest achievements in Egyptian engineering are the Great Pyramid of Giza, the Sphinx, the statues of Ramesses II at Memphis and Luxor (both of which are perfectly symmetrical – which attests to the Egyptian skill at mathematics), the Temple of Abu Simbel, and the many obelisks that were carved out of the solid rock.

The tools that they developed for the construction and engineering achievements were, and are, symbols of Egyptian genius. The lathe was fundamental to the success and skill of Egyptian engineers. Egyptian cutting tools for quarrying rock and later shaping that rock into the desired object were far and above anything that would follow. These cutting tools were made out of diorite, a stone harder than iron. The Egyptians also invented a tubular drill that was not only strong and sharp enough to carve into stone, but could also withstand the weight of the rock into which the drill was cutting. Cutting tools were also developed that enabled Egyptian stone cutters to drill into stone to produce the accurate 'pictures' that have survived to the present day. These were also produced with mathematical precision. The Egyptians transported cut stone weighing many tonnes from the quarry at Aswan to wherever they wished to build their monuments and other projects. Interestingly, many of the methods of construction are still not fully understood today. Much of the knowledge died with the Egyptians, and what they did with the tools they developed cannot be duplicated today or only with great difficulty.

The Development of the Army

The armies that developed in Old Kingdom Egypt (c.2649–c.2150BCE) went through the 'armed mob' phase that marked the beginnings of most of the armies of ancient kingdoms and empires. The Sumerians, Babylonians, Israelites and Hittites – as well as the Egyptians – all went through this period of development. As the armies grew in experience, expertise, size and strength, however, their commanders came to see the need for improved training and organization, while themselves developing an understanding of the science of warfare and leadership.

Soldiers of the Old and Middle Kingdom periods were conscripted, and in the beginning their armies were more a militia called up for

▼ The great temple of Ramesses II, carved into the rock face at Abu Simbel. A smaller rock temple nearby was dedicated to his wife Queen Nefertari.

THE MIGHT OF ANCIENT EGYPT

▲ *Fresco depicting the army receiving rations, from the Tomb of Userhet, Thebes. Userhet was a royal scribe of Amenhotep II, in the 18th Dynasty.*

emergencies than a professional military organization. Training was hard and would be considered brutal today; protective armour was almost non-existent and weapons were simple if effective. The lack of a regular and reliable standing army was undoubtedly one of the reasons that both the Old and Middle Kingdoms eventually failed.

In the 16th century BCE, pharaohs, senior generals and government civil servants realized, with the restoration of central rule, that the nation's future survival might also depend on the effectiveness of its army. The army and navy were put on a regular footing, and through training and practice, became a professional military organization that defended the kingdom year round and was always ready to do the pharaoh's bidding. The New Kingdom had undoubtedly the best armies fielded by the ancient Egyptians in 3,000 years of history.

The new professional army was an almost universal service: personnel would not serve exclusively in either the army or the navy, but would be assigned to either depending on the situation. They served where needed. That being the case, and because the lifeline of the vital Nile River had to be defended, the Egyptian navy became as necessary as the army to the kingdom's survival.

In addition to seagoing warships, new river craft were built, which were manned and maintained in peacetime, although over time it became increasingly evident that the Egyptian army and navy would need to be repeatedly sent away on campaign, either to defend the kingdom from hostile neighbours or to embark on new campaigns of conquest of their own.

Army Organization

There were two main branches of the Egyptian army – the infantry and the mounted arm, which was a chariot corps; the latter was considered the elite group. Infantrymen were organized first in what would today be called 'platoons' of 50 men each. The junior officer in the army was the commander of this basic unit. The 'platoon' was further divided into five 'squads' of ten men each, with an experienced soldier commanding each squad. An Egyptian company consisted of up to five platoons, four or five being the usual number in each infantry company. Next, the infantry 'battalion' was made up of several companies and these were further organized into regiments of several battalions; regiments would be organized into divisions commanded by general officers. Egyptian divisions were usually named after deities.

The Egyptian chariot arm was the elite of the army of the New Kingdom. Organized into units of 50, the chariot corps was considered the Egyptian 'aristocratic' arm as it rode into battle, avoiding the dust and sweaty manoeuvrings of the 'crunchies', the basic infantrymen. The chariot arm was flamboyant and could be decisive on the battlefield through shock and élan. It was also the place where an ambitious officer could make a name for himself and advance further, either in the army or the government.

As in earlier eras, training in the New Kingdom was hard, and the discipline imposed on recruits and conscripts could be harsh. The treatment of deserters, if caught, was brutal: their families were also subject to punishment and would have suffered under the 'hard heel' of the army and the government.

In terms of logistics, troops on campaign carried basic supplies but were expected to augment their meagre rations and supplies by foraging – and looting. Necessary fodder for the animals, horses, asses and camels that travelled with the army was foraged. On campaign, they were expected to live off the land.

EGYPT'S NEIGHBOURS AND ENEMIES

◀ A relief from Memphis c.1250BCE shows Ramesses II capturing enemies: a Nubian, a Libyan and a Syrian.

In the periods before the New Kingdom (c.1550–c.1070BCE) the Egyptians had three principal groups of neighbours and enemies. To the west, across the desert, were the Libyans; to the south were the Nubians; and to the north were the peoples of the Levant and the Sinai, who posed a significant threat to the northeastern border of the kingdom. In addition, there were also internal threats to the kingdom from the regions that now and then attempted to separate from the centralized government and which formed autonomous regions within the borders of Egypt.

The Egyptians had an involved and at times productive relationship with their external enemies. Some groups fought alongside the Egyptians as mercenaries. The Nubians and Libyans both fought with the Egyptian army in this way. The Sherden (thought by scholars to be originally from Sardinia and one of the peoples proposed as the source of the Sea Peoples) fought in the army of Ramesses II at the Battle of Kadesh in c.1275BCE. The Egyptian army and navy were also significantly influenced by their enemies in the design of weapons, armour, chariots and galleys.

The Hyksos

The Hyksos, who ruled in Egypt from c.1640BCE to c.1550BCE, introduced the chariot, weapons made and cast of bronze, and the composite bow. Both the chariot and the composite bow revolutionized Egyptian warfare. It is significant that there was more than one large quiver of arrows in Egyptian chariots from this period on, which indicates not only that the chariot was being used as a mobile missile launcher, but also that for Egyptian chariot troops the bow was the weapon of choice and not the spear or javelin.

The Mitanni

These emerged as a force in northern Mesopotamia in the 16th century BCE when several small states unified

▶ A miniature painted wooden troop of Nubian archers was found in the tomb of Mesehti at Assiout, c.2061–2010BCE. Nubians were mercenaries and auxiliaries in the Egyptian army as well as foes. The 40 wooden Nubian figures walk in four rows, with short kilts, decorated in red, yellow and green. (See also page 77.)

▶ Bas-relief showing two of Egypt's enemies, the Libyans and Mesopotamians, in the New Kingdom Temple of Ramesses III, Medinet Habu in Thebes. The geographical position of Egypt left the country open to invasion on all sides by multiple enemies.

under their rule. They were feared and respected by the Egyptians and Hittites, and the three kingdoms came into conflict in the territories where their interests and claims overlapped, especially in Palestine. The Mitanni were caught between the two expanding neighbouring kingdoms and, despite their superiority in many military categories, were eventually brought to defeat.

Like the Hyksos, the Mitanni had developed the use of the chariot as a military weapon. Their military strength was centred on the horse and the chariot and the military elite who used them, who were known as the *maryannu* ('young warriors').

The maryannu often wore lamellar and scale armour. This was copied by the Egyptians and Hittites. The maryannu armoured both the chariot driver and his accompanying bowman. The armour covered the chest and torso, coming down to mid-thigh and sometimes almost to the ankles. Their helmets were iron or lamellar/scale armour; the chariots themselves were partially armoured on the sides. The driver was equipped with an efficiently designed rectangular shield. The horses were also protected around the throat and the chest. The maryannu chariot bowmen carried their arrows in quivers strapped to their backs.

The Sea Peoples

Around 1250–1200BCE the civilizations and kingdoms of the Near East underwent a cataclysm. The 'Sea Peoples' – shipborne invaders – swept through the region, ravaging,

▶ This section of a stone relief at Abu Simbel, built as a lasting monument to Ramesses II to commemorate his victory at the battle of Kadesh, shows his Nubian prisoners of war.

destroying and moving on, either damaging existing kingdoms so that they never or barely recovered or else destroying them outright.

The Sea Peoples defeated the Hittite empire, which at this time was allied to the Egyptian pharaoh, Ramesses II. The Egyptians fought two battles against these invaders: the first under Pharaoh Merneptah (c.1213–c.1203BCE) and the second under Ramesses III (c.1184–c.1153BCE).

The origin and identity of the Sea Peoples is not known for certain. There are several references to them in Egyptian sources and various theories among historians as to who they were and where they came from. One hypothesis is that they originated among ancient ethnic Greek peoples of Mycenaean or Minoan origin; another suggests that they were a coastal people known as the Lukka from western Anatolia; a third is that they were the Sherden from Sardinia. Whatever their origin, the Sea Peoples were a formidable enemy and a major disruption to the existing societies, kingdoms and empires of the Near East and North Africa.

TIMELINE OF ANCIENT EGYPT

*c.*3300BCE: The Bronze Age in the Near East begins.

*c.*3150BCE: Upper and Lower Egypt are united by Narmer (also identified as Menes).

*c.*2925BCE: The Early Dynastic (or Archaic or Thinite) period begins.

*c.*2670BCE: The Step Pyramid of Djoser, the earliest known pyramid, was built in the 3rd Dynasty.

*c.*2649BCE–: The Old Kingdom begins, the period when the remainder of the pyramids were constructed, including Saqqara and the Great Pyramid of Giza. (During the later Middle Kingdom few pyramids were built as they were being raided for treasure, and so pharaohs were buried in secret in the Valley of the Kings.)

*c.*2150BCE: The Old Kingdom in Egypt collapses, probably because of a natural disaster such as long drought. The First Intermediate Period begins, with two competing Dynasties.

*c.*2030BCE: The Middle Kingdom begins. Mentuhotep II reunifies the

▼ *The Palermo Stone, a fragment with hieroglyphic inscription, from the Royal Annals of the 5th-Dynasty Old Kingdom.*

kingdom and establishes Thebes as the capital (later moved to Itjtawy).

*c.*1640BCE: The Second Intermediate Period begins. The Hyksos, a Semitic people, take control of Lower Egypt.

*c.*1550BCE: Ahmose I becomes Pharaoh in Upper Egypt, overpowers the Hyksos, and founds the 18th Dynasty. The New Kingdom of Egypt, also referred to as the Egyptian empire, considered to be its golden age, a time of wealth, prosperity and power, begins.

*c.*1525–*c.*1504BCE: The reign of Pharaoh Amenhotep I. He begins a campaign in Syria to expand Egypt.

*c.*1504–*c.*1492BCE: The reign of Thutmose I. He leads an Egyptian army as far as the Euphrates River on a campaign of conquest in Mesopotamia against the Kingdom of the Mitanni.

*c.*1492–*c.*1479BCE: Thutmose II is in power.

*c.*1479–*c.*1458BCE: Thutmose II's wife and half-sister, Hatshepsut, becomes regent for Thutmose III (aged 2 when his father died) and then co-ruler. She constructs a unique funerary temple in Thebes.

*c.*1479–*c.*1425BCE: The reign of Pharaoh Thutmose III.

*c.*1457BCE: In the celebrated Battle of Megiddo, Thutmose III defeats a Canaanite confederation, expanding the Egyptian empire into Palestine.

▲ *The fertile banks of the Nile have been fundamental to settlement through millennia. A New Kingdom wall painting.*

*c.*1455BCE: Thutmose leads the Egyptian army across the River Euphrates to defeat the Mitanni.

*c.*1427–*c.*1400BCE: Amenhotep II is in power. For the last two years of his father Thutmose III's reign he is co-regent. He campaigns in both Canaan and Syria, waging an almost annual war against the Mitanni for control of the Middle East.

*c.*1400–*c.*1390BCE: Amenhotep's son reigns as Thutmose IV. He concludes a peace treaty with the Mitanni.

*c.*1390–*c.*1352BCE: The reign of Pharaoh Amenhotep III. The son of Thutmose IV, he accedes to the throne at the age of around 12 years.

*c.*1353–*c.*1336BCE: The reign of Pharaoh Amenhotep IV, who became known as Akhenaten in 1349BCE, who finally destroys the Mitanni and establishes the first monotheistic religion. The name Akhenaten means 'the one who is effective for the sun god Aten'.

*c.*1336–*c.*1327BCE: The reign of Pharaoh Tutankhamun.

*c.*1327–*c.*1323BCE: The reign of Pharaoh Ay.

*c.*1323–*c.*1295BCE: The reign of Pharaoh Horemheb. He had been a general in the army of Tutankhamun, in command of the troops in northern Egypt. As pharaoh he appoints several priests and officials from among his former army colleagues rather than from the families traditionally associated with these prestigious roles.

c.1295–c.1294BCE: The short reign of Pharaoh Ramesses I marks the beginning of the 19th Dynasty.

c.1294–c.1279BCE: Pharaoh Seti I rules. He leads the Egyptian army into Canaan and the Levant and fights the Hittites. He has many military successes but is overshadowed in history by his son, Ramesses II.

c.1279–c.1213BCE: The reign of Pharaoh Ramesses II. He campaigns to the north in Palestine against the Hittites. The exodus of the Jews from Egypt – as described in the biblical book of *Exodus* – is thought by some historians to have taken place under Ramesses II; some suggest it took place later, in the 12th century BCE.

c.1275BCE: Ramesses II leads the Egyptian army to what is recorded as a victory in the Battle of Kadesh against the Hittites.

c.1258BCE: Ramesses signs a peace treaty with Hittite king, Hattusilis III.

c.1250–1200BCE: From the 12th century BCE the Sea Peoples, especially the Philistines, land and finally settle in Palestine, called Canaan during this period. The invaders cause havoc in the Levant: the result is the near collapse of any political order in the region.

c.1213–c.1203BCE: Ramesses's 13th son, Merneptah, is in power. A period of great upheaval in Egypt follows the death of Merneptah.

1200BCE: The end of the Bronze Age and the beginning of the Iron Age. This allowed a technological revolution with stronger tools and weapons.

c.1186–c.1184BCE: The short reign of Pharaoh Setnakhte marks the beginning of the 20th Dynasty.

c.1184–c.1153BCE: The reign of Pharaoh Ramesses III.

c.1180BCE: Ramesses III drives back the invasion of the Sea Peoples.

c.1070BCE: The end of the reign of Pharaoh Ramesses XI marks the end of the New Kingdom.

▲ *Queen Hatshepsut, joint ruler of Egypt with Thutmose III in the 18th Dynasty.*

c.1070BCE: The Third Intermediate Period begins.

1006–968BCE: In Israel, King David succeeds King Saul. During his reign the Israelites create an empire that might have extended from the border of Egypt to the Euphrates River.

924BCE: The now-divided Israeli kingdoms of Judah and Israel are invaded by Shishak I of Egypt.

671–663BCE: The Assyrians repeatedly invade Egypt.

609BCE: Judah and Egypt go to war against each other. Meeting at Megiddo, Josiah is killed in action and his army is defeated against the Egyptians commanded by the Pharaoh Necho.

525BCE: Egypt is conquered by the Persians under Cambyses. The Persians rule for over a hundred years, and again for a decade in 343BCE.

332BCE: The Persian empire is conquered by Alexander the Great. Palestine becomes a part of the new Macedonian empire, and Alexander prepares to campaign against Egypt.

301–200BCE: After the death of Alexander, Palestine comes under the rule of the Ptolemaic dynasty in Egypt.

198BCE: Antiochus III of Syria invades Palestine and takes it from Egypt.

170BCE: The first Syrian campaign against Egypt by Antiochus IV.

30BCE: Egypt is conquered by the Romans under Octavian (later Caesar Augustus) and becomes a colony.

Egyptian Dynasties

The time before the Early Dynastic Period is generally referred to as the Predynastic Period. Historians also suggest the Protodynastic Period or 0 (zero) Dynasty for the Nagada III period from c.3200BCE. Upper and Lower Egypt were united before the Early Dynastic Period. In Egyptology dates are debated; these follow the Metropolitan Museum of Art, USA.

Early Dynastic (Archaic) Period c.2925–c.2649BCE
First Dynasty c.2925–c.2775BCE
Second Dynasty c.2775–c.2649BCE

Old Kingdom c.2649–c.2150BCE
Third Dynasty c.2649–c.2575BCE
Fourth Dynasty c.2575–c.2465BCE
Fifth Dynasty c.2465–c.2323BCE
Sixth Dynasty c.2323–c.2150BCE

First Intermediate Period c.2150–c.2030BCE
Seventh and Eighth Dynasties c.2150–c.2130BCE
Ninth Dynasty c.2130–2080BCE
Tenth Dynasty c.2080–c.2030BCE
Eleventh Dynasty (first half) c.2124–c.2030BCE

Middle Kingdom c.2030–c.1640BCE
Eleventh Dynasty (second half) c.2030–c.1981BCE
Twelfth Dynasty c.1981–c.1802BCE
Thirteenth Dynasty c.1802–c.1640BCE

Second Intermediate Period c.1640–c.1550BCE
Fourteenth to Sixteenth Dynasties c.1640–c.1535BCE
Seventeenth Dynasty c.1635–c.1550BCE

New Kingdom c.1550–c.1070BCE
Eighteenth Dynasty c.1550–c.1295BCE
Nineteenth Dynasty c.1295–c.1186BCE
Twentieth Dynasty c.1186–c.1070BCE

Third Intermediate Period c.1070–c.713BCE
Twenty-first to Twenty-fourth Dynasties, including periods of concurrent rule

Late Kingdom c.713–332BCE
Twenty-fifth to Thirtieth Dynasties

Graeco-Roman Period 332BCE–395CE
Macedonian 332–304BCE
Ptolemaic 304–30BCE

Roman Period 30BCE–395CE

Eastern Roman Period 395–642CE

WARRIORS OF THE OLD KINGDOM

The Campaigns of Snefru

For centuries the rulers of Egypt fought their neighbours in Nubia and Libya. The Palermo Stone (see page 72) is a slab of black basalt inscribed with royal annals of the Old Kingdom period; we know from its hieroglyphic inscriptions that the Egyptian army embarked on a military campaign in Nubia in the reign of the Old Kingdom Pharaoh Snefru, founder of the 4th Dynasty (reigned c.2575–c.2551BCE).

A central part of military strategy in the Old Kingdom was the building of fortified settlements to protect borders and subdue troublesome populations – and a key role for the militias was therefore manning and defending the forts. At Buhen on the west bank of the Nile, north of the Second Cataract in Nubia, the army garrisoned a large fort. (The site is today submerged beneath Lake Nasser.) Evidence suggests this fort was established in the reign of Snefru. The fort's main purpose was probably to establish a buffer zone facing the south and to protect trade routes in the region. Soldiers needed to defend the fort's walls with spear and bow and arrows, and to fight at closer quarters with battle-axe if necessary.

According to Royal Annals, Snefru captured a great deal of booty on his Nubian campaign. He also led the army into battle against the Libyans. A later tradition suggests he conquered the Sinai peninsula; there are reliefs showing him in turquoise mines in Sinai. His reign was subsequently

▼ **INFANTRYMAN**
This infantryman is dressed in what is essentially civilian clothing. He is armed with spear and shield.

▲ **NUBIAN MERCENARY**
Egypt had a long association with the Nubians, both as enemies and as employees. As in all the ancient kingdoms, mercenaries played an important role in the militias and armies of Ancient Egypt. This bowman is simply clad, but he does wear some colour which may be a clan identification.

celebrated in Ancient Egypt as a golden age, of peace at home and success in wars of conquest abroad. He built two pyramids at Dahshur (southwest of Cairo) that are still standing today. Military success abroad made these ambitious building schemes possible: he brought home 11,000 prisoners from Libya and 7,000 from Nubia and used these people as enslaved labour; he also carried back from Sinai, Nubia and Libya the building materials used in the construction of the pyramids.

▼ **Standard Bearer**
Symbols of animals were popular totems for standards and on this example the coloured streamers were probably meant as unit identification.

▶ **Axeman**
This infantryman is another example of the simple clothing worn in the field. He is armed with the animal-hide-covered pentagon shield and an early axe, and a small dagger is strapped to his wrist.

Arms and Armour

In Old Kingdom Egypt the pharaoh had no standing army. The governor of each administrative division (*nome*) raised a militia to fight when needed. The pharaoh led what was essentially a militia army into war.

The men in these militias were generally from the poorest sections of society. They were clothed and equipped in a military version of civilian dress, designed for comfort in a desert environment. Infantrymen often wore little more than a loincloth, with some frontal protection of the groin.

Arms and equipment were generally kept to a minimum. Soldiers did not usually wear helmets or armour, although many did carry an oblong, pentagon-shaped shield. Native spearmen had a rectangular shield. Most militia members used a simple, one-piece bow that was effective at close range – this probably did not exceed 60m (200ft). They also had access to crude bronze battle-axes, throw sticks, daggers and spears.

The militia carried standards for unit identification: troops could identify with their unit standard and ensure that it was adequately defended in combat. Historians cannot be certain whether unit standards were viewed with devotion in the manner of Roman eagles in a later age; but since the standards represented Egyptian deities or pharaohs, their protection in combat was probably considered a matter of the highest importance. A standard bearer carried a short weapon, such as a bronze-headed axe, to defend himself and the standard.

While the Egyptians fought both the Libyans to the west and the Nubians to the south, they also employed them as mercenaries. All three peoples were more or less equal in weapons and ancillary equipment.

MIDDLE KINGDOM TROOPS

Reunification of the Empire

The period after 2000BCE saw the reunification of Egypt at the close of the years historians label the First Intermediate Period (c.2150–c.2030BCE) and the beginning of the Middle Kingdom (c.2030–c.1640BCE). The country had been divided between 10th-Dynasty rulers based at Heracleopolis Magna and 11th-Dynasty monarchs at Thebes.

Annals state that Pharaoh Mentuhotep II (reigned c.2051–c.2030BCE) led his army against Heracleopolis Magna in the fourteenth year of his reign (so around 2037BCE) and ousted the rival rulers. As a result he took the name 'Uniter of the Two Lands' and was later honoured as founder of the Middle Kingdom.

Mentuhotep II made Thebes the capital of his reunited kingdom and built a great complex of tombs and a temple there; he also raised several temples in Upper Egypt, where he had reliefs carved depicting his military triumphs. In politics he was practical: he allowed many local governors to remain in place so long as they swore loyalty to him. He also led his troops against Bedouin raiders in the Nile Delta and established firm control in northern Nubia, which he made part of his own kingdom. Nubia was also a military target of 12th-Dynasty Pharaoh Sesostris (Senwosret) I (1961–1917BCE), who led a series of campaigns in Lower Nubia and took control of territory there as far as the Second Cataract of the Nile. He established a series of fortresses manned by an occupying force to keep the locals under control. We also know, from an inscription of his successor, that he campaigned in Syria and Palestine.

▼ NUBIAN ARCHER
This is another example of the Egyptian employment of Nubian allies as archers. Armed with an Egyptian-style bow, he wears a skull cap with feather. His 'kilt' is an animal skin with tail still attached.

◀ INFANTRYMAN
The Egyptian troops of the Middle Kingdom became more sophisticated in dress as well as arms and equipment. All now wear head coverings to protect them from the sun and this striped example seems to have been the most popular. There is still no body armour, but there is protection for the groin area. This infantryman is armed only with a spear.

MIDDLE KINGDOM TROOPS

▼ **STANDARD BEARER**
The standard this man is carrying appears to be a falcon, which was a royal symbol in Egypt. He is unarmed and unarmoured, so one would assume there would be an another guard in combat situations to protect him and the standard. Most, if not all, of the ancient armies grew to understand the value of standards for identification on the battlefield and also as a symbol of loyalty and unit pride.

Uniforms of the Middle Kingdom

The Egyptians of the Old Kingdom wore a type of loincloth or kilt, had little or no clothing to cover their torso and went into battle barefoot. In the Middle Kingdom, Egyptian soldiers still wore at times what was essentially a short kilt or loincloth, but it sometimes came down almost to the knee. It allowed freedom of movement because it was neither tight-fitting nor restrictive, suited to a desert climate.

By the beginning of the Middle Kingdom soldiers wore a type of headwear, sometimes striped, sometimes solid in colour, that gave protection from the sun and the elements and some meagre element of defence against edged weapons. They began to wear a short-sleeved shirt or tunic rather than fight with a naked torso; over the shirt, armour was now coming into use for the more elite infantrymen and chariot troops of the Egyptian army. The Egyptian army still usually went barefoot on the march.

The Nubians and Libyans who either fought against the Egyptians or were allied to and fought alongside them wore basically tribal clothing, which was of some type of cloth such as linen or animal skin. When the Nubians' loincloths were made from the skin of the big African cats – such as leopards, cheetahs or lions – the tails would sometimes be kept attached for effect.

Tomb of Mesehti

There is an excellent, if somewhat unusual, reference source for how the Egyptian infantryman looked during the period cusping the Old and Middle Kingdoms. This is from a tomb, probably that of the 11th-Dynasty priest Mesheti in c.2000 BCE, with its many painted wooden miniatures of warriors. The heavy infantry are armed with long spears and the typical Egyptian shield of the period, the shields having at least five different designs on them, probably depicting examples of different units. The light infantry miniatures depict Nubian bowmen armed with the bow and carrying their complement of arrows in the right hand, the bows in their left. The tomb was found at Assiout in Upper Egypt.

▶ *Wooden Nubian miniature figures were found in the 11th-Dynasty tomb of Mesehti in Assiout. The carefully painted spearmen had hide-covered shields and white skirts. Each figure was individually carved and painted. (See also page 70.)*

▶ *Early Middle Kingdom relief depicting the pharaoh Mentuhotep II slaying a prisoner with a distinctive knobkerrie-style weapon.*

▼ OFFICER
This Egyptian officer wears an odd style of headdress in order to be identified positively by his own side. He wears a colourful and stylized belt which is also a indicator of rank. He is armed with a knobkerrie.

Improved Arms and Armour

The core of the army in this Middle Kingdom period was a group of veteran heavy infantry armed with bronze short sword and spear. These experienced long-service troops are thought to have overseen the training of new recruits. That the Egyptian army at this period understood the need for instructors for the army's raw intake indicates a change in attitude that would later lead to the professionalism of the army of the New Kingdom.

As the Egyptian army became more professional, not only did weapons become more sophisticated and better made, but the soldier's personal protection became a concern for Egyptian commanders. The Egyptian spearman, the mainstay of their infantry, came to be armoured with a linen cuirass and more elaborate protection in the groin and belly. The simple loincloth became larger, with padded armour made of several layers of linen to protect the loins. A padded, sleeveless 'cuirass' was developed and used to protect the chest and belly. Middle Kingdom troops did not wear helmets, but the distinctive Egyptian headgear was padded to give some protection to the skull.

The shield was simple, of wooden construction with a single handle to hold and use it. This limited its use as a weapon and because it was flat in shape, it was probably only used to block the weapons of the infantryman's opponent and not as an offensive weapon – as the Greeks and Romans would later come to use their shields for attack.

A relatively short bronze spear was the main weapon, with a curved or straight dagger or a short sword, also bronze, being used for personal

▼ SPEARMAN
A padded linen jerkin offers some protection in a melée and perhaps from arrows. His spear has a counterweight at the base which could double as a skull-cracker.

defence if the spear – or the spear and shield together – were lost. Without the double arm and handhold of later models, the shield must have been awkward to wield and quite possibly difficult to hold on to in a melée.

The early Egyptian bow was constructed in a 'V' shape. While sufficient as a missile weapon, it was definitely inferior to the composite bow with which many of Egypt's enemies were armed by this time. The Egyptians soon copied the technology of the powerful and innovative composite bow and issued it to their troops. It was especially effective in the hands of veteran chariot troops, which made them mobile archer platforms.

Egyptian infantry may have worn footwear on the march, but many references show them barefoot for combat. This might indicate that their feet were so tough that not wearing footwear in combat was an advantage.

Egyptian Infantry on Campaign

As in earlier time periods, the usual Egyptian conscript at the close of the Middle Kingdom wore a simple loincloth, possibly with stiffened linen or cotton armour, constructed of several layers of cloth or possibly quilted for better protection. He carried a spear and shield.

When on campaign, the Egyptian soldier would carry his personal items with him wrapped in what would later be called a blanket roll. The personal items would be carefully laid on a blanket and rolled up and tied off at the ends to secure it and ensure that the enclosed items would not fall out. It was shaped somewhat like a horseshoe. The soldier would place it over his head and shoulder, and wear it across his body. It was comfortable, enabled the soldier to carry his personal items securely, and if worn in combat provide some protection against missile weapons, edged weapons and polearms.

◀ **Spearman**
This spearman is wearing a padded jerkin, as well as padded groin protector; in addition to his spear he carries a wooden shield. A curved edged weapon is also conveniently carried in his belt.

▶ **Archer**
This native Egyptian archer is armed with a composite bow, but no other weapon. He is well-clothed compared to some of his comrades and wears feathers in his headband.

Armies of the Late Middle Kingdom

At the close of the Middle Kingdom, foreign influence brought major changes to the Egyptian way of war. The Hyksos, a Semitic people from the northwest who took over Lower Egypt in the Second Intermediate Period, introduced the war chariot (see page 90). The Mitanni, founders of an empire in northern Mesopotamia, also made their influence felt – and their use of lamellar armour (made from plates stitched together in rows) was copied by the Egyptians. The plates, or scales, were of bronze and were stitched to the undergarment and provided excellent protection to

▼ INFANTRYMAN
This spearman carries a shield as well as short spear. There is a hole to look through at the top of the shield so that he can hold it up to his face and still see what is going on.

▲ ARCHER
This is a well-equipped archer with a cuirass as well as a sword to protect himself in close combat. He does not have a composite bow, but this appears to be a second-generation development even though it is still constructed out of one piece of wood.

the wearer. However, the lamellar armour was not impenetrable and both edged weapons and well-made arrows could penetrate the armour in close combat.

As the Egyptian armies of antiquity had no cavalry, their mounted arm consisted completely of their chariot-borne troops. In c.1600BCE the Egyptians fought from their chariots with spear and bow, both being employed as missile weapons.

Arms and Armour

The Egyptian use of archers in combat was simple and effective: deployed in mass, they showered the enemy with lethal missiles. They aimed not only to cause casualties but also to create disorder in enemy units, distracting and upsetting them and making them vulnerable to an infantry attack. The bow was the most effective missile weapon of the ancient armies. The Egyptian bowman wore light armour or no armour at all. He was armed with his bow, a quiver of arrows and perhaps a dagger for self-defence. The line between what was a dagger and what was a short sword was somewhat hazy. The Hyksos brought new types of daggers into use. These weapons were wide-bladed, with no hilt, and were designed for thrusting, like the later sword that developed from them. Daggers gradually became longer, cast in bronze, and were the forerunners of the short sword.

The infantryman wore a typical Egyptian headdress, usually of striped linen; it was stiffened to keep its shape if necessary.

▶ **Officer**
This elaborately dressed sword bearer is an officer or a man of high rank. His dress clearly marks him as an important personage and it could denote him as a type of guardsman for the pharaoh.

◀ **Standard Bearer**
This well-clothed soldier carries a ram's head standard. He wears a tunic as well as the Egyptian 'kilt' and typical headgear. He is armed for self-defence with a weapon that is undoubtedly for stabbing as well as clubbing.

▼ The Middle Kingdom Great Chief Khnumhotep II's tomb at Beni Hasan is noted for its wall paintings of nomadic traders, considered to represent Hyksos delegates bringing offerings to the deceased. The Hyksos themselves were of Semitic and Asiatic descent, settling in the Nile Delta and then ruling Egypt in the 15th and 16th Dynasties.

THE ARMY OF THE NEW KINGDOM

The establishment of the New Kingdom in *c.*1550BCE brought in a new army. This was set up on a permanent basis and became professional in both name and practice. Military clothing was now more elaborate and armour became much more common for the infantry, even though armour would not often not be worn in combat, even by the senior officers. Weapons, cast in iron, were much more modern and sophisticated. New Kingdom rulers developed a professional, long-service army that was better armed and equipped than any Egyptian army that had come before.

Scale armour was used, especially by the archers in the chariot arm. However, most infantrymen wore linen armour, along with a linen headdress; they were armed with an improved bow, spears and lances, and scythe-shaped close-combat weapons. The bow was now the composite type, copied from that of the Mitanni, and instead of being constructed in one piece as was the earlier bow in the Middle Kingdom, it was now constructed of both wood and horn giving it greater strength and hitting power as well as increased range. It also required more strength to pull the bowstring, to give full force to the new advantage of construction.

The Egyptian shield was now almost rectangular in shape, but the top was rounded. It could be of a simple wooden construction, but could also be reinforced by bronze on the face of the shield, usually in bronze disks.

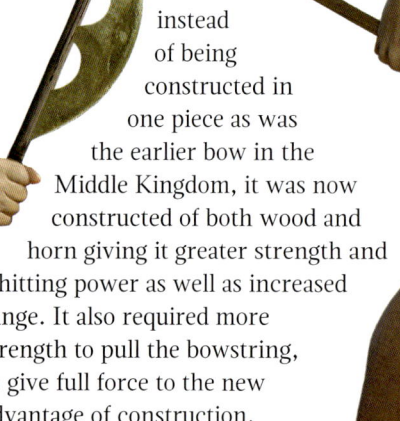

◀ **ARMOURED INFANTRYMAN**
This well-armed and well-armoured infantryman is wearing a leather harness or cuirass as well as a leather helmet which would protect him from glancing blows but not direct strikes from edged weapons or polearms. His arms are spear and axe.

▲ **INFANTRYMAN**
This well-equipped heavy infantryman has a linen jerkin along with a helmet and the padded groin protector. He has the wooden, hide-covered shield, and wields the dangerous-looking cutting weapon with knobkerrie, this time as a polearm.

Ahmose I and the New Military State

At the start of the New Kingdom Ahmose I (reigned c.1550–c.1525BCE), founder of the 18th Dynasty, not only completed the expulsion of the Hyksos that had been begun by his brother Kamose but also led the Egyptian army into Palestine – as well as reasserting Egyptian control over Nubia. He embarked on these campaigns after consolidating his rule, attacking and destroying Avaris, a great stronghold of the Hyksos in the eastern part of the Nile Delta. He forced the former rulers out of the country altogether; then he campaigned in the south of Palestine and laid siege to Sharuhen (Tell el-Far'ah), laying the foundations for an Egyptian empire. In the south he campaigned as far as Buhen. He appointed an official named Overseer of the Southern Foreign Lands to manage these conquered territories.

Ahmose's reign saw the establishment of a military class loyal to the pharaoh. He gave captives and other spoils of war to his key officers and his soldiers, who took the prisoners into service as slaves. Ahmose set New Kingdom Egypt on the way to becoming a military state and a multicultural empire.

Campaigns of Thutmose III and the Battle of Megiddo

Around 80 years later, Thutmose III (reigned c.1479–1425BCE) led an army of infantry and chariot units of 10,000–20,000 men to victory at the celebrated Battle of Megiddo in c.1457BCE. The campaign was recorded in inscriptions of the temple he built at Karnak in Thebes, based on a first-hand journal kept by the pharaoh's scribe Tjaneni.

Thutmose marched north to confront the King of Kadesh in Syria, who was leading a revolt by a confederation of Canaanites and Mitanni and the King of Megiddo (now an archaeological site in northern Israel). On this campaign Thutmose showed considerable daring and confidence in the New Kingdom army. Approaching Megiddo, he surprised the rebels by taking the most difficult and dangerous of three possible routes, a narrow pass that forced his army to travel in single file and made them vulnerable to attack; because this route was so difficult, the city's defenders had left it unguarded and the Egyptians, led by Thutmose in person, passed safely through and took up a strong position near Megiddo.

Next the Egyptian army – with around 10,000 infantry and 1,000 chariots – met and defeated the defenders of the city of Megiddo in open battle outside of the city. Thutmose skilfully deployed his army in three wings, and led it into a decisive attack on the rebel army. The rebels were decisively routed, but their remnants withdrew into Megiddo, forcing Thutmose to besiege the city. Beginning siege operations, Thutmose's engineers directed the construction of a ditch and palisade to isolate Megiddo from outside assistance. Thutmose gained the city after a siege of eight months. The loot and spoils seized by the Egyptian army were significant. Thutmose took advantage of the successful siege to resupply and re-equip his army. The Karnak inscriptions record that among many other spoils, the Egyptians carried home from Megiddo almost 1,000 chariots and 500 bows, as well as the royal chariot and armour of the King of Megiddo. Afterwards Thutmose took several other cities in the region, including Kadesh, and took control of a number of strategically valuable ports in Phoenicia along the Mediterranean coast. In c.1455BCE he led a meticulously executed campaign to conquer the Kingdom of the Mitanni, beyond the River Euphrates. Oxcarts carried pontoon boats across Syria and were used to transport his army across the river. The army of the Mitanni must have been trounced in the ensuing battle, although no details survive, but we do know that the King of the Mitanni fled and Thutmose took prisoner several hundred soldiers and – he claims – thirty members of the king's harem.

▶ **ARMOURED INFANTRYMAN**
This heavy infantryman is armoured from head to hip in leather scales and carries a wooden rectangular shield and a somewhat primitive axe. The reconstruction of the scale hood is hypothetical; the feather is probably a unit identifier.

Thutmose led no fewer than seventeen further campaigns in his long reign and established secure rule over Egypt's imperial possessions in Asia.

Armoured Infantry

Some sources state that the Egyptian infantry still went into combat unarmoured because of the climate in which they fought. However, there is also evidence that some ordinary Egyptian troops – in addition to the senior officers and the pharaoh – wore armour in combat.

Armour developed over time and its shape, functionality and utility could have been copied from Egypt's enemies. Certainly chariot troops would be more heavily armoured than infantry, but the tendency to use armoured infantry also progressed. The infantryman of the New Kingdom was well-armed and -armoured compared to earlier soldiers. The infantrymen of c.1300BCE typically wore a type of simple mesh armour over the usual kilt, with groin protection. He had belly and chest protection in the form of stiffened or reinforced linen wrapped around his body, which could also be used as bandages if wounded. He wore a cuirass with the over-the-shoulder supports made either of leather or of stiffened linen and probably padded for added protection. This armour was placed over the shoulder that was not protected by the shield. The shield was sometimes in the shape of a modified trapezoid, with the usual circular top, and was constructed of wood and animal hide.

The short spear was the main weapon used, but a battle-axe often supplemented his spear. Some infantry were armed with a long, undoubtedly heavy, machete-like weapon together with a protective shield.

Helmets could be of stiffened cloth or leather and provided better

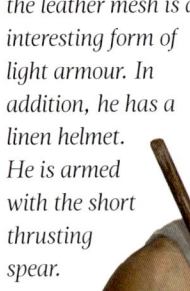

▼ INFANTRYMAN
This soldier is armoured and accoutered with stiffened linen armour over a kilt; the leather mesh is an interesting form of light armour. In addition, he has a linen helmet. He is armed with the short thrusting spear.

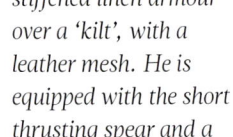

◄ SPEARMAN
This spearman has stiffened linen armour over a 'kilt', with a leather mesh. He is equipped with the short thrusting spear and a wooden shield covered with animal hide.

THE ARMY OF THE NEW KINGDOM

protection than previous head coverings. Some infantrymen might even have a bronze helmet.

Archers

Whether armed with the simple early bow or the later and much more deadly composite bow, the appearance of the native Egyptian archer did not change much over the passage of time. The big event technologically in the ancient world was the changeover from the Bronze Age to the Iron Age around 1200 BCE, and this affected archers with the introduction of iron arrowheads of various types. The Nubians alternated between either fighting for or fighting against the Egyptians. They were stalwart enemies, and then useful allies. The Nubians who fought with the Egyptians as allies or mercenaries excelled as bowmen and gave an additional flexibility to the Egyptian army as a whole. They were armed with long bows supposedly 2m (6ft) in length and – according to accounts – constructed of 'palm blades'. This seems a little fantastic; it might have been intended to signify palm wood. Their arrows were made of reed and tipped with sharpened stone.

The Nubians were, in addition, armed with lance-like spears, the lance tip being made from the sharpened horns of the gazelle. One of the traditional weapons of the eastern Africans, the knobkerrie, was also carried by the Nubians.

▶ **Archer**
This archer is sparsely equipped and not armoured other than the groin protection; he has no sidearm, and carries the early type of simple Egyptian bow. However, his arrow sheaf and strap appear quite advanced.

◀ **Archer**
This archer wears no armour except for the traditional padded groin protection. He carries a stave bow and a leather arrow quiver. Noteworthy is the cap of his quiver, seen here removed and attached to the quiver by a leather thong.

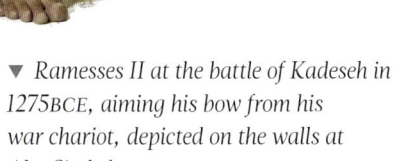

▼ *Ramesses II at the battle of Kadeseh in 1275 BCE, aiming his bow from his war chariot, depicted on the walls at Abu Simbel.*

Guardsman

Egyptian guard units of this period are well documented. A guard officer was typically equipped with a shield that had two handholds for better control, usually rectangular in shape, with a rounded top. In a guard unit the shields were richly decorated; the markings denoted the bearer's status.

The guardsman was armed with an iron sword without a handguard: even without such a precaution, this new model of a short, straight sword was a great improvement over previous edged weapons used by Egyptian soldiers. A skilfully used short sword and a well-handled shield make a deadly combination – as would later be demonstrated by the Roman legions and the Spanish 'sword-and-buckler' men of the Renaissance period.

Battle Standards

Egyptian standards were similar to early Sumerian standards: animal symbols were used atop the pole that was carried by the standard bearer. The animal symbols were totem-like in their use and were carried at the head of the units. Along with the ubiquitous falcon, which may have been the personal symbol of the pharaoh, the jackal and various other birds were used. Later, non-animal symbols were used to designate different units, such as the feather and the fan, but standards that appeared to be abstract were also used. From around 1279 BCE (roughly the start of Ramesses II's reign) a standard with the appearance of a pair of hands raised in supplication or prayer was used by at least one unit.

In this period the Egyptian standard bearer was often equipped with an armoured vest that came to mid-thigh or almost to the knees. It was of scale or lamellar armour, which indicated the influence of the Mittani on Egyptian military dress and equipment. He wore a typical Egyptian headdress, which gave a layer of defence against blows to the head and some protection against the elements, especially the back of the neck from the sun. He carried a shield with elaborate additions to its front. He might also have worn a short sword suspended by a waist belt, the sword hanging on his left side.

The biblical phrase 'terrible as an army with banners', from the *Song of Solomon*, is an apt one. Armies of the

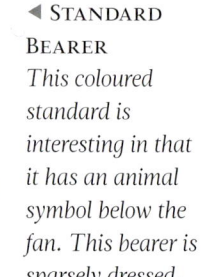

◀ **Standard Bearer**
This coloured standard is interesting in that it has an animal symbol below the fan. This bearer is sparsely dressed.

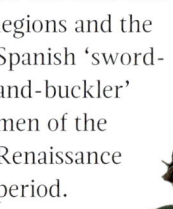

◀ **Guard Officer**
This officer is wearing an expensive overvest which doubles as armour and is most likely made of leather. He is uncovered here, but in the field of battle he would wear headgear, most probably an armoured helmet.

THE ARMY OF THE NEW KINGDOM

ancient world traditionally employed banners, flags and other symbols on poles to intimidate their enemies. Other important purposes were to identify units and to serve as an inspiration and rallying point for warriors on the battlefield after a melée or if a unit was defeated or had to retreat.

Standards were carried down to the company level, and may have been carried at the platoon level also. Some sources believe that the platoon commander would carry the standard. Typical standards of the period include fans that possibly represented the rays of the sun, and so honoured the sun god; a surviving image of one showed a fan with a lion underneath, which might represent a specific unit. The feather was used as a chariot unit standard. An image of the falcon-headed war god Montu was also used on a military standard. Montu generally carried the disc of the sun in his headdress, a symbol of the pharaoh's all-conquering spirit.

▼ **STANDARD BEARER**
This standard bearer was issued headgear and armour, though he does not appear to have a weapon for self-defence. He does have a shield, however. Undoubtedly armed troops would be detailed to protect him so that the standard would not be lost in combat. In an emergency, the standard itself could be used as a weapon for self-defence.

▶ **STANDARD BEARER**
There is no animal likeness on this standard above or below the fan, which tends to infer that the fan is the most important part. This bearer is unarmoured and unarmed.

1 2

▲ **FALCON AND FEATHER**
Both of these emblems would be called finials today as they would be on the top of whatever standard they were attached to. On the other hand, they could themselves be the standard, the falcon being a royal emblem.

Musicians

Most armies through history have employed musicians of some type. Martial music can inspire one's own troops and at the same time strike fear into an enemy. Musicians can be either combatants or personnel hired merely to provide the music required and who tend to disappear when the serious business of the day begins to take place.

Egyptian drummers accompanied their units into combat in the field and the drum was used for signalling as well as giving a steady beat to regulate units on the march. The Egyptian trumpet had a limited range of notes, but was still used for signalling in battle with specific trumpet calls being developed to manage the movements of the units in combat. Both drummers and trumpeters had to be trained and have their calls to hand immediately, for making a mistake or using the wrong call could be disastrous in the middle of a melée or while trying to execute the commander's plan of action.

▶ **Military Drummer**
This drummer has an outsized drum, which is probably African in origin and is carried slung across the body. Apparently, the Egyptian musicians assigned to the army were not armed, not even for self-defence. The conclusion can be drawn that while they would accompany the army on campaign, they were not expected to join the combat.

▲ **Trumpet Player**
The Egyptians used a primitive form of trumpet, though it seems more advanced than that used by the Greeks. At the very least it is recognizable as a brass instrument, whereas the early Greek instrument of this type was not. Trumpets of some type have been part of the 'music' attached to the army for millennia and had then, as now, an important role.

◀ **Trumpeter (far left)** *A fragment of a painted relief of a trumpeter, found on a limestone wall dating to the reign of Akhenaten.*

THE ARMY OF THE NEW KINGDOM

A good courier system was vital for communications and it is evident that the Egyptians realized this and employed a system for this purpose. Couriers would be lightly armed for self-defence and might even wear light armour. Their purpose was to keep communications open, and not to engage in combat unless required by their mission. Therefore, while the Egyptians did not develop a cavalry force in their army, they did recognize that the horse was of use in other ways than merely as teams for chariots.

◀ **Courier**
Even though the Egyptians did not use cavalry, evidence suggests that they did use couriers mounted on horses. This also suggests that equitation was not a common Egyptian skill and that couriers had to be taught how to ride before being assigned to their role.

Mounted Couriers

Horses were not native to Egypt or the countries of the Levant and were expensive to import. Chariot troops were the only mounted troops in the army, therefore, and the mounted arm were considered to be the elite of the army. However, the horse was still employed during the New Kingdom in a variety of other roles, such as carrying couriers either on the battlefield or between separate units in different theatres of war.

▶ *The Ancient Egyptians did not have a tradition of horse riding, but a military relay rider was depicted on a wall relief of the New Kingdom tomb of Horemheb, in the 18th Dynasty. The rider holds a message baton in one arm and the reins in another.*

EGYPTIAN WAR CHARIOTS

The first Egyptian chariots were somewhat crude, although they had progressed a great deal from the early Sumerian 'war wagons'. The wheels were now spoked, and during this period the wheels had six spokes. These early Egyptian chariots were lightly built, with a low barrier around the cabin area that was sturdy enough to hold the arrow sheaths for the archer in the two-man crew. The barrier also provided a little protection.

The driver, or charioteer, doubled as a shield bearer, leaving him only one hand to control the two-horse team. He was unarmoured and probably only wore clothing from the waist down. The bowman wore lamellar armour, copied from the Mitanni. He was trained to be able to hit his targets with the chariot at speed, which also accounts for the light construction of the chariot itself, the Egyptians preferring speed over protection.

New Kingdom War Chariots

The Egyptians experimented with using wheels with eight spokes in their war chariots, but these were discarded as unserviceable and the six-spoked wheels retained. In chariots of the New Kingdom (c.1550–c.1070 BCE) the driver was basically unarmoured, but the archer wore light armour, metal scales sewn to a tunic, and a helmet to match. This form of armour was lighter than that used previously; the influence of the Mitanni remains clear – there is no doubt that the Egyptians were open to learning from their enemies.

The horse team now had much better protection, as the horses were the larger and more likely target of the enemy chariot troops and much easier to hit than any individual in the chariot itself when moving at speed. Killing or wounding the chariot team would put the chariot out of action and effectively negate the advantage of the enemy chariots. The crew would either be hurt or killed in the ensuing

◄ **EARLY WAR CHARIOT**
The arrangement of driver and archer in the two-man chariot is standard throughout the chariot world, the archer being armoured in this case. The lamellar and scale armour was copied by the Egyptians from the Mitanni; the armour covered the chest and torso, coming down to mid-thigh and sometimes almost to the ankles.

▶ **War Chariot of Thutmose III**
Thutmose III (c.1479–c.1425BCE) might have been the most successful commander in the field in Egyptian history. There are weapon holders attached to each side of the chariot.

crash and the chariot damaged or destroyed. The horses' padded body armour gave some protection from enemy missile weapons. The horses' eyes were protected with a type of blinders and their upper neck with a covering made from animal skins.

The chariot runners had to be in excellent physical shape for their demanding duties. They were to follow their assigned chariots on foot, and their main mission was to catch and kill any enemy chariot crew who had been dismounted during the action.

The Chariots of Amenhotep III

18th-Dynasty pharaoh Amenhotep III (reigned c.1390–c.1352BCE) was probably the first ancient Egyptian ruler to establish war chariots as a separate unit in his army. He created an elite corps of charioteers and made Yuya, his father-in-law, lieutenant commander of this corps. Amenhotep himself led a campaign into Nubia in the fifth year of his reign. This victory was commemorated in three stelae discovered near Aswan (now in the south of Egypt). The inscription describes dramatically how Amenhotep led the campaign to crush a rebellion in the Kingdom of Kush: he was an 'angry-eyed lion whose sharp claws grabbed wicked Kush, who stamped on all its leaders in their gentle valleys, they being thrown down in their own lifeblood, one lying on top of another.'

▼ *A detail from a victory stele of Amenhotep III depicting the pharaoh in his war chariot.*

▼ **Chariot of Ramesses II**
This is an excellent example of the evolved Egyptian chariot. Well-built and sturdy, it has the axle placed at the rear and connected to the yoke for harnessing the horses. Weapons were carried in the quivers at the side of the chariot, slanted at an angle for easy access. The pharaoh would have an assigned driver.

The Chariots of Ramesses II

As the army's commander-in-chief, the pharaoh typically led his troops into battle. In his royal war chariot a ruler such as Ramesses II (reigned c.1279–c.1213BCE) cut a commanding figure leading the chariot attack and employing his bow to subdue enemies.

Ramesses was an imposing soldier: his appearance in his armour and war regalia, including his blue crown, was magnificent. He wore cross-chest belts and protection around his neck and throat; his driver was unarmoured. Ramses was armed with a sword and his bow, with plenty of arrows. As well as leading his chariot forces in combat, he would also take part in the fighting as a participant in the melée that usually accompanied the clash of contesting chariot forces.

▼ **War Chariot**
The driver would drive with one hand and hold his shield to protect the fighter to his right. The Egyptian chariot was elegant and well-built, sturdy and very manoeuvrable.

EGYPTIAN WAR CHARIOTS

The pharaoh's horse team was magnificently fitted out: there was no way that Ramesses's men would not recognize his chariot even in the dust and mess of a melée. The headdress of the horse team was particularly noteworthy. The chariot itself was of the same light construction as those used by the rank and file, built for speed and mobility. There was no extra protection for the pharaoh – he would take his chances in combat in the same way as his troops. With a driver, the pharaoh could fight from his chariot while leading the squadrons.

Blades were sometimes fitted on the harness across the shoulders of the horses that pulled the royal war chariot. They were clearly designed to discourage enemy troops from trying to mount the horse team to capture or disable the pharaoh's chariot.

In the Egyptian war chariots of this period the placement of the axle at the very rear of the cabin was key. It made it possible to turn the chariot at speed and in tight angles in the heat of battle. The chariot had a case mounted on its side in which the crew could store the long, powerful composite bows when they were not needed.

▼ *Ramesses II in his chariot with bow and arrow at the Battle of Kadesh. Reconstruction of wall painting from the Great Temple, Abu Simbel.*

◀ **CHARIOT RUNNER**
Runners followed chariots on foot in order to capture or kill any enemy warrior or soldier left on the ground after the chariot attack. This runner is lightly accoutered in order to be able to move swiftly, but he does wear an Egyptian helmet. He is armed with a short spear and a wooden, hide-covered shield.

The Chariot Battle of Kadesh

When Ramesses II led his troops northwards in his celebrated attack on the Hittite stronghold of Kadesh in c.1275BCE his army was organized into separate infantry and chariot units. This was a large, well-trained and equipped army: each of these four units was probably 5,000-strong. Ramesses planned his campaign against Kadesh carefully, sending a force to take control of the seaport of Simyra while the remainder of his troops forded the River Orontes then made a stealthy approach towards Kadesh through a wood. He believed himself to have the upper hand because two captured spies had misinformed him that the main Hittite army was stationed at Aleppo. However, he discovered that the Hittites were hidden behind the city of Kadesh. He sent couriers to summon reinforcements from Simyra.

The battle is well documented on the Egyptian side because Ramesses made sure records of his handling of the battle, and resistance when initially overcome, were widely circulated: temple carvings on no fewer than five temples in Nubia and Egypt were supplemented by a poetic account on papyrus. When the Hittites burst forth from their hiding place, for a time they overwhelmed the Egyptian advance guard. At Kadesh the Hittites employed at least 2,500 chariots, each with three-man crews, the Egyptians having only two men per chariot. The

94 ARMIES OF ANCIENT EGYPT

◀ CHARIOT WITH CREW
This rear view shows the positioning of the driver and fighter, as well as the wide wheel base of the chariot itself, and the arrangement of the arrow quivers. The fighter on the right wears a full set of Egyptian armour and helmet.

▶ EGYPTIAN CHARIOT
This is a rank and file chariot manned by a lightly accoutered crew. While this chariot is not as expensively equipped and caparisoned as that of the pharaoh, it is still constructed in the same way, and having the axle in the rear of the chariot allowed it to have a narrower turning radius which gave it a decisive advantage manoeuvring against the enemy in the field.

▲ *An elephant carved into sandstone at the 3rd-century BCE Nubian temple complex of Musawwarat es-Sufra in what is now Sudan.*

battle was desperate: Ramesses and his household chariots were fighting for their very survival. The Hittites failed to exploit their initial advantage and when the Egyptians were reinforced during the fighting by the troops from Simyra, the initiative in the fighting shifted to them. Ramesses drove the Hittites back, and by his account won a decisive victory.

According to one of Ramesses's accounts of the battle, as recorded on papyrus, he won the struggle with the help of the god Amun, who declared: 'I go forward with you/I am your father and my hand supports you/I triumph over one hundred thousand of your enemy.' The battle – though so much celebrated – was in fact a draw. The pharaoh's failure to decisively defeat the Hittites encouraged rebellion against Egyptian rule by different peoples in northern Palestine and southern Syria. Further, war continued between the Egyptians and Hittites for another sixteen years after Kadesh. Eventually, in 1258 BCE, a peace treaty was signed between Ramesses and the Hittite king, Hattusilis III. This treaty survives in both Egyptian and Hittite versions; the world's oldest surviving peace treaty in military history. (A copy is kept in the United Nations building in New York, United States.)

War Elephants

Egyptians of the late New Kingdom are believed to have made a limited use of war elephants. They had access to African elephants through their expeditions southwards into Nubia and Ethiopia. The fighting platform on such an elephant held two or three men, and the bow and arrows along with javelins were the weapons of choice. The 'driver' was in the open at the front and somewhat vulnerable to arrows, spears and other forms of attack. The elephant was a dangerous weapon: if the driver were killed, the elephant might run amok in the middle of combat. This would, of course, be disastrous for the soldiers mounted behind him unless they could regain control of the animal – and probably spelt catastrophe for the army spread out on the battlefield in the elephant's path. An uncontrolled elephant could completely disrupt an army's forward momentum in an attack.

▼ **War Elephant**
The Egyptian war elephants were assigned a three-man crew which included an unarmed driver sitting immediately behind the elephant's head, and two men in the fighting tower on the elephant's back. Two men, one with spear and one with bow, occupied the fighting tower.

EGYPT'S ENEMIES

The Ancient Egyptians' imperial ambitions brought them into conflict with a range of enemies from across the area of operations, including the Libyans, Canaanites, Phoenicians and Israelites – not to mention the ill-defined Sea Peoples.

The Libyans
Enemies of Ancient Egypt from across the desert to the west of the kingdom, the Libyans were fierce, warlike tribesmen, but crudely armed and armoured and not so well organized as the Egyptians. They were essentially cross-border raiders for profit and their battle clothing was minimal, habitually being merely enough to cover and provide basic protection for the groin. They were often armed with Egyptian weapons taken in previous raids and ambuscades, but they also fought using weapons captured from other enemies. In particular, they were known for having iron swords.

One notable item used by the Libyans was a large, cloak-like garment worn for protection from the elements. The Libyans undoubtedly 'lived' in the large garment as desert nights could be cold. Libyans generally were bearded, with a tribal hairstyle, decorated with feathers and beads. They wore no shoes or boots.

The Libyans would later be part of the Persian empire and were described by the 5th-century BCE Greek historian Herodotus. In the time of Herodotus, the Libyans wore leather garments and were armed with heat-sharpened javelins. Other non-Libyan northern Africans were also noted by Herodotus: these wore a distinctive type of headdress made from a skinned horsehead complete with the mane and ears, the ears placed so as to stand up from the head piece. They also carried an odd type of shield that was made from the skin of a crane.

◀ LIBYAN INFANTRYMAN
More tribal warrior than soldier, the Libyans encountered on the battlefield were aggressive enemies who were defeated by the discipline and fighting ability of the Egyptians. This warrior's sparse dress is indicative of his tribal status. From time to time the Egyptians employed Libyan auxiliaries in their armies, as they also did Nubian auxiliaries.

▲ LIBYAN ARCHER
Like his comrade-in-arms, this archer is lightly dressed for desert warfare, and he carries the early type of Egyptian stave bow. His animal-skin cloak would serve to keep him warm as desert nights could be notoriously cold. His only other equipment is his arrow quiver.

The Canaanites

These people were a completely different calibre of opponent to the Libyans. They inhabited parts of Palestine and Syria and were identified in Egyptian sources of the 15th century BCE as Canaanites and their territory as Canaan. They fought desperately for their land and heritage against all comers, the Israelites and Egyptians among them. Unfortunately for the Canaanites, their land was the traditional and logical invasion route into Egypt, as well as the route taken by Egyptians heading north against the Hittites. They occupied an unenviable strategic position. Their territories were taken by the Israelites in the late Bronze Age around 1300BCE.

The influence of the Mitanni of northern Mesopotamia on the army of the Canaanites was quite definite. The Canaanites used a light chariot similar, if not identical, to that of the Mitanni, and they were armed and armoured similarly to the Mitanni. They were also influenced by the armies of Ancient Egypt who marched through their lands. They wore an Egyptian-style 'kilt' and an Egyptian type of linen armour. They also had calf and ankle-length 'robes' and as arms carried only the early Egyptian-type V-shaped bow. Their shields were rectangular and made from wood and wicker.

◀ CANAANITE WAR CHARIOT
The Egyptians modelled their chariots on those of the Canaanites. The simplicity of design, as well as structural strength and the relative light weight, aided their production. This type of chariot would be drawn by two horses and have a crew of two. The Canaanites placed their chariot axles in the middle of the carriage portion, which made for a relatively wide turning radius.

◀ CANAANITE INFANTRYMAN
The Canaanites are thought to be some of the original inhabitants of the Levant in what would later be known as Palestine. They were conquered by the Egyptians, and were similarly in conflict with the early Israelites. Their dress and weapons were similar to the Israelites.

▶ CANAANITE ARCHER
This is a Canaanite maryannu ('young warrior') and he is clothed in the long skirt-like garment that indicates his high-status among the Canaanites. He is armed with a wicker shield and bow, but has no other armour and no visible headgear. He is not equipped for hand-to-hand fighting.

The Sea Peoples, Philistines and Sherden

The Sea Peoples were warlike migrants, shipborne invaders who swept through the Near East around 1250–1200 BCE. They used a variety of weapons and equipment, probably a mixture of arms and armour from the different peoples that made up their ravaging horde. Their spears and swords were worn attached to a baldric over the shoulder; some of their helmets featured animal horns as decoration. Troops armed and equipped in this way were employed by the Egyptians as elite troops in an earlier period.

One of the contingents of the Sea Peoples may have consisted of the Sherden, a people from Sardinia who at one time supplied soldiers to the Egyptian pharaoh as his personal bodyguard. They carried a round shield and a long sword very different from that used by the native Egyptian troops. Their armour was of either leather or metal, and was in a design

▶ **Warrior of the Sea Peoples**
The Sea Peoples constituted a national threat to all of the nations with which they came into contact, but they were notably defeated by the Egyptians. Undoubtedly, they were searching for 'living space' for themselves. Their arms and equipment consisted of straightforward leather helmet, short sword and spear. The horns on the helmet were probably only decorative.

▲ **Philistine Infantryman**
Some believe that the Sea Peoples at some time evolved into the Philistines who formed a kingdom in Canaan. They were similiarly accoutered and equipped and their odd headdress evolved from the headdress of some of the Sea Peoples. This infantryman has leather upper body armour, an excellent spear and a round bronze-faced shield.

unique to the Sherden, being shown in Ancient Egyptian reliefs as overlapping bands across the chest and torso. Their helmets were round – or conical – in shape and were horned with a spike at the top of the helmet.

The biblical Philistines were one of the Sea Peoples and were originally of Aegean origin. According to biblical tradition, as expressed in the books of *Deuteronomy* and *Jeremiah*, they were from Caphtor – tentatively identified by scholars as Crete. They were part of the invading force of Sea Peoples that was driven back by Ramesses III in c.1180BCE and afterwards settled in the coastal region of Palestine, south of modern Tel Aviv. There they carved out a kingdom based on five cities – Gaza, Ashkelon, Ashdod, Gath and Ekron – and were in almost constant conflict with the ancient Israelites, who fought them during the period of the Israelite Judges, before the time of the Hebrew kings. Their territory was called Philistia ('Territory of the Philistines') – the origin of the modern name Palestine.

The Philistines were variously armed and armoured, but had a somewhat uniform appearance, especially with their distinctive headgear. Both Philistines and Sherden were valued as mercenaries by different ancient kings and armies.

The 19th-Dynasty Pharaoh Merneptah (reigned c.1213–c.1203BCE), a son of Ramesses II, defeated a combined force of Libyans and Sea Peoples in c.1209BCE. An account of the battle in an inscription beside the sixth pylon at the Temple of Karnak is only one of four surviving reports of this encounter: from the Karnak inscription, we know that Meryre, king of Libya, led an attack in combination with Sea Peoples in the western part of the Nile Delta, aiming to attack Memphis and Heliopolis. This forced Merneptah – said in the inscription to be 'enraged like a lion' – to take the battle to the invaders. The battle lasted six hours. Merneptah held back his infantry and chariots and sent forward his archers. According to the inscription, the Egyptian bowmen were protected by the god Amun, who was like a shield over them. With or without divine help, the archers were a formidable force and the rain of arrows broke the invaders' will to fight. Finally King Meryre fled, the invading army lost its discipline and Merneptah let loose the chariots and infantry. They overran the demoralized remnants of the Libyans and Sea Peoples: 6,000 of their army were left dead and Merneptah took 9,000 more as prisoners. He settled many of these prisoners in camps for use as mercenaries.

The Sea Peoples disappeared as suddenly as they arrived in the Middle East. Apparently, they mixed with other, more established, peoples and eventually 'produced' the Philistines.

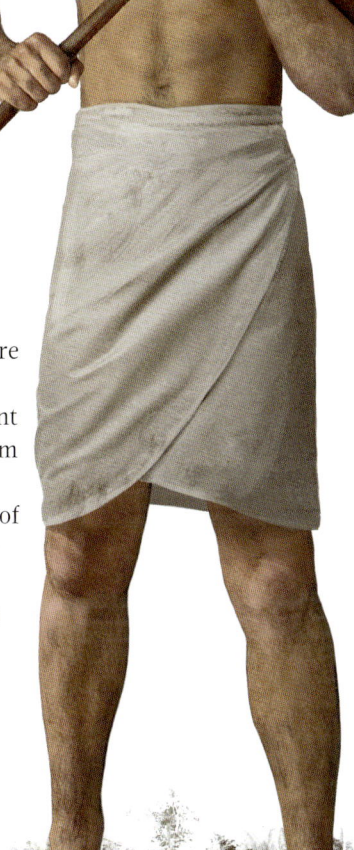

▲ ISRAELITE WARRIOR
The simple attire and spear is typical. It was the Israelite Judge Samson who slew 1,000 Philistine soldiers 'with the jawbone of an ass', and the two peoples were traditional enemies. The Israelite shepherd David, who became the second king, slew the Philistine giant Goliath by flinging the stone to stun him then cutting off his head.

▼ *The Merneptah Stele, found at Karnak in Thebes, is a black granite slab 3m (10ft) high. At the top, the god Amun is depicted giving a sword to the pharaoh. The text below glorifies Merneptah's victory over the Libyans and Sea Peoples. It is also known as the Israel Stele, as it gives the first-known usage of the name Israel (see page 101).*

The Phoenicians

Ancient sailors and colonizers, the Phoenicians were noted more as seamen than as soldiers. They were based in coastal parts of what is now Lebanon from around 3000 BCE; they are thought by scholars to have come originally from the Persian Gulf and established a thriving centre of trade, with their principal cities being Tyre, Sidon and Berot (modern Beirut). Archaeological finds in the ancient port of Byblos (modern Jbeil, about 30km [20 miles] north of Beirut) demonstrate that the Phoenicians were trading with the Ancient Egyptians from the Egyptian 4th Dynasty (c.2575–c.2465 BCE) onwards. At various times, Egyptian forces clashed with the Phoenicians and in time they achieved control of the region.

In the first millennium BCE the Phoenicians established many trading settlements, including Jaffa and Acre in what is now Israel and Carthage in northern Africa (now a suburb of Tunis in Tunisia). The Phoenicians were expert seamen and shipbuilders, and they were employed as naval forces for different kingdoms during the ancient period, including Persia and Macedon. However, they did also have land infantry – typically lightly armed with a spear and wearing only a loincloth.

The Israelites

Aggressive, organized and usually well led, the Ancient Israelites were some of the most formidable warriors of the period – certainly by the time of Solomon, king of a united Israel in the 10th century BCE. The original Israelite armies were probably unarmoured and their members armed themselves with anything and everything they could lay their hands on. They eventually equipped themselves with a great variety of types and styles of arms and armour, as they would seize those items of military equipment captured and looted from their early conquests, beginning with the ingenious mining operations and assault

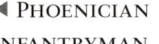
◀ PHOENICIAN INFANTRYMAN
This lightly equipped and accoutered infantryman, armed with short sword and shield and helmet of sorts, is ready for combat either aboard ship or ashore as necessary. The personal equipment of this warrior is almost identical to that used by the warriors of the Sea Peoples, most notably the Philistines.

▲ JOSHUA
This famous leader of the nation of Israel after the passing of Moses; some of his soldiering is chronicled in the Old Testament. 'Armed' with his ram's horn and burning torch, he is prepared to lead his people against any and all opposition.

on Jericho as described in the biblical book of Joshua. The ram horns blown by the priests in the army at the climax of this encounter (Joshua 6:1–27) were a typical signalling device of many unique to the Sherden, being shown in Ancient Egyptian reliefs as overlapping bands across the chest and torso. Their helmets were round – or conical – in shape and were horned with a spike at the top of the helmet.

The biblical Philistines were one of the Sea Peoples and were originally of Aegean origin. According to biblical tradition, as expressed in the books of *Deuteronomy* and *Jeremiah*, they were from Caphtor – tentatively identified by scholars as Crete. They were part of the invading force of Sea Peoples that was driven back by Ramesses III in c.1180BCE and afterwards settled in the coastal region of Palestine, south of modern Tel Aviv. There they carved out a kingdom based on five cities – Gaza, Ashkelon, Ashdod, Gath and Ekron – and were in almost constant conflict with the ancient Israelites, who fought them during the period of the Israelite Judges, before the time of the Hebrew kings. Their territory was called Philistia ('Territory of the Philistines') – the origin of the modern name Palestine.

The Philistines were variously armed and armoured, but had a somewhat uniform appearance, especially with their distinctive headgear. Both Philistines and Sherden were valued as mercenaries by different ancient kings and armies.

The 19th-Dynasty Pharaoh Merneptah (reigned c.1213–c.1203BCE), a son of Ramesses II, defeated a combined force of Libyans and Sea Peoples in c.1209BCE. An account of the battle in an inscription beside the sixth pylon at the Temple of Karnak is only one of four surviving reports of this encounter: from the Karnak inscription, we know that Meryre, king of Libya, led an attack in combination with Sea Peoples in the western part of the Nile Delta, aiming to attack Memphis and Heliopolis. This forced Merneptah – said in the inscription to be 'enraged like a lion' – to take the battle to the invaders. The battle lasted six hours. Merneptah held back his infantry and chariots and sent forward his archers. According to the inscription, the Egyptian bowmen were protected by the god Amun, who was like a shield over them. With or without divine help, the archers were a formidable force and the rain of arrows broke the invaders' will to fight. Finally King Meryre fled, the invading army lost its discipline and Merneptah let loose the chariots and infantry. They overran the demoralized remnants of the Libyans and Sea Peoples: 6,000 of their army were left dead and Merneptah took 9,000 more as prisoners. He settled many of these prisoners in camps for use as mercenaries.

The Sea Peoples disappeared as suddenly as they arrived in the Middle East. Apparently, they mixed with other, more established, peoples and eventually 'produced' the Philistines.

▲ **ISRAELITE WARRIOR**
The simple attire and spear is typical. It was the Israelite Judge Samson who slew 1,000 Philistine soldiers 'with the jawbone of an ass', and the two peoples were traditional enemies. The Israelite shepherd David, who became the second king, slew the Philistine giant Goliath by flinging the stone to stun him then cutting off his head.

▼ *The Merneptah Stele, found at Karnak in Thebes, is a black granite slab 3m (10ft) high. At the top, the god Amun is depicted giving a sword to the pharaoh. The text below glorifies Merneptah's victory over the Libyans and Sea Peoples. It is also known as the Israel Stele, as it gives the first-known usage of the name Israel (see page 101).*

The Phoenicians

Ancient sailors and colonizers, the Phoenicians were noted more as seamen than as soldiers. They were based in coastal parts of what is now Lebanon from around 3000BCE; they are thought by scholars to have come originally from the Persian Gulf and established a thriving centre of trade, with their principal cities being Tyre, Sidon and Berot (modern Beirut). Archaeological finds in the ancient port of Byblos (modern Jbeil, about 30km [20 miles] north of Beirut) demonstrate that the Phoenicians were trading with the Ancient Egyptians from the Egyptian 4th Dynasty (c.2575–c.2465BCE) onwards. At various times, Egyptian forces clashed with the Phoenicians and in time they achieved control of the region.

In the first millennium BCE the Phoenicians established many trading settlements, including Jaffa and Acre in what is now Israel and Carthage in northern Africa (now a suburb of Tunis in Tunisia). The Phoenicians were expert seamen and shipbuilders, and they were employed as naval forces for different kingdoms during the ancient period, including Persia and Macedon. However, they did also have land infantry – typically lightly armed with a spear and wearing only a loincloth.

The Israelites

Aggressive, organized and usually well led, the Ancient Israelites were some of the most formidable warriors of the period – certainly by the time of Solomon, king of a united Israel in the 10th century BCE. The original Israelite armies were probably unarmoured and their members armed themselves with anything and everything they could lay their hands on.

They eventually equipped themselves with a great variety of types and styles of arms and armour, as they would seize those items of military equipment captured and looted from their early conquests, beginning with the ingenious mining operations and assault

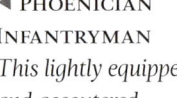

◀ PHOENICIAN INFANTRYMAN
This lightly equipped and accoutered infantryman, armed with short sword and shield and helmet of sorts, is ready for combat either aboard ship or ashore as necessary. The personal equipment of this warrior is almost identical to that used by the warriors of the Sea Peoples, most notably the Philistines.

▲ JOSHUA
This famous leader of the nation of Israel after the passing of Moses; some of his soldiering is chronicled in the Old Testament. 'Armed' with his ram's horn and burning torch, he is prepared to lead his people against any and all opposition.

on Jericho as described in the biblical book of Joshua. The ram horns blown by the priests in the army at the climax of this encounter (Joshua 6:1–27) were a typical signalling device of many

EGYPT'S ENEMIES 101

◀ **ISRAELITE NOBLE**
This infantryman wears a one-armed cloak, undoubtedly for warmth and protection from the elements. His left arm remains free of any encumbrance, to use his spear with ease.

▶ **ISRAELITE ARCHER**
Clothed only in a kilt or 'wraparound' this light infantryman is simply armed with his bow and quiver, with no sidearms for self-defence if the situation turned against him.

alliance is found on the Israel Stele (see page 99). The stele is so-called because it contains the earliest surviving use of the word 'Israel' – in the context of a description of Merneptah's military campaign in Palestine shortly after the 1209 battle. The inscription reads: 'Israel is desolate and has no seed'. (The exodus of the Jews from Egypt – as described in the biblical book of Exodus – is reckoned by some scholars to have taken place during the reign of Merneptah's father Ramesses II.)

ancient peoples, especially those who raised and herded flocks of sheep.

The Israelite infantry had three arms – heavy infantry, light infantry and archers. Israelite light infantry included skilled slingers. The Israelites developed the use of the horse with the army, and both chariot units as well as cavalry were employed. The Israelite cavalry developed into an effective mounted arm, and, if not classed as an elite unit, it was a very important part of the Israelite army which was used to great advantage by Israelite commanders.

The Canaanite chariot impressed the early Israelites and they copied it for their own use. As their expertise grew, chariots were used in conjuction with cavalry.

Pharaoh Merneptah, the same ruler who defeated the Libyan-Sea Peoples alliance in c.1209BCE, also won a victory over the Israelites at around the same time. One of the four accounts of the battle against the Libyan-led

THE EGYPTIAN NAVY

The Egyptians were great pioneers of boat- and shipbuilding. Evidence suggests they invented the sail in c.3500BCE, as boats with sails were depicted on pottery from this period. They also developed the first navy.

Merchant Ships and Warships

Ancient peoples who had access to the sea – including the Minoans, Greeks and Phoenicians, as well as the Egyptians – were not slow to understand that sea power brought clear advantages to build overseas trade and to found colonies. Pharaoh Ramesses III (reigned c.1184–c.1153BCE) put his navy to good use in defeating the invasion of the Sea Peoples at the Battle of the Delta in c.1180BCE, but he also used marine power for commercial activity: in his reign he dispatched a seagoing trade expedition to the Land of Punt, in the coastal region of modern Somalia. Marine trade with Punt was well established by this time; the 18th-Dynasty pharaoh Hatshepsut (c.1479–1458BC) had kept a trading fleet on the Red Sea and used marine shipping to carry out a commercial expedition to Punt that is documented in reliefs at her mortuary temple at Deir el-Bahri.

Once peoples had developed a functioning merchant marine, they saw that they needed a navy to protect it and to project power. In disputes warships delivered many defensive and strategic advantages. Often, in practice, warships were merely merchant vessels with armed troops aboard for protection against attacks.

Later the galley – a swift vessel mainly powered by banks of oars – was developed: this was eventually equipped with a bronze or iron ram, its main weapon. Ramming an enemy vessel was the primary tactic of ancient naval warfare; boarding the vessel was ancillary to ramming and sinking it.

First Egyptian Boats

There is archeological evidence that the Assyrians used inflated animal bladders to cross rivers. The earliest boats were built of various materials such as papyrus and reeds, before progressing to wood. The Egyptians were building boats and ships of papyrus and reeds by c.1400BCE, then pioneered the building of ships using wooden planks, the hull being smooth and the ship's ribs being added inside the hull after the planking was completed. As wooden-hulled ships evolved, the planks were cut to a specific shape and then fitted together. Later, a method of construction was developed in which the hull planks overlapped, called clinker-building, and this method made for much stronger hulls, although the overall appearance was no

▲ NAVAL ARCHER
This early naval archer is in a traditional mode of dress. Lightly clothed and armed, he wears no armour except for padded groin protection. He carries a stave bow and a hide-covered arrow quiver, and his head covering is a typical Egyptian cloth.

◀ *Egyptian wall painting from the Old Kingdom tomb of In Snefru Ishtef at Dahshur, depicting two ships with bipod masts, c.2500–2000BCE.*

longer smooth and looked somewhat like siding on a modern house. The two means of propulsion were oars and sails, the sails fixed to a mast in the middle of the ship, amidships. The sail was attached to the mast by a crosspiece, the yardarm.

▲ **River Craft**
This is an example of what the Egyptians developed for commerce along the Nile. From this their warships would develop – first as converted merchantmen and then as purposely designed galleys.

▼ **Ocean-going Vessel**
From the basic design of the river craft the Egyptians developed seagoing merchantmen that were able with little difficulty to venture into the Mediterranean for trade and transport, and then fighting. They look similar in design although the seagoing vessels would be more robust.

▶ **Tyrian Warship**
Built by the city of Tyre, this was a purpose-built Phoenician warship of sturdy construction with the addition of a large ram.

Enemy Vessels

The warships of the Egyptians' opponents and contemporaries such as the Hittites were generally sail-powered. These vessels were probably developed from merchant ships – or actually were merchant ships. Their single large sail was attached to one mast. They were not as graceful as their Egyptian counterparts, and were awkward to manoeuvre in naval combat. Researchers have shown that while a square sail made life difficult in the close encounters of a sea battle, it was a benefit in other situations and allowed the ships to sail close to the wind.

The ships used by the city-state of Ugarit were based on a merchantman design. Their primary means of propulsion was wind and sail, similar to the ships of their opponents, the Sea Peoples. These ships were not as box-like as those of the Sea Peoples, but they were nonetheless a far cry from the graceful and functional lines of the Egyptian galleys.

The Minoan galley was similar to later Egyptian vessels. Its lines were straight; these ships were powered by oars and sail, with a single mast standing amidships. This vessel may have been designed as a warship or for raiding; it was probably also used as a merchantman from time to time.

◀ **Minoan Galley**
This early galley was designed and built specifically for warfare during the Bronze Age in Crete. It was not used for trading or commerce, but for raiding and perhaps even for piracy. It was not strongly built, but was light and swift, powered either with oars or the large sail on the ship's single mast.

The Tyrians, from the port city of Tyre along the Lebanese coast, were excellent sailors who designed and built seaworthy vessels for trade and warfare. They were much in demand by land-locked peoples to furnish vessels for hire and use. It was the Tyrians who foiled Alexander the Great of Macedon in the great siege of Tyre he conducted in 332BCE. The great Macedonian war leader finally overcame the determined Tyrian defence in July of that year. The Tyrians and Phoenicians discovered that directly ramming an enemy vessel at a ninety-degree angle could damage the ram, if not lose it completely, which would then damage the ship, leaving it in a sinking condition and out of action. They learned to ram at an angle less than ninety degrees to the enemy ship.

Naval Crews

Infantry detailed for service with the fleet were clothed, armed and equipped largely as they were for service on land. In point of fact, any Egyptian unit or individual could be assigned service in the navy. The basic categories of archer and spearman were the same whether in army and navy, and an individual archer or spearman would not look out of place in either service.

Crewmen typically wore the usual Egyptian kilt and a striped shirt with sleeves reinforced by padding or layers of stiffened linen. The headgear gave protection against the elements; becoming helmet-shaped, it was conical, but still with the neck protection of Egyptian headwear.

The arms and armour were as usual, and were not modified for sea or riverine service. A naval archer

▲ **Hittite Warship**
The Hittites developed their own warships, this one being the type that was provided to the Hittite overlords by the people of the city of Ugarit, a port city in northern Syria that had been conquered by the Hittites when they expanded southward from Asia Minor. It was with this type of warship that the Hittites would engage the invading Sea Peoples.

used the strong composite bow, with the arrow quiver worn at the hip and a baldric instead of a belt. The spear and shield were intended for close combat, either for boarding an enemy vessel or defending a ship against enemy boarders. The bowmen and spearmen were trained to act together, the archers employed to deplete the crew of an enemy vessel as the captain closed the distance with the enemy ship and to provide critical fire support for the spearmen as they boarded or defended their ship. The spearmen would also provide protection for their supporting bowmen with their shields and presence.

The infantry were armed in a very basic manner with a crude battle-axe, and a shield with a modified rectangular shape with a gently pointed top. There was only one handle for the shield, a bar across the top, which would undoubtedly inhibit the dexterous use of the shield as a

◀ **Naval Spearman**
Lightly accoutered for sea duty, this Egyptian spearman did not wear armour, except for a helmet, nor did he have any other weapons besides his spear and shield. The hide-covered shield was standard for Egyptian soldiers either on land or afloat.

defensive or offensive weapon. For close self-defence the infantryman would have a dagger strapped to his wrist. Here he could access it easily and perhaps provide a nasty surprise for his enemy in a melée if he was unarmed and lost his axe and shield.

The Battle of the Delta

The Egyptian navy was crucial to Pharaoh Ramesses III's victory over the invading Sea Peoples in c.1180BCE. Faced with the Sea Peoples' potentially lethal southward approach on two fronts, by land and sea, Ramesses confronted them with a land army in Palestine and with the navy in the Nile Delta. The naval victory in the Battle of the Delta is depicted in reliefs carved in Ramesses's mortuary temple at Madinat Habu in Thebes. In a battle, the square sails of the warships made them difficult to manoeuvre, so both navies had their sails reefed and relied on their oarmen for movement.

Ramesses judged that his fleet would be defeated in an open battle at sea, so plotted an ambush in the Nile Delta. Once the Sea Peoples' ships came close to shore, the previously hidden Egyptian vessels emerged

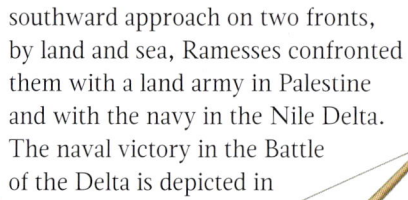

▲ **WARSHIP OF THE SEA PEOPLES**
The Sea Peoples became a dangerous adversary as they were searching for land after having, probably, been driven out of their homeland by someone else. Their ships were not graceful, and the tactic used by the Sea Peoples was to board and attempt to fight as they did on land. This usually did not work with the Egyptians, who shot them down with their long-range bows.

◀ **NAVAL ARCHER**
Lightly clothed and equipped, the archer did not wear armour on sea duty, with the exception of his helmet. His one-piece stave bow and sheaf of arrows were his only weapon. The Egyptian archers showed their superiority over the naval forces of the Sea Peoples.

to hem them in. The key Egyptian advantage lay in their archers, who were lined up along the shore and on their ships: the Sea Peoples relied on ferocious hand-to-hand fighting once ships were close enough for boarding, but they could not get close enough under a hail of Egyptian arrows. Moreover they had no long-range missile weapons with which to attack and drive back the Egyptian archers.

Having cleared the decks of the Sea Peoples' vessels with volleys of arrows let loose by the ranks of skilled archers, the Egyptians then used oar power to get among the enemy ships and capsize them. Some of the invaders were killed in hand-to-hand fighting on board the vessels, others captured, others dragged to shore and finished off there. In his temple inscriptions Ramesses declared proudly 'Those who arrived at my boundaries...

THE EGYPTIAN NAVY

▲ **Egyptian War Galley**
This shows the ultimate development of Egyptian warship. It was still modelled on their merchant ships but with the conspicuous ram for capsizing enemy ships. They outclassed the ships of the Sea Peoples, whose only hope to defeat the Egyptian navy was to overwhelm it by numbers.

▼ **Phoenician Warship**
The Phoenicians were the first mercantile nation to trade with other Mediterranean peoples. Consequently, they developed a navy, and designed an excellent galley to protect their merchant fleet and colonies around the Mediterranean.

were hauled out, overturned and cast low upon the shore; killed and thrown into heaps from one end to the other, while all their belongings floated upon the waters.'

The ships of Ramesses III were a development of the early Egyptian river craft and can be classed as galleys. They were designed as warships and were the epitome of ship design and technology of the period. They were oar-powered and were also capable of using their one large sail on the galleys one mast for power. However, Egyptian seapower went into decline, if not almost total eclipse, with the fall of the New Kingdom around 1085BCE. Beginning around 900BCE, the Phoenicians – a trading, colonizing and seagoing people – revived the idea of seapower; from their pioneering work, the Greeks developed a battle- and war-winning warship.

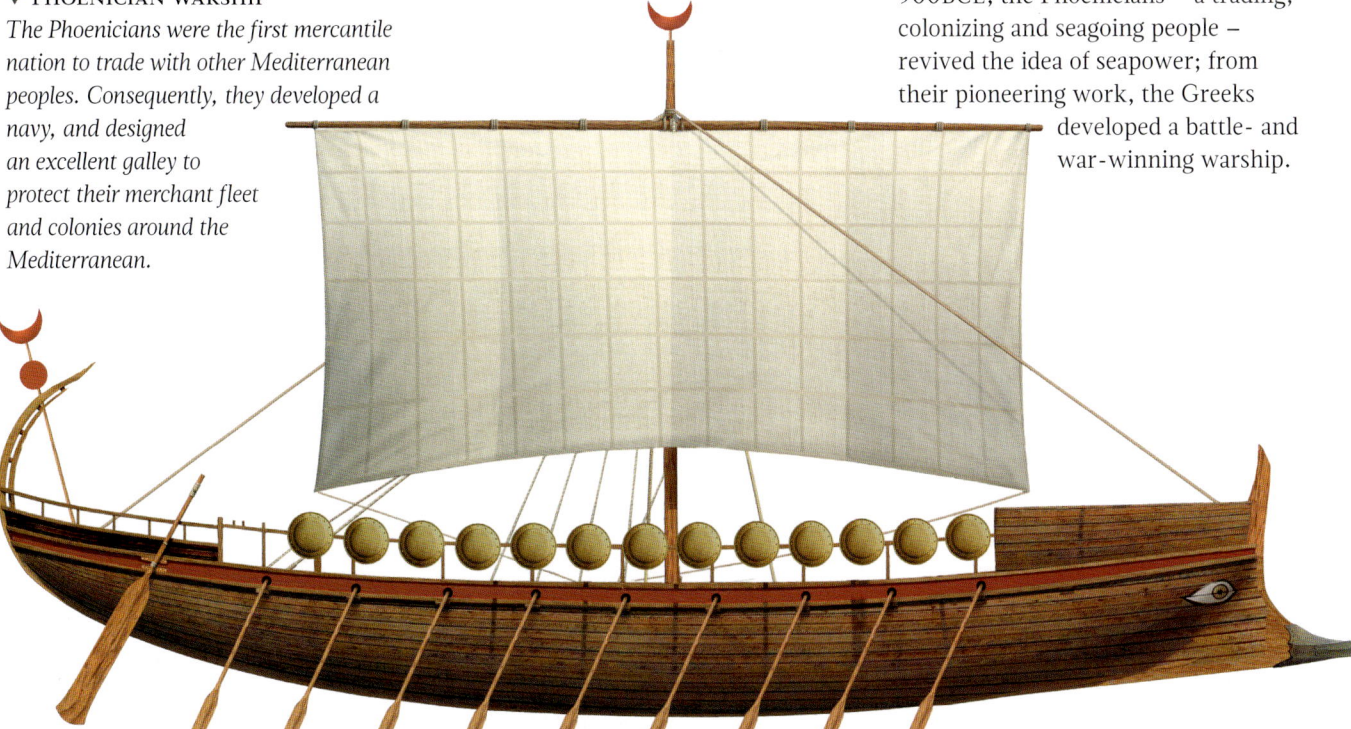

ARMS AND ARMOUR

The principal weapons used by the Ancient Egyptians and their enemies were the bow and the spear. Armour, initially more or less nonexistent, developed greatly over the period.

Edged Weapons
The Egyptians' edged weapons varied according to period as well as to preference. They consisted of swords, daggers and axes of many designs. Swords were usually of two types: the earlier one was a scythe-like weapon that could be deadly in the hands of an expert, but was awkward for an inexperienced infantryman to use; the second, later, type was a traditional straight sword that was easier to carry and use – its simple design made it deadly even in the hands of a newly recruited man. Other types included a broad-bladed sword shaped somewhat like a machete, and a slightly curved sword used by some of the infantry.

Egyptian daggers were common, but usually carried only by senior personnel, either officers or members of the royalty and the pharaoh's household. The daggers were wide-bladed; they looked more like a small short sword than what people would usually associate with a dagger design today.

Egyptian axes began as a piece of metal strapped to a handle, little better than a club. As metallurgical skill increased, the axes became much more deadly: they developed from the crude model used in the Old Kingdom to a more sophisticated and better constructed type by the time of the New Kingdom. They could be wielded

▲ *Soldiers in Queen Hatshepsut's expedition to the Land of Punt, carrying battle-axes along with standards and palm fronds. Temple of Hathor, Deir el-Bahari, c.1490BCE.*

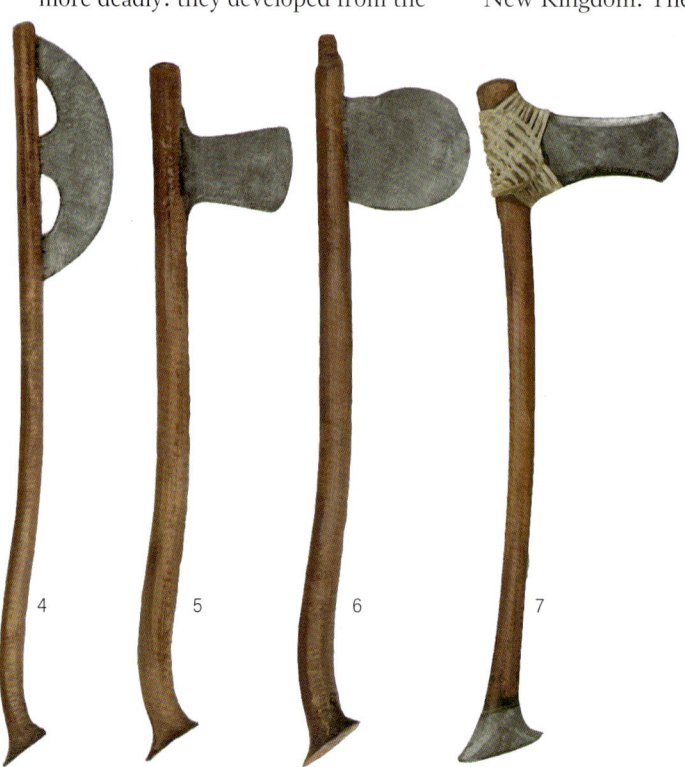

◀ AXES
Numbers 1 through 7 show some types of axes used in combat in Egypt and the Levant, with number 4 probably being the most sophisticated and deadly when wielded by a skilled warrior.

ARMS AND ARMOUR 109

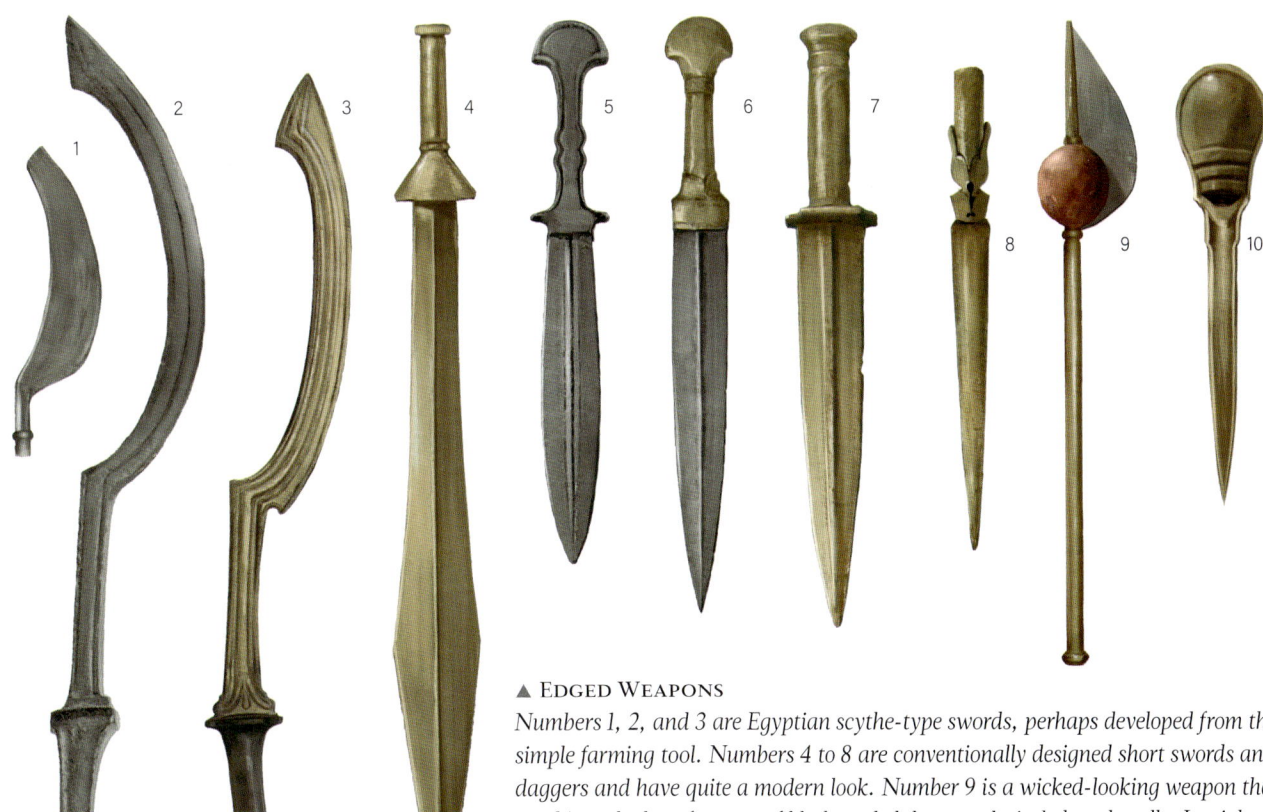

▲ Edged Weapons
Numbers 1, 2, and 3 are Egyptian scythe-type swords, perhaps developed from the simple farming tool. Numbers 4 to 8 are conventionally designed short swords and daggers and have quite a modern look. Number 9 is a wicked-looking weapon that combines the best features of blade and club on a relatively long handle. It might have been made in two versions – one short for close fighting and one somewhat longer for use as a polearm. Number 10 is a short sword or dagger with the hilt in the shape of what would later be referred to as a knobkerrie, for braining your opponent (though holding it by the blade to accomplish that could be questionable).

and employed along with the shield, or they could be converted to a missile weapon by throwing them.

Missile Weapons

While the Egyptian army did not have javelins per se, they did use throwing spears that for all intents and purposes were javelins. They could be accurately thrown from a moving chariot with practice.

Another missile weapon the Egyptians employed was a boomerang-like throwing stick that took practice to become skilled with. It was highly effective and deadly at short range. This was a form of weapon found widely in ancient cultures, where it was put to use – as it was by the Egyptians – in hunting as well as in battle. There are tomb reliefs of Egyptians using the stick in birdhunting.

The throwing stick was in use from the Predynastic Period (c.3100BCE) onwards, and remained in regular use by Egyptian soldiers right through to the end of the New Kingdom. The throwing stick was not so lethal as a sling-launched stone, but it could stun or knock down an enemy, and in extremis, such as in a melée, it undoubtedly could be used as a club.

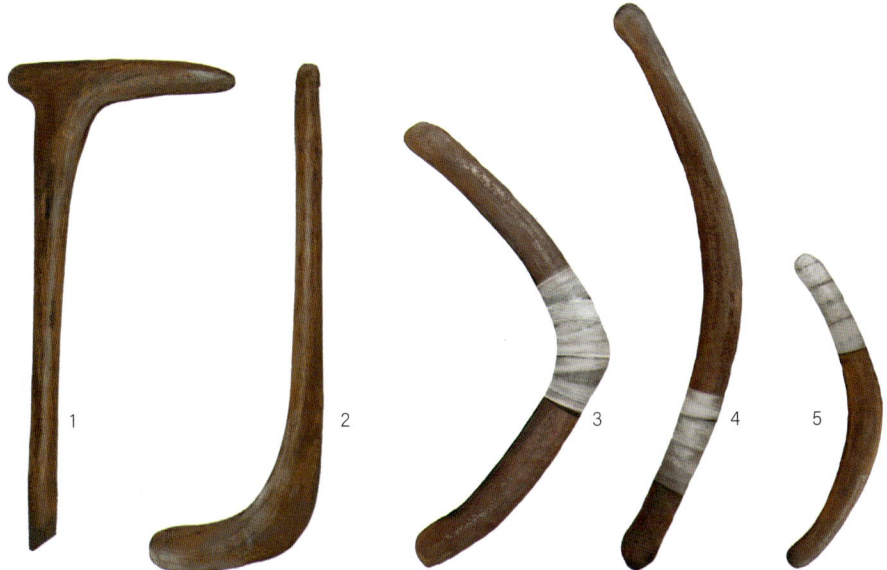

◀ Throwing sticks
The throwing sticks 1 to 5 are specifically Egyptian weapons of the Old Kingdom. They would be thrown directly at an opponent and, if possible, recovered later and reused.

Bows and Arrows

The bow was the Egyptian army's main missile weapon. Employed on foot by infantrymen or by mounted men on chariots, it was a highly effective weapon. Usually it was a large, laminated bow that had been copied from Egypt's enemies among the Semitic tribes in what is now Palestine. It was a powerful weapon with a useful range and had excellent penetration. The composite bow, much stronger and having a longer range than the simple one-piece Egyptian bow, was introduced to Egypt by the Hyksos. However the one-piece, or stave, bow was still used in the New Kingdom.

Armour

The Egyptians initially had sparse armour: the design was very elegant, being two pieces that went one over each shoulder, crossing in the centre of the chest. Later, scale and lamellar armour was brought into use, probably because of contact with the Mitanni and the Hittites.

In all ancient armies, a cross-fertilization of arms, armour and equipment was common. Victorious armies seized enemy weapons, armour and other equipment and put them to use – this was only practical, since the production of arms and armour was challenging and expensive. New designs could thus easily be tried out and, if effective, copied. As the

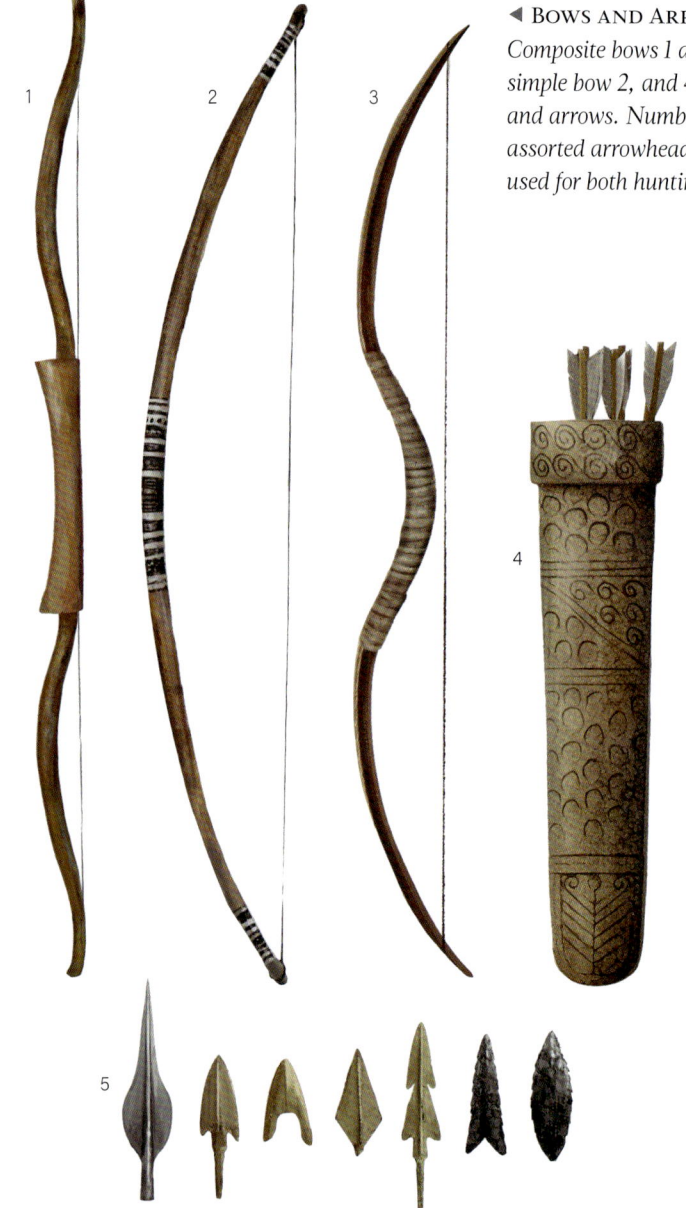

◀ BOWS AND ARROWS
Composite bows 1 and 3 flank a simple bow 2, and 4 shows a quiver and arrows. Number 5 shows assorted arrowheads that could be used for both hunting and warfare.

Iron Age dawned around 1200BCE, it appears that the new technology that produced stronger iron arms and armour did not immediately make older bronze equivalents obsolete. Bronze armour and weapons, especially helmets, carried over for some time during the early Iron Age in the armies of the Near East, especially in those armies, such as the early Israelites, that were weapons-poor and had primarily to use captured arms and armour until they could produce their own in quantity.

◀ *Archers, shown in a hunt, from the mortuary temple of Ramesses III in the New Kingdom.*

Shields

The Egyptian arched shield developed over time, finally including a leather strap that allowed the infantryman to sling the shield over his shoulder – leaving his arms free. Because of that, polearms could then be wielded with two hands. The shield could also then be slung on the infantryman's back on the march, which allowed a better march rate for the army and was less fatiguing for the individual infantryman.

The round shield type was later in the period and would come into more general use among belligerents as metallurgy improved. The ultimate in this type of shield would be the Greek hoplon, which was not only used as protection, but as a weapon along with the spear and sword.

▼ SHIELDS
Numbers 1, 3, and 5 are wooden shields that are covered with animal hides. Number 2 appears to have a very early type of metal boss on the otherwise completely wooden shield. Numbers 4 and 6 show the back of two wooden shields with simple and unsophisticated handles for the bearer to wield. Number 7 is an early form of metal-coated shield which would make all others obsolete; this is what the Philistines carried. Number 8 is a Canaanite shield constructed of wicker, which would later be common in the Persian empire but which would prove to be nearly worthless when facing the much better armed and armoured hoplites of Greece.

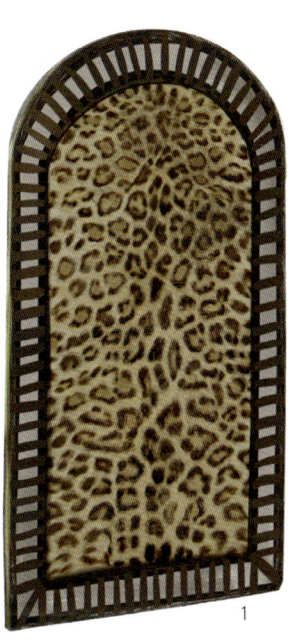
1

2

3

4

5

6

7

8

ARMIES OF ANCIENT GREECE

The resolute resistance of the hoplite, or heavy infantryman, was crucial to the survival of the Greek city-states when they were twice invaded by Persia in the 5th century BCE. In the celebrated Battle of Thermopylae on 20 August 480BCE, a solid phalanx of Greece's finest infantrymen – from the city-state of Sparta – held the narrow pass against the invading Persians despite being heavily outnumbered. The infantrymen in the Spartan phalanx, locking their shields and thrusting forward their spears, presented an immovable wall. They not only held their ground against the Persian troops, but also fought back against them, slaughtering large numbers of invaders. The Greek army employed chariots and cavalry as necessary, and developed an extremely effective navy, but it was the infantry – the hoplite, wearing helmet, cuirass and greaves and armed with an imposingly long spear and circular wooden shield – who was the army's principal weapon. To the hoplite goes the credit for saving Greece from the incursions from the east, and without him – if Greece had not endured to then influence the Romans – Europe would have developed very differently.

▲ *Detail of a terracotta Corinthian vase showing a hoplite battle, c.600BCE. Noteworthy are the different style of helmets on both sides of the engagement as well as the personal devices on the hoplons (shields).*

◄ *Cavalcade, or horsemen, on the south frieze of the Parthenon, sculpted by Phidias in c.447–433BCE. Holes indicate where the bridles and reins would have been attached on the original marble relief.*

FROM THE MINOANS TO THE CITY-STATE

The history of Ancient Greece began long before the glory of the Battle of Thermopylae. The earliest Ancient Greek settlements took place around 7000BCE in Crete and in the region of Thessaly in northern mainland Greece. Around c.3100BCE the Bronze Age developed on the Greek mainland and on Crete, and settlement probably began in the Cyclades, a group of around 30 islands in the Aegean Sea. The Bronze Age refers to the era in which people moved from the crude tools and weapons of stone to the development of metallurgy and the ability to make tools and weapons of bronze, an alloy of copper and tin; it also saw the beginnings of urban life and of writing.

▼ Rugged terrain contributed to the creation of separate Greek city-states as well as the development of a sea trade. From lucrative merchant trade, city-states such as Athens grew into maritime powers within Greece and against invaders.

◄ A Mycenaean krater depicting soldiers departing for battle, from the 12th century BCE. These are the Greeks of the Iliad that besieged and took Troy.

The Minoans

In c.3000BCE the Minoan civilization was beginning to flourish in Crete. This civilization, which endured until after 1500BCE, subsequently vanished from history – and was only discovered in the early 20th century by British archaeologist Sir Arthur Evans through his excavation of the great palace at Knossos on Crete and of associated 'Minoan' artefacts there and throughout the Mediterranean. Evans named the culture 'Minoan' from the name of a mythical Cretan king, Minos. In c.2000BCE these people constructed the first great palaces on Crete, including Knossos. They began to colonize other parts of the Aegean around 1700BCE, using force if resistance was encountered. During this period, the Cycladic islands came under Minoan influence.

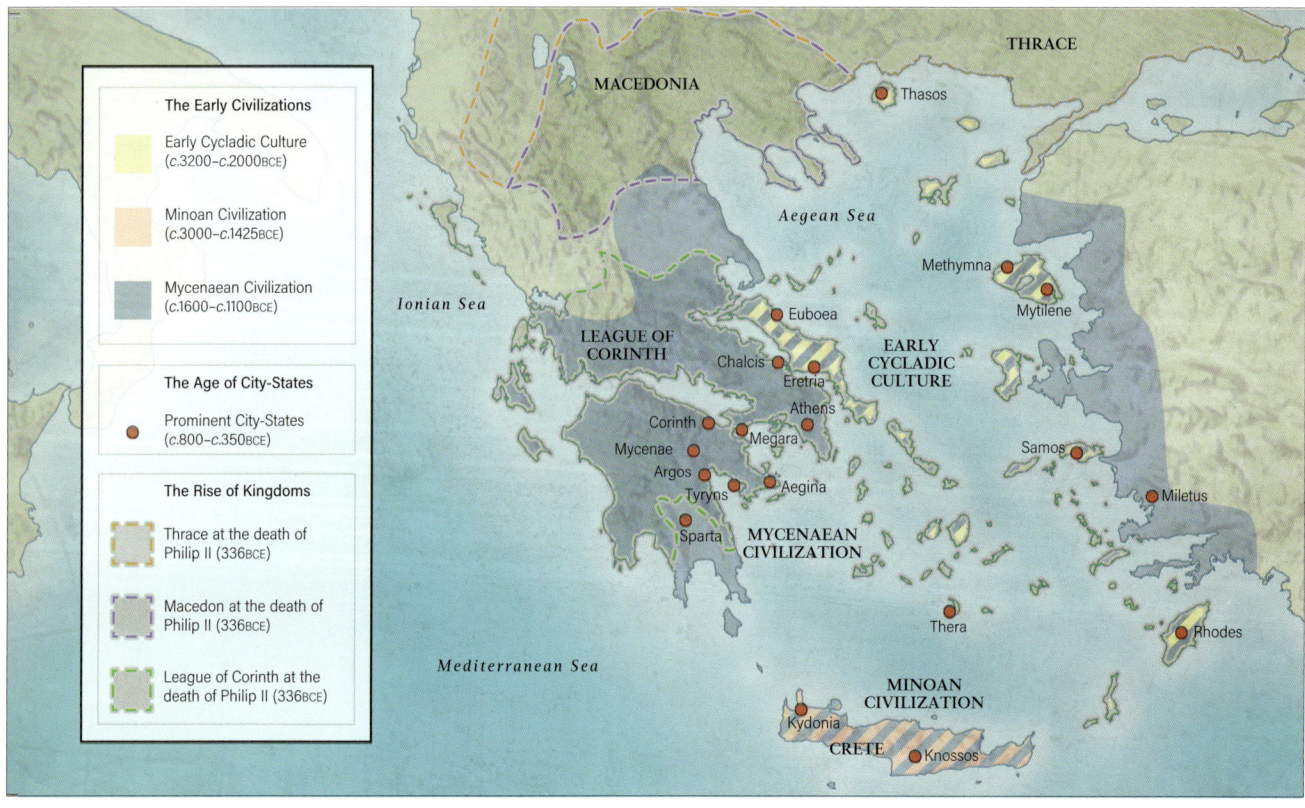

The Mycenaeans

An Indo-European migration from Central and Northern Europe south into Greece occurred between 2000BCE and 1800BCE. This coincided with the migration of the same ethnic groups that migrated to and occupied Thrace. These peoples occupied the entire Greek peninsula as well as the outlying islands, and assimilated with the native peoples already there, and the race that emerged from the migrations and assimilations were the Achaeans or Mycenaeans, the early Greeks.

The Mycenaeans began as a tribal group who eventually evolved into a more sophisticated society with definite social strata, ruled by a type of early monarch. They came to be known as the Mycenaeans, from the military stronghold of Mycenae – around 90km (56 miles) to the southwest of Athens in the Peloponnese peninsula, in southern Greece. Their civilization, at first strongly influenced by the Minoans, lasted from c.1600BCE to c.1100BCE.

In 1500BCE the Minoan civilization was dealt a death blow by a series of natural disasters, probably earthquakes and tsunamis from the volcanic eruption at Thera (Santorini), that destroyed its capital Knossos. The Mycenaeans were quick to take advantage, invading and conquering Crete from the mainland.

'Greek Dark Ages'

The Mycenaean culture lasted until the end of the Bronze Age in Greece, and ended in a period sometimes referred to as the 'Bronze Age collapse'. A great upheaval occurred, but historians are not completely sure what happened or what caused the collapse. The Mycenaeans had certainly weakened themselves through internal strife; their major kingdoms – Thebes, Tiryns, Pylos and Mycenae – were in a state of almost constant warfare, which left the culture divided and susceptible to invasion and conquest.

▶ *The ruins of the Erechtheion today, on the Acropolis above the city of Athens.*

▶ *The symmetrical double-headed axe of ancient Crete, the labrys, on a decorated palatial Minoan vase, c.1450–1400BCE.*

One possible reason for the Bronze Age collapse was an attack by the Sea Peoples, the groups of seafarers who caused havoc throughout much of the eastern Mediterranean and twice struck Ancient Egypt in the 13th and 12th centuries BCE. According to this theory, the Sea Peoples (who may have hailed from Sardinia, Sicily or Anatolia) overran the weakened Mycenaean civilization. However, as described elsewhere, some scholars think the Mycenaeans were themselves the Sea Peoples – which indicates the degree of uncertainty.

At this time of upheaval the so-called 'Dorian invasion' also occurred. The Dorians may have been an ethnic Greek tribe that migrated into Mycenaean territory, speaking a language that was a different dialect from the one spoken by the Mycenaeans. However, the Dorian event may not reflect an invasion or aggressive migration at all, but simply a cultural shift. Either way, it marks a time at which an early set of dialects and traditions were replaced by a newer set, one which prevailed through the classical period in Greece.

This period of drastic change at the close of the Mycenaean civilization around 1200BCE to 800BCE is also referred to as the 'Greek Dark Ages'. The Mycenaean culture was shattered: society largely broke down; cities were destroyed, and tribal living was once again taken up by the survivors of the upheaval. Organized society was disrupted, if not destroyed, and the population of Greece reduced.

Rise of the City-State

Around 800BCE, the Greeks began to recover and by 600BCE society was again organized. The Greek city-states developed. During this period the well-trained, heavily armed and armoured Greek hoplite arose – and an entire military system was built around him. The most important

▲ *A red-figure kylix, or drinking vessel, illustrating a battle scene between a hoplite, carrying a round shield with Pegasus motif, and a bearded Persian, 460BCE.*

city-states were Thebes, Corinth, Athens and Sparta. Thessaly was also a powerful city-state, but was isolated in the mountains.

The Greeks were not a united people, being loyal to their city-states and not any central Greek authority, but when a threat arose that endangered them all, the city-states would unite temporarily to face the external enemy. When the threat subsided or was defeated, the individual city-states would once again look after their own interests and war among themselves. This situation continued until Greece was conquered by the Macedonians under Philip II.

Ancient Greece can rightly be called the cradle of democracy and the basis for Western civilization.

▶ *Greek helmets came in many designs, but this is a classic hoplite one, a Corinthian-style bronze helmet from the Necropolis at Agia Paraskevi (Thessaloniki), c.500BCE.*

The political system adopted by most Greeks was the city-state. This was not only dictated by the Greek culture and temperament, but by the terrain and geography of Greece itself. The city-states developed separately and differently – some were run as oligarchies and some as democracies – but the disaster for Greece was the Peloponnesian Wars, which ruined many of the city-states.

The Greek Regions

Ancient Greece was divided into different regions. The major areas were Attica, Boeotia, the Peloponnese, and the Greek islands in the Aegean Sea. Boeotia was located in central Greece and the people who lived there, no matter what city-state they belonged to, were generally referred to as Boeotians. Attica was the area in central Greece in which Athens was located. The Peloponnese was southern Greece, where Sparta and the other southern city-states were located. When the Greek confederations or alliances among city-states were formed after the Persian Wars in c.478BCE, they were established in these geographic regions. Some of the smaller Greek city-states were founded and thrived on the islands in the Aegean Sea, such as Melos, north of Crete.

Sparta, located in the Peloponnese, south of Athens, was a military city-state that fielded the best-trained and best-disciplined army in Greece. It was also known as Lacedaemon, so the Spartans are frequently referred to as the 'Lacedaemonians'. Prior to the rise of Athens as the great cultural centre, Sparta was the leading Greek city-state.

In the city-state of Athens, democracy, rule by the people, first came about in 508BCE. Athens – located in the geographical area known as Attica – would remain essentially a democracy until 322BCE at the conclusion of the Lamian War. Athens was at its most powerful, both militarily and culturally, during the Age of Pericles in the mid-5th century BCE. This period was also known as the 'Golden Age of Athens'. The Athenians and their allies would fight Sparta and her allies in the cataclysm known as the Peloponnesian Wars, finally being defeated by Sparta.

Persian Invasions

The greatest threat to ancient Greece before the onset of the Peloponnesian Wars were the two invasions of Greece by the Persian empire in 490BCE and 480BCE. The catalyst for the Persian

▲ *Pericles was the master strategist of Athens in the Peloponnesian War, but died of the plague that swept through the city.*

invasions was the military aid that Athens sent to the Ionian Greeks in Asia Minor, colonies established earlier from the Greek mainland, in their revolt against the Persians in 499BCE. Bent on vengeance, the Persian king Darius I invaded Greece. In 490BCE his army met the army of Athens and her allies at Marathon, and was decisively defeated.

Thermopylae and Salamis

Ten years later, in 480BCE, Darius's son Xerxes invaded Greece with a huge army and a supporting navy but again met grief at the hands of the Greeks. Expertly delayed by the Spartans and other small Greek contingents at Thermopylae, the Persians finally forced the pass, destroying the 300 Spartans to a man, but were later overwhelmed by a Greek coalition led by another Spartan contingent. The Persian navy was then defeated by the combined Greek fleet, led by the excellent Athenian navy, at Salamis. Xerxes's dreams of conquest and vengeance were shattered.

The Peloponnesian Wars

The Greeks committed the equivalent of national suicide after the Persian Wars, when the city-states engaged in internecine warfare for dominance on the Greek peninsula. The major warring parties were Sparta, the leading land power in Greece, and Athens, the country's foremost naval power. Other Greek city-states allied themselves with one or the other, forming confederations that varied during the wars.

Both Sparta and Athens formed what were in effect empires. The Hellenic League, the original alliance among the city-states, became the Delian League, headed by Athens. The League came into existence in 478BCE and had more than 150 member city-states. The original purpose was to continue the war with Persia. The member city-states were not always in agreement with Athens' goals; they would sometimes come into direct conflict with Athens, and Athens' imperial pretensions were a main cause of the Peloponnesian Wars between c.431 and 404BCE.

Athens had formed the Delian League, later commonly known as the Athenian empire, based on its naval strength. It fortified the territory between the city-state and its naval harbour at Piraeus, on the coast to the southwest. Sparta was the leader and dominant military state of what had become known as the Peloponnesian League in southern Greece where Sparta was located. City-states joined Sparta for self-protection and to maintain at least a semblance of independence. The member-cities of the League, among other things, pledged one-third of their military power to the alliance in case of war.

The wars dragged on for more than 30 years and exhausted all parties. The result of the conflicts was twofold. They paved the way for Sparta – despite being the victor, as exhausted as Athens – to be defeated by Thebes at Leuctra in 371BCE, and also set the stage for the rise of the warlike kingdom to the north, Macedon, and its warrior king Philip II.

▼ *Soldiers in combat, possibly a Spartan and Athenian, during the Peloponnesian War, on a late 5th century BCE gravestone.*

TIMELINE OF ANCIENT GREECE

*c.*3000BCE: The Minoan civilization first emerges on Crete. It was not a Greek culture and they developed their own language. Other Aegean islands are occupied by the Minoans.

*c.*3000–2000BCE: The early Bronze Age or Aegean Bronze Age. This coincides with the Early Cycladic Culture (3200–2000BCE) and Early Helladic Period (3000–2000BCE).

*c.*2000BCE: The Minoans erect their great palace on Crete, Knossos. Their civilization spreads to other parts of the Mediterranean; the Minoan Palatial Age is 2000–1750BCE.

*c.*2000–1800BCE: Indo-European and Celtic migration from Central and Northern Europe into Greece.

*c.*1600BCE: Rise of the Mycenaean civilization, whose people were also referred to as Achaeans, Danaans and Argives by their descendants. The Mycenaeans were ethnic Greeks.

*c.*1425BCE: Collapse of Knossos and the Minoan civilization. The Mycenaeans become dominant.

*c.*1400BCE: Achaeans sail to Cyprus and maintain a presence on the island.

*c.*1250BCE: The construction of the Lion Gate at Mycenae.

*c.*1200BCE: Dorian Greeks continue to migrate and expand their culture and influence in the eastern Mediterranean.

*c.*1194–1184BCE: The Mycenaean army and fleet assail Troy in what probably began as a trade dispute. They destroy the city of Troy after a ten-year siege.

*c.*1100BCE: The Mycenaean civilization comes to an end with the destruction of the citadel of Mycenae; the start of the Greek 'Dark Ages'.

*c.*800–480BCE: The Archaic Period, and the rise and organization of the Greek city-state.

*c.*800BCE: Greek colonization across the Mediterranean begins and lasts until *c.*450BCE. There were two types of Greek colonies. The first were permanent city-states, based on the model of the Greek homeland but independent states. The second were trading colonies which were populated not only by Greeks, but people from other states who traded there.

776BCE: The first Olympiad is organized and staged in Greece.

757–738BCE: The emerging city-state of Sparta is victorious in its first war against Messenia. In Athens, the status and office of Archon (ruler) is reduced to ten years. Charops is the first Archon under the new ruling.

754BCE: Polydorus is king of Sparta.

753BCE: The first Greek colony in Italy, Cumae, is founded.

735BCE: Perdiccas of Argos conquers Macedon and becomes its king. A Greek colony in Sicily is founded.

725BCE: The Lelantine War begins between the city-states of Chalcis and Eretria, not ending until the mid 600s.

719BCE: Polydorus, king of Sparta, is assassinated by Polymarchus.

*c.*700BCE: The development of hoplite warfare and the adoption of the bireme and trireme galleys in Greek navies. The probable period of Homer's writing of the *Iliad* and the *Odyssey*, usually dated to the late 8th century or early 7th century BCE.

690BCE: Pheidon assumes power in Argos, becoming tyrant.

687BCE: The position of Archon in Athens is now made an annual office open to any qualified Athenian citizen.

*c.*685–665BCE: Sparta again defeats Messenia, in the Second Messenian War. The defeated Messenian population is enslaved as the Helots.

680BCE: Coinage is introduced to Greece. This led to the rise of a thriving mercantile class in the Greek city-states which threatened the rule of the aristocratic class.

664BCE: According to Thucydides, the first Greek naval battles occur.

650BCE: The militarization of the city-state of Sparta is complete: a permanent serf class supported the male citizenry, all of whom were required to undertake military training, forming a permanent warrior class.

642–634BCE: A Greek colony is established in Libya.

630BCE: People from Thera establish a colony in Cyrene, North Africa.

▼ *Detail of a phalanx battle on an Attic black-figure Tyrrhenic amphora, c.560BCE.*

621BCE: The Athenian lawgiver, Draco, writes a new law code that contains severe punishments, including the death penalty. The term 'draconian' is coined.
594BCE: Solon became Archon of Athens. He is credited with laying the legal basis of democracy in Athens.
569BCE: The Greek states of Lydia, Cyrene and Samos ally themselves with the Egyptian pharaoh Amasis II. A Greek trading colony is established at Naucratis in the Nile Delta.
565BCE: Athenian general Peisistratos organizes the Diakrioi, a political party composed of poor people.
561BCE: Peisistratos creates an autocracy in Athens; in later years he is twice deposed and then restored to power.
546BCE: Croesus, the rich king of Lydia, is defeated and captured by the Persians at Sardis. Cyrus the Great wins the battle of the Halys River and captures Sardis as well.
535BCE: The sea battle of Alalia off Corsica occurs between Phocaean Greeks and the Carthaginians and Etruscans.
521BCE: Darius I is King of Persia.
513–12BCE: Darius campaigns in Scythia and conquers Thrace.
510BCE: Pythagoras establishes a mathematical school. The Athenians, with the help of Sparta, overthrow the tyranny of Hippias, the eldest son of Peisistratos, who had been conspiring with the Persians. Athens becomes a democracy.
507BCE: Cleisthenes, a noted reformer, restores and increases democracy in Athens.
499BCE: The Ionians revolt against the Persians.
498BCE: Sardis is taken and burned by the Greeks.
497BCE: Cyprus revolts against the Persians, and is defeated by Darius.
495BCE: Pericles, one of the most outstanding statesmen and military commanders in Athenian history, is born.
494BCE: Sparta defeats Argos and is now the most powerful city-state in that part of Greece.
490BCE: The Persians invade Greece but are defeated by the Athenians at the battle of Marathon.
486BCE: Xerxes becomes the king of Persia.
480–323BCE: The Classical Period of Ancient Greece.
480BCE: In the second Persian invasion, the Spartans and their allies defend the pass at Thermopylae, delaying the Persian army's advance into Greece. The Persian navy is badly defeated at the Battle of Salamis.
479BCE: Athens forms the Delian League, an alliance of city-states on the Aegean coast. Athens 'converts' the confederation into an Athenian empire, and Sparta forms the Peloponnesian League in response.
478–429BCE: The celebrated 'Golden Age of Athens' begins, between the end of the Persian Wars and the beginning of the Peloponnesian Wars. It was noted as the age of Athenian hegemony in Greece, and the time when Athens transformed from a democratic city-state into an empire in power, influence and authority.
449BCE: Greek historian Herodotus writes his History of the Persian Wars.
448BCE: The Acropolis is rebuilt by architects Ictinus and Callicrates.
443BCE: The Thirty Years' Peace ends. The city-states of Sparta, Corinth, Megara and Aegina form an alliance against the city-states of Athens, Corfu, Leontini and Rhegium.

▲ *Ancient Attic cavalry, as depicted in marble relief on the west frieze of the Parthenon c.447–433BCE.*

435BCE: The statue of Zeus at Elis is completed by the sculptor Phidias.
431–404BCE: The Peloponnesian Wars between Athens and Sparta (and allies) were fought in three phases.
430BCE: The plague kills a quarter of the population of Athens, putting the city at a great disadvantage in the war.
429BCE: The death of Pericles. The Golden Age of Athens, also known as the 'Age of Pericles', ends.
428BCE: Attica is invaded for the third time. Birth of philosopher Plato.
412BCE: Sparta allies itself with Persia. A new Spartan fleet begins naval operations against the weakened Athenian fleet in the Aegean.
405BCE: Despite its history of seafaring success, the Battle of Aegospotami ends with the destruction of the Athenian fleet. Athens is blockaded.
404BCE: Athens surrenders to Sparta.
399BCE: Socrates dies.
347BCE: Plato, the philospher, dies.
338BCE: Philip II of Macedon defeats Athens and Thebes, and establishes the League of Corinth.
336BCE: Alexander succeeds his father in Macedon.
323–146BCE: The Hellenistic Period of Ancient Greece.

THE MINOANS AND EARLY GREEKS

The Minoans preceded the Greeks in cultural development, arms and armour, as well as in fortifications. Builders of fine palaces and a capital at Knossos on Crete by c.2000BCE, they developed a great civilization while the Greeks on the mainland were still living in groups herding sheep and goats in the hills.

The Minoan civilization used bronze weapons – swords and battle-axes being the preferred type. Most Minoans wore a linen loincloth into battle, padded somewhat like an Ancient Egyptian loincloth of the period. Some wore body armour. Higher-ranking members of the Minoan army wore a bell-shaped cuirass; others had a linen vest that was worn to cover the chest and fitted over the head and was reinforced usually by bronze disks – this was inferior in design to the bell-shaped cuirass, however, and offered less protection.

Sword, Spear and Bow

Like early Mycenaeans, the Minoans were usually armed with a straight short sword and a spear. They carried the short sword in a scabbard suspended from a baldric, which was slung from the right shoulder. They also used large shields, generally either rectangular or shaped like a figure of eight that covered the body from the ground to the neck. They had helmets with cheek pieces; the conical-shaped helmets were usually decorated with coloured horsehair plumes that were placed in the centre. The Minoans knew of the bow and employed it in

◀ **WARRIOR**
This is an early Indo-European warrior from the southern Balkans, dating from about 2300BCE. His helmet, which is his only armour, is probably made from some type of organic material. He is armed with a spear and either a dagger or a type of short sword, carried in a sheath slung from a baldric. His 'kilt' is of cloth.

▶ **MINOAN WARRIOR**
This infantryman is from about 1500BCE. He wears a metal cuirass and an elaborate helmet with plume. Armed with sword and spear, he still carries the older figure of eight shield. His greaves are of metal and the advances in metallurgy are apparent.

combat. The bows of this era were of two types. The first was a simple, one-piece instrument that might sometimes have been braced with glued-on animal sinew. The second, more advanced, design was a composite bow constructed of wood, animal sinew and horn, the whole held together by glue. Minoans used arrows made of wood, with arrowheads fashioned from obsidian or flint; metal arrowheads were unknown during the period.

▶ **Warrior**
This infantryman who resembles an early Celt is an 'immigrant' to Greece, probably an Indo-European. He dates from about 1800 BCE and is well clothed and armed, with a sword and a large figure of eight shield. His only armour, however, is his helmet, of the boar tusk type, and greaves.

Mycenaeans often fought without clothing, although they sometimes wore a short, kilt-like garment along with a shirt or one-piece tunic that was belted. The later Greeks maintained the kilt-like lower garment and short-sleeved shirt under armour; some cavalrymen wore the same without armour, a wide-brimmed civilian hat, and a military cloak. Greek light infantry, including archers, would seldom if ever wear armour, although some would carry shields, similar to, if not the same as, the hoplon.

Minoans at Sea

Being a seafaring people, the Minoans carried on a lively sea trade. They built and employed an early type of war galley, which they manned and sailed with skill and admirable seamanship.

◀ **Minoan Prince**
This royal personage wears a linen breastplate reinforced with bronze plates and is simply armed with axe and a small rectangular shield, easier to use than the typical figure of eight type, especially in a hand-to-hand contest. His clothing is typically Minoan and his cap is topped by three peacock feathers.

They aggressively patrolled their sea lanes against pirates, who they would attack on sight to protect their maritime trade.

Minoan ships had one row of oars and a centred, mounted mast with one yardarm or crosstree and one square sail (see page 104). The lines were straight and these ships were powered by both oars and sail: when under oar power, especially in combat, the yardarm and sail were stored in line with the ship to cut down on drag. This kind of ship was similar to Egyptian vessels. The Minoans were not averse to borrowing ideas.

THE MYCENAEANS

Like other armies of the 2nd millennium BCE who came from the Mediterranean and Near East, early Mycenaean warriors wore either the usual civilian clothing or 'specialized' military clothing derived from what was worn by the general population. Typically mild weather in the region meant that clothing was often sparse: many early Greeks are pictured on the vases of the period completely without clothing, while warriors/soldiers are depicted wearing minimal armour and equipment and sometimes, again, no clothing at all.

This could not have been good policy or practice: fighting without the protection of clothing meant a warrior was undoubtedly more vulnerable to minor as well as mortal wounds than he would be if he wore clothing and at least a minimal amount of armoured protection. However, it should be noted that arms and armour were expensive and time-consuming to produce and could quickly bankrupt the state if it were engaged in continual warfare. As in other cultures of the ancient world, Mycenaean warriors therefore often fought in less than ideal attire, and with any kind of weapon available, including those seized from the enemy or gathered up as spoils of war. As equipment and military clothing developed, infantrymen were armed with an all-purpose spear and a short sword or dagger, with the scabbard either

◀ **Heavy Spearman**
This infantryman only wears a helmet for armour, made out of boars' tusks. His shield is large enough to cover his body in combat, and while clothing and armour are minimal, he is well-armed with sword and spear.

▼ **Armoured Spearman**
This infantryman of a later age is well-armoured as well as well-armed with spear and shield. He wears a horned helmet and his leather 'kilt' is reinforced with metal studs. He wears a full cuirass as well as greaves to protect his lower legs. His helmet is decorated with boars' tusks and a plume.

THE MYCENAEANS

▲ LIGHT SPEARMAN
This light infantryman is well-armed with sword and thrusting spear, but, with the exception of the helmet and linen greaves as well as a leather covering for his 'kilt', he is unarmoured. As usual for the period, his helmet is covered in slivers of boars' tusks.

suspended from the shoulder by a baldric or worn with a belt around the waist. The earlier light infantry usually wore at least a kilt-like garment, often with nothing covering the upper body. They might wear a boar tusk helmet, but carried no shield.

Later, more heavily armed and armoured infantrymen had a bronze cuirass, an early model of the 'muscle cuirass' that would become standard in the hoplite armies of the Greek city-states. These men wore a kilt fitted with circular brass studs. They had sandals and bronze greaves and carried a semi-circular, crescent-shaped shield that they used in combat in conjunction with the spear.

Mounted Cavalry

The Mycenaeans fielded both cavalry and mounted infantry – a type of soldier later known as a dragoon – who used his horse for transportation but dismounted to fight on foot. By around 1200BCE the cavalryman or mounted infantryman (see overleaf) was typically equipped with a plain bronze two-piece cuirass and wore a conical bronze helmet, that would have been adorned with a decoration to indicate his unit, usually some type of feather, and had moveable cheek pieces. He wore bronze greaves over sandals, an early precursor of the cavalry boot. Under the sandals he might sport long woollen socks, and a type of knee protection also made from wool. He carried a short sword and scabbard that was suspended from a baldric worn over the right shoulder and positioned on the left hip.

▶ CHARIOT DRIVER
This man is holding the bit and reins of one of the horses in his chariot team. He is lightly dressed and his only armour is his helmet and a padded cuirass made out of cloth. His duty was to drive, not to fight, and he may or may not be protected by a shield held by another crewman, if there was room enough in the chariot.

Horse furniture comprised a simple saddlecloth, with no saddle, together with a bit, leather bridle and reins. We know from contemporary depictions that mounted men and cavalry sat farther back on the horse than they would have done if they had had a saddle: a position that made it easier to stay on the horse and also much more comfortable than sitting closer to the horse's withers or shoulder. They gripped the horse with their knees.

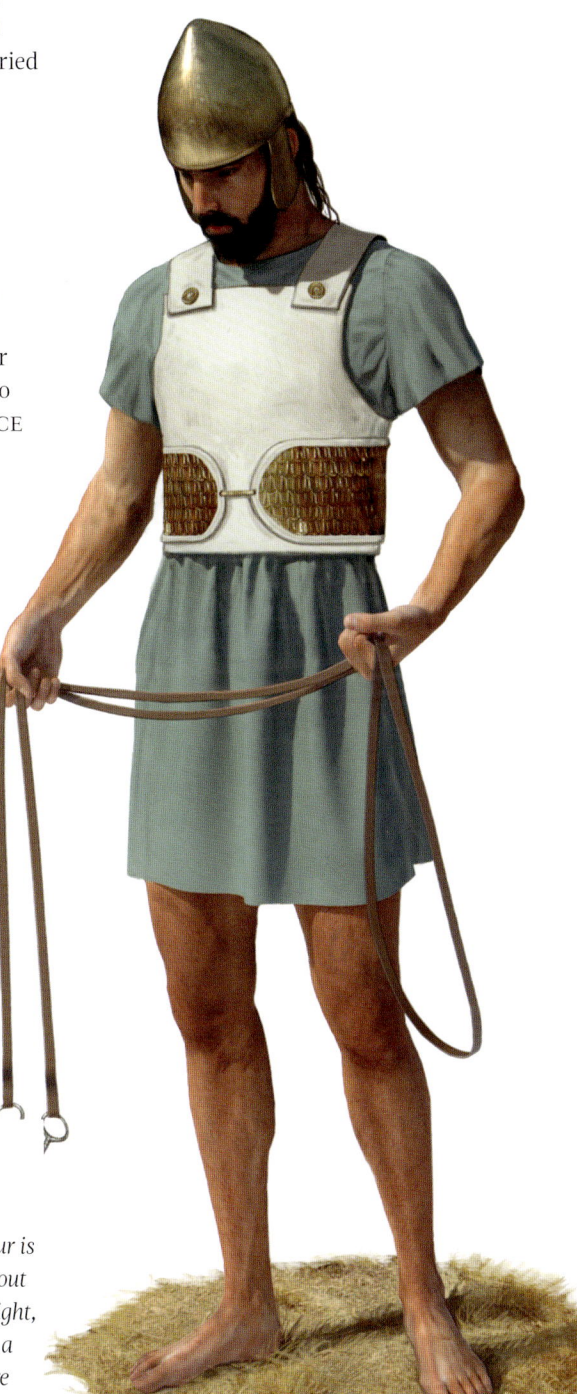

These mounted warriors must have been skilled horsemen: riding a horse without a saddle while armed and equipped is certainly an interesting proposition.

Two-Wheeled War Chariots

The mountainous terrain of mainland Greece was not conducive to large-scale chariot armies or operations, and the Mycenaeans used chariots sparingly. Grecian terrain was neither natural cavalry or chariot country: further, chariots were high-maintenance pieces of military equipment and were expensive.

What chariots they did deploy were four-spoke wheel and two- or four-horse teams. The two-man crew consisted of a driver and a warrior, the driver unarmoured except for a helmet constructed of boars' tusks. Conical in shape, this was adorned with a horsehair plume, dyed to reflect either the wearer's tastes or to designate a unit or family affiliation. The warrior was equipped with a bronze-plate panoply (full-body armour), helmet and greaves, which must have been very heavy and awkward to fight in, especially in a melée or in dismounted hand-to-hand combat. It was also highly inelegant compared to later Greek armour, but no doubt afforded the wearer a significant amount of protection.

The two-horse team was unprotected, having only a basic leather harness-bridle, bit and reins. This horse equipment was simple and functional, but could be much more elaborate – depending on who owned the chariot. The richness of the harness, the saddlecloths of the horse team and how the horses themselves were 'decorated' depended on the desires of the chariot's owner and how much he could afford to spend on the harness.

▶ CAVALRYMAN
This cavalryman wears a full cuirass, and his sword and scabbard are worn on a sling across the body. A helmet and greaves complete his armour; the feather was probably an indicator of his unit. The saddle is primitive and may only be a saddlecloth with a girth.

▼ Two-Wheeled Chariot and Warrior

This light two-horse chariot was not very sturdy, and the four-spoke wheels would not have been able to stand much stress. The warrior was probably a commander or royalty; his Dendra panoply armour, however uncomfortable and with little articulation, would be expensive (see also 126).

The effectively unenclosed 'rail' chariot of the Mycenaeans, manned by two crewmen, was in use in the 16th century BCE, following the simpler 'box' chariot of the 17th century BCE. The crewmen wore leather or bronze cuirasses that were much better made than the older panoply of interconnected bronze plates, leather probably being preferred as lighter and easier to fight in. Metalworking had progressed to the point that bronze conical helmets with cheek pieces could now be manufactured.

The driver wore a leather cuirass and a bronze helmet and the warrior wore a bronze cuirass and helmet. He was armed with a sword slung from a baldric from the right shoulder and a round shield, not yet the hoplon of the later hoplite, but functional enough. The warrior also had bronze greaves. In some cases troops merely used their chariots to get to the battlefield, where the warriors dismounted and took up formation to fight. The driver/charioteer stayed with the chariot.

Four-Wheeled War Chariots

The light, four-wheeled chariots used by the Mycenaeans may have been influenced by the Sumerian version of the four-wheeled chariot, but the construction of the Mycenaean version was much lighter and used a four-spoked wheel. The four-wheeled chariot was much more stable than the early versions of the two-wheeled.

The type of wheel was important. Solid wheels without spokes were sturdy, but they were also heavy, adding to the overall weight of the vehicle and the strain on the chariot team when in motion. The size of the wheels was also critical. Smaller wheels had trouble traversing uneven and broken ground, where a larger wheel was more effective. On muddy and wet ground, smaller wheels

▶ Four-Wheeled Chariot

The open-backed four-wheeled chariot was drawn by two horses. The officer standing by his vehicle is both well-dressed and well-equipped, wearing a full cuirass and decorated helmet. Armed with a sword, he is barefoot, probably because he will be in his chariot.

would almost certainly bog down, while larger wheels, especially spoked wheels, had a much better chance of coping with difficult terrain without getting stuck. Wheel size determined mobility and the speed of the vehicle when in motion.

Warriors fighting from the chariot would lead with their spear, just like their counterparts on the ground. They wore a sword and scabbard suspended by a baldric. The difficulty with body armour in the Bronze Age was that because of the technological restrictions in terms of metallurgy armour was heavy, rarely well fitted and sometimes so bulky as to restrict movement. Round, dome-shaped helmets were the best-designed of the period, although others less well-designed were also worn. Warriors sometimes wore shoes into battle, but not always; bronze greaves provided valuable protection for the lower leg. Warriors wore leg wrappings with greaves or without. Tunics were often long-sleeved.

◀ **Fully-Armoured Warrior**
This warrior might be a commander of some rank. The armour is in Dendra panoply style, so-named for the all-body armour of bronze plates found in a tomb in Dendra. The armour is awkward, and along with the figure of eight shield makes for a heavy load. The helmet is faced with boars' tusks and he is armed with a period (1400BCE) sword and scabbard.

▲ **Noble Warrior**
This infantryman is wearing more servicable armour, a simpler helmet, and a smaller and handier shield. His greaves are practical, as is his cuirass. He is armed with a sword and is well-equipped for hand-to-hand fighting.

THE MYCENAEANS

▼ **Heavy Infantryman**
This spearman has an interesting tiara-type helmet along with spear and shield, the latter being well-suited for close combat. His simple but effective cuirass is made of overlapping metal plates, as is his armoured 'apron.' His shield is suspended around his neck and shoulders with a leather strap, so he is less likely to lose it during fighting.

Arms and Armour

The Mycenaean warriors wore bronze cuirasses of varying designs, both two-piece and one-piece, and these were hinged on one side for ease of taking on and off. They also had greaves. Some warriors wore complete body armour designed to protect the entire body in the close combat demanded in phalanx-type fighting.

Mycenaeans wore bronze helmets that were constructed, at least on the outer layer, of boars' tusks over a lighter frame. Plumes of different-coloured horsehair adorned the helmets of various units. Headwear and helmets came in a plethora of designs and shapes: at least 27 have been identified by historians. They were decorated not only with the horsehair plumes, but also with feathers, horns and short plumage, which gave an interesting dimension to the designs. Some of the helmet designs were found among the Sea Peoples who ravaged parts of the Near East in *c.*1200BCE as well as among the biblical Philistines. As we have seen, the Mycenaeans have been suggested as possible candidates when historians speculate on the origin and identity of the Sea Peoples. Conversely, some writers have suggested that the Mycenaeans were one of the targets of the Sea Peoples' raids and destruction, and fought against them for their very survival.

▶ **Noble Warrior**
This expensively accoutered stalwart is equipped with a full cuirass along with a functional helmet with trailing plume. He is armed with sword, and an elaborately carved spear. His colourful 'kilt' completes the outfit with the exception of the stiffened linen greaves.

The Mycenaeans fought first with spears and only afterwards with sword and shield. The later spears were short, not as tall as their bearers, and heavy. They usually had a straight, smooth shaft, but spears of the same size with circular-designed shafts were also used. Both types were heavy. The Mycenaeans also employed a bronze battle-axe, similar to the early Egyptian battle-axe, although better designed and constructed, and more lethal. They carried long and short straight swords, wearing them in a scabbard attached to the body by a baldric slung over the right shoulder. They also took short daggers into battle; these were carried along with the sword.

Mycenaean shields came in various shapes and sizes, some large enough to cover the body from neck to ankle; they were heavy and undoubtedly awkward to use, requiring training and constant practice to use them to advantage in combat.

In the *Iliad* Homer describes how the warrior Ajax, strongest of all the Mycenaeans, used a giant shield made from a layer of bronze and seven cowhides as his principal weapon. He often fought side by side with his brother Teucer, who was a skilled bowman; Ajax wielded his shield while Teucer dispatched arrows at the enemy. Ajax also fought with great skill using the long Mycenaean spear: in a day-long battle with the greatest Trojan warrior, Hector, he used the spear to effect and also attacked Hector with a rock; the two warriors fought one another to a standstill. In another later encounter, among the Mycenaean ships, Ajax demonstrated agility with the spear, leaping from ship to ship to keep Hector at bay.

Some warriors had shields in a figure of eight design, some were rectangular, others circular with a crescent cut-out, some a simple circular shape, and still others a design that was symmetrical but concave on the sides and convex on the top and bottom. These shields – especially the small, circular ones – were fitted with a strap called a baldric, that was used to sling the shield over the shoulder both in combat and when not in use.

Origins of the Phalanx

Homer referred to the Greek fighting formation *c.*1200BCE as a 'phalanx', however this is an anachronism. The phalanx formation, in which the hoplite was formed in closed ranks, eight in depth, with linked shields and with the first three ranks projecting their shields forwards, was probably not developed until *c.*800BCE. This later date was about the time that Homer's poem was created and performed, so the word phalanx would have been familiar to his audience. But, although they would not have used that precise term, the Mycenaeans who went to fight against Troy could possibly have used an earlier version of the formation in the battle.

Troy, Homer, and the 1,000 Ships

The Mycenaeans are most famous in history for the ten-year siege of the city of Troy, in northwest Asia Minor. Homer's epic poems, the *Iliad* and the *Odyssey*, tell of the terrible war with Troy and the journey home for the Mycenaean survivors, but were written *c.*700BCE, more than 400 years after the destruction of Troy. The existence of Homer himself, as a single author, has been called into question by some historians, and of course many of the details in Homer's works reflect the practice of his own time and not that of the time of the fall of Troy.

In the 1860s the excavations of Englishman Frank Calvert and German Heinrich Schliemann uncovered remains of a city at Hisarlik in Anatolia that was rebuilt many times in a short timespan: one of the archaeological levels is generally accepted as the Troy of Homer and the Mycenaeans. The 'city' appears to have been built and rebuilt during nine

◀ **Warrior**
This warrior is a chariot rider and his elaborate helmet and crest undoubtedly mark him as a personage of importance, if not a commander. He is lightly armoured, but is armed with sword and spear, the spear being employed for stabbing rather than throwing.

THE MYCENAEANS

▲ *The Greek phalanx was a formidable war machine; soldiers marched in formation in full armour wearing helmets, cuirasses, greaves, shields and spears.*

periods, the last one being a Greek city that was later occupied by the Romans. The first five cities stood on the site between 3000BCE and 1900BCE, based on the best information gathered by archaeologists. The sixth city on the site was wrecked by an earthquake sometime in the period 1900BCE to 1300BCE. The seventh city is probably the Troy of the *Iliad*, built on the ruins of the sixth city, as its remains show that it was destroyed by fire, which could be the result of a siege and sack. This city was placed around 1240BCE, in the timeframe in which historians believe the attack by the Mycenaeans took place, between 1220 and 1180BCE.

The cause of the war between Troy and the Mycenaeans is not actually known. Homer, who was not a historian but a storyteller, gave the reason as Helen's abduction by Paris, the son of King Priam of Troy. Menelaus, Helen's infuriated husband, asked his brother, King Agamemnon, for aid and a great fleet of 1,000 ships set sail for Troy in a major military expedition to bring Helen home; they besieged Troy for ten years, before winning control of the city. In Homer's imaginative epics, which were performed over several nights of declaimed poetry to audiences at elite banquets, it was the Mycenaeans who defeated and destroyed Troy, the celebrated city in Anatolia (modern Turkey). Homer called the Greeks who besieged Troy the 'Achaeans'. Yet the area he described as their zone of operations – from the Greek mainland and western isles to Crete and Rhodes – is that occupied by the Mycenaean culture, as revealed by archaeology. It makes sense therefore to identify the Achaeans of Homer with the Mycenaeans of history.

The story of the Trojan War is a legend celebrated not only by Homer but also more widely in Greek and Latin literatures, not least in the *Aeneid* (*c*.30BCE) of the Roman poet Virgil.

▶ **HEAVY INFANTRYMAN**
An infantryman armed with sword and figure of eight shield, this warrior wears a distinctive style of helmet; the skull of the helmet is of the usual design, but the boar tusks were becoming a common decoration during this period.

Mycenaean Strategy

As the siege of Troy was described by Homer and in other classical sources, the Mycenaeans did not initially use military strategy to any great extent. Many of the military encounters described were single combat between heroic warriors – not least between the greatest Mycenaean warrior, Achilles, and the Trojan hero, Hector. At the end of this encounter, in which Achilles finally dispatched Hector with one great neck blow, Achilles tied Hector to his chariot and gloried in hauling him around the battlefield.

However, the physical strength of the warrior hero could only do so much; the Mycenaeans could not achieve any

▼ Spearman

Armour is becoming simpler and, apparently, infantrymen are being more functionally armed. This spearman has a full cuirass and a helmet with plume, and is armed only with a spear, which may indicate that he is of second-rank.

▼ Swordsman

This infantryman has a small, functional shield to protect himself and is armed only with a sword. He does wear greaves, and his 'kilt' is reinforced by bronze disks, but he does not have a cuirass. These may be indications that he is a light infantryman who would be employed to skirmish ahead of the main infantry line. His helmet is similar to the spearman's, with the addition of the boars' tusks.

lasting victory by such means. The siege is said to have lasted for ten years – partly because Troy's walls were so strong. In the end the Greeks needed a different quality, strategic intelligence, to win out. The decisive moment of the conflict is celebrated as one of the greatest examples of strategy in military history.

Mycenaean warrior Odysseus was famed for his *metis*, a Greek word meaning cunning intelligence. In Homer's *Odyssey*, Odysseus commissioned a fellow-Mycenaean named Epeius to build a great hollow wooden horse, large enough to contain hidden warriors. The Mycenaeans left the horse outside the walls of Troy and then retreated to the nearby island of Tenedos, giving the impression that they had abandoned the siege. The Trojans,

THE MYCENAEANS 131

◀ Musician
The Greeks usually, if not always, were accompanied by musicians on campaign and in battle. They were not, however, soldiers and were not expected to fight. They dressed in normal civilian clothing and carried only their instruments on campaign. They were usually boys and were not yet fighting men.

▼ Swordsman
This shield-bearing swordsman does not have a spear, and his shield is still of the old figure of eight type. He wears a cuirass similar to the spearman, along with a helmet made of slivers of boars' tusks and topped by a plume, the colour of which might indicate his unit. While he does wear greaves, he is barefoot like the spearman. These are examples of early Greek warriors; the helmets are not yet made of bronze, there are no hoplons, and the weaponry is not sophisticated.

overjoyed that the siege has been lifted, decided that the horse was an offering to the goddess Athena and hauled it into their previously impregnable city. At night the Mycenaean fleet returned from Tenedos and the hidden soldiers clambered out from within the horse and opened the city gates. The Mycenaean warriors, wielding shield and spear, with swords in reserve, poured into Troy and brought the war to an end, killing King Priam and his surviving sons. It needed a ruse, an act of deception, to bring them victory.

The ten-year war exhausted the Mycenaeans, however, and their pole position as a Mediterranean power rapidly declined. They returned home to their city-states weakened, and never recovered.

THE RISE OF THE GREEK PHALANX

Ancient Greek warfare was highly stylized in the era c.900–700BCE. Both sides had to consent to engage in battle before it took place. The two armies would draw themselves up in their respective phalanxes and would approach each other closed up and ready to fight. The two armies would break into a trot and then a run: the front ranks would present their spears to their enemies and the 'shock', or collision, of the two phalanxes must have been terrific.

Stylized the warfare might have been, but it was bloody, deadly and undoubtedly exhausting. Generalship would count for little, while training, skill in weapons handling and endurance would be paramount.

Fighting in Formation

The phalanx formation, which developed around 800BCE, came into existence because of the widespread use of a new shield – the large, round hoplon. Because of its shape soldiers who used it, soon called 'hoplites', could now fight in close order, and it was ranks of hoplites that made up

▼ **Warrior**
With less armour and still carrying the older-type shield, this may be either a light infantryman or a second-rank soldier.

◀ **Proto-Hoplite**
With the exception of the older-style shield, this infantryman is a forerunner of what the hoplite would become.

the ranks of the phalanx. The hoplite was a heavy armoured infantryman and the phalanx allowed these heavy infantrymen to lock shields and present a shield wall punctuated by a hedge of spear points. If its members stayed firm, this formation could stop an enemy attack in its tracks and if it advanced successfully it could drive the enemy from the field.

The phalanx at this time was usually, but not exclusively, made up of files of hoplites eight men deep. A file was composed of troops from front to rear, and a rank was from left to right of the formation. Therefore, each hoplite belonged both to a file and a rank. The original organization of the phalanx is not known for certain, but the generally accepted opinion among historians is that the original formation consisted of four units of 25 hoplites each; the unit commander was in the front of the left file, while his second in command was alone in the rear of the formation. In each sub-unit, there were three files of eight hoplites each.

The phalanx as formed was used in two formations. First, an open formation with a relatively wide space between files was used for manoeuvring before contact with the enemy was made. Once the decision was made to attack, the phalanx would close up with only about 1m (3ft) between hoplites, and then a shield wall was presented to the enemy.

The phalanx was rectangular in shape. Its detailed formation could vary. The width of the formation was not always uniform, either: it could vary from one city-state to another, as well as being sometimes dictated by the terrain. The phalanx worked best on flat, open terrain, and was not suited to undulating or mountainous terrain. The development of light troops would take these factors into consideration and would cover, or screen, the phalanx on the battlefield.

In the phalanx, the hoplite carried his hoplon on the left and his spear on the right. Whether an individual hoplite was right- or left-handed was irrelevant. The use of the spear with the right hand and the shield with the left covered not only the individual hoplite with his own shield, but it also partially covered the man to the hoplite's left. This procedure also tended to have the phalanx veer somewhat to the right, that being the normal tendency. This could cause problems on the battlefield if it was not adjusted by the commanders.

Brought to its peak by Philip II, King of Macedon, the phalanx was the primary Greek and Macedonian infantry-fighting formation for more than 600 years until it was finally outmanoeuvred, outfought and overwhelmed by the Roman manipular legion at the Battle of Pydna in 148BCE.

◀ **WARRIOR**
The older, seemingly top-heavy, helmet and little or no body armour probably indicates a light infantryman. He carries the shorter javelin and not the 'regulation' spear carried by the armoured hoplite. However, he now carries a round shield, a forerunner of the hoplon. With the development of the round, bronze-faced hoplon, the closed ranks of the phalanx would become the dominant infantry formation in the ancient world until it was finally overcome by the Roman Legion.

GREEKS AGAINST PERSIANS, AND THE BATTLE OF MARATHON

When the Athenians – supported by allies from the Greek city of Plataea – won a crushing victory over the invading Persians at Marathon in 490BCE, their triumph relied on the tactical nous of Athenian general Miltiades and the excellent implementation of his plan by his infantrymen in their phalanxes, but also proving that the long Greek spear, sword and armour were superior in battle to the weapons and equipment of the Persians.

The Persian empire was at the height of its power. Emperor Darius invaded the Greek mainland in 490BCE after an attempt two years before had been frustrated by a storm that devastated his fleet. Faced with a Persian army of around 15,000, the Athenians sent for help to their rival city-state, Sparta. According to the nearly contemporary historian Herodotus (c.484–420BCE), a runner powered across 240km (150 miles) in just two days to ask for aid, but the Spartans were engaged in a religious festival and did not come.

Reinforced with a contingent of 1,000 from Plataea, an Athenian army of 10,000 men took the field on the plain of Marathon. The Greeks had been understandably nervous at facing the intimidating Persian cavalry on an open plain, but when Miltiades learned that the Persian

◀ ATHENIAN CAVALRYMAN
The costume of this Athenian cavalryman, especially the headgear, is based on that of the Thessalian horsemen who were the best in Greece and an example to follow for all the others. He is lightly armed and not armoured.

▶ SAMIAN HOPLITE
This hoplite from Samos is in full panoply with the exception of his footwear, usually not worn on the march. His armour and weapons are typical of a hoplite anywhere in Greece, and as he is at his ease, he wears his helmet cocked back on his head.

cavalry was not with the army, he ordered an attack on the Persian infantry. Miltiades deployed a battle line that was reinforced on the flanks. When the Persians attacked in the apparently weak centre of the Greek line, the Greek flanks wheeled around and encircled the invaders.

Surrounded, the Persian troops panicked and fled back towards their ships. In the ensuing carnage, they lost 6,400 men to the Greeks' 192. Legend has it that in the Greeks' moment of triumph, Miltiades dispatched a runner to carry the good news to Athens. The story goes that this man covered the necessary c.40km (25 miles) so quickly because of the importance of the message, that after arriving and declaiming the good news in a single word, 'Victory', he dropped dead on the spot; and this story is the 'founding myth' of the marathon 26-mile 385-yard running race.

Arms and Armour

Armies of the different Greek city-states wore whatever armour was available. This led to a variety of appearances, individually and in formation. Plumes and horsehair crests were often varied, and sometimes they were not used or worn. They were removeable, although the attachment was a permanent part of the helmet. Plumes were useful not only for identification, but to also present a martial and imposing appearance to the enemy: they would magnify the hoplites' height, and add to the nervousness of their enemies before coming into spear range.

Shields developed and improved in shape; round shields were balanced and easy to use, much easier than the older figure of eight shield. Bronze cuirasses were now better made, and easier and more comfortable to wear. Generally speaking, the cuirasses offered good protection against polearms, edged weapons and missile weapons.

The arms and equipment carried by the Greek hoplite consisted of helmet, cuirass, greaves, spear, sword and scabbard, together with the hoplon shield. There was also a common type of shoe or 'boot' worn in combat. However, the Greek hoplite would often go barefoot on the march, carrying his footwear.

There were three common Greek helmets during this period, the favourite being the Corinthian model (see page 163). This was a solid piece of brass that had been hammered into the desired shape. It enclosed the entire head down to the neck in the rear as well as both cheeks. The eyes, mouth and chin were open and a nasal piece protected the nose. The ears were enclosed, which made hearing commands difficult in the heat of combat – this problem would be partially remedied in later helmets of this type. The horsehair crest was attached to the helmet from front to rear and was often of a solid colour – red was a favourite,

▶ **CAVALRYMAN**
This cloaked cavalryman differs from the Athenian horseman in that instead of the wide-brimmed hat he wears the pilos, the simple helmet that both cavalry and infantry would wear later in the period.

however it could also be made up of alternating colours. There were variations to the Corinthian helmet such as having movable cheek guards, but the different models were closely evolved from the original and were recognisably of the same basic type.

The Chalcidian helmet was a development of the Corinthian helmet, as well as an improvement on it. The sides were modified in design so that the ears were exposed, solving the hearing problem when in combat.

The third helmet used was the simple, conical-shaped pilos helmet, which was a departure from the classical Greek helmets. It protected the head from the forehead up, and had no protection for the cheeks, back of the neck or face. There was no crest or plumes. A leather strap kept the helmet attached if struck.

The cuirass was originally of two types, both of bronze. The first, the 'bell cuirass', was somewhat awkward; the second, more comfortable, design was the 'muscle cuirass'. Both were attached by a combination of hooks and straps and either came in two halves, or was hinged on one side to make a single piece overall.

By the time of the Greco-Persian wars (492–449 BCE), a newer, much lighter cuirass had been developed, made of stiffened layers of linen or other 'soft' material and glued together to form an almost form-fitting piece of armour. There was also a skirt to protect the lower belly and groin, cut into strips after construction for ease of movement. A leather

▼ **Hoplite**
This is a Spartan hoplite as he would be in line of battle or a melée after breaking or losing his spear. The Corinthian helmet is without the comb, otherwise he appears 'regulation'. Noteworthy is the device on his shield which was particular to Sparta.

▶ **Hoplite**
A well-armed hoplite with a distinctive sword that is wider toward the tip. He has the usual hoplon and spear, but no armour except for his later-model helmet with horsehair comb and cheek pieces.

GREEKS AGAINST PERSIANS, AND THE BATTLE OF MARATHON 137

▼ ARGIVE HOPLITE
This hoplite wears a red tunic that matches the horsehair crest on his Attic helmet. Armed with spear and hoplon, the hydra symbol was distinctive of Argos.

cuirass was also worn and both the linen and leather cuirass allowed greater freedom of movement for the individual hoplite and swifter manoeuvre by a phalanx. Sometimes, scale or lamellar armour, probably adopted from that used by the Persians or other enemies, was used to reinforce portions of the linen cuirass.

The greaves were also of bronze and went from ankle to cover the knee in front, and stopped below the knee at the back. They were eventually attached to the legs by leather straps. Earlier models were not, and used a type of 'spring' device for attachment. Some were shaped to follow the lines of the knee and the muscles of the calf.

The well-designed Greek spear was between 2–3m (6–10ft) in length. Like the later Macedonian sarissa, it was balanced by a bronze butt piece that was also pointed and could be used as a weapon – particularly useful if the head of the spear broke off in combat. The grip of the spear was bound with leather straps. The hoplite wielded the spear overarm and one-handed, in conjunction with the hoplon.

The hoplite's sword was 60cm (24in) long. A double-edged weapon, it was auxiliary to the spear and was used for stabbing and slashing.

The scabbard was constructed of wood and encased in leather.

The shield (hoplon) was 90cm (3ft) in diameter, and heavy to hold. It was not only used as protection in the phalanx, but also as a weapon, as the later Roman rectangular shield was. The basic hoplon was of wood, faced with bronze and the inside lined with leather. There were two straps inside, the first large strap was on the edge of the hoplon, through which the hoplite put his arm. Across from this, and almost to the opposite edge of the shield, was a much smaller hand strap, from which the hoplite controlled his hoplon.

▶ HOPLITE
This fully equipped hoplite is in full panoply and is armed with sword, hoplon, and spear. His particularly fine decorated shield can be a clan symbol, a symbol from his city-state, or a personal emblem. The scale armour around his middle reinforces his linen cuirass.

THE SPARTANS AND THERMOPYLAE

After Darius was defeated at Marathon in 490BCE, the Persians had withdrawn from Greece, but ten years later they mounted a second invasion. In the pass of Thermopylae, about 135km (84 miles) northwest of Athens, the Greeks mounted a heroic defence in 480BCE against the invading Persian army, commanded by Xerxes, the new Persian king (reigned 486–465BCE). An alliance of Greek city-states was formed to defend the region: Sparta had command of the army, and Athens was in control of the navy. About 7,000 Greek infantry, most of them hoplites, were dispatched to delay the Persian army's advance into Greece and took up defensive positions at the Pass of Thermopylae, a position which largely negated the huge Persian numerical advantage.

The heart of the Greek defence was 300 Spartan hoplites led by their king, Leonidas. The Spartans and their allies repeatedly defeated the best troops that Xerxes could throw against them, and even got the better of the most elite of Persian troops, 'the Immortals'. Numbers in the narrow pass were less important than skill and tactics. The Spartans and other Greeks outclassed their more numerous opponents. They were better and more heavily armoured, their arms and equipment were vastly superior to

◀ Leonidas
This is the king of Sparta who commanded the Greeks at Thermopylae, including his personal contingent of 300 Spartans; he led these Spartans in a fight to the death against an overwhelming army of Persians. He is armed and armoured in hoplite fashion. His spear is equipped with a metal tip on the butt end, the standard style of the Spartan hoplites.

▶ Hoplite
This Spartan hoplite is fully equipped for battle as he is wearing footwear. Oddly, he does not have a horsehair comb on his Corinthian helmet. Spartan hoplites of this period were uniformly equipped and accoutered.

THE SPARTANS AND THERMOPYLAE

▼ Hoplite
This fully equipped hoplite wears a substantial shaped helmet with comb. He wears a metal cuirass and carries the normal hoplon, as well as a sword and spear, which is equipped with an iron tip on the butt end.

▲ *Spartan military training started from youth, and was tough and unforgiving.*

The Greek Contingents at Thermopylae, 480BCE

Contingent/Demonym	Strength
Spartans	300
Tegeans	500
Mantineans	500
Orchomenians	120
Arcadians	1000
Corinthians	400
Phleiousians	200
Mycenaeans	80
Thespians	700
Thebans	400
Phocaeans	1000
Opuntian Locrians	1000*
Total	**6200****

*Herodotus states that the Opuntian Locrians 'had come in full force', so this total is an estimate.
**The highest estimate of the Greeks in the Pass of Thermopylae is 7000, so Herodotus' numbers are probably close to the combined total.

those of the Persians, and they were highly trained in the classic Greek tactic of the phalanx — the solid shield wall, studded with iron spear points, of trained, professional and steady infantry that would stand until annihilated or ordered to retreat.

Initially, the Greeks were successful against Persian threats and frontal assaults. But a traitor showed the Persians a trail around the flank of the pass, and this put them in the rear of the Greek position. Now it was only a matter of time before the Greeks were annihilated.

When Leonidas learned about the treachery that led the Persians around his position, he ordered the bulk of the 7,000 Greeks to retreat while he with his core of 300 Spartans set themselves to defend the pass and hold off the Persians for as long as possible. As the Persian infantry attacked to his front, he led the Spartan infantry in a counter-attack, during which he was killed in the fierce fighting.

Summoned by Xerxes to give up the body of their king and leader, in return for their lives, the Spartans refused and withdrew to a hillock in the pass. Surrounded and fired upon from all sides by Persian bowmen, the Spartans died to a man, defiant to the end.

Aftermath of Thermopylae

The Spartans' valiant stand at Thermopylae may have ended in their defeat, but it rallied the Greeks to fight the Persians and defend their homeland. When the Greek and Persian navies clashed at Salamis the Greeks, commanded by Themistocles, were victorious and established naval supremacy over the Persians. The Persian king, Xerxes, accepted personal defeat and returned home, leaving an army in Greece commanded by Mardonios.

The Persians were later decisively defeated at Plataea in 479BCE by an allied force of Spartans, Athenians and Tegeans (people from Tegea in the Peloponnese). The Persian commander was killed in the field.

The Spartan Phalanx

The stand of Leonidas and the 300 Spartans at the Pass of Thermopylae is celebrated as the foremost example of Spartan steadfastness, discipline and skill. The Spartan hoplite was undoubtedly the best soldier in Ancient Greece for centuries.

There are two primary sources for the organization of the Spartan phalanx: the Greek historian Thucydides (c.460–c.404BCE) in his history of the Peloponnesian Wars, and his fellow Greek Xenophon (c.430–c.350BCE), the author of the Greek history, *Hellenika*. Both Thucydides and Xenophon were soldiers and 'trailed a pike' in the phalanx; both of their versions of the Spartan phalanx will be presented.

According to Thucydides, the basic unit of the Spartan phalanx was the *enomotia*, which was commanded by an *enomotarch*. The *enomotia* consisted of 32 hoplites, in four files of eight each. Four *enomotia* would make up a *pentekostys*, which was commanded by a *pentekonter*. Four *pentekostys* would then form a *lochos*, which was commanded by a *lochagos*. Lastly, seven *lochoi* would be grouped together to form the Spartan army in the field at full strength. That army could be commanded by one of the two Spartan kings, though occasionally both would take the field. Sometimes a commander would be appointed by the kings.

Xenophon's version differs from that of Thucydides in that he states that there were only two *enomotia* in the *pentekostys* and that only two *pentekostys* made up the next level of command, the *lochos*. Further, Xenophon states that four *lochoi* made up a *mora*. The *mora* was commanded by a *polemarch*. Six *morae* then made up the Spartan army in the field. The strength of a *mora* ranged from 500 to 900 hoplites; the army then being fielded had a strength of between 3,000 and 5,400 hoplites. The Spartans also fielded light troops as well as auxiliary cavalrymen.

Xenophon – Soldier Historian

Author, historian and soldier, Xenophon was a multi-talented Greek who left substantial written records of the period. His most famous work, *Anabasis* ('March Upcountry') recounted the experiences of the 10,000 Greek mercenaries who, finding their Persian prince and employer, Cyrus the Younger, dead in a victorious battle, made the decision to march home from Asia Minor to avoid annihilation at the hands of the new Persian king, Artaxerxes.

Xenophon was an Athenian, but seems to have preferred the Spartans

◀ **XENOPHON**
The soldier-historian Xenophon was one of the commanders of the famous 10,000 Greek mercenaries who left the Persian army after their Persian commander was killed in action and before other Persians could massacre them. They decided to go home and their epic march is a tribute to their professionalism, innate toughness, and the discipline for which Greek hoplites were famous. Xenophon was an Athenian, but it appears that he preferred the traditions of Sparta.

THE SPARTANS AND THERMOPYLAE

◀ MUSICIAN
This Spartan musician is a piper. The musicians that accompanied the army wore simple civilian clothing and while there are suspicions that they dressed in red, that is not actually known. It is quite probable that they helped with the wounded after a battle.

Persians were trained hoplites from different city-states: their panoplies, especially the artwork and symbols on their shields, identified their home city-state. This gave a varied appearance to the phalanxes and other formations in which they were lined up.

Xenophon's experiences as a junior officer or a hoplite in the service of Cyrus the Younger, and then as a replacement commander after the Greek senior officers were treacherously murdered by the Persians of Artaxerxes, illustrate how the Greek military system actually functioned. Sometimes senior officers in the field were appointed, but Xenophon's narrative describes how Greek hoplites were not discouraged by the loss of their commanders and steadfastly continued with their mission by electing new commanders. This illustrates a military system that could function within what is now known as a 'chain of command' and also demonstrates the innate toughness of the Greek hoplites, even in a group that could not be expected to be a cohesive military unit since its members came from different city-states across Greece. They had the same background and experience as soldiers and warriors, and displayed soldierly virtues of professionalism, moral courage and the willingness to endure.

▶ MUSICIAN
This Spartan musician would accompany the army on campaign and might also play them into battle. He is playing the Greek trumpet, which is quite a simple instrument in appearance.

Spartan Traditions

The city-state of Sparta is renowned above all for being a military state. Healthy male children were trained as soldiers from a young age. Justly famous for the defence of Thermopylae, the Spartans were the only military city-state in Greece. Preeminent in land warfare, as Athens was at sea, Sparta was famed for her military traditions.

Sparta was built on the banks of the River Eurotas in a part of the Peloponnese known as Laconia. Sparta

to his native people. This did not endear him to his fellow Athenians. He was a brave and innovative soldier who did more than his assigned duty. Somewhat uniquely among his fellow Greeks, Xenophon was through experience and training an expert horseman and also wrote a treatise on the horse and mounted troops.

Born too late to participate in the Greco-Persian Wars, Xenophon gave service as a mercenary with the Persians. This was somewhat typical of Greeks in his period. Those Greeks who signed up as mercenaries with the was probably founded in the 10th century BCE and had finally developed by c.650BCE to be the foremost power on land in Greece, her hoplites being superior in organization, training and leadership to the armies of any other Greek city-state, including Athens.

Spartan society was stratified and divided into different classes, four levels being recognized and observed: Spartiates, Mothakes, Perioikoi and Helots. The

▲ *Detail from a Corinthian polychrome vase, c.620BCE, depicting a battle between two hoplite phalanxes. Both sides in this depiction are uniformed and equipped almost identically. The only differences shown are the designs on the shields, which are probably personal to each hoplite.*

Spartiates were native-born Spartans, who were granted the full rights of Spartan citizenship. Mothakes were Spartans who had been naturalized citizens and were not native-born. Perioikoi were freemen but without Spartan citizenship, while the Helots were state-owned serfs or slaves from Peloponnesian areas taken or controlled by Sparta. Only the highest social class, the Spartiates, were trained as Spartan hoplites, but the other classes, especially the helots, would accompany the army on campaign and fulfiled necessary positions, including that of light infantry.

The Spartan Hoplite

The Spartan panoply was similar to that of the hoplites of other city-states in Greece, with a few exceptions. The weapons and hoplon were basically the same, as were cuirass, greaves, footwear and helmet. There were two main differences: the crest of the helmet was usually worn parallel to the shoulders (as was that of the later Roman centurions in a sign of their rank) and was usually red, although there are suggestions that it might occasionally have been multicoloured

◄ SPARTAN OFFICER
This fully equipped hoplite might be an officer of some type because of the transverse horsehair comb on his helmet. This would distinguish him from the men that he commanded and led. This type of crest would later be adopted by the Roman centurion and fulfil the same purpose.

THE SPARTANS AND THERMOPYLAE

(as were as the crests of other city-states). When it was multicoloured, two colours were alternated on the crest.

Spartan hoplites were known for their long hair. Herodotus records that when the Spartan hoplites were waiting for the Persians to attack at Thermopylae, they kept agile by taking exercise and prepared for battle by combing their long hair.

The second main difference was that the Spartan hoplites wore red military cloaks that were uniform in design and colour. They were not worn in combat, as that would hinder the use of the hoplite's weapons. As the Spartan phalanx developed, it was usual for the Spartans to walk forward to contact with the enemy, usually preceded by their musicians. Their pace would undoubtedly increase before shock (physical contact with the enemy), but apparently they did not break into a trot or run before they came into close contact with their enemies.

▼ **SPARTAN HOPLITE**
This is a Spartan hoplite from the late Peloponnesian War. Body armour became scarce and the hoplites were more simply dressed and equipped. He has his hoplon, spear and probably a sword, but the only armour he possesses is a helmet.

▲ **HOPLITE**
This is another fully equipped hoplite, probably another Spartan. He has a comb crest on his Corinthian helmet. His linen cuirass is simple and elegant, and he has the usual weapons and equipment of spear, hoplon and sword.

ARMIES AND NAVIES, AND THE SIEGE OF SYRACUSE

Fighting between the armies and navies of the two opposing leagues in Greece in the 4th century BCE differed from the hoplite warfare that had characterized earlier Greek conflicts. The traditional methods entailed encounters between armies of heavily armed and armoured hoplites on flat, open terrain that facilitated the use and employment of the phalanx. But now there was also fighting in varying terrain that demanded more lightly armed and armoured troops to engage with the enemy in woods, and allow them to lay or escape from ambushes. Missile weapons, such as the bow and the sling, were used more often and with greater effect.

The lightly armoured infantry often had the traditional arms of the hoplite. However, the Greek hoplite of the mid to late 4th century BCE was armoured less heavily than his classical predecessor had been during the Persian Wars of the previous century. Armour had become lighter, and many times the only armour worn was a simple conical helmet.

Fast-moving Troops

Greek cavalry was used more often for raids and ambushes. The hoplite was deployed in conjunction with light infantry and missile troops, attacking under the umbrella of well-aimed missile weapons from the supporting archers and slingers, and protecting the missile troops in close order when

▼ **Hoplite**
This hoplite is wearing the older panoply, and is uniformed, armed and equipped in the traditional manner even though it would be almost prohibitively expensive.

▼ **Spartan Hoplite**
The marking on his hoplon and his red clothing identify this as a Spartan from the late 4th century BCE. His panoply is simplified and the Phrygian helmet is a marked departure from earlier practice.

The Siege of Syracuse c.416–413 BCE

During this period the Greeks developed siege expertise greater even than what the Assyrians had achieved. Philip of Macedon and his son Alexander would later build on these developments in their siege warfare.

One of the greatest sieges of the period was an attempt by the Athenians to take the island of Sicily and its strategic city of Syracuse, which served as a base and source of supply for the Spartans and their allies. The hard-fighting Syracusans were helped by the scientist and mathematician Archimedes, who employed his ingenuity in developing their own siege engines to defeat the Athenian fleet.

The Athenians dispatched an expeditionary force of at least 50,000 men with a fleet to take Syracuse. They constructed siege works in order to cut the city off from outside aid. The city garrison was gradually failing in its desperate attempts to defend their city, when the Spartan general Gylippos arrived in 414 BCE to take over the defence. Gylippos immediately seized the initiative from the Athenians and went on the offensive. He built better defences that counteracted the Athenian siege works and prevented the Athenians from penetrating into the city.

The Athenian fleet, which was attempting to storm the city from the harbour, was trapped by the Syracusans – who stretched a chain across the harbour mouth, preventing the Athenian ships from escaping. The Athenians were forced to abandon their fleet: they attempted to escape overland, but were pursued and repeatedly defeated. Of the 50,000 men who began the expedition, only 7,000 survived to be captured by the Syracusans. The Athenian commanders were immediately executed, and the men in their army sentenced to work as slaves in the stone quarries of Syracuse. This overwhelming defeat ruined Athens militarily and ensured the final victory of Sparta.

▼ HOPLITE
This more traditionally equipped hoplite with full panoply harkens back to an earlier period. The skirt at the bottom of his hoplon gives protection in combat to the lower legs.

▲ BAGGAGE MAN
This non-combatant was necessary for any army to employ. All armies had baggage and supplies to carry, and the use of baggage men, in another time known as train troops, was critical for success in the field. Their laborious service allowed the soldiers to live and fight on campaign. They were often employed as servants for the hoplites, sometimes seven for one hoplite. Sometimes they would join in the fighting if the situation became desperate.

threatened by opposing infantry and cavalry. Naval warfare became much more common, even for the Spartans, and seaborne forces conducted raids along hostile coastlines as well as engaging enemy fleets at sea. Infantry were often used as marines.

INTERNECINE WARFARE, GREEKS AND THRACIANS

Over time, the panoply of the Greek hoplite was lightened and simplified, armour was diminished and the overall protection of the individual hoplite greatly reduced. Bronze cuirasses, as we have seen, gave way to linen cuirasses. These were constructed of layers of linen cut to a pattern and glued together.

At the waist, the hoplite wore strips of either bronze or linen that protected the groin from spear or sword thrusts. The Corinthian helmet was very common, but Greek helmets were being improved from the original design – especially by opening up the face in order to allow the hoplite to see his surroundings better and by removing part of the helmet around the ear so that he could hear. These changes gave the hoplite a better chance of survival, especially if the phalanxes broke and fighting degenerated into a melée.

Greek armies employed a plethora of designs depicting animals, gods or families on their hoplons. The Spartans only had one, an inverted 'V' shape. A colourful cloth extension was added to the bottom of the hoplon, designed to protect the legs from missile weapons.

◀ **Archer**
This archer is not only well-armed with composite bow and quiver of arrows, but he is also well-armoured. His headgear is an animal skin and head, which could be worn as a trophy or for some peculiarity of his unit.

▶ **Hoplite**
This hoplite wears a fully enclosed Corinthian helmet, carries his hoplon and is armed for close combat with a sword. His armour is a metal cuirass and greaves. A military cloak would be removed as a hindrance when engaged in combat.

The Thracian Enemy

Thracians from the Balkans and eastern Europe were part of the Persian army. They were some of the army's best light infantry. Expert javelin men, they were adept at skirmishing. Their clothing consisted

of animal skin, with their headgear made from fox and their footwear from fawn skin. They wore practical tunics and cloaks that were called *zeiras* and were usually multicoloured. In addition to their javelins, Thracians were also armed with a crescent-shaped shield, which allowed a degree of self-protection that Greek peltasts did not have (see page 155).

The Peltast

Essentially the Greek peltast was a light infantryman, who may or may not have worn a helmet but was otherwise unarmoured, and armed only with a circular shield and a spear or javelin. Often the Greek peltasts were not equipped with a shield and only with javelins, and were then used as missile troops.

Greek peltasts came to be an important part of warfare, especially in the Peloponnesian Wars when armour became either lighter or was done away with entirely, except for the shield and simplified helmet, and there came to be less difference between the hoplite and the peltast in military appearance.

When fighting the Thracians however, whose peltasts were better armed and equipped, the native Greek peltasts were at a distinct disadvantage.

◀ **Light Infantryman**
This javelin thrower wears an older-style helmet with a high comb, but he does carry a hoplon along with his javelin. Sometimes spears would be equipped with an iron tip on the butt end which could be used as a spear point if the actual one broke in combat.

▲ **Hoplite**
This hoplite has the cloth extension on the hoplon. He wears a metal cuirass, and has his sword (behind the fabric) and spear. His helmet has an unusual shape and comb.

IPHICRATES AND THE BATTLE OF LECHAEUM

In the late 5th and early 4th century BCE, Greek city-states were embroiled in a series of bitter conflicts. In the wake of the Peloponnesian War (431–404BCE) between Athens and Sparta, the Corinthian War (395–387BCE) pitted Sparta against an alliance of Thebes, Athens, Corinth and Argos. The Athenian general Iphicrates won several victories using mobile light infantry or peltasts – notably in the Battle of Lechaeum near Corinth in 390BCE when he almost wiped out a regiment from Sparta.

By reducing the infantryman's protective armour, Iphicrates made him more mobile. The peltast wore no body armour except a plain iron conical helmet with cheek pieces. He carried a light, oval wicker shield and was armed with a spear, short sword, and perhaps javelins. The name peltast came from that for the smaller shield, the *pelta*.

Iphicrates also modified the armour of the hoplites in his army. The hoplite's shield, though still constructed of wood and bronze, was smaller and lighter; the soldier did without heavy metal greaves, instead wearing a new type of boot, which covered, and was laced up above, the ankle. The boots were called *iphicratids* after their inventor (see example on opposite page). The hoplite did not wear a cuirass, instead having a type of quilted vest. His helmet was of a more modern construction and design, taken from the Phrygian or Thracian types.

In the Battle of Lechaeum 390BCE Iphicrates used repeated assaults by his peltasts to drive back the heavier and slower-moving battalion of hoplites from Sparta. The battle began after the Spartan army near Corinth divided as a contingent of men from Amyclae were being escorted homewards to take part in a religious festival. At a point near Corinth the Spartan cavalry carried on with the men from Amyclae while the hoplites turned back. At this point wave after wave of peltast members of an Athenian garrison in Lechaeum swept out to attack

▶ **ATHENIAN CAVALRYMAN**
These cavalrymen had not advanced or changed much at all from the Persian and Peloponnesian Wars. This one wears the Boeotian helmet and is armed with lance and sword. They were still auxiliary troops, the hoplites being the main fighting arm.

the hoplites with spears and javelins. When the Spartan troops fell back to a nearby hilltop, the Athenian hoplites marched out to give battle and at this point the Spartans fled. Iphicrates then won several victories around Corinth.

Athenian Cavalry

Because the terrain of Greece is not conducive to large-scale cavalry operations, Greek cavalry was not considered to be of high combat value and was a secondary arm to the hoplite.

The arms and equipment of the Athenian cavalry were basic, and they were not used as a main fighting arm on the battlefield as the excellent Macedonian cavalry would be. The Greeks fielded no horse archers, and the Greek cavalrymen were armed with either spears or javelins and probably would have carried short swords for fighting in a melée.

Slingers

Troops skilled in the use of the sling were classified as light infantry. They were seldom if ever armoured. They operated in front of the phalanx to skirmish with the light troops of the opposing force. They usually engaged the light troops of the enemy and probably would have little or no effect on hoplites in formation in a phalanx. Slingers were a feature of Greek and Near Eastern warfare for centuries. The sling was a basic missile weapon, undoubtedly older than the bow, and in the hands of an experienced slinger, a deadly, relatively short-ranged weapon. Slingers sometimes also carried a dagger or short sword.

▲ **Slinger**
Slingers were light infantrymen who would be employed to skirmish with the opposing light troops before the phalanx was sent forward. They were usually unarmoured and wore only light clothing, and they were armed only with their sling and stone bag, which would be filled with specially selected stones chosen for their roundness and aeronautic capability. Sometimes they might be issued a light shield for self-defence from the enemy light troops.

▶ **Iphicratean Hoplite**
This hoplite is in a later form of panoply, a precursor of the Macedonian phalangite of Philip II. His cuirass is either padded linen or cotton. It was comfortable but did not provide the protection of scale armour, stiffened linen or a muscle cuirass. The spear has become quite a bit longer.

THE THEBAN PHALANX, AND THE BATTLE OF LEUCTRA

The Thebans decisively defeated the Spartans, and destroyed their dominance as the preeminent infantry in Greece, at the Battle of Leuctra in 371BCE. The Theban solution to the problem of Sparta's dominance was both organizational and tactical.

Epaminondas, the Theban commander, attacked in a novel formation (see panel) that would later be used by Frederick the Great in the Seven Years' War (1756–63CE). It meant that the Theban infantry on the Theban left wing came face to face with the Spartan infantry on the Spartan right wing. The normal practice was for a phalanx of hoplites to be between eight and ten men deep. But Epaminondas increased the depth of his left flank phalanx to at least 50, so that when it struck the Spartan line, it would overwhelm it not only through the shock of impact, but by weight – outnumbering the enemy. This was not a permanent change to the usual organization of the phalanx, but a tactical modification employed in a specific situation. In addition Epaminondas deployed his epilektoi to support the left phalanx.

The shock of the Theban left-flank phalanx shattered the opposing Spartan phalanx, even though this was the cream of the Spartan army. The successive shocks of the echeloned, smaller phalanxes (the ones arrayed back to the right) as they followed through stunned the Spartans and their allies. Epaminondas and his new tactics ended Spartan superiority in Greece.

These tactics were profoundly influential. Both Philip II and Alexander the Great drew inspiration from Epaminondas's innovation in their own battlefield tactics – notably by concentrating force, refusing to engage on one flank, and combining infantry and cavalry in a single assault. Military historians point out that Epaminondas himself was influenced by the bold and groundbreaking military tactics used by fellow Theban Pagondas at the Battle of Delium in 424BCE in the Peloponnesian War.

▶ **Thessalian Cavalryman**
The Thessalians, who fielded the best cavalry of Greece, lived on a flat area bordering Thebes; they often provided excellent mercenary auxiliary mounted contingents to the Thebans.

◀ **Theban Hoplite**
The spear is now longer, giving greater reach on the battlefield, and is turning into what would become the sarissa. It has the iron butt piece. His other armour is simple with a muscle cuirass, helmet, and greaves with added knee protection.

▶ **Theban Hoplite (far right)**
The older helmet style combined with the bronze muscle cuirass is an interesting combination. He is also armed and equipped with bronze greaves, hoplon, and sword with scabbard and baldric.

THE THEBAN PHALANX, AND THE BATTLE OF LEUCTRA

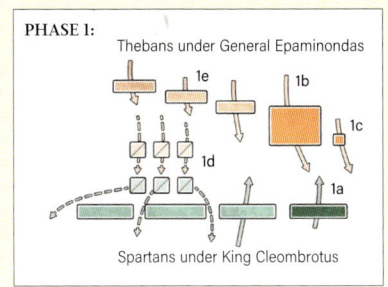

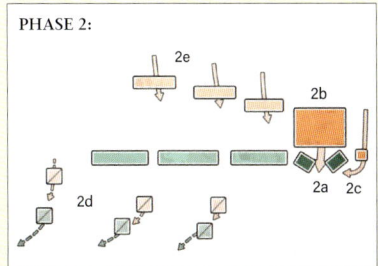

The Battle of Leuctra 371BCE
1a: The Spartans were arranged in four phalanxes, 8–12 men deep. The more vunerable right was considered a place of honour, for the elite troops.
1b: The Thebans broke dramatically with this tradition at Leuctra, massing a narrower but 50-deep column on their left flank, opposite the more exposed if experienced Spartan right.
1c: The concentration of force on the Theban left was further reinforced by a mobile elite force, the Sacred Band.
1d: The cavalry engaged.
1e: The weaker Theban right advances slowly but does not engage, protecting the exposed flank of the massed Theban phalanx.
2a-e: The concentration of Theban force onto one critical point crushes the Spartan elite.

The Sacred Band of Thebes
The military forces of Thebes included an elite guard corps of chosen soldiers ('epilektoi'): the Sacred Band. This consisted of just 300 men, who lived and trained in pairs. Such select warriors, whose ranks included important personalities like Epaminondas, were mostly tasked with protecting the democratic government of Thebes from internal rebellions. The Sacred Band was completely annihilated by the Macedonians at the Battle of Chaeronea (338BCE).

Battle of Mantinea
Epaminondas was killed in action at Mantinea, despite defeating both the Spartans and Athenians, as well as their allied Greek city-states. The Thebans were allied to the Boeotian League and Arcadia, while the allies of the Spartans and Athenians were the Elians and Mantineans. The Spartans were commanded by their king, Agesilaus II. Thebes and Sparta were unable to recover from this battle. When Epaminondas was mortally wounded, he encouraged the Thebans to conclude peace, even though they had won the battle. Both sides were so weakened cumulatively by incessant fighting that it paved the way for Philip of Macedon to conquer Greece.

Hoplite Armour
The Theban hoplites won undying fame under Epaminondas and the famous victory at Leuctra. The hoplite of this period would have fought with a heavy spear between 5–7m (16–23ft) in length and about 2.5cm (1in) in diameter. His shield was attached to his left arm, but was moved by way of a strap around his neck. His lower legs were protected by strap-on greaves and he wore a Thracian helmet.

The Greek armies of this period – after the defeats of the two Persian invasions and the internal struggles of the Peloponnesian Wars – were quite different to those of earlier times. Their arms and armour became simpler, and the hoplites, while still relying on the hoplon and the spear, were not as well-armoured as they had once been.

▲ *Epaminondas defends Pelopidas at the battle of Mantinea, in a 1910 lithograph by William Rainey.*

NEIGHBOURS AND ENEMIES OF GREECE

Bold traders and colonizers, the Ancient Greeks had many encounters with peoples around the Eastern Mediterranean, as well as further north through Anatolia and central Europe. These included the Phrygians of Anatolia (modern Turkey), the Scythians from the Eurasian steppes, the Thracians from the region of the Black Sea, and the Celts of central Europe.

Phrygians

The Phrygian kingdom had its capital at Gordium (modern Yassihuyuk in the Ankara Province of Turkey) in the valley of the Sakarya River in west-central Anatolia. Its roots went back at least to the time of the Trojan War, but it was at the height of its power and extent in c.720–675BCE before it was made part of first the Lydian and then the Persian empire.

Phrygian infantry were armed and armoured similarly to the Ancient Greeks, wearing iron helmets with horsehair crests as well as leather and iron breastplates or cuirasses. They carried round or irregularly shaped shields and wore tunics that came down to mid-thigh; leg coverings and boots finished their clothing. They carried spears along with the shield and also a short sword suspended from a baldric hung from their right shoulder.

Phrygian cavalrymen were armed with a composite bow and a spear, along with a sword. They were not armoured and wore a cloth hat that later became known as the 'Phrygian cap'. This design later evolved into a helmet worn by the Macedonian phalangites (heavy infantry).

Scythians

The Scythians were nomads and raiders who caused the Greeks a great deal of trouble through the ancient period.

◀ PHRYGIAN ARMOURED INFANTRYMAN
This heavy infantryman is reminiscent of the Greek hoplites in both appearance and armament, especially his shield. His helmet is of an older pattern, but he is well-clothed and well-shod and appears to have stiffened linen greaves.

▲ SCYTHIAN ARMOURED INFANTRYMAN
Scythian infantry would also be armoured, wearing the typical scale armour that the Scythians favoured. His shield is of an odd design, being constructed of wood but in a shape reminiscent of the older Greek figure of eight shield. His iron helmet and weapons are typical of the period and he is also well-clothed and well-shod.

NEIGHBOURS AND ENEMIES OF GREECE

▲ Coating from a short sword showing highly skilled Scythian metalwork. 4th century BCE.

▼ SCYTHIAN HORSE ARCHER
This horseman is armed with the powerful composite bow of the steppes. Here he is unarmoured, but the Scythian cavalrymen also wore advanced scale armour which usually indicated a difference between light and heavy cavalry. However, it can be assumed that some light cavalrymen would be partially armoured.

They were skilled metalworkers and probably influenced the Celts in their acquired skill in metallurgy. Like the Persians, the Scythians wore an early type of trousers. While some of their troops certainly fought on foot, the Scythians really made their mark as horsemen and skilled cavalrymen.

Scythian infantry wore a round iron helmet, not conical in shape but more closely fitted to the head. They wore a cuirass of scale armour and their tunic fell as far as the knee. They wore trousers similar to those of the Medes and Persians and carried swords and axes, along with an irregularly shaped shield, different from that of the Phrygians.

Scythian cavalrymen were also armed with sword, spear and composite bow and wore either light armour or no armour at all. The cavalryman's headgear was a soft cap similar to that of the Phrygians, but they also had access to a metal helmet of iron, usually rounded. Sometimes the Phrygian soft cap was stiffened and then covered with metal plates to form a makeshift helmet. Some of the Scythians wore no head-covering at all, save for coloured headbands that probably served

▲ PHYRGIAN LIGHT CAVALRYMAN
This light cavalryman is a horse archer, who is also armed with a lance. He is well-clothed and his dress is typical of civilian dress in Phrygia, including the tell-tale headwear known as the 'Phrygian cap'.

154 ARMIES OF ANCIENT GREECE

as a means of identification for regrouping in the heat of battle. They also fought expertly with lances in conjunction with the shield or on their own.

Scythian shields came in a variety of shapes, small enough to be used effectively on horseback, and were usually either rectangular in shape or circular with a crescent cut out of the top. This latter shape facilitated the shields' use by members of the cavalry.

The Scythian horses were both armoured and 'decorated'; the quality of metalworking being very high, their horses were also adorned with metal objects.

Soldiers wore greaves to protect their lower legs while mounted, and had boots or shoes. They used bows while mounted. These were composite bows – chosen for their strength and range – that were small enough to be used with ease while mounted.

Naturally enough, as in other armies of the ancient world, Scythian noblemen and commanders were dressed and armoured more ornately than the men they commanded.

Thracians

The Thracians were a tribal society of Indo-European origin. They may have coalesced from as many as 40 different tribes that lived in the lands north of Greece and south of what is now Russia. Some of the tribes lived across the Hellespont in Asia Minor. The Thracians occupied territory that was along the main invasion route into Greece that was used by the Persians, Celts, Macedonians and Greeks.

The Thracians were fiercely independent and warlike. They caused considerable trouble to those with whom they came into contact in their own lands. They also frequently hired themselves out as mercenaries. They were employed as mercenaries by the Persians in Xerxes's invasion of Greece in 480 BCE.

▲ **THRACIAN HORSE ARCHER**
Most of the Thracian cavalry was the mounted version of the infantry peltast, armed with the same shield and javelins, but they would also field skilled horse archers. This one is from the Getae (a tribe of the Thracians).

▶ **LIGHT CAVALRYMAN**
This Thracian horseman is armed like his infantry brethren with light shield and javelin. He is unarmoured but an excellent light cavalryman, forming a formidable duo alongside a horse archer.

NEIGHBOURS AND ENEMIES OF GREECE

The Thracian tribes lived in the hills as well as on the steppes and were noted, like the Scythians, to be expert horsemen and excellent cavalrymen. Before the coming of the Macedonians, the Thracians occupied some of the lands that later became Macedonia. The Macedonians drove the Thracians from their new lands.

Thracians were formidable opponents and enemies. Armed and armoured much like the Ancient Greeks, they fought both on foot and on horseback, and their light infantry, their peltasts, were skilled infantryman who excelled in skirmishing and raiding.

The Thracian cavalry wore armour and helmets of Phrygian design and were generally of two types. The heavy cavalry were armed with lance and straight sword and their armour was of the scale and lamellar type. The light cavalry consisted of lightly armed and very mobile horse archers, who were skilled at working with the armoured Thracian cavalry and were expert bowmen and worked well with their own light infantry. The mounted archers were excellent light cavalry and generally wore no armour. Their arrows were thought to be the best of their kind.

After the Greco-Persian wars, in around 460BCE, the Odrysai – probably the most powerful Thracian tribe – founded a kingdom based on the central Thracian plain. They established their capital city, Seuthopolis – the only Thracian city of record – at what is now Kazanlak in central Bulgaria. (The actual site of the original city is now at the bottom of the Koprinka Reservoir.) The city was greatly influenced by the Greek cities to the south, and may have been destroyed when the Celts invaded the area in 279BCE. The Thracians were finally overcome and conquered by the Romans in 46CE.

▲ **TRUMPETER**
This Thracian trumpeter would be mounted in order to follow his mounted commander closely on campaign and in combat. He is armoured with a cuirass and helmet with horsehair crest and is armed with the long cavalry sword. Like any competent trumpeter, he would also guard his commander's back in combat, especially in a melée.

▶ **THRACIAN PELTAST**
This Thracian light infantryman was armed with a javelin which was thrown. These peltasts, named after their light shield, the pelte, were superior to the usual Greek light infantrymen who were similarly armed. The peltast was the principal fighting man of a Thracian army, and wore traditional Thracian hunting clothing.

▲ Celtic War Chariot
The Celts were another warlike people who developed and used their own style of chariot on the battlefield. This was not a vehicle made only for transportation; it was used as a combat vehicle and the Celtic crew of the chariot would fight from it if the terrain permitted. The chariot is pulled by a pair of horses and is open in front and to the rear.

Celts

The Celts probably originally came from north of the Alps. They were an advanced people, who thrived in the Iron Age. Aggressive and warlike, they traded, or raided, for profit. From central Europe they expanded through western Europe, including modern-day France and Spain, into northern Italy and southeastern Europe, the Balkans and Greece – and across the Bosporus into Asia Minor, where three Celtic tribes moved and settled. They also crossed the English Channel into Britain and Ireland. Their expansion affected the development of Macedon and northern Greece.

The Celts were a tribal people: their loyalty was to the tribe, the clan and the family and not to an overarching Celtic identity. As early as 700 BCE Celtic chieftains in the region of Austria were trading with the Greeks:

▶ Celtic Warrior
The Celts were great individual fighters; not soldiers in the professional sense, but warriors in the greatest sense. This one is lightly armed and not armoured at all, which could be common in the early incursions into Greece of the Celts.

jars and other vessels of bronze and pottery from Greece have been found in graves of Celtic chieftains at the site of Hallstatt.

The Celts reached their period of greatest influence and power c.300 BCE. In 279 BCE Celts from what is now France made inroads into the region of Greece, perhaps driven southwards by overpopulation or as a result of famine, or perhaps through a desire for wealth and space.

The Celts raided into Greece and fought any and all peoples with whom they came into contact. A Celtic force reputedly numbering 150,000 infantry and 15,000 cavalry met a collation of Athenians, Aetolians (from the mountainous region of Aetolia), Boeotians (from central Greece)

and others at the Pass of Thermopylae. The Celtic chieftain Brennus sent a detachment to attack Aetolia (on the north of the Gulf of Corinth) and this weakened the defenders because the Aetolians departed to guard their homes. The Celts found a way around the pass and went on to attack and sack Delphi, but were defeated and Brennus was killed; the remnants of the Celtic army later suffered another heavy defeat at the hands of a Greek army containing troops from Thessaly.

After that, the Celts saw their power and influence begin to decline, mostly because of the growing power of Rome. This decline was not sudden, but took place over many decades. In the Punic Wars of 264–146BCE the Celts rallied to the standard of Carthage, a city-state in north Africa near modern Tunis in Tunisia, to fight against Rome. It would be the Romans who would finally and devastatingly defeat the Celts in Gaul and Britain.

The Celts were excellent metalworkers and produced fine armour and weapons. They wore iron helmets and their armour was either scale or, later, chain mail, and the equal of the Greek arms and armour. They built great hillforts as places to take cover. They were skilled poets and musicians. Their long broadsword, called a *spatha* by the Romans, was later adopted by Rome for its cavalry, because it had a much longer reach than the Roman infantry sword, the *gladius*.

▲ CELTIC MOUNTED WARRIOR
Celtic mounted troops were not usually cavalry, and the horse was used as transportation for the warrior to dismount and then fight on foot. Later, as the Celts came into contact with enemies who did employ cavalry, they developed their own to counter them. This horseman is armed with a long sword, that the Romans would later call a spatha, and an oval shield better-suited for mounted warfare.

◀ CELTIC STANDARD BEARER
Like other ancient armies, the Celts took standards into combat for the usual reasons – identification and to be used as a rallying point after a melée. Animal images were favoured.

NAVAL POWER AND THE BATTLE OF SALAMIS

The Greeks surpassed every other power in the Ancient World in naval development until the rise of Carthage; they clearly demonstrated that prowess against the second Persian invasion of Greece at the Battle of Salamis in 480BCE, where, outnumbered in galleys, the Greeks crushed the Persian fleet while the Persian king Xerxes was forced to watch from the shoreline. The Greek galley, the famous trireme, was 'state of the art' in the period.

The predecessors to the Greek galleys were the *penteconter* and the *hecatonter*. The former was galley-like in design with clean lines and a single line of oars and had the upswept stern that was beginning to be common to all Greek ship designs.

The bow did not have a ram, which would come later, but it did have a pointed 'cutwater' that was similar in appearance at a distance to a ram.

The larger *hecatonter* had two rows of oars, but was similar in both design and appearance to the *penteconter*. Both ships had a central mast and a large sail and were renowned for being swift and easy to manoeuvre.

Two smaller, similarly designed Greek vessels were the *triaconter* and the *samaina*. The *triaconter* had one row of oars, the *samaina* two rows, the first a single row of 15 on each side and the latter two rows of 13. Again, both had the centrally mounted mast with one large sail.

The Trireme

The first galleys or triremes were probably built in Greece around 700BCE. They are certainly mentioned as early as 550BCE. The design of the ship, however, was probably developed by the Phoenicians. When Athens had a windfall of mined silver from Attica, this funding was used to build a fleet, on the recommendation of the far-sighted Athenian Themistocles, a staunch proponent of naval strength and

▲ **Penteconter**
This ship was employed in early Greece, before 500BCE. She had a single bank of oars and the oarsmen sat on benches built into the hull without being covered by the deck as in later warships. The penteconter was not equipped with a ram, but had a structure on the hull called a 'cutwater.' The hulls were coated in black pitch.

▼ **Hecatonter**
The hecatonter was developed from the penteconter and had two rows of oarsmen, 25 to a row. The arrangement of the oarsmen was more sophisticated than that of the penteconter, the oarsmen being staggered and the oars of the lower rows now resting on a gunwale. There were probably 20 seaman and officers who ran the ship.

power. Possessing just 70 warships in 490BCE, by 481BCE Athens possessed a modern fleet of triremes that numbered at least 200 first-class ships. It was this building programme that enabled Athens, with support of the other city-states with available ships, to put a fleet to sea to oppose the Persian invasion in 480BCE and to rally the available Greek triremes to face the Persians at the Battle of Salamis and defeat the Persian fleet.

The Greek trireme was designed to fight its opponents at sea by ramming them, and then if possible to board the opposing vessel. The trireme was highly manoeuvrable and was propelled by three banks of oars. While the trireme had at least one and usually two masts, these could be dismantled and left ashore if combat was imminent. The crew of a trireme numbered 200 – 16 seamen who handled the ship, 14 naval infantry, and 170 oarsmen.

The trireme was an excellent warship, but had a problem with seaworthiness: in rough seas or bad weather, it had a significant risk of capsizing. On the other hand, the trireme could be beached easily for repairs or in bad weather and did not require a built-up harbour in which to seek shelter.

The trireme was also used as a military transport when necessary, carrying supplies, horses and other material

▲ SAMAINA
This was an early Greek vessel with 25 oars to each side arranged in two rows. It was heavily built towards the bow, probably to give it the capability to ram, but also to give it the ability to carry cargo. It had a full deck which allowed the crew to fight their vessel more easily, and the oarsmen were also protected by the deck. The samaina was made obsolete by the larger, faster, and more efficient galleys.

▼ TRIACONTER
This was a smaller vessel with only 32 oarsmen, plus the helm. They were of the same design as the other Greek galleys, only smaller, and they were probably armed with a ram. The triaconter was used as the 'eyes' of the fleet as well as carrying dispatches and would also be employed to search and rescue sailors from sunk or damaged galleys. The triaconter was fast and manoeuvrable which enabled it to avoid being rammed by larger galleys.

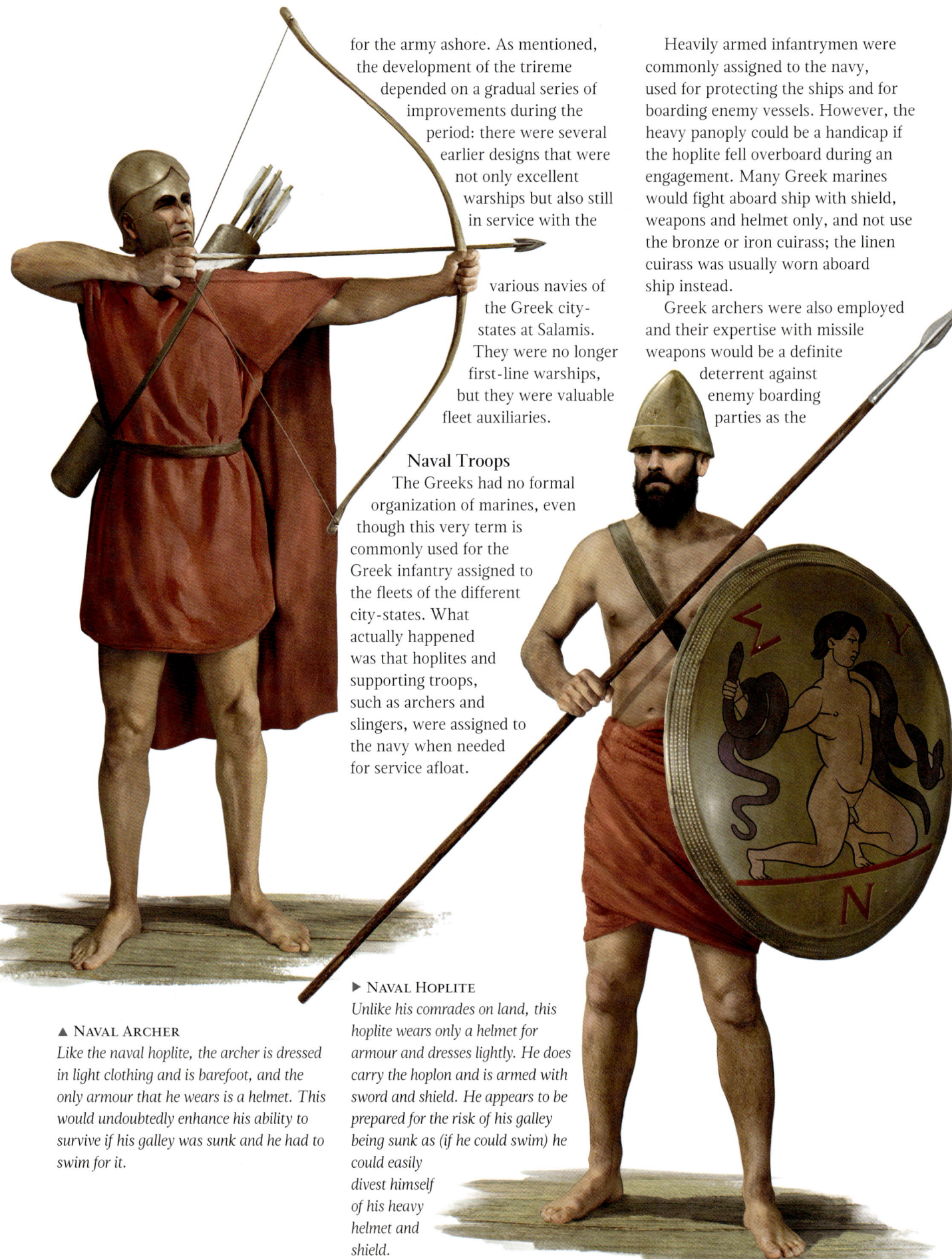

for the army ashore. As mentioned, the development of the trireme depended on a gradual series of improvements during the period: there were several earlier designs that were not only excellent warships but also still in service with the various navies of the Greek city-states at Salamis. They were no longer first-line warships, but they were valuable fleet auxiliaries.

Naval Troops

The Greeks had no formal organization of marines, even though this very term is commonly used for the Greek infantry assigned to the fleets of the different city-states. What actually happened was that hoplites and supporting troops, such as archers and slingers, were assigned to the navy when needed for service afloat.

Heavily armed infantrymen were commonly assigned to the navy, used for protecting the ships and for boarding enemy vessels. However, the heavy panoply could be a handicap if the hoplite fell overboard during an engagement. Many Greek marines would fight aboard ship with shield, weapons and helmet only, and not use the bronze or iron cuirass; the linen cuirass was usually worn aboard ship instead.

Greek archers were also employed and their expertise with missile weapons would be a definite deterrent against enemy boarding parties as the

▲ **Naval Archer**
Like the naval hoplite, the archer is dressed in light clothing and is barefoot, and the only armour that he wears is a helmet. This would undoubtedly enhance his ability to survive if his galley was sunk and he had to swim for it.

▶ **Naval Hoplite**
Unlike his comrades on land, this hoplite wears only a helmet for armour and dresses lightly. He does carry the hoplon and is armed with sword and shield. He appears to be prepared for the risk of his galley being sunk as (if he could swim) he could easily divest himself of his heavy helmet and shield.

Greek Fleet at Battle of Salamis

Contingent	Number of Ships
Athenians	180
Lacedaemonians	16
Corinthians	40
Sicyonians	15
Epidaurians	10
Troizenians	5
Hermionians	3
Megarians	20
Ambraciots	7
Leucadians	3
Aeginetans	30
Chalcidians	20
Eretrians	7
Keians	2
Naxians	4
Styrians	2
Kythnians	1
Total	**365**

galleys closed in. Whether or not the hoplites were competent swimmers is unknown, but undoubtedly many losses at sea came from drowning.

Naval Tactics

Three basic tactics were employed in naval warfare involving galleys or similar ship types. Opposing fleets would usually approach in a single or a double rank of galleys, depending on how much room was available for manoeuvre and also on the manner of command and control that was being exercised by the fleet commanders.

The first manoeuvre was the *periplus*, used when the fleets approached each other in line. In order to disrupt or put the opposing fleet into disorder, one of the fleets would extend its line and attempt to outflank the opposing fleet and attack the galleys on one end of the enemy's line. The second was the *diekplus*. Instead of attacking in line, the enemy fleet would be approached and attacked in a single column, or line ahead. The lead ship would aim for the space between two of the galleys in the enemy's line and at the last moment of the approach attack one of the two target galleys, breaking the enemy's line and allowing the following galleys to get through the enemy's line and begin a melée.

The third tactic was defensive in nature. The defending fleet would form a circle, the *kyklos*, with the rams of each galley pointing outward. Command and control galleys would be in the centre of the circle, also pointing ram outward. This formation was designed to entice the enemy to attack, and then to break the attack and begin the melée.

The Battle of Salamis 480 BCE

After the Battle of Thermopylae the Greeks knew that in spite of their navy being newly reinforced by more than 100 galleys, they were still going to be heavily outnumbered by the Persians; they had to find a place in which Persian numerical superiority would be largely negated and then entice the Persians to attack them there. The Greek commanders wanted to trap and destroy the Persian fleet, which might force Xerxes to leave for good.

At Salamis the Athenian commander Themistocles, with just 365 vessels at his disposal, faced a vastly larger Persian fleet that contained around 800 galleys. He relied on tactical cunning to get the better of the invaders, luring the Persians into straits of Salamis between the island of that name and the port of Athens. In these restricted waters the Persian galleys found it difficult to manoeuvre, and were vulnerable. The Greek triremes repeatedly rammed their opposite numbers. The Greeks lost just 40 of their vessels while sinking some 300 of the Persian vessels. The remainder of the Persian fleet scattered. The invasion was at an end, thanks to the success of the Athenian trireme.

▶ **ATHENIAN TRIREME**
The trireme had three banks of oars and one or two masts, which were lowered in combat. Built for speed and manoeuvrability, its main weapon was the ram built into the bow.

ARMS AND ARMOUR

The development of arms and armour by the Greek city-states encapsulates the history of classical weapons. They were copied well into the modern era; classical helmet designs as well as full and half cuirasses were used until, and after, the Napoleonic period.

Greek body armour principally consisted of a bronze or iron cuirass. Later a leather or stiffened cloth cuirass was developed. The cuirass consisted of both breast and back plates and came in many designs. Early attempts from the Minoans and Mycenaeans at body armour, though effective, were clumsy and definitely not handsome. The Greek muscled cuirass, quite different and more modern, fastened over the shoulders and was more comfortable, which facilitated movement. The bronze muscle cuirass gave excellent protection to the chest and back, and the kilt protected the hoplite from the waist to mid-thigh.

Warriors wore bronze or iron greaves to protect their lower legs. These had a leather backing and could either completely cover the calf, both front and rear, or be made merely to cover the front of the lower leg.

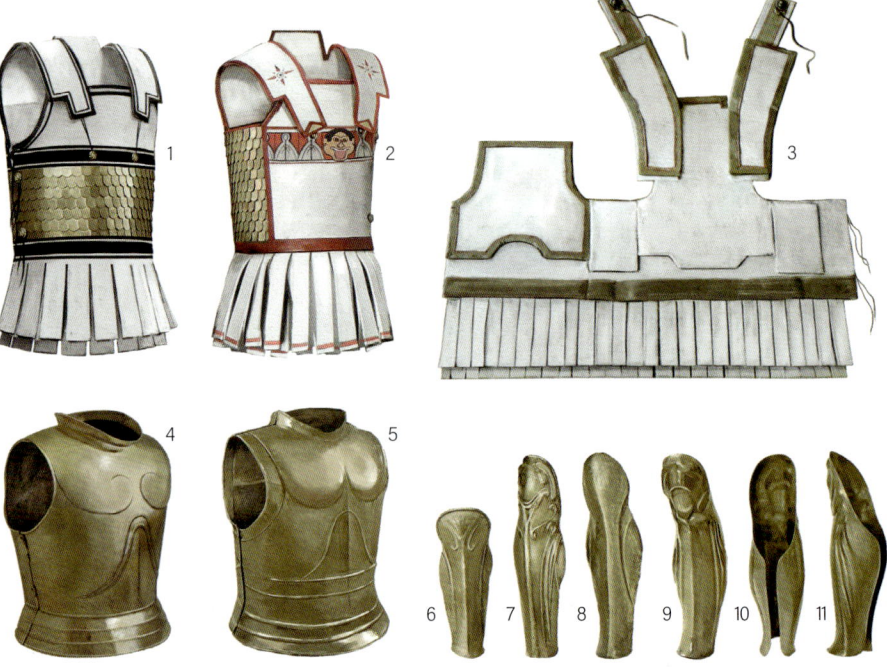

▲ BODY ARMOUR
The typical linen cuirass is shown in 1 and 2, with an exploded view in 3 to show the construction of the armour. Two versions of the bronze muscle cuirass are shown in 4 and 5, and a selection of bronze leg greaves in 6 to 11. Greaves were needed to protect the legs because this part of the body was not covered by the shield or hoplon.

▼ SHIELDS
The round, concave, bronze-covered Greek shield, the hoplon, gave the hoplite his name. Numbers 1–3 show the different arrangements on the inside of the shields to hold them. Individual Greeks, Greek city-states and units might have their own devices painted on the outside for identification purposes in combat (4–8).

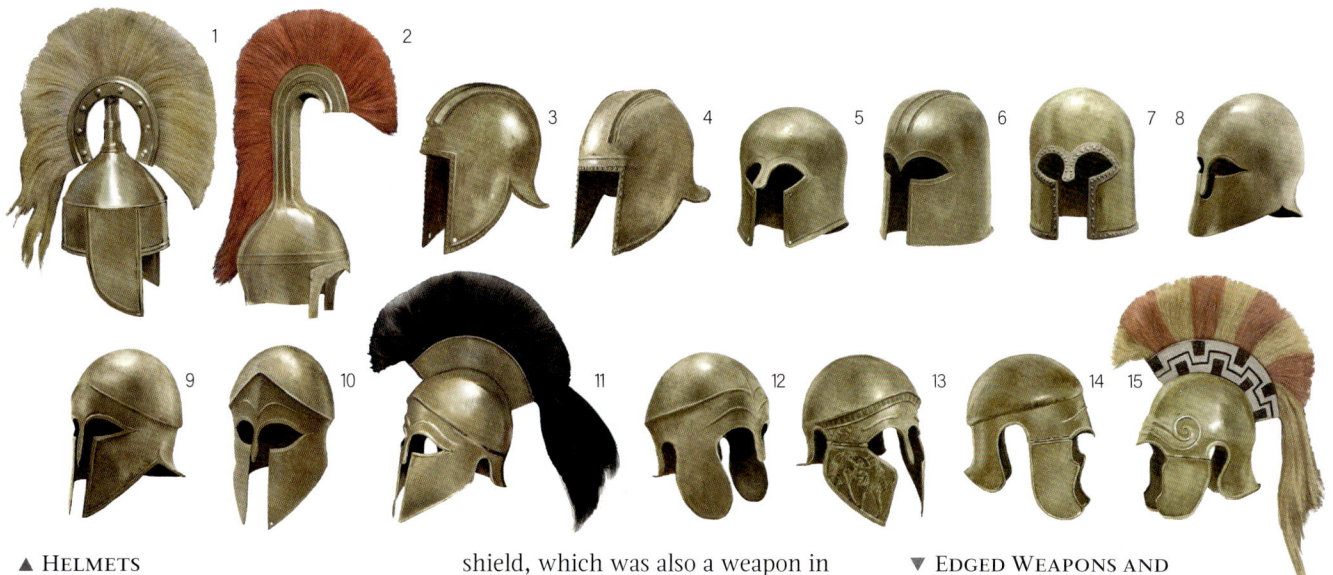

▲ Helmets

The classical Greek Corinthian helmets developed from somewhat ornate beginnings (1,2) which undoubtedly had to be top-heavy. They did serve a purpose, the design and colour being forms of identification in combat among the dust and mess. From those beginnings, the less ornate but more functional helmet derived (3–10). In almost all of these examples, the face and head are completely protected, which limited visibility for the wearer. A comb with horsehair crest and tail was later added (11), and helmets developed (12–15) where the face was open for better visibility but the cheek sides were still protected. 15 has an ornate crest.

Missile Weapons

The Greeks used the usual variety of ancient weapons, first of bronze, then of iron. Greek missile weapons were the bow, sling and spear. The Greek bow was short, powerful and drawn to the chest. Sometimes the Greek bow was made of two deers' horns made to fit together; it was a very difficult bow to string and required some skill to accomplish that task alone. The sling, in all the long period of its use, remained a simple weapon that needed a skilled slinger to be effective.

Spear and Sword

The main weapon of the hoplite was the spear, typically between 2–3m/6–10ft long. It was grasped using a leather grip in the centre of the spear and usually used for thrusting in conjunction with the round hoplon shield, which was also a weapon in line of battle. When thrown the spear could reach a distance of 6–9m (20–30ft). The shield was carried in the left hand, leaving the right hand free to use the thrusting spear, with the shield not only protecting its bearer, but the hoplite to his left. The solid line of shields with the spear as the offensive weapon of the phalanx was almost unbeatable if the phalanx remained unbroken.

Of secondary importance to the spear was the hoplite's sword, worn on the left side and of different designs. It was a short sword. The hoplon was constructed of wood, faced in bronze and had two handles on the inside of the shield so that it could be controlled properly in the phalanx.

Head Protection

The classical Greek helmet went through many stages of development. The first were quite similar to those of other ancient peoples: conical in shape, sometimes with a short coloured plume on the top. The helmet was designed to protect the head including the face, although this cut down the field of vision. Colourful horsehair plumes adorned the helmet, sometimes of a single solid colour, such as blue or red, or of black and white or other contrasting colours.

Light troops wore leather helmets and animal skins, or no headwear at all, while the hoplites in infantry formations wore heavier, more protective full bronze helmets.

▼ Edged Weapons and Polearms

The Greeks favoured the spear as their polearm of choice (1, 8–12). Swords (2, 4–6) were of varying designs throughout the period. Daggers were of many types, but (3) is typical of those carried, if they were carried at all. Sword scabbards (7) were usually of leather with metal fittings.

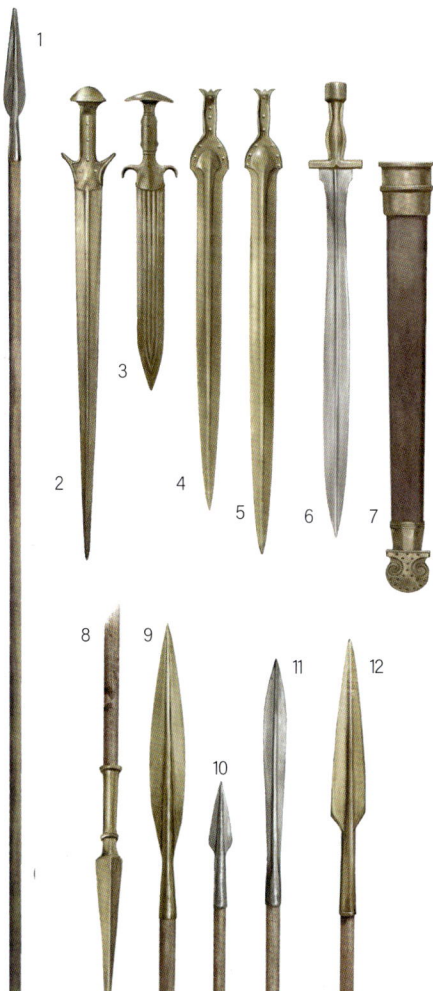

ARMIES OF THE PERSIAN EMPIRE

The Persians were an Indo-European people whose rise eclipsed the empires that had come before them in the territory centred on the Tigris and Euphrates rivers that lies westwards of the Iranian plateau. Long dominated by the Medes, the Persians rose to be in the ascendant in this area for more than 200 years, and established an empire that was huge, superbly well administered and modern. When this power finally fell to Alexander the Great, he kept the internal organization of the Persians intact, realising it was an excellent system to control these vast lands. This was not the end of the Persian empire; it rose again after Alexander's empire was broken up shortly after his death, and Persia would rival the Eastern Roman empire well into the 7th century CE, until, exhausted by constant warfare and defeat at the hands of the Eastern Roman Emperor Heraclius, it would finally succumb to the march of the new power in the East – Islam.

▲ *King Darius I, on a limestone bas-relief from the Treasury at Persepolis, c.515BCE. The courtiers' dress is unusual in that it shows a shirt-type of clothing worn. Perhaps this is court dress for formal occasions in audience to the king.*

◄ *Frieze depicting archers of the Persian king's guard, from the Palace of Darius the Great at Persepolis, in a mosaic of polychrome glazed brick tiles. These Immortals are interesting in that their dress is similar but not uniform, and show a range of the arms used, including both spear and bow with sheath.*

THE RISE AND FALL OF PERSIA

In c.553BCE the Persian prince Cyrus led an uprising of the Persians against the Median empire ruled by his maternal grandfather Astyages. His relationship to Astyages did not stop him taking the crown of the Medes and joining it to that of the Persians. He went on to found the great Persian Achaemenid empire, the largest empire known to history up to this point, which endured until its conquest by Alexander in 331BCE.

The Achaemenid empire sought to conquer Ancient Greece, but failed to do so each time it invaded, defeated by a temporary alliance of Greek city-states: in 490BCE the campaign culminated in Athenian victory at the Battle of Marathon; in 480–479BCE there were three important battles, the Greek stand at the Pass of Thermopylae, the naval battle of Salamis and the final Greek land victory at Plataea.

The Achaemenid empire was also the power that was invaded by Alexander of Macedon (the youthful general known to history as Alexander the Great) and his near-invincible army of Macedonians and Greeks. Alexander conquered all that Cyrus and his successors had built.

The Achaemenid Dynasty

The dynasty founded by Cyrus the Great was named after his grandfather, Achaemenes. Cyrus's father was Cambyses I, referred to as 'Great King'. Cyrus II (Cyrus the Great) was probably born between 600 and 590BCE; he was named for *his* grandfather, who was Cyrus I of Persia. When Cyrus succeeded to the Persian leadership upon the death of

▼ *Map showing the different satrapies into which the Persian empire was divided for administrative purposes.*

▲ *Croesus' rich kingdom of Lydia in Asia Minor was the first to fall to the Persian advance. Defeated by Cyrus the Great of Persia in 547BCE, Croesus was, according to Herodotus, put on a pyre to be burned, a scene shown on this vase c.480BCE.*

his father in 559BCE, the Persians owed their allegiance to the Medes, who were sovereign over both Media and Persia. Cyrus organized a revolt against the Medes in 553BCE and by 550BCE had conquered them, now becoming their overlord and founding the Persian empire, becoming officially king of Persia.

The subjugation of the Medes that began Cyrus's wars of conquest would not end until the further conquests of his son Cambyses II after Cyrus's death. The Lydians were conquered by Cyrus in a campaign that included the besieging and capture of their capital at Sardis in 547BCE. Their king Croesus was, it is said, put on a pyre but saved by rain and a change of heart by Cyrus. The Lydians revolted the following year, but their rebellion was suppressed. Asia Minor and Palestine were also conquered by the Persians.

The Emergence of Empire

With the conquest of Babylon in 539BCE, Cyrus assumed the grandiloquent titles of the King of Sumer, Akkad and Babylon, as well as 'King of the four corners of the world'. This was not all bombast, as Cyrus ruled the largest empire in the history of the world up to this point. When he died in 530BCE, his empire ran from India to Asia Minor and south to Palestine. It would be up to his son and successor, Cambyses II, to extend Persian conquests into Egypt. Cyrus's son ruled for only seven years, being succeeded by his brother Bardiya who did not have the talent to rule as well as his brother and father had done.

Cyrus was probably killed in combat against the Massagetae, a tribal people in the eastern marches of the empire. Details of his death vary, depending on the chronicler, and one story states that Cyrus died peacefully in his bed, but it appears most likely that he died on the battlefield fighting either the Dahae or the Massagetae, and his body was returned home to his capital city, Pasargadae, by his troops. It was interned in a golden coffin in a large tomb, that still stands.

Cyrus was celebrated as a ruler, a general and a lawgiver. He is credited with issuing a directive, known as the Cyrus Cylinder, which was probably the first proclamation of basic human rights in history. Merciful and just to the peoples he conquered, Cyrus was known for respecting the traditions, religions, customs and laws of the lands that were conquered and absorbed into the new Persian empire. He is renowned also as the king who returned the Jews to their homeland after their enforced captivity in Babylon, issuing two 'Edicts of Restoration' for this purpose. He was celebrated in the Bible: in the Old Testament book of Ezra he is called an agent of the Lord, and after his death he was the subject of an essay on the ideal ruler written by Greek historian Xenophon (c.430–c.354BCE).

Cyrus oversaw a centralized bureaucracy that administered his multicultural empire efficiently and, usually, justly. He organized the empire into satrapies (provinces), each ruled by a satrap (governor). This effective and innovative system lasted as long as the empire and was generally kept intact even when the empire fell to Alexander the Great.

▲ The tomb of Cyrus the Great at Pasargadae, in what is now Fars province in northern Iran. The simple construction is like an early ziggurat.

Persia Against Greece

With the exception of Cyrus's son Cambyses II, who succeeded him, none of the Persian kings who followed Cyrus were as successful in their military operations as Cyrus had been. Darius I was also considered a good and competent king, even though he was defeated in his invasion of Greece at the Battle of Marathon in 490BCE. Before the invasion of Greece, Darius had campaigned against the Scythians, but since the Scythians were nomads and had

▶ Cyrus the Great, called the father of his people by the ancient Persians, was a tolerant monarch. This tinted engraving by Gustave Doré depicts Cyrus returning the sacred objects of the Hebrews. He issued an edict allowing the Jews to return to their homeland.

▲ The Royal Guard depicted in a bas-relief at Tachara, or the Palace of Darius, in Persepolis.

▼ A relief on a doorway of the Hall of the Hundred Columns depicting King Xerxes with two attendants, one of whom shades him from the sun. Persepolis 460BCE.

neither cities nor land, the Persian army could not force their foes into a decisive battle on their own terms, and Darius had to give up the campaign. Instead, he turned on Greece, unsuccessfully invading it in 490BCE.

Xerxes, the son of Darius, in the hope of avenging and exceeding his father, recruited and built up a huge army for the time and invaded Greece again in 480BCE. He crossed the Hellespont, the narrow body of water that separates Europe and Asia, on a 'bridge of boats', which was actually a huge pontoon bridge. Xerxes was an excellent king and organizer, but he was no general, and being held up for about a week by 7,000 Greek hoplites at the Pass of Thermopylae (including the 300 Spartans who have gone down in history) was a major setback for the invasion even though the Persians were eventually victorious, and annihilated the Spartan contingent that remained at the pass. Later, Xerxes watched his fleet being destroyed by a smaller, better-led Greek fleet under the leadership of the Athenians, whose city Xerxes had destroyed. After he returned to Persia from the failure of the Battle of Salamis, the remnant of army he left in Greece was heavily defeated at the Battle of Plataea.

Battle of Issus

The Battle of Issus in 333BCE was the second of Alexander's battles against the Persian empire, although it was the first time that he faced the Persian king Darius III in combat. Issus is in what is now southern Turkey; the two armies faced each other across the River Pinarus. Alexander's left flank was resting on the Gulf of Issus and on his right flank were the Amanus Mountains.

The battle itself was fought on a flat, open plain and the river was clearly fordable. The Macedonians were incensed prior to battle, as Darius had captured their base camp and maimed or slaughtered Macedonian sick and wounded. Those who were not murdered had their right hands sliced off. The Macedonians were outnumbered, and Darius was reinforced by 10,000 Greek mercenaries who were probably his most steady troops. Alexander personally commanded the Macedonian right while his trusted subordinate, Parmenion, commanded the Macedonian left. Interestingly, Alexander launched his main attack against the Persian left, while the Persians attacked Parmenion's troops on the Macedonian left.

Alexander led the Macedonian attack with his heavy cavalry and his trusted Companions. Parmenion was hard-pressed by the Persian attack against him, but his troops, while giving ground, did not break. Meanwhile, Alexander and his cavalry, supported by the vaunted infantry in phalanx, shattered the Persian left flank, causing panic in the Persian army and routing the Persians facing them. Wheeling to the left against the Persian centre, Alexander saw Darius in his chariot. Darius's brother, Oxyathres, attempted to stop the Macedonians but failed, and the Persian army broke up and fled, along with their king. The Persians left behind a camp full of riches and other booty. Alexander would face Darius once more, but Darius was thereafter murdered by one of his own men.

Defeat and Collapse

The Persian empire fell to Alexander the Great, but he adopted many of its customs and traditions, marrying his generals to Persian women and making its capital, Babylon, his main residence. After Alexander's death in 323BCE his vast and disparate empire was divided up among his leading generals, known as the Successors.

What was left of the Persian empire was finally defeated after long wars with the Eastern Romans under the Emperor Heraclius, and was so exhausted by the protracted warring that the remnants of empire quickly fell to the Islamic onslaught that followed shortly after. What is interesting, nonetheless, is the seeming resilience of the Persian state despite repeated defeats by the Greeks and Alexander.

▲ The Behistun Inscription is carved into limestone cliffs. Dating from 521BCE, a large relief depicts Darius I, with his bow and lance carriers behind, judging defeated prisoners; the last one wears a Scythian cap. The inscription is given in three cuneiform scripts, so providing a key to those languages.

▼ The Battle of Salamis, 480BCE, between the navies of Greece and Persia, in an 1882 oil painting by Konstantinos Volanakis.

TIMELINE OF THE PERSIAN EMPIRE

c.600BCE: Cyrus (who will be Cyrus II) is born in the old province of Anshan. He is the son of Cambyses I, who is the younger son of Cyrus I.
586–539BCE: A resurgent Babylon conquers the Israelites.
572BCE: Nebuchadezzar II conquers Assyria and establishes the new Babylonian empire.
559BCE: Cyrus II takes power as King of the Persians after the death of his grandfather Cyrus I. He forms an army with which he will add conquests to his kingdom.
c.553–550BCE: Cyrus II, with his new army, revolts against Media and unifies the Persians with the Medes.
549BCE: Cyrus II founds the Achaemenid Persian empire after conquering Ecbatana, capital of Media.
547BCE: Sardis is captured by Cyrus II after defeating King Croesus of Lydia on the Halys River.

▼ *The grand staircase of the Palace of Darius I at Persepolis, the ceremonial capital of the immense Persian empire.*

539BCE: Cyrus II wins the battle of Opis and then takes Babylon. He is now known as Cyrus the Great.
530BCE: Cyrus II is killed in action against the Massagetae; Cambyses II, his eldest son, succeeds to the throne.
525BCE: Cambyses II attacks and defeats the Egyptian army at Pelusium, adding Egypt to the empire. He successfully organizes a navy to operate in the Nile Delta in support of the army.
524BCE: Cambyses attacks Kush, but fails to conquer it.
522BCE: Cambyses dies in Syria, and is succeeded by Darius I, who seizes power after a period of internal revolt. Darius is of the Achaemenid family.
516–512BCE: Darius campaigns in Scythia and then completes the conquest of Thrace.
499BCE: The Ionian revolt against the Persians begins.
498BCE: Sardis is captured and burned by the rebel Ionian Greeks.
497BCE: Darius defeats a revolt on Cyprus, returning it to Persian rule.

494BCE: The Persians defeat the Ionian fleet at Lade and destroy Miletus, crushing the Ionian revolt. Because mainland Greeks supported the Ionian revolt, Darius plans an invasion of mainland Greece.
493BCE: The Persians win at Malene.
492BCE: Severe storms badly damage the Persian fleet near Mount Athos. The Persian general Mardonios is defeated in Thrace.
491BCE: Darius I gives an ultimatum to the Greek city-states: submit to Persian rule or be destroyed.
490BCE: The two commanders of the Persian fleet, Datis and Artaphernes, cross the Aegean in order to land troops in Greece. The Persians are defeated at the Battle of Marathon.
486BCE: Xerxes becomes king of Persia upon the death of his father Darius. Egypt revolts.
485BCE: Babylon revolts against Persian rule.
480BCE: In the second Persian invasion of Greece, the Spartans and their allies defend the pass at

▲ *The ruins of the Palace of Darius I, Persepolis, in present-day Iran.*

Thermopylae against the Persian army. The Spartans are defeated but the battle delays the Persian advance into Greece, and inflicts severe losses. The Persian navy is badly defeated at the Battle of Salamis.

479BCE: The Persian army under Mardonios is defeated by the Greeks at Plataea, and Mardonios is killed in action. The Persian invasion is halted.

465BCE: Xerxes is assassinated. His son Artaxerxes assumes the throne.

454BCE: An Athenian expeditionary force in Egypt is destroyed by the Persians.

▼ *A cylinder seal depicting King Darius I in a chariot hunting lions. The winged disk of the god Ahura Mazda is above.*

449BCE: Peace is established between Persia and the Greek city-states.

431–404BCE: The Peloponnesian Wars were fought between Athens and its allies, and Sparta and its allies.

408BCE: Cyrus (known as Cyrus the Younger), a younger son of the Persian king Darius II, assumes power over the Persian provinces in Asia Minor.

405BCE: The death of Darius II.

401BCE: Cyrus leads a revolt against the new Persian king, his elder brother Artaxerxes II. His army includes a Greek mercenary force, the famous 'Ten Thousand'. Cyrus is killed in the Battle of Cunaxa against Artaxerxes even though his army is victorious. The Persian empire continues in its gradual decline.

338BCE: Court eunuch Bagoas poisons Artaxerxes III and then his son Artaxerxses IV.

336BCE: Darius III becomes King of Kings in Persia. In Macedonia, Philip II is assassinated and Alexander ascends the throne of Macedon.

334BCE: Alexander defeats the Persians at the Battle of Granicus.

333BCE: Alexander defeats Darius III at the Battle of Issus.

331BCE: After taking the city of Tyre in 332BCE as well as invading Egypt, Alexander defeats Darius at the Battle of Gaugamela. Darius plans to continue his resistance in the eastern satrapies (Sogdia and Bactria), but he is assassinated by his own commanders as part of a coup organized by the powerful satrap Bessus. Persia is now part of Alexander the Great's empire.

The Kings of Persia and Media

Cyaxeres 'King of the Medes and Persians' reigned 625-585BCE

Cyrus I 'King of Anshan in Persia' reigned 600-580BCE

Astyages 'King of the Medes and Persians' reigned 585-550BCE

Cambyses I 'the Great King' reigned in Anshan c.580- c.559BCE

The Kings of The Persian (Achaemenid) Empire

Cyrus II 'the Great/Elder' reigned c.559-530BCE

Cambyses II reigned 530-522BCE

Darius I 'the Great' reigned 522-486BCE

Xerxes I 'the Great' reigned 486-465BCE

Artaxerxes I reigned 465-424BCE

Darius II reigned 424-405BCE

Artaxerxes II reigned 405-358BCE

Artaxerxes III reigned 358-338BCE

Artaxerxes IV reigned 338-336BCE

Darius III reigned 336-330BCE

ORGANIZATION OF THE PERSIAN EMPIRE AND ARMY

The Persian empire was a stratified society, with the Persian nobility at the top of the social ladder, followed by the 'bondsmen', with the slaves bringing up the rear. The arrangement has been characterized by some as feudal in nature and makeup. The organization of the empire was complex but well managed.

Persian Satrapies

The Persians called their provinces satrapies; their governors, satraps. There are five different calculations of the number of the provinces of the Persian empire. The authors of these five versions are Darius I, Herodotus, Darius III, Xerxes and Greek historian Arrian (died 180BCE). Respectively, they list the number of satrapies as 22, 23, 25, 25 and 24. These slight changes in the numbers occurred mainly for two reasons: new conquests by the Persians, and the reorganization of the satrapies in order to be more efficient to govern and control.

The internal organization of the Persian empire prior to its conquest by Alexander and the Macedonian army was efficient, highly organized, and loyal to the central government. It was administered in a generally fair manner and the structure itself was a model of how to govern a large transnational empire. It was obviously also admired by the Macedonians who had no experience in governing such a large tract of land with diverse populations that had their own

Persian Satrapies and Modern Locations

Sometimes the larger satrapies were divided into smaller satrapies to make governing them easier and to lessen the power of the individual satrap.

Satrapy	Modern Location	Ancient People
Arabia	The Arabian Peninsula	Arabs
Arachosia	Southern Afghanistan and Pakistan	Arachosians
Aria	Afghanistan	Arians
Armenia	Turkey	Haykians
Assyria	Iran, Iraq, Turkey, Syria	Assyrians
Babylonia	Iraq	Babylonians
Bactria	Northern Afghanistan	Bactrians
Cappadocia	Central Anatolia, Turkey	Cappadocians
Caria	Western Anatolia, modern Turkey	Carians
Carmania	Iran	Carmanians
Chorasmia	Part of ancient Persia/Iran	Chorasmians
Dahae	Iran, east of the Caspian Sea	Dahaeans
Drangiana (Sarangia)	Parts of Afghanistan and Pakistan	Sarangians
Ecbatana	Part of Iran and Turkey	Ecbatanans
Egypt	Egypt	Egyptians
Elam	Iran	Elamites
Ethiopia	Ethiopia, Eritrea	Nubians
Gandara	Afghanistan	Gandarans
Hyrcania	Iran	Hyrcanians
India	Western India and Pakistan	Indians
Ionia	Coastal Anatolia, Turkey	Ionian Greeks
Libya	North African coast, present-day Libya	Libyans
Lydia	Western Asia Minor, Turkey	Lydians
Maka	Bahrain, Qatar, UAE, parts of Oman, and Pakistan (Sindh Province)	Arabs
Makran	Southern Sindh, Balochistan, Pakistan, Iran, along the coast of the Arabian sea and the Gulf of Oman	Makranians
Media	Parts of Iran and Turkey	Medes
Mesopotamia	Iraq, Kuwait, Turkey, parts of Syria	Babylonians, et al
Parthia	Northeastern Iran	Parthians
Persia (Persis)	Iran	Persians
Sacae	Kazakhstan-Scythian tribes, Iranian origin	Saca/Scythians
Sattagydia	Sindh region of Pakistan	Sattagydians
Scythia	Northern coast of the Black Sea	Scythians
Sogdia/Sogdiana (Samarkand)	Tajikistand and Uzbekistan	Sogdians
Susa	Iran (royal city)	Susans/Elamites
Thrace	Parts of Bulgaria, Greece and Turkey	Thracians

▼ *Detail of a bas-relief of a Persian archer showing the carved top of the bow in the shape of a duck's head.*

ORGANIZATION OF THE PERSIAN EMPIRE AND ARMY 173

traditions and way of life, and its internal organization was therefore left alone by Alexander and his commanders after they defeated the Persian armies and claimed control of the empire.

Army Size

For the second Persian invasion of Greece in 480BCE, the huge Persian army was composed of contingents of the indigenous peoples that made up the multicultural Persian empire. The invasion took place under the leadership of Persian king Xerxes, son of Darius the Great, whose army had been defeated by the Athenians at Marathon ten years earlier.

There is no certain number of the strength of the different contingents of the Persian army. Greek historian Herodotus stated that the size of the Persian army that invaded Greece was 1,700,000 infantry, 80,000 cavalry and 20,000 camel-mounted troops. However, these numbers are probably exaggerated.

A more accurate estimate of the strength of the Persian army is about 200,000–300,000 in total; some historians argue that the actual figure was as low as 30,000, but that is surely too small a number, since we know that the Immortals, the Persian army's elite troops, numbered 10,000 men before any other units are considered.

Army Structure

The Persian army was organized in regular units or regiments (each called a *hazarabam*), each of 1000 men. Every regiment had ten subunits or companies (each called a *sataba*) of 100 men. A company was divided into ten subunits of ten men each, a *dathaba*. The regiment was commanded by a *hazarapatis*, the company by a *satapatis*. The higher organization, a division formed from ten regiments, was called a *baivarabam* and contained 10,000 men. The commander of a Persian division was called a *baivarapatis*.

There is evidence that units were not always kept at full strength – a common feature of all armies, then or now. This was especially true of units on the Persian frontiers, far from the centre of the empire and their traditional recruiting areas. The one Persian division that would always be kept up to full strength was the elite guard, the Immortals (in Persian, *Amrtaka*). The Persian army contained tribal, regional and ethnic contingents who were under their own officers, but overall national contingents were always commanded by trusted Persian senior officers. The Persians and Medes were the best-trained, best-equipped and best-led contingents of the army and were directed by trusted, efficient combat veterans – some of whom were related to the ruling house.

◄ IMMORTAL STANDARD BEARER
This bearer carries the royal standard of the falcon. His clothing is that of the Immortals, who were not only guardsmen at the royal palace but accompanied the king on campaign. His colourful shield is typical of the Immortals and the army of the period.

THE PERSIAN COMMAND AND ARMY ELITE

The Achaemenid empire was founded by Cyrus II in 550BCE. Cyrus was one of the great kings of the ancient world and the empire he founded developed an efficient governmental bureaucracy where some of the high-ranking court officials also held senior commands in the Persian army.

The Hazarapatis and Spearbearers

One of the highest-ranking officials was the Hazarapatis, who, depending on who held the office, might be termed 'the greatest Persian' after the king himself. The Hazarapatis was not only a courtier or bureaucrat, he was also the commander of the Spearbearers Regiment of the Persian army. Those in this elite unit, not belonging to the Persian Immortals, were granted the privilege of wearing royal clothing. They also bore the royal standard of red flag decorated with the royal falcon. It was not rare for Spearbearers to receive gifts from the monarch in the form of highly-decorated weapons. The entire regiment, including the Hazarapatis, carried a hoplon to demonstrate their high status.

'King of Kings'

When in command, Xerxes was decked out in the finest garb – its splendour only fitting for a ruler who claimed the title 'King of Kings'. To witness the performance of his navy against the Greeks at Salamis, he even had a large dais or throne set up for him on the shore overlooking the sea action.

◄ XERXES I
Xerxes, the son of Darius I, organized and led the second Persian invasion of the Grecian mainland, and was finally defeated at the naval battle of Salamis. Here he is wearing the lavish robes and headgear of a Persian monarch.

► IMMORTAL
The king's division was made up of ten regiments of Immortals, each regiment being 1,000 guardsmen. Though the Immortals are usually considered to be picked men, some were not considered to be elite troops.

Persian Senior Command

The Persian commanders were responsible not only for leading the army on campaign and in combat, but also for its organization and the administration. It is notable that these general officers possessed considerable skill in organizing and assembling so large a force for a foreign invasion; they must have had very good administrative skills to keep the army supplied, equipped and fed. These officers also appointed the commanders of all units from the leaders of the smallest basic unit, the *decarchs*, who commanded ten men, to the *hecatonarchs*, who commanded a unit of 100, to the *chiliarchs*, who commanded 1,000 men, and to the division commanders, the *myriarchs*, who commanded 10,000 men.

Reliable Persian commanders were placed in authority over the various national units and contingents from all over the empire, including those from India, North Africa (Egyptians, Libyans and Nubians – whom the Persians called 'Ethiopians'). Greek historian Herodotus named the senior Persian commanders as Gergis, Megabyzus, Masistes, Smerdomenes, Mardonios and Tritantaichmes. Although usually not mentioned, they are the senior Persian generals who organized and led the army into Greece and were responsible for the operations and logistics of that immense effort. Smerdomenes and Tritantaichmes were both related to Xerxes, being sons of the late king Darius's brothers, which may explain why Tritantaichmes was not penalized by the king for his father Artabanos's opposition to the invasion. (His father, of course, was proved correct.)

◀ **Immortal**
This fully armed and equipped infantryman from one of the Immortal regiments carries both a Persian composite bow and arrow quiver, and is also equipped with a spear. His headgear is an alternate to the crown-like cap, and is a form of the Persian tiara. His dress marks him as a member of the Persian king's bodyguard.

▼ **Immortal**
This is a member of the king's division, the Immortals (as pictured in Darius' palace in Susa on glazed-brick friezes, see page 164). He is in formal palace wear along with the usual spear and bow. Each unit of the Royal Guard dressed in a distinctive colour.

The Immortals

The elite regiment that formed the core of the Persian army from Darius I to Darius III, the Immortals, was famous for the gold its members wore or carried on their person. Some of this precious metal was perhaps looted by the Spartans after they had humiliated the notionally invincible Immortals at the Pass of Thermopylae in 480BCE. Invincible or otherwise, the Immortals were considered an essential part of the Persian military system. Their strength was always maintained at 10,000, no matter the circumstances: this is why they were called 'Immortals', because their numbers were always kept to full strength, and if a member of the troop died on a campaign or engagement he would be replaced without delay. At the time of the invasions of Greece, the commander of the Immortals was Hydarnes, a subordinate trusted by the king.

The elite corps were organized sometimes by the colour of their clothing – blue, red and others if necessary. This would make it easy to identify the different regiments on the battlefield in the middle of the melée, and the casualties.

The Immortals sometimes wore – usually as formal or court wear – ankle-length robes along with their arms and equipment.

◂ **IMMORTAL STANDARD BEARER**
By his dress and shield, as well as his headgear, this infantryman clearly belongs to one of the Immortal regiments. His standard is that of the Persian royal falcon and he does not appear to be armed, though undoubtedly he would have at least a sword on campaign and might also be armed with a bow.

▲ *Relief carving of Immortals on the walls of the palace in Persepolis built by Xerxes I and Artaxerxes I in the 5th century BCE.*

On his head an Immortal wore a Persian tiara, a type of headgear that protected him from the elements, but failed to offer much resistance to a determined blow from an iron weapon. The tiara was worn two ways: a person of royal blood wore the tiara straight up on top of his head, but a commoner wore the headgear with its top flopped over, rather along the lines of a beret.

The Persians and Medes who made up the bulk of the Persian army and gave it a solid core of reliable troops had not only what would be considered 'full dress' in modern times, but also a 'field' or 'campaign dress'. An Immortal infantryman in the Persian version of field dress would wear patterned trousers and multi-coloured tunic with a figure of eight wicker shield, which was usually covered with hide. This type of shield was adequate for the type of warfare to which the Persians were accustomed, the kind of engagement typical in Asia and in Eastern Europe; but against the Greeks and later the Macedonians, who were better-armed and -armoured, this Persian shield proved inadequate as it did not stop the thrust of the iron weapons used by those troops.

An Immortal wore a cuirass of scale armour under his tunic. Like all Persian or Median infantry, the elite Immortals carried a powerful composite bow, which was their main weapon. In fighting the well-protected Greek hoplites however, the bow proved largely ineffective. The Immortals also carried a short sword or dagger similar to the Greek type, and a short thrusting spear. The spear had an iron head and a spherical counterweight cast in silver. (Officers in the Immortal corps had a gold counterweight.) Tactically, although the Immortals were professional soldiers, and were tough, well-trained and hard-fighting troops, they were no match for the Greeks massed in the phalanx, and in a melée were at a distinct disadvantage.

The Immortals had their own logistical system and support, separate from the rest of the army. On campaign the Immortals were followed by a supply wagon train containing carriages, mules and camels and carrying personal servants and concubines as well as food and war materials. The food supplies were of higher quality than the fare provided for the rest of the army, reserved for soldiers in the Immortals.

Persian Standards

Persian standard bearers carried their unit standard alongside or near their commander. This not only identified the unit and allowed unit-members to know where their standard was, but also located the position of the unit commander – enabling men to rally after a melée or if they became broken up in battle.

Some standards do not appear to have been a flag, *per se*, but more a fixed emblem used to identify the different units. Persian standard bearers appear to have worn animal skins, as those of Rome would also in a later age. While some standards were rigid, many were more flag than identifier and definitely represented a step in the development of military standards. They were well made, probably from richly embroidered cloth. The king's standard was carried by a picked man, one of the king's bodyguards armed as an infantryman with the exception of a spear. He had a shield and carried a composite bow. For self-protection, the standard bearer would also carry either a dagger or a short sword. His standard would stay close to the king, to denote the king's position in the field. The personal standard of Cyrus the Great was a falcon (a symbol also used by the ancient Egyptians, who depicted the god Horus as a man with a falcon's head), with wings spread and the head turned to its left. The border of the standard was alternate black and sky blue triangles, all on on a sky blue field. King Xerxes's standard was a version of Cyrus the Great's falcon standard, except that the main colour was red, instead of Cyrus's sky blue.

▶ **STANDARD BEARER**
The brightly striped clothing of Median origin marks out this infantryman as a standard bearer. The wolfskin headdress was also common attire for a Persian standard bearer. They were also at times armed with a bow and quiver of arrows, but in this case he carries a multi-coloured striped shield and sword.

Military Training

Persian military training was compulsory for both the nobility and the 'bondsmen'. Greek historians Herodotus (c.484–430BCE) and Xenophon (c.430–c.354BCE) both remarked on the quality of Persian training and military organization. Strabo (64BCE–23CE), a later Greek historian, philosopher and geographer, also commented on the methods used for the raising and training of the Persian army. Persian children probably began their military training by the time they were five years old, when they were introduced to horsemanship and archery, the two most valued skills in the Persian army.

Elite Infantrymen

Contemporary Persian artefacts demonstrate the full panoply (body armour) of Persian elite infantrymen, together with the arms, armour and equipment of the regular Persian and Median infantry who invaded Greece under Darius I and Xerxes in 490 and 480BCE or fought the armies of Alexander the Great in the 4th century BCE. This was not, however,

◀ **Immortal**
This infantryman is in full field kit, ready for march or combat. He carries the Persian figure of eight wicker shield along with his spear, his main weapon of choice. He would also have a bow and quiver and a short sword. His headgear is a tiara.

▼ **Guard Infantryman**
This is the typical dress of a guardsman when not on campaign. The long robes were eventually abandoned by the Achaemenid troops, the usual wartime attire then being Median trousers and a knee-length tunic.

THE PERSIAN COMMAND AND ARMY ELITE

◀ Relief carving of Persian guards from the walls of Persepolis, the ceremonial capital of the Achaemenid empire in the 5th century BCE. Of particular note is the uniformity of dress and headgear as well as shields and spears.

the campaign dress of these troops. These infantrymen were armed with spear, composite bow and sword and equipped with a shield, this being of different shapes and designs, from a simple rectangular wicker shield to the more complicated figure of eight shield, so-called by modern historians and authors became of its elliptical shape, with a crescent cut out of each side midway down the shield.

As in all ancient armies, the Persian senior-ranking officers were clothed, armed and equipped in a more elaborate style than the troops they led. They could thus be seen and quickly identified by their troops on the battlefield. Their body protection consisted either of scale armour, composed of metal plates sewn onto a leather or padded undergarment, or lamellar armour, perhaps in the form of an armoured shirt worn over a leather or padded undergarment. Some might wear an elaborate, easily identified helmet – often in the Greek style favoured by their enemy.

The lower-ranking Persian officers, however, of the smaller national contingents, were dressed, equipped and armed more similarly to the men they commanded; whereas the Persian commanders wore Persian and Median dress, the national contingents were commanded by native officers who wore clothing that reflected their local origin or satrapy.

This general lack of uniformity of dress as well as arms and armour among the many Persian contingents was 'normal' for an army of this level of cultural diversity. It meant the army as a whole was non-cohesive, unlike the Greeks. Greek contingents, even hailing from the different city-states, would enjoy a uniformity and sophistication of arms and armour not seen in the Persian force.

▶ OFFICER
This officer is in off-duty camp dress of trousers and tunic along with a Phrygian-type cap and a military cloak. He is armed with both a dagger and a sword along with leather belt and baldric. In combat the cloak would not be worn, and the officer might have some type of armour to protect his torso and probably a shield as well.

Persian Battle Array

Along with the foot archers and slingers, the Persian army typically deployed the light infantry in the front, with the cavalry on the flanks and the heavy infantry in support. If necessary, the Persian missile troops would be supported by the elite *sparabara*, who would form a shield wall to protect the archers and light infantry spearmen while they were in action. This was especially essential in certain tactical situations because the Persian bowmen were not trained in hand-to-hand combat and it is quite probable that the slingers were not either. The commanding officer would typically choose a point in the centre ground, preferably on raised ground, where he was best protected and could direct the engagement with the enemy.

The archers and slingers fired, then the heavy infantry marched forward, fighting with sword and spear, with cavalry support from the flanks. When the army encountered Greek hoplites, these tactics were less than effective: the well-armoured hoplites were not bothered by arrows or the stone or lead missiles sent over by the archers and slingers, and in hand-to-hand combat could overcome the Persians, not because they were braver but because they were better armed and equipped.

The Persian infantry were known for their commitment and bravery when fighting for a gifted general, but if the general was killed or captured then the infantrymen were liable to break and flee. There was certainly honour to be won on the battlefield: the commander would note down the names of those who particularly distinguished themselves in combat. Both Darius and Xerxes had their royal scribe beside them in major battles to keep a written record of the names of those who fought bravely.

The Army on Campaign

The Persian army usually embarked on campaign in the early part of spring. As it marched, the royal standard and religious symbols were carried in the army's centre. There were chariots sacred to the gods Ahura Mazda and Mithra, surrounded by chanting priests. When possible supplies were prepared and stored along the route of the march in guarded reserve areas, but baggage trains also came along with the marching troops. Mounted scouts rode ahead of the main body of the army. The king and his commanders had an efficient system in place, of couriers and fire-towers to send and receive messages.

The Persians did not tend to march or attack by night. The army would encamp on flat ground, digging out a ditch and putting up a sand-bag barrier around the site. If they encountered rivers, they used rafts or bridges of boats, if they could not ride and march across. The logistic efforts must have been immense.

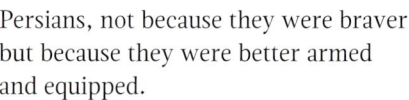

◀ **SPARABARA**
The sparabara were derived from the earlier Persian archer pair, where one would be the bowman and the other would carry a spara or pavise, a large shield used to protect the archer when firing. The sparabara, Persian for 'pavise bearers', carried the large rectangular shield as shown and in this case wore scale armour that protected the torso as well as spear and sword.

THE PERSIAN COMMAND AND ARMY ELITE

A Variety of Uniform

The Persian army's arms and armour, as well as major equipment, was not consistent. Each different contingent would be armed and equipped as they would be in their home territory. The Persian troops were more used to fighting in the east, so would have been ill prepared to encounter the identically armed and armoured Greeks and Macedonians. For example, the Persians for the most part would be equipped with wicker shields that could not stop a Greek or Macedonian javelin or spear, and the infantry would be at a great disadvantage having to face the massed Greek or Macedonian phalanx. Greek arms and armour would have a robustness not seen in the Persian ranks. The Persians would sometimes make up for this shortcoming by repurposing captured Greek equipment.

▲ IMMORTAL OFFICER
The officers of the Immortals, like the men they commanded and led, wore armour but usually over their tunics. This officer does not, however, wear a helmet, instead wearing the native Persian headgear sometimes referred to as a tiara.

◄ IMMORTAL
This is a fully armed and equipped man from one of the Immortal regiments ready for field service. Persian heavy infantry, especially the Immortals, would be armed with both bow and spear, although it might have been awkward to have both in certain situations. His sword is attached to his belt. This soldier is carrying the older-type wicker shield.

THE PERSIAN CAVALRY

The cavalry was essential to the success of the Persian army from the time of Cyrus the Great onwards. Along with the archers, cavalrymen could be considered the elite of the army. While they were certainly superior to the Greek horsemen they faced in 480BCE, the Persian cavalry met their match in the mobile mounted troops of the Macedonian armies of Philip and Alexander 150 years later.

The Cavalry under Xerxes

Greek historian Herodotus noted that the Persian cavalry in Xerxes' army of invasion in 480BCE numbered 80,000 men. While that total is probably too many, as was Herodotus's estimate for the total strength of the Persians, the true number was undoubtedly a high one.

Native Persian horsemen in this army were dressed, armed and equipped in the same manner as the Persian infantry. Likewise, amongst the national groupings, the cavalries of the Medes and Kissians were equipped and dressed just like their respective infantries. Some Persian cavalry wore an elaborate metal helmet of iron or bronze with a horsehair crest that ran from front to rear on its top.

The cavalry contingents of the various satrapies rode with their own infantry, with the exception of those contingents mounted on camels. Camels and horses did not get along, probably because of the smells of the different animals or the habit the camels had of spitting.

The commanders of the Persian cavalry under Xerxes in the campaign against Greece in 480BCE were the generals Tithaeus and Harmamithres.

▶ **HEAVY CAVALRYMAN**
This cavalryman is uniformed in typical Persian-style clothing and his armour is of brass scales over a linen jerkin. While here he is only armed with a sword, he would normally carry javelins that would be thrown while mounted.

THE PERSIAN CAVALRY

A third man, Pharnuches, had been appointed but before the expedition set out to invade the Greek mainland, he was badly hurt when he was thrown from his horse: a dog had run between the horses legs and startled Pharnuches's mount, the horse rearing and the general being violently thrown off. Pharnuches vomited blood. He was so angry at the horse's actions that he ordered his servants to kill the animal. Pharnuches developed pneumonia or consumption and did not participate in the expedition. He was discharged from his position of responsibility.

Mercenary Cavalry

Many if not all the national contingents in the army of 480 BCE supplied cavalry. The Persian mercenary cavalry was partly composed of light cavalry armed with a rope lasso, together with a short sword or dagger for self defence. Some of these light horsemen also carried a battle-axe for close combat.

Notable among the national cavalry contingents were the Sagartians. They were armed with iron daggers, but that was their only conventional weapon. Their main weapon was neither lance nor bow, but lasso, made of plaited leather, with a loop at one end. In combat, the Sagartians would engage the enemy by throwing their lassos from the saddle in an attempt to catch either the enemy soldier or horse with the loop. If they caught their target, they would drag the rider or horse towards them, then kill the near-helpless enemy or animal – who was unable to move properly while entangled in the loop of the lasso. In the order of battle of the army, the Sagartians were brigaded and/or attached to the Persian horse. The Sagartian cavalry, like their infantry, wore a type of Persian dress that had been influenced by the Paktyikans (from what is now southeast Afghanistan). Other Asian tribes allied to or owing allegiance to the Persian king provided cavalry that were armed, equipped, dressed and armoured in the same manner as their respective infantry, for

▲ **MERCENARY CAVALRYMAN**
This light cavalryman could be a Sagartian, a member of a nomadic tribe that fought with what was in effect a lasso. As well as a dagger, they could also be armed with an axe. Other Nomadic tribes in eastern Persia as well as central Asia also used the lasso.

▶ **LIGHT CAVALRYMAN**
This is a light horseman from a nomadic tribe, probably from central Asia or perhaps Anatolia. His horsemanship would be excellent. He is lightly armed with a spear; he does not carry a shield or wear body armour.

184 ARMIES OF THE PERSIAN EMPIRE

▲ A 19th-century tinted engraving visualizes King Cyrus I. In reality the king would be unlikely to lead troops in battle in such formal dress.

instance the Indians, Caspians, Bactrians, Parikanians and Arabs. The Libyans, whose mounted arm consisted only of chariots, were also the same in appearance and armament as their infantry.

The Indian mounted arm was the most diverse in the Persian army. Its members were equipped with chariots, but also mounted on horses. The teams for the chariots were composed of either horses or wild asses. The mounted contingents of the Arabs, Caspians and Parikanians were all mounted on camels. Camel-mounted troops were considered cavalry and did engage on the battlefield in mounted action, even against horse-mounted cavalry. The camel was kept in use for at least as long as the horse by armies or armies that employed mounted troops.

The Cavalry of Cyrus the Younger

In the early 5th century BCE elite cavalry served in the bodyguard of the prince and satrap of Lydia and Ionia, Cyrus the Younger, who attempted to unseat his elder brother Artaxerxes II (reigned 404–358BCE) from the Persian throne. These troops wore a cuirass of stiffened linen and scale armour, together with loose-fitting

◀ GUARD CAVALRYMAN
This horseman is one of the troopers that formed the bodyguard of Cyrus the Younger and the Greek influence is quite evident, especially with the Greek-style helmet and plume. His armour and that of his horse is of linen reinforced with bronze scales. He is armed with javelins and would most probably also be armed with a Greek sword. Clothing and equipment were generally consistent for this era of the Persian empire.

◀ Light Cavalryman

Dressed in Median-style clothing as all or nearly all Persian cavalry were, this light cavalryman, intended for skirmishing, scouting, and pursuing a broken enemy, is armed only with javelins which could be thrown while mounted. He has neither armour nor shield. His kit would be relatively inexpensive, contrary to that of the heavy cavalry or horse archers. Persian light cavalry were probably recruited from the outlying satrapies.

▼ Light Cavalryman/ Horse Archer

Persian cavalrymen often wore Median clothing as it was much more suited for wear by mounted troops. This was the usual practice in the Persian army, no matter what the troops' ethnicity, or to what satrap they belonged.

scale armour on the legs, soft boots and bronze plumed helmets.

They carried a short sword similar to the Greek 60cm (2ft) model, and javelins for throwing. The 'saddle' on their mount was little more than a thick blanket. Their horse was partially armoured, equipped with a bronze chaffron and a scale armour skirt that covered its chest. The bridle and head harness were of leather with brass reinforcements.

The Light Cavalry

The Persian light cavalryman was equipped with lance and composite bow, together with large quiver, but carried no shield. He was generally unarmoured – and could be classed as a light horse archer. His clothing was of at least two types. He might wear either a knee-length robe or a short tunic and trousers of multicoloured cloth. A longer robe was probably not comfortable or easy to manage for a mounted warrior. The multicoloured trousers were probably a unit identifier. The tunic and trousers could match, but that was not required. He wore a Persian tiara.

Persian light cavalry could be variously armed depending on what part of the empire they were recruited from. Even then, their arms could vary in each unit. Light cavalry, while usually wearing typical Persian armour, might also 'adopt' captured Greek armour, such as a light linen cuirass.

The Macedonian Impact

At the beginning of the Macedonian invasion in 330 BCE, the Persians probably underestimated the Macedonian cavalry. They were soon surprised, and very unpleasantly, when they met the Macedonian cavalry on the battlefield. The Persians had met their match. As good as the horsemen were, they were not the equal of the Macedonian mounted arm, notably the Companion cavalry commanded by Alexander, who were the elite of the Macedonian army.

Persian cavalrymen did not usually wear elaborate armour or a helmet. When they did, in this period, the helmet was influenced by Greek design. They carried an oddly shaped cut-out crescent shield (see page 198) whose unusual design may be attributed to its connection to some of the minor contingents within the huge Persian empire.

The Persian cuirass, though still of scale armour, would later develop into lamellar armour, covering both the front and back of the horseman, and this would later develop into the fully armoured heavy cavalryman, the cataphract, which style would also be adopted by the Eastern Romans. The later addition of the stirrup, unknown at this time, would make the cataphract a very effective offensive weapon.

▲ **LIGHT CAVALRYMAN**
The cloak of this light cavalryman has an inside lining of leopardskin. He is armed and equipped as a typical light cavalryman with lance and sword and his shabraque is impressively embroidered. The horse panoply was simple but elegant. The horse's tack was composed of a simple bridle, an iron bit and leather reins. There was no saddle, but a heavy saddle blanket eased the cavalryman's discomfort when moving at speed.

▶ **LIGHT CAVALRYMAN**
This light horseman is armed only with a spear or lance, putting him at a disadvantage against an armoured combatant in a melée. His embroidered shabraque is noteworthy. National cavalry units were often locally recruited.

◄ CHARIOT
The heavy Persian chariot drawn by four horses is reminiscent of the older Assyrian chariot that was part of their mounted arm. The Persian chariot, however, was most probably not used for combat but for the king to use as a mobile command post.

► HEAVY CAVALRYMAN
As this example shows, the Persians were also developing armoured heavy cavalry. This was greatly influenced by contemporary 'cataphracts', the extra-heavy cavalry that was raised by Achaemenid monarchs in the frontier regions of Bactria and Sogdia.

The Persian Chariots

When Persian prince Cyrus the Younger led a revolt against his brother King Artaxerxes II, he employed chariots with scythe-like blades attached to the wheel hubs in the field. These could be a powerfully effective weapon in a charge against both cavalry and infantry since they could brutally dismember both horses and men.

The Persians may have been the first army to develop and use the quadriga, a four-horse team for larger chariots, although there is evidence that the Assyrians had earlier made use of a quadriga with their heavy-wheeled chariots (see page 54). But the Persians certainly invented scythe-equipped chariots. Naturally enough, if these chariots were not deployed sensibly, they could be as great a danger to your own troops as to the enemy. An out-of-control horse team due to either accident or casualties among the chariot's crew would undoubtedly pose a threat to troops on both sides.

Persian chariot crews were armoured in scale or lamellar armour. They did not wear helmets, but soft headgear, perhaps of Phrygian design. All members of the two- to three-man crew were armed save the driver: they carried a composite bow or javelin, or both.

THE PERSIAN LIGHT INFANTRY

Achaemenid Infantry

The army of the empire that fought for Cyrus and his successors contained contingents with differing battledress and weapons from across the vast territories the Persian kings governed. The Persians and Medes themselves were largely dressed and armed alike – indeed, according to Greek historian Herodotus, the two groups were so much alike on the battlefield as to be indistinguishable.

The dress, arms and equipment Herodotus saw were largely adopted by the Persians from the Medes. Their headgear was not a helmet, but a soft hat called a tiara, which was similar to an Arab headdress. They wore multicoloured trousers that reached as far as their ankles. Their tunics, which came down to mid-thigh and sometimes almost to their knees, were also multicoloured.

They wore chest and back armour, which was either scale or lamellar and was attached to a type of undershirt and worn under their tunics.

Their footwear was a type of moccasin and tied at the ankle. They were armed with a short thrusting spear and wicker shields that were not strong or robust enough to withstand the iron weapons of the Greeks. They were also armed with long bows, along with quivers that were worn on their backs. Their arrows were made from swamp reeds and had iron heads.

Local Differences

The Persian empire established by Cyrus II (the Great) conquered and absorbed the ancient empires and peoples that preceded the rising of the Persians and Medes. By that assimilation, older, traditional clothing, arms and equipment were extended in use among the new subject peoples – not only was using traditional weapons and equipment comfortable for them, but it also saved expenditure for their new Persian rulers.

Later, as the empire became consolidated and the government more firmly established, greater uniformity was enforced in weapons, arms and equipment. Nevertheless at the time of the second Persian invasion of Greece in 480BCE – when the huge Persian army consisted of national contingents from the entire empire, as well as the usual mainstay of Persians and Medes – native clothing, arms, weapons and military equipment were still in use, with national contingents differently

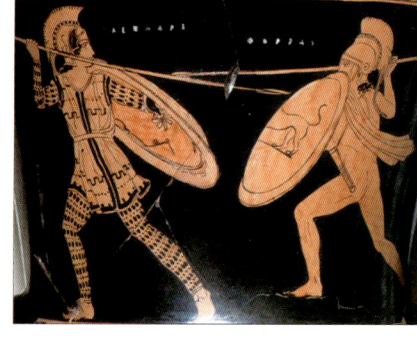

▲ This vase shows a Persian soldier almost running away from the attacking Greek hoplite. Persians were fine soldiers, despite defeats on land and sea in 480BCE and 479BCE, but Greek hoplites were better infantry than their Persian counterparts, as was demonstrated at the battle of Plataea.

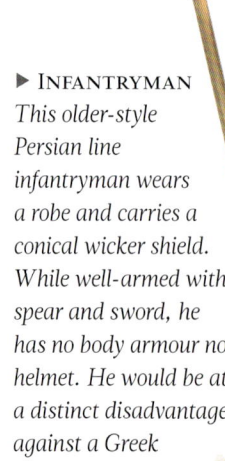

▶ INFANTRYMAN
This older-style Persian line infantryman wears a robe and carries a conical wicker shield. While well-armed with spear and sword, he has no body armour nor helmet. He would be at a distinct disadvantage against a Greek hoplite.

dressed and equipped depending on their origins.

In the multicultural imperial army, the Bactrian contingent wore clothing and headgear similar to the Medes. They were armed with both bows and short, thrusting spears, the bows being constructed of reeds, which appears to have been a popular method and material for making bows in Asia.

Clothing and Weapons

The infantryman wore a type of cloth cuirass that was reinforced with metal. There was a progressive use of scale and lamellar armour over linen cuirasses. The soldiers were usually dressed in two types of clothing: in one case, a short tunic and trousers; in the other, a robe worn over a tunic.

The infantry did not wear a helmet, but the usual tiara. This tiara headpiece would be worn flopped over, to denote non-royal status. Among the different contingents, the tiara was the normal headgear for the Persians and Medes; those of Arab origin wore turbans, while other troops preferred conical iron helmets – which gave excellent protection for the head. Persian infantry were armed with a composite bow and quiver that was worn on their backs. The arrows were made from swamp reeds and had iron heads.

So-armed, the infantry would consider their bow to be their primary arm, which would put them at a disadvantage in close combat with Greek or Macedonian infantry. They were also armed with a short thrusting spear and wicker shield that was not strong or robust enough to withstand the iron weapons of the Greeks. The troops carried a

▶ **Infantryman**
This line infantryman is more modern in appearance, having adopted Median clothing of tunic and trousers, but he is still without armour of any kind. His shield is an older figure of eight wooden type, but he is typically armed with sword and spear.

▲ **Light Infantryman**
This javelin man carries two or three. He is unarmoured, but does wear the now-usual Median dress. He also carries for self-defence an unusually-shaped sword, which is a derivative of the Lycian sickle sword.

short spear, a short sword or dagger on the right side, and a shield that could be round, oblong, rectangular or an irregularly shaped shield that was probably Phrygian in origin.

Two secondary weapons used by the Persians were the battle-axe and a small war-hammer. The axe was very modern in appearance and would have been familiar to a Western medieval knight. The small war-hammer was very effective in close combat against an enemy that wore iron helmets.

Improved Protection

As time progressed and experience against the heavily armoured Greek infantry left its mark, Persian infantry and cavalry became more heavily armoured themselves, and weapons and equipment were modified. Metal scales were affixed to the linen cuirass, sewn into the fabric so that they

◀ **KARDAKE INFANTRYMAN**
Kardakes were Persian 'imitation hoplites', heavy infantrymen equipped with hoplite shields, created during the late empire to face the Greeks on equal terms. This heavy infantryman has a cuirass, this time of stiffened or reinforced linen. He is armed with the usual spear, a sword with a baldric, and round, metal-faced shield.

▼ **ARMOURED INFANTRYMAN**
This well-equipped and very well-armed infantryman wears scale armour that covers the torso and he is armed with a stout spear with a round counterweight on the butt. His shield is covered in metal and he also carries a sword. On his head he wears the typical Persian tiara. These two infantrymen's cuirasses definitely show Greek influence.

overlapped and provided adequate protection against arrows and edged weapons. The shields used became more rounded – very similar to the Greek hoplon shield – and were used in conjunction with the short thrusting spear. This still put them at a disadvantage against the Macedonian hypaspists and phalangites, but it was a great improvement over the wicker shields. Combining their new armour with a round shield, a Persian infantryman was able at least to hold his own against the Macedonian heavy infantry, if he was properly led.

Archers

The Persians completely outclassed their Greek and Macedonian opponents in fielding and employing large numbers of skilled archers.

The army utilized archers in large numbers from various satrapies. Their skill and training varied according to which province the troops were recruited from. The Medes were undoubtedly skilled archers, and

▲ *Black-figure pottery plate depicting an archer in Persian dress, 6th century BCE.*

Median dress is often seen where a Persian archer is depicted. Long trousers, tight at the ankle, along with a long-skirted tunic, were usually worn in a variety of colours and the tunic sleeves were drawn tight at the wrist, which undoubtedly helped when shooting. Sashes of various colours were worn around the archer's waist.

Headgear was as varied as the provinces from which the archers came. Most common was probably the popular Phrygian cap which also could offer protection for the ears and side of the head and face.

Armour was usually not worn, as archers were light infantry, but sometimes it was used to offer at least some protection when employed as a skirmisher and in the line of battle. Some Persian foot archers in the later years of the empire were also equipped with a round shield similar to the Greek hoplon.

When using the bow, the foot archer wore his shield across his back – an arrangement that allowed him to move freely and easily in using the bow, while also providing welcome protection for the bowman's back.

Persian Immortals were also armed with a bow and a quiver of arrows along with the spear and sidearms. The quiver for all archers was designed to carry both the bow and the arrows.

The Persians employed horse archers effectively and these may have been the best trained and skilled in the army. Not only did they have

◀ **Archer**
This well-equipped bowman is dressed in Median style and could very well be a dismounted horse archer. His headgear is the Persian tiara and he carries a simple bow, not a composite one. For self-defence in close combat he carries an axe.

▶ **Archer**
This well-equipped archer not only is armed with a powerful composite bow, but also has a sword and shield. Typically for the Persian army, he does not have any body armour. His headgear is what appears to be a form of Phrygian cap.

▶ **Archer**
This bowman is a light infantryman, intended for skirmishing, and would be supported by other light infantry armed with spears and shields. He wears no armour, but his quiver is large enough to also carry his composite bow. The quiver also has a top to protect both his bow and arrows when not in use.

to be competent horsemen, but they had to be able to shoot effectively when moving at speed. Whether they employed what would later be known as the 'Parthian shot' (turning on the horse and shooting over the horse's hindquarters) is relatively unknown. However, it is not doubted that at least some of them could perform this impressive manoeuvre.

Composite Bows

As already mentioned, there were various types of bows used by Persian archers and there was no army-wide standard used. The composite bow, when properly constructed, was undoubtedly the best and it required a strong, skilled archer to use one effectively.

The Persians, like the Scythians, used a composite bow constructed of bone and wood, with the different parts glued together. It was used by both infantry and cavalry. The Greeks and others used a simpler bow, not so powerful or long-ranged as the composite bow, but effective enough within its range. Along with the sling and the javelin, the bow – of whatever type – was the principal missile weapon of the Ancient World and remained so until the advent of gunpowder on European battlefields in the 14th century CE.

THE PERSIAN LIGHT INFANTRY

▼ **Archer**
This is a Median archer, as is evident from his distinctive headdress. His composite bow and quiver of arrows are both carried together and he is also armed with a spear. His quiver would usually be carried over the shoulder with a leather strap, but in this case it is attached at the waist.

◄ **Archer**
This well-turned out bowman is not only well-clothed and well-shod, but he has a linen cuirass of Greek type which suits his function in combat very well. It offers him good protection yet is light and comfortable enough to give him freedom of movement. His composite bow and quiver are Persian in design and he is also armed with a formidable dagger or short sword.

▶ The Parthian shot became famous through history, as evidenced by this 19th-century French illustration. It is probable that some Persian archers did execute this skilful technique.

GREEK MERCENARIES IN THE SERVICE OF PERSIA

Along with almost every ancient army, the Persians employed mercenaries to supplement their regular army and its national contingents. Greek mercenaries were the ones most frequently recruited. Without doubt, the most celebrated Greek mercenary troops to serve the Persians were the 10,000 who fought for Prince Cyrus the Younger in his attempt to take the Persian throne from his brother, Artaxerxes II; those who made the 'March of the Ten Thousand' homeward to Greece after the Battle of Cunaxa in 401BCE, as described by Greek historian Xenophon in his work *Anabasis*.

The Battle of Cunaxa and 'The March of the Ten Thousand'

In 401BCE Cyrus's cavalry lined up alongside 10,000 Greek mercenaries in the Battle of Cunaxa. The rebel Cyrus won against Artaxerxes, but was killed by a javelin thrust during the battle when he attempted to take the fight

◀ GREEK MERCENARY
The Persians employed Greek hoplite mercenaries against Alexander. They were armed and equipped as typical hoplites of the period, though they would be outclassed by the Macedonian phalangites mainly because of the length of their spears, being shorter than the Macedonian sarissas. Alexander would show no mercy to them when they fought against him, and thousands were slaughtered at the Battle of Issus.

▲ *The 10,000 Greek mercenaries were forced to flee back to Greece to escape retribution after Cyrus's defeat at the Battle of Cunaxa in 401BCE. As recorded by Xenophon, on seeing the sea, they cried out 'Thalatta, Thalatta!' ('The sea, the sea!'). Litho by Bernard Granville Baker, 1901.*

personally to his brother. Cyrus was later found under a heap of slain enemy troops. After his death, the rebel forces fled, save the Greeks, who did not know that Cyrus had died and fought on, winning the battle.

Since their employer was now dead, the Greeks were offered a truce by Artaxerxes. They agreed to enter into negotiations, and the senior Greek commanders went to the Persian camp to meet with the representatives of Artaxerxes, led by Tissaphernes. The Greek commander Clearchus was accompanied by his immediate subordinate commanders, five generals and 20 captains, and escorted by 200 hoplites. Lulled into a false sense of security by the Persians, Clearchus and the five generals were captured, and his men were surprised and murdered by Persian cavalrymen lying in ambush; the 200 hoplites were slaughtered almost to a man. One badly wounded survivor, Niarchos the Arcadian, made it back to alert the Greeks in their camp, stammered out his warning before dying from his wounds. The furious Greeks stood to arms. Clearchus and his five generals were beheaded by the Persians.

Persian cavalry was ranging in the plain between the two encampments, hunting down every Greek they could find. The Greek hoplites, watching from their camp as the Persian cavalry came closer to them, immediately sprang to arms at an alarm and prepared to fight. The Persians demanded their surrender, announcing that Clearchus and the others had been killed and that the Greeks should give themselves up to the conditional mercy of the Persian king, Artaxerxes.

Having witnessed what Persian 'mercy' was like, the defiant Greeks told the Persians to be gone, and quickly prepared to march or fight. After the Persians had left the Greeks elected new commanders, one of whom was the young Athenian Xenophon (c.430–c.354BCE), the later historian and author of the chronicle of the Greeks return home, *Anabasis* ('March Upcountry'). Under their new commanders, the 10,000 Greeks marched for home. That they brought their troops out is an inspiring story of courage, leadership, and fortitude. Xenophon records the joyful moment when the 10,000 (by then actually far fewer) finally saw the sea signifying their escape (the southern coast of the Black Sea), whereupon they shouted 'Thalatta! Thalatta!' ('The sea! The sea!').

Greek Mercenary Armour

After Alexander's invasion of the Persian empire, the Greek mercenary infantry who served Darius III, and who were defeated and destroyed by the Macedonians, were armed and basically equipped according to the reforms of the Athenian general Iphicrates (c.418–c.353BCE), who improved the equipment of Greek mercenaries.

Under Iphicrates's reforms, the hoplite panoply (body armour) was made simpler and lighter, with the helmet also redesigned to be less massive and without its horsehair crest. The new helmet design was better suited to troops who fought in close order, because it meant that they could see more clearly and had better peripheral vision, and while the ears and cheeks were protected, there was less metal around the ears – which made it much easier to hear directions or instructions on the battlefield.

The hoplon shield was made somewhat smaller, but the typical Greek short sword remained unchanged, and the traditional spear remained about the same length, at 3m (10ft) – this put the hoplite mercenaries at a distinct disadvantage when engaging with the Macedonian heavy infantry who were armed with the sarissa, which was 5.4–6m (18–20ft) long. This was demonstrated at the Battle of Granicus, where the Greek mercenaries in the army of Darius III were destroyed by the combined action of the Macedonian phalangites and Alexander's Companion cavalry. This battle included a direct encounter between the Greek mercenaries and the Macedonian spearmen in which the longer reach of the sarissa was a decisive factor and enabled the Macedonians to inflict fatal wounds on the Greeks while themselves remaining in safety.

◀ **IMITATION HOPLITE (KARDAKE)**
The Persians realized through hard experience that their wicker and wooden shields were not effective against Greek hoplites. This round, metal-faced shield, similar to a hoplon, was adopted for their heavy infantry. This 'Kardake' soldier also has a leather cuirass with brass studs and would also have a sword. He still wears, though, a Phrygian-type soft headdress.

NATIONAL CONTIGENTS IN A MULTICULTURAL ARMY

The backbone of the Persian army lay in the large numbers of Persians and Medes organized in permanent units, but they were complemented by national contingents from the empire whose members served as auxiliaries. They boosted the army's numbers, but probably did not increase its quality. The fact that the national contingents were all commanded by trusted Persian senior officers is an indication that the subject national contingents were not considered to be as reliable as the native Persians and Medes.

Native Persians and Medes were usually armed with a composite bow and arrow quiver, in addition to their other weapons, but national contingents may or may not have had archers, depending on their place of origin. Their weapons and equipment were issued at home and not by the Persian authorities. For instance some, such as the Indians, always had skilled archers, but others did not. Some of the national or tribal contingents of the Persian army might even come to fight virtually unarmoured – each warrior being equipped only with a spear and shield and perhaps having tribal markings on his face.

The minor contingents in the Persian army in 480BCE included the Caspians, Sarangians, Pakytes, Parikanians and Otians – who were variously armed with reed bows, swords and daggers and spears.

The Sarangians were noted as being armed with the same type of spear that the Medes used. These units were usually tribal and were clothed in animal skin cloaks. The Sarangians were known for wearing knee-high boots and clothing dyed in bright colours.

The Arabian contingent wore their loose, native clothing tied with a belt. They were armed with long bows, probably of a composite design. The Egyptian, Libyan and Nubian troops – whom the Persians called 'Ethiopians' – were like some other early warlike peoples, such as the Celts of Europe, in that they painted their bodies before going into battle. The 'Ethiopians' would coat one half of their body with chalk, and the other with a red-ochre pigment.

There were many other minor contingents assembled by the Persians for the invasion of mainland Greece under Xerxes. The Paphlagonians, Ligyeans, Matienans, Mariandyni and the Syrians were all dressed alike and their arms and equipment were similar if not exactly the same. All were armed with short thrusting spears along with small shields and they wore a plaited helmet. Their arms included javelins and daggers, and they wore boots that came up to the middle of their calves.

Some of the contingents that accompanied the invasion were armed and equipped similarly to the Greeks. The Lydians were an example. The Mysians were a similar contingent, but were less impressively armed, with fire-sharpened javelins. Two additional contingents, the Chalybes

▶ **TAKABARA INFANTRYMAN**
This soldier is a 'Takabara', or Persian 'imitation peltast'. The shield is the same used by the Thracian peltasts. The fully armed and equipped infantryman is armed with a crescent-shaped shield with a painted falcon design. His sword hangs from a baldric and he also has a leather belt. He wears a tiara.

National Contingents in a Multicultural Army

Persian Subject Peoples

These are some of the peoples, including tribal and nomadic, that fell within the Persian empire and which fielded contingents to fight for the king in his campaigns.

Arians Satrapy near Parthia and the city of Susa.
Bactrians Central Asia.
Chalybes Central Asia.
Chorasmians A satrapy under the governance of the Satrap of Parthia.
Cilicians Western Asia Minor.
Colchian Western Caucasus and Georgia.
Dadikai Central Asia near India.
Gandarians Central Asia, near India – usually identified with the Sarangians.
Lasonians Central Asia.
Ligyeans Central Asia.
Lycian Southern Asia Minor along the Mediterranean coast.
Lydians The kingdom east of Ionia in Asia Minor. The old kingdom of Lydia encompassed the entire area of western Anatolia. Sardis was the capital of the Persian satrapy of Lydia.
Makrones India.
Mares Near or western India.
Mariandyni West or central Asia.
Matienans Eastern Asia, now in India.
Milians Anatolia in Asia Minor
Moschians Georgia in Central Asia.
Mossynoikians Asia Minor; fought beside Xenophon and the 10,000.
Mysians Western Asia Minor.
Otians Central Asia.
Paktyians Southeast Afghanistan
Pakytes Western Asia Minor near Ionia.
Paphlagonians A region on the Black Sea Coast in north-central Anatolia in Asia Minor, this was bordered by Bithynia on the west and Pontus on the east. The region was separated from Phrygia by the Bithynian Olympus. The western boundary was Parthenius river and the eastern boundary Halys river.
Parikanians From Media, near Persia.
Phrygia and
Pamphylia Western Asia.
Pisidians Located in Asia Minor, bordering ancient Lydia.
Sagartions Central Asia.
Sarangians Central Asia near India.
Sogdians Central Asia southeast of the Aral Sea.
Tibareni Coast of the Black Sea.

▶ NOBLE WARRIOR
This fighter from one of the satraps could be called up during an emergency. He is armoured but lightly armed, with a war-hammer and probably an edged weapon under his coat.

composite bow of Lycian design. The Moschians, Makrones, Mossynoikians and Tibareni were also armed and equipped similarly, with shields and short spears that had an unusually large spearhead. The Mares contingent used the javelin in conjunction with small shields made of leather. The Colchian contingent also carried small hide shields along with a short thrusting spear, and carried knives. The contingents of the Arians, and the Pisidians, wore Greek-style bronze helmets, but with an ox's horns and ears, also of bronze, attached to the helmet along with a crest. Both contingents used shields made from the hides of oxen as well as spears, used for both hunting and warfare.

The Lasonians and the Cilicians used the same clothing and equipment. The Milians' main weapon was a short spear, although some of them used the Lycian bow, which was a

◀ *Red-figure plate showing a Persian mounted archer, inscribed 'Miltiades kalos', from the 6th century BCE.*

Dadikai, Gandarians, Chorasmians and Sogdians were all equipped and uniformed in the same manner as the Bactrians. The only difference between these contingents was that the Areians carried the same type of bow as the Medes.

▼ Horse Archer
This light cavalryman, probably from the satrapies or quite possibly a nomad, was still a skilled archer even when the horse was at speed. His weapon is the strong composite bow and a sidearm of some type, sword, dagger, or axe, would also be carried.

A Persian army that was made up of troops from all of the satrapies undoubtedly presented a colourful mix of peoples on the march. Horses, mules, donkeys, and camels were all present in the field force, and were either used for combat troops (horses and camels) or for the army's transport and baggage (mules, donkeys, and camels). It was Achaemenid policy to exploit the combat capabilities of their multi-ethnic empire.

▲ Cavalryman
The elaborate helmet and shield indicate this is a provincial cavalryman from Phrygia. Some, but not most, Persian horsemen, did carry a shield, which was a late addition to the equipment of the excellent Persian cavalry. This soldier is armed with the usual javelins and sword; he also wears a padded linen jerkin which was light armour in the true sense as it provided only marginal protection against edged or missile weapons. He is clearly developing into the Persian form of cuirassier.

The Use of Camels

The Asian contingents, as well as the Arabs, used camels for transport and combat. The two-humped camel, called the Bactrian camel, originated in Bactria (the satrapy that corresponds to northern Afghanistan). It was uncomfortable to ride and difficult to mount. The Arabs used the more familiar dromedary or single-humped camel. The dromedary was an excellent military animal both for transport and for mounted combat. The camel could go for days without water, and would remain a workhorse, so to speak, for military units of various nations for thousands of years.

A dromedary unit could usually outmarch a horse-mounted unit, and the dromedary was better able to survive and operate in the desert than a horse. Furthermore, the dromedary was capable of covering a great distance at a comfortable gait, although it did not provide a comfortable ride for troops who were not used to being camel-mounted. Dromedaries enjoyed a height advantage compared to horse-mounted units, and were also more able than the horse to carry two soldiers without tiring quickly.

▼ **Camel-Mounted Infantry**
The Persians used Bactrian (two-humped) camels as both baggage animals in the army's train and for carrying fighting troops. Here two infantrymen are mounted in a small howdah from which they might be able to fight. They might also dismount to fight on foot.

THE PERSIAN ARMY AGAINST ALEXANDER AND AFTER

Immortals

In this period certain units of the Persian Immortals – the first ranking of elite troops – were distinguished from others by the collars and the hems of their tunics, as well as the central strip down the front of the tunic, which would be in the unit

▼ Hazarapatis

This was not the title of the unit, but of the person himself. This officer was the regimental commander of the regiment of Spearbearers and a powerful personage within the Persian empire, quite possibly the second most powerful man in the empire next to the king. As such, he is clothed, armed, and equipped as an elite infantryman.

▼ Sparabara

The term sparabara translates as 'shield bearers'. This example of the sparabara is armed with long spear and sword, and the large rectangular shield ('spara') from which their name comes. The design of the shield motif matches that of this warrior's Median clothing.

colours. This was a new practice in the Persian army and appears to have been one of the first examples in military history of the later practice, found especially in European armies, of identifying different units by their facing (collar, cuffs, coat-tails and lapels) colours.

Sparabara

The second-ranking unit among the elite of the Persian infantry, *sparabaras* were next in importance to the Immortals. These infantrymen, armed with 1.8m (6ft) spears and rectangular shields, formed the front line of the Persian battle array, employed to create what would later be considered a 'shield wall' from behind which archers were deployed.

The infantry were more than competent archers. A leather belt worn at the waist below their armour drew in the tunic. On their belts they usually carried a dagger for self-defence in a melée if they lost their shields and spears; they might also or instead have been armed with a short sword. Their edged weapons were worn on their right side. The Persian horse archer was considered an elite among the overall excellent Persian cavalry arm.

Standard Bearer and Hazarapatis

The royal standard bearer of Persia in this period carried either the original royal standard of a falcon on a blue field (from the period of Cyrus the Great) or on a red field (Xerxes), or a modification of that design.

The hazarapatis, a senior officer of the Persian army, was identified by his clothing and distinctive shield and accoutrements – notably by the blue stripe on his tunic. He was the regimental commander of the elite Spearbearers; the commander of this unit at the time of Darius III was Mazaios, who was described as second only to the king in the army. Mazaois was also satrap of Cilicia – it was not unusual for a leading official to hold an appointment while also keeping his role as satrap.

Darius III

The last king of the Achaemenid Persian empire, King Darius III (336–330BCE) was humbled and defeated by Alexander the Great, at Issus and then at Gaugamela.

Darius had been placed on the imperial throne in 336BCE by the vizier (chief minister) of the Achaemenid empire, Bagoas. Darius was then known as Artashata: a great-nephew of the previous king, Artaxerxes III, he was working as a royal courier. Bagoas saw him as an easily manipulated figurehead, and put him in power after killing Artaxerxes and all his sons. However, Darius asserted his independence and when Bagoas tried to poison him, overcame this 'kingmaker' and forced him to drink the poison himself. Artashata then took the name Darius III to rule as king.

Darius was now free to make his mark in history, but signally failed to do so. He was an inept ruler and cowardly in battle: he twice turned tail and fled from the battlefields on which he had been defeated by Alexander the Great. Fleeing to Ecbatana and Bactria after Gaugamela, Darius was murdered by his own relative, Bessus, the satrap of Bactria, where his body was found shortly afterwards by the advancing and victorious Macedonians. His death signalled the end for the Persian empire.

◄ ROYAL STANDARD BEARER
This Immortal standard bearer is dressed and equipped for field service. He wears the now-standard Median dress of trousers and knee-length tunic and carries a sword and a round, metal-faced shield.

The Battle of Issus

Darius may have been involved in the assassination of Philip II of Macedon in 336BCE. Whether or not this was the case, he was roundly humiliated by Philip's son, Alexander the Great. At the Battle of Issus (now in southern Turkey) in 333BCE Alexander deployed his Macedonian army with the cavalry on the wings and the infantry in the centre on the opposite bank of the River Pinarus (perhaps the modern Payas River) to Darius's troops. Alexander himself led the attack across the river and smashed the left wing of Darius's army before attacking the Greek mercenaries who were in the centre of the Persian line. Defeat for the Persians looked inevitable and in the confusion Darius fled, abandoning his family to the mercy of Alexander. In his haste he abandoned his chariot, royal bow and kingly mantle – which were all gathered up by the victorious Alexander. Left without a commander, the bulk of the Persian army also fled; Alexander's biographer Arrian reports that the victory was so easy that the Macedonians lost only 450 soldiers.

Darius made two attempts to negotiate peace, offering to cede to Alexander all Achaemenid territory lying to the west of the Euphrates. He also said he was willing to pay a great ransom for his family and proposed Alexander take the hand of his daughter in marriage. But Alexander was in no mood to make peace.

The Battle of Gaugamela

At the Battle of Gaugamela, Darius was forced to rely chiefly on his 10,000 Immortals and around 2,000 Greek mercenaries. The rest of his infantry were poorly equipped and far less effective – although there was a contingent of relatively well-armed Armenians. For this reason the vast discrepancy in numbers between the great Persian and smaller Macedonian armies made less difference than it might have done had levels of arms and training been more equally matched.

As was traditional in a Persian army, Darius as royal commander took up position in the centre of the battle line with the Immortals and close to the Greek mercenaries. In the end he was left vulnerable because so much of his cavalry was drawn forward and outward by Alexander's manoeuvres: Alexander rode with his Companions to the extreme right of the battle line to draw the Persian cavalry away from the centre before he himself hit hard in that central area and took out Darius's royal guard. Battle was rejoined at a site to the east of what is now Mosul, in northern Iraq, on 1 October 331BCE. Despite greatly outnumbering the Macedonian invaders, Darius's Persian army was routed: Alexander sent cavalry, javelin troops and archers against the Persian left wing and then repulsed an attack by the fearsome Persian scythed chariots in the centre of his line. Darius's cavalry poured forward, leaving his infantry exposed, and Alexander and his elite

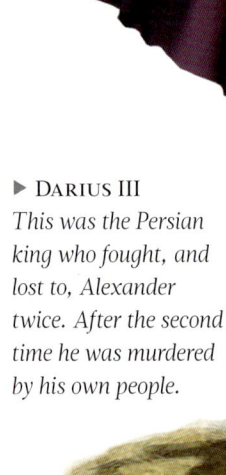

▶ DARIUS III
This was the Persian king who fought, and lost to, Alexander twice. After the second time he was murdered by his own people.

▼ *Darius fighting Alexander in the Battle of Issus, a detail from the 'Alexander mosaic' in the ruins of Pompeii (see also page 219). Darius is pictured in some distress in his chariot. Depending on the progress of a battle the king would either be mounted on his horse or in his chariot.*

Companions cavalry capitalized, striking hard at the Persian centre and then again at the wings and rear.

When Darius fled, his army was reduced to panic and, in retreat, was cut to pieces by the triumphant Macedonians. Darius got safely to Ecbatana and then took flight again when he heard of Alexander's approach. He was finally put out of his misery when he was assassinated by Bessus, the satrap of Bactria.

Outmanoeuvred by Bessus and the chief of his own royal guard, Nabarzanes, Darius was bound with ropes and thrown in a cattle cart, while his captors attempted to rouse the Persian troops for another attack on Alexander. When Alexander arrived on the scene with a small force, Bessus and Nabarzanes killed Darius with their own spears.

▲ *The envoys of Alexander the Great dress the gardener Abdalonymos (here, an old man) with the Insignia of the Magnificence of Sidon, as imagined by the painter Nikolaus Knüpfer, c.1645–1650CE.*

King Abdalonymus of Sidon

Persian senior officers were generally clothed in a manner commensurate with their rank. King Abdalonymus was a different case; his dress was typical of what a senior Persian officer might wear on campaign. He was of the royal house of Sidon (a city in Lebanon) and when King Straton II was deposed by Alexander, he had been working as a gardener. Abdalonymus came to the throne because Alexander gave his great friend Hephaestion the task of choosing the new king of Sidon. Hephaestion tried to bestow the honour on two brothers with whom he was staying, but they said the crown could only be passed to one of royal blood. They pointed out Abdalonymus, reduced by poverty. Alexander interviewed him and was pleased by the wisdom he showed in conversation, so confirmed the appointment. The magnificent marble 'Alexander Sarcophagus', found near Sidon and now in the Archaeological Museum in Istanbul, is believed to have belonged to Abdalonymus. The sides are decorated with carvings of Alexander fighting and hunting lions (see also pages 23 and 212).

◀ **KING ABDALONYMUS**
Abdalonymus became king of Sidon and an ally of Alexander the Great after his predecessor, Straton II, was deposed by Alexander. The troops of Sidon under Abdalonymus retained Persian dress, weapons, and organization.

Later Immortal Uniform

The Immortals' name came not from their combat prowess, which was considerable, but from the fact that they were always kept up to strength. Combat losses were usually quickly replaced so the overall strength was always at 10,000. Being household as well as combat troops kept their appearance consistent and well-turned-out. Their commanders were usually physically close to the king on campaign and on the battlefield, both for protection and for the ability to be committed to a crisis in a battle when necessary. They could always be counted on in combat, and they were respected within the army, though the favoritism shown to them could cause resentment in the regular army. They were probably feared by the national contingents.

They were armed and equipped as the rest of the army, and finding their shields and armour inferior to that of the Greeks and later the Macedonians was undoubtedly a shock to the regiments. The Persians were accustomed to fighting in Asia, not in Western Europe, and their way of war was quite different. Deficiences in arms and armour were made up on campaign as the Immortals and the rest of the Persian army learned from defeat, but not quickly enough to survive the Macedonian onslaught.

◀ **Immortal Axeman**
This lightly armed soldier of one of the Immortal regiments has no armour, bears a wooden shield, and is armed with only an axe. It might be assumed that he has already lost or broken his spear in battle.

▼ **Immortal Light Spearman**
This Immortal, from yet another of the ten regiments, is much better armed than the preceding example, with spear and sword, but he still carries a wooden shield that is not metal-faced. His cloak is noteworthy for the leopardskin lining.

THE PERSIAN ARMY AGAINST ALEXANDER AND AFTER

▼ **IMMORTAL HEAVY SPEARMAN**
This is an excellent example of an Immortal in field service or combat dress. He wears a Greek-type linen cuirass and is well armed with sword and spear. His shield, however, is outdated, being made of wood and not faced with metal. Uniformity of dress, armour and arms in the huge Persian army was difficult due to the different tribes and regions that the soldiers came from. The Immortals, however, were uniformed alike whether in the field or on palace duty.

The elite Immortals in the time of Darius III were more simply armed and dressed than in earlier eras. They had a round shield, with a crescent portion at the top cut out and a type of early battle-axe. Their outfit exemplified either a relaxation of standards or a dearth of available weaponry because of the toll taken by the long series of battles against the Macedonians and Greeks of Alexander's army. The soft head covering contained a section that could be stretched across the lower face to keep dust and wind at bay.

There was an elite within the elite among the Immortals. This upper tier of guards was dressed in yellow tunics with blue-purple trim and collars, and trousers. Perhaps a select regiment of bowmen, they were employed in conjunction with the Spearbearers Regiment (see page 174). The spearbearers formed a shield wall behind which the archers would deploy, to loose their arrows at the enemy formations. They were also armed with round shields and as secondary weapons carried the excellent Persian battle-axe.

◄ **IMMORTAL ARCHER**
This bowman is lightly equipped. He is well-clothed in typical Persian colourful trousers and tunic and has what appears to be a leopardskin cloak. He is armed with the usual composite bow.

THE PERSIAN NAVY

Navies, in the ancient world as in the modern, were developed for two reasons. First, to protect the commerce of the nation or city state. Second, to counter an enemy that already had a navy. Both of these types of navies could or would also support land operations of the army.

The navies of the Greek city states such as Athens were created to project seapower against their enemies, to both intimidate their enemies and to move the army where it was needed and supply it after it was ashore. The Persian empire was a land power, and supporting land operations was the primary mission for its navy.

When Cambyses II, the son and successor of Cyrus II, invaded Egypt, a huge undertaking that consumed most of his short reign, he and his generals realized that to attack this country by land across its arid landscape, they would have to be supported and

▼ *The Phoenicians were a fine seafaring people who traded along the Mediterranean coast. Their warships were an important part of the Persian naval force. Bas-relief on 4th-century BCE stone sarcophagus.*

resupplied by sea. In addition, the Egyptians had an efficient navy that could block Persian movements and isolate the army. Cambyses built a fleet of ships that could efficiently support the Persian army ashore and meet the Egyptians on close to an equal basis at sea. The 26th-Dynasty Egyptian pharaoh Ahmose II (reigned 570–526BCE) defended his lands against the Persians with an excellent fleet, but was nonetheless defeated by Cambyses and Egypt was conquered by the Persians.

Ancient navies deployed infantry as part of their ships' companies. Their tasks were: to defend their vessel against enemy boarding parties; to board enemy ships in order to incapacitate them or seize them; and to provide naval landing parties for limited deployment ashore for a variety of missions. The tendency is for modern authors, especially English-speaking, to describe these infantrymen as 'marines' in the sense of, say, the United States Marine Corps and the British Royal Marines. However ancient 'marines' were typically personnel detailed from the army for service at sea and were not a separate organization.

Persian Naval Contingents 480BCE	
Contingent	**Number of Warships**
Phoenicians and Syrians	300
Egyptians	200
Cyprians	150
Cilicians	100
Lycians	50
Pamphylians	30
Dorians	30
Carians	70
Ionians	100
Aegean Islanders	17
Aeolians	60
Pontic Region	100
Total	**1,207**

The Trireme

The epitome of the galley-type warship of the period, the trireme was used by all of the major naval powers of the time. The ship was approximately 38–40m (125–135ft) long with a beam of 3–4m (10–13ft). It had a draught of 1–1.2m (3–4ft) and the oar length was 4.2–4.5m (14–15ft). Its main weapon was the bronze-coated ram at the bow of the vessel.

The trireme evolved from Phoenician warships which were originally powered by a single row of oars on either side. The Phoenician version of the trireme was higher than the Greek version and had a much more rounded bow. Furthermore, the Phoenician ram was horn-shaped and underwater, whereas the Greek ram was more blunt, somewhat resembling a clenched fist, and was positioned low on the bow so as to appear to be on the surface of the water.

The trireme was constructed from the outside of the hull inwards, termed the 'shell-first' method. The hull was constructed and shaped with the planking, which was adjoining. This method is described in Homer's Odyssey. The wood used for galley construction was specific for the

▲ **Trireme Galley**
The Phoenician trireme, the design of which was employed wholesale by the Persian navy, was higher than the Greek trireme and had only one mast, instead of the Greek standard two. The bow above the ram was much more rounded than the Greek equivalent, and shields were hung on the sides as shown.

different parts of the galley. Cedar was used for the ship's mainmast not only because the tree was tall, but because it was both elastic and very durable. Cypress was used to construct the hull. This wood is both strong and elastic, and very durable in withstanding the elements of weather and sea. Oak was not used because it is heavy, and galleys needed to be light and strong.

Whereas Greek triremes had a mainmast and a smaller foremast, the Phoenicians constructed their galleys with only a mainmast, which had one yardarm to which was attached the ship's mainsail. The mast, as in the Greek triremes, would be lowered and secured at times of combat, the galley then relying on the three banks of oars for speed and manoeuvring.

The main, and perhaps only weapon, of the trireme was the ship's ram. The two masts were lowered for combat, and only used when the wind was up and there was no immediate chance of combat.

The Ships' Crews

The crew of a trireme was approximately 200, 170 of them being rowers. In the navies of the Greek city states, the oarsmen were not slaves but were highly trained professional seamen who were drawn from the Greek lower classes. The Persians may have used the same system.

The oarsmen were arranged on three levels on each side of the ship and of the 30 remaining crewmen, about half were marines (hoplites and archers) and the others were crewman who sailed the ship. The rudder was actually two oars manned by one crewman.

Persian Naval Logistics

In addition to the warships assembled and deployed by Xerxes and his naval commanders for the invasion of Greece, Herodotus states that there were 3,000 non-combatant support ships. These were supply vessels and horse-transport boats for the Persian cavalry, supply train and chariot teams. Camels were also transported. The number may seem high, but transporting a large army, as well as having the capacity to build a bridge of boats across the Hellespont, as Xerxes did during his campaign, would require many support vessels.

▼ **Bireme Galley**
This predecessor to the faster, more deadly trireme was a Phoenician development. The ship had a Phoenician-type ram, as did the trireme, which was underwater when the ship was underway. The design was identical to the Phoenician trireme and when underway it was probably difficult to tell them apart. At Salamis, no biremes were evident in the Persian fleet.

Naval Clothing and Equipment

In this multicultural force, there was a great deal of variety in weapons and battledress. The fighting contingent of a large percentage of the Persian navy consisted of Phoenicians recruited to fight as shipboard marines, trained to board enemy vessels after ramming and to defend their own ship in close engagements. The arms and armour of these marines was significant and consisted of a white linen cuirass, Greek-style crested helmet, round shield, and a variety of weapons. The linen cuirass protected the torso, and it was cut into strips from the waist down to facilitate movement in a confined space. The helmet was bronze with a horsehair crest and cheek pieces.

The weapons carried were of three types: a single-edged curved sword that was carried in a leather scabbard, javelins, and a curious two-headed 'boarding spear'. The latter consisted of a straight arm which was a spear and a curved arm useful in boarding operations which acted as a hook. The marine probably did not have any footwear or boots, being able to walk barefoot on the planked deck.

The Egyptians wore helmets and cuirasses and were equipped with a large shield, battle-axe and a spear. They also carried a knife or short sword. The Cyprians, from the island of Cyprus, wore a type of felt cap; their commanders wore turbans. The Cyprians had migrated to Cyprus from mainland Greece, Phoenicia and Ethiopia. The Cilicians were dressed in woollen tunics and wore a type of native helmet. Their shields were made of rawhide and they were armed with short swords and javelins. The Lycians (ethnic Greeks from

▶ **Rower**
Most of the crew of the Persian galleys, like their Greek counterparts, were the rowers. They were unarmed, and wore no armour, only a loincloth, and no footwear. They were not slaves, but seamen with one job – to propel the ship when the wind had died and the sail became worthless. Their 'weapon' was a 4.5m (15ft) heavy oar.

◀ **Naval Infantry**
Many of the marines, or naval infantry, manning the Persian fleet were armed and equipped along the model of the Greek hoplite, but some of them, such as here, were Phoenicians. The helmet and shield were definitely influenced by the Greek infantry and they were armed with a single-edged sickle sword, javelins, and a curiously designed boarding spear. They wore a linen cuirass and a wraparound undergarment.

Crete) wore goatskin cloaks and felt caps adorned with feathers, together with cuirasses and greaves; they fought with bows and javelins. Their arrows were featherless and made from reeds.

Several contingents in the navy were dressed and equipped 'in the Greek manner'. Some of these were Greeks who had allied with invading and conquering Persians. Such contingents included the Pamphylians (reputedly descended from the Trojans who had been defeated and scattered when Troy fell to the Greeks), the Dorians (ethnic Greeks who had been transplanted to Asia Minor), the Aegean Islanders, and the Ionians (ethnic Greeks from the region of Achaea who had allied themselves with the Persians). The Carians (from western Anatolia) used traditional Greek battledress and weapons, but

Persian Fleet Commanders

The Persians put some of their best troops – Persians, Medes and Sacae (Scythians) – on board ship to serve as naval infantry. The native contingents who served with the Persians were in theory commanded by their own officers and commanders. In reality, the Persians put in place a general who held the actual power of command, and the foreign contingent commanders followed their orders.

The two senior Persian fleet commanders at the time of Xerxes' invasion in 480BCE were Prexaspes and Megabyzus. In support were Achaemenes, who was in command of the Egyptian naval contingent; and Ariabignes, who commanded the contingents from Caria and Ionia. Arguably the best of the Persian naval commanders – mentioned as such by Xerxes himself – was Queen Artemisia of Halicarnassus. Born of a Halicarnassian father and a Cretan mother, she took command of her flotilla of five galleys after her husband's death. She had a son of military age, but decided to take command herself and to support the empire. Artemisia's ships were manned by her own Halicarnassians as well as men from Kos, Nisyros and Kalymna. Her flotilla was held in the highest esteem by Xerxes because of its state of readiness and expertise at sea. Her performance at Salamis was distinguished and she brought out her flotilla intact from the disaster.

The Battle of Salamis 480BCE

The defining naval action of the period was the battle of Salamis where the Greek fleet trapped Xerxes' fleet and decisively defeated the Persians, inflicting heavy losses in both ships and men. Cambyses' creation of the Persian navy, using the Phoenicians as a basis for the fleet, had made Persia a naval power in the eastern Mediterranean. However, the Persian navy, though well organized and large, was not the best or most efficient of the period. Like the Persian army it was composed of sailors and marines from across the empire and was not a cohesive fighting force. Being composed of personnel from throughout the satrapies, and commanded by Persian admirals and ships' captains, the multi-national force could not match the cohesive combined Greek fleet, and was enticed into a trap in the straits of Salamis. The destruction of the fleet was witnessed by Xerxes from the shore.

▼ ARTEMISIA
Both the Carian Queen and an admiral in the Persian Navy, commanding a flotilla of five galleys which had a very high reputation of efficiency and courage. She was the only female commander in the Persian fleet.

▲ NAVAL ARCHER
Both the Greeks and Persians employed Scythian mercenaries as archers, and they would be wearing their native clothing aboard ship. Both skilled and efficient, they were armed with the Scythian composite bow and the typical wide Scythian quiver. They might also have a double-edged short sword and sometimes an iron battle-axe.

were also armed with daggers and the older scythe. The Aeolians were yet another contingent of ethnic Greeks who were armed and equipped as the other 'Greek' contingents within the Persian fleet. One small contingent of these, from Abydos, did not accompany the fleet to the Greek mainland but were detailed to maintain watch over the bridges across the Hellespont after the Persian army moved on.

ARMS AND ARMOUR

Persian armour and defensive equipment did not match that of the Greeks and Macedonians. While Persian infantry did possess scale armour, often – more used to fighting ill-equipped enemies in Asia Minor and the Middle East – they wore only their usual clothing, which was designed for fighting in their home climate and terrain and not against heavily armed and armoured infantry. The bows were excellent, as were the Persian archers. The lack of armour, though, was a definite handicap when fighting western-style armies. The Persians did learn from their defeats at the hands of the Greeks, and weapons and arms did improve; the hoplon was later adopted by some units, such as the Spearbearers Regiment. The most critical weakness of the Persian army, however, was the lack of uniformity and training among the different peoples in the army itself. Not all of the units were trained the same way, whether they were infantry or cavalry, and the lack of uniformity in defensive

◀ *Two Persian infantryman, the man on the right being a Mede with the Median distinctive headdress. The Persian, who might be an Immortal, carries a distinctive shield reminiscent of the older figure of eight shield.*

▼ **Helmets**
Numbers 1 and 2 are bronze helmets of typical patterns from Asia Minor and Persia; numbers 3 and 4 are cavalry helmets. Cavalry helmets are more elaborate, both for decoration and to provide more protection for the wearer in a melée.

weaponry such as shields, led to different methods of fighting against Greek and Macedonian infantry who were, in contrast, cohesive and well-trained in the same system.

At least some of the Persian troops were familiar with the Greek method of waging war and of employing heavily armed and armoured infantry. However, the Persians, Medes and Kissians who formed the bulk of the most trusted troops in the Persian army had not been able to adopt the

▲ **Shields**
Numbers 5 to 7 are large wooden shields probably used to protect archers. Number 8 is an example of the typical wicker shield; 9 is the much superior round shield, based on the hoplon, faced with iron – adopted after repeated defeats at the hand of the Greeks.

◀ **Missile Weapons**
Numbers 1 and 2 are examples of the excellent Persian composite bow. Number 3 is the scabbard which carried both the bow and the arrows, usually used by horse archers.

▶ **Polearms**
Numbers 1 and 2 are spears with a counterweight at the butt end which was useful in hand-to-hand combat; 3 is a type of javelin; the leather strap was used in throwing, to increase the range of the weapon. Number 4 is a model of spear which had an iron-shod butt, useful if the spear broke in combat.

equipment of their Greek foes before being handed a very pointed lesson in the advantages of the Greek 'way of war' at Marathon in 490BCE, and at Thermopylae and Plataea in 479BCE.

Armour

The Persians wore cuirasses of leather or stiffened cloth, but these were not of the calibre of those worn by the troops they would face in the Greek wars or against the Macedonians of Alexander the Great. Persian protective clothing included both lamellar and scale armour, but many Persian troops were not armoured – mainly those from the outlying areas of the empire such as the Indians, Ethiopians and Libyans. Asian troops who were either ethnic Greeks or had come into contact with the Greek hoplites did wear some if not all of the Greek panoply. The Persians also used Greek mercenaries, such as Xenophon's famous 'Ten Thousand' in c.400BCE, who Darius employed against Alexander and his Macedonians.

Shields

The Persians often used symmetrical oval or rectangular shields of wicker instead of the wooden shields faced with iron or bronze employed by the Greeks and Macedonians. The wicker shields provided little or no protection against the spears of the hoplites and pikes of the phalangites: the Greeks and Macedonians would go through a Persian formation equipped in this manner with the greatest of ease.

The national contingents of the huge Persian armies used a variety of shields of different shapes. Wood and wicker were favourite construction materials. Designs included figure of eight shields, and round shields with a crescent shape cut out. The Persians also fought with captured shields and equipment. Some cavalrymen used asymmetrical shields of Eastern designs. However these were difficult to wield while mounted, without significant practice and experience.

Weapons

The Persians were armed with spears and swords that matched those of their enemies and while they may have been underprotected, they were definitely not underarmed. They fielded excellent archers, both on horse and on foot, armed with a powerful composite bow. In fact, it was the Persian archers who finished off the Spartans in the Battle of Thermopylae.

The Persians carried a variety of weapons, including the spear, and they were also armed, depending on their

▲ **Edged Weapons**
Numbers 5 and 6 are two examples of period swords, 5 being bronze, 6 being iron and more modern-looking. Spears 1, 2 and 4 are balanced with counterweights at the butt. Number 3 is noteworthy in that it has a sling which would be worn over the arm so that it would not be lost during a melée.

ethnic group, with the short sword, the battle-axe and knobkerrie. The latter was a wooden club with a knot of wood on the end, used to brain an opponent: it was made from a single piece of wood, taken and fashioned from a tree root.

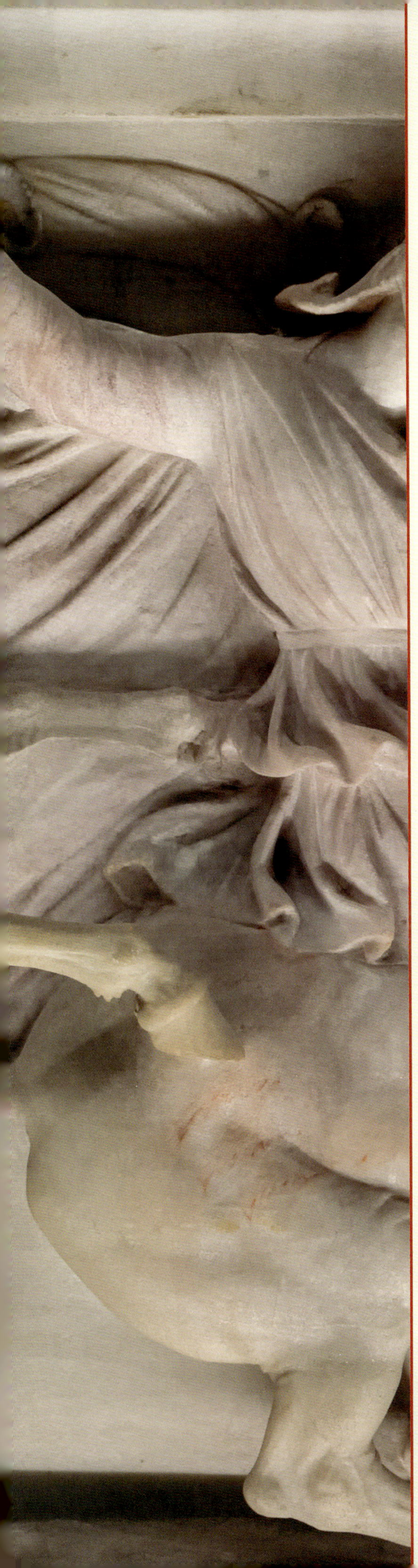

ARMIES OF ALEXANDER

On 1 October 331BCE Alexander of Macedon won a great victory over Darius III of Persia in the Battle of Gaugamela (near modern Mosul, Iraq). This triumph signalled the end of the Persian Achaemenid empire. Alexander, aged just 25 and already the ruler of Greece, Asia Minor and Egypt, was now poised to become 'King of Kings' in Persia. He had just eight years to live but he dedicated the remainder of his life to a near-continuous 17,000-km (10,500-mile) military campaign that created one of the greatest empires known to history.

The army that Alexander commanded was built by his father Philip II of Macedon. One great advantage that the Macedonian army would have over its opponents was the excellent cavalry arm that evolved from their natural ability with horses. Philip created a balanced force of infantry and cavalry, and supported the two with an impressive engineering arm. The army that Philip created, and that Alexander used with skill and dedication, was undoubtedly the best army of the ancient world until the advent of Rome and the creation of the Roman Legion.

▲ *Alexander cutting the Gordian knot, as painted by Jean-Simon Berthélemy. The oracle in a myth stated that whoever could undo the impossibly tangled knot would rule Asia.*

◀ *Alexander on a lion hunt, depicted on the 4th-century BCE Alexander Sarcophagus.*

PHILIP II AND THE RISE OF MACEDONIA

Philip II is one of the most underestimated soldiers and kings in history. He is usually only known as the father of Alexander the Great; people remember that he was assassinated by a disaffected bodyguard, propelling Alexander to become king of Macedon at a young age. Philip was a king intent on improving his mountainous kingdom and on creating a first-class army. He was also an excellent soldier himself and a competent general whose border campaigns secured the boundaries of his kingdom and established Macedon and eventually Greece as the base for his greater ambition – the invasion and defeat of the Persian empire.

Philip defeated the Greeks, and was acclaimed as their overlord, ostensibly uniting the peninsula under Macedonian leadership. The two most powerful city-states of the time were the naval power of Athens and the land power of Sparta, which possessed the best army in Greece. The city-state in the ascendant would change from time to time; in the Peloponnesian Wars (431–404BCE), Athens was completely defeated by Sparta. Sometimes other states, such as Thebes, would become the most powerful – notably when Thebans under the leadership of Epaminondas decisively defeated the Spartans at Leuctra in 371BCE.

The next period of Greek history was to be dominated by Macedon under the leadership of first Philip II and then his son Alexander.

Theban Lessons

Philip was held hostage in Thebes in his youth from 368BCE to 365BCE, when the Theban general was Epaminondas, who had led the Thebans to victory over Sparta at Leuctra. This victory, which made Thebes the leading city-state in Greece, led to the so-called and short-lived Theban hegemony. Epaminondas schooled Philip both in diplomacy and military matters. This would later come back to haunt Thebes when Philip led a Macedonian army against the city.

Philip returned to Macedon in 364BCE. Five years later, he became Philip II of Macedon. Originally third in line for the throne, Philip became king after both his elder brothers, Alexander II and Perdiccas III, died. He was faced with a grim situation, both externally and internally. In eastern Macedonia, the Thracians and Paeonians were running amok, raiding and pillaging the countryside. The Athenians had landed a Macedonian pretender to the throne, Argeus, on the coast at Methoni and were encouraging his cause and backing up his claim with an army of 3,000 hoplites.

Philip was equal to the emergency. He bought-off the Thracians and Paeonians, and turned on the Athenians, defeating them decisively in 359BCE, and ending the pretender's claims to the throne of Macedon.

Military Reforms

Now that the immediate threats to Macedon were dealt with, Philip concentrated on rebuilding and retraining the army. Then, having strengthened his military arm, he turned to deal with further threats to Macedon. He remodelled the admirable Greek phalanx to suit the Macedonian way of fighting, lengthened the reach of the Greek spear by developing the sarissa, and turned the Macedonian army into a professional fighting force of full-time soldiers. The combination of the excellent Macedonian cavalry

◀ Pella was Macedonia's new capital, chosen by king Archelaus in 413BCE, leaving Aegae as the ceremonial centre. It was in Pella that the young Alexander III was born and grew up while his father Philip II extended his power.

PHILIP II AND THE RISE OF MACEDONIA

▲ A bust of Philip II of Macedon, a Roman copy of a Greek original, 3rd-century BCE.

and the reformed and retrained Macedonian infantry would become nearly invincible on the battlefields commanded first by Philip and later by his son Alexander.

During this period Philip also solved the internal political problems of the kingdom. These actions not only confirmed his position as king, but also brought internal stability to the kingdom.

Taking on the City-States

Next Philip marched against the Illyrians, in 358BCE. The following year he defeated them, his army killing more than 7,000 of the enemy. With this victory, Philip extended the boundaries of Macedon.

Problems with Athens caused war between the two states, and prompted Macedon to seek support from other Greek states. Philip gained lost Macedonian territory, and one of his generals, Parmenion, again defeated the Illyrians. While directing the siege of Methone, an Athenian-controlled city, Philip was badly wounded in the face and lost an eye. Methone fell in 354BCE. In the meantime, Philip's son Alexander had been born, in 356BCE.

For the next sixteen years, 354–338BCE, Philip continued his campaigns to secure Macedonia's borders and to subjugate the Greek peninsula. Finally, only Sparta stood in the way of Philip's goal of conquest, security and domination. Macedonian hegemony moved steadily down the Greek peninsula. Philip gained Thessaly, as well as the Chalcidian peninsula; the city of Olynthus and others on the peninsula were razed to the ground.

Thebes was convinced to ally itself with Philip after the eastern areas belonging to Thebes submitted to him. Athens continued to be a thorn in Philip's side, but peace was finally made in 347BCE. The one apparent hold-out against Philip in Greece was Sparta. Sparta was not what it once was, but recognition of the famous Spartan toughness caused Philip to send a warning to Sparta that "if" Philip attacked and defeated the Spartans, he would ensure that the surviving Spartans would be sold into slavery and would remain enslaved "forever". The Spartans, remembering their martial heritage and traditions, merely answered Philip's threat with a one-word reply: "If".

For the time being Philip let the Spartans be, and continued his campaigns against the remaining threats to Macedon. In 345BCE while campaigning against the Ardiaei, an Illyrian people who lived on the Adriatic coast, and their king Pleuratus, Philip was again badly wounded, this time in the leg, leaving him with a permanent limp.

▲ The assassination of Philip II in 336BCE by Pausanias of Orestis, during a procession into the theatre.

The Final Conquest of Greece

Philip turned north in 342BCE and fought a campaign against the Scythians, taking the fortified settlement of Eumolpia, which was held by the Thracians. Two years later, Philip failed in sieges against Perinthus and Byzantium on the Bosphorus, which led to a hopeful resurgence against Macedon by the Greeks. Philip put paid to those hopes by decisively defeating the Greeks at the Battle of Chaeronea in 338BCE. Alexander fought alongside his father, aged 18, and was placed on the left commanding the elite Companion cavalry. Philip advanced, then suddenly seemed to flee, fooling the Athenians who pursued, leaving a gap through which Alexander charged.

The next year the League of Corinth was formed with Philip as *hegemon*, or leader, pledging not to go to war against each other unless it was to suppress a revolution among its members. Philip was at the pinnacle of his power. His plan was war against Persia, but he was then assassinated.

◄ This cuirass, or body armour, belonged to Philip II of Macedon, the father of Alexander the Great. It was made of iron and the craftsmanship is evident. It was Philip who created the Macedonian army that made Alexander's campaigns possible.

ALEXANDER AND THE CONQUEST OF PERSIA

Alexander III of Macedon – the man known to history as Alexander the Great, who conquered the known world by the age of 33 – owed the basis of his successes to his father, Philip. Alexander was a great captain, an expert in the use of the Macedonian army, a general who was never defeated, but it was Philip who handed him the army that was Macedonia's instrument of conquest.

Philip carefully trained Alexander to be able to command and lead an army in the field, and ensured that he was properly educated, recruiting the philosopher Aristotle to be Alexander's tutor. Aristotle served in this position for two years. He ensured that Alexander was taught geography and natural science and encouraged his love of reading.

As a young man Alexander accompanied his father in his later campaigns. Philip's overriding ambition was to invade and conquer Persia, but before he could depart on this adventure, he was assassinated. It was now Alexander's turn.

▼ *The Battle of Granicus painted in 1665 by Charles Le Brun, visualizing Alexander's first battle against the Persian king Darius III in 334BCE.*

The Great Expedition

After subduing the Greeks in their homeland, Alexander proceeded to fulfil his father's lifelong ambition of conquering the Persian empire. The Persian empire was huge and wealthy, with an excellent infrastructure, both materially and governmentally. Alexander's campaigns, the battles and sieges, were an unbroken string of successes.

Alexander's initial task was to quell uprisings within Greece. First, in 335BCE, he subdued the Triballians, whom he pursued across the Danube. He then moved against the Illyrians in the north-west frontier, then marched his army 800km/500miles south in two weeks to take and destroy the city of Thebes. After this, the Greeks did not rebel further, and Alexander could look east to Persia once more.

At the Battle of Granicus in 334BCE Alexander fought his first engagement with the Persian army under Darius III. He had invaded the Persian empire by crossing the Hellespont into Asia and advanced mostly along the northern coastline of Asia Minor, visiting the site of ancient Troy along the way. The superior training of the Macedonian heavy infantry and the demonstrable superiority of the

▲ *A bust of Alexander, in fact a Roman copy of the original by Lysippus, shows the dynamism and ruthlessness of the young conqueror.*

Macedonian cavalry gave Alexander victory over the Persians, although he also showed typical boldness and battlefield acumen.

At Issus in 333BCE Alexander triumphed at his next encounter with Darius III, routing the Persians, and then conquering Phrygia, Lycia, Caria, and Pamphylia. In 332BCE he captured the island city of Tyre, long thought invincible, after one of

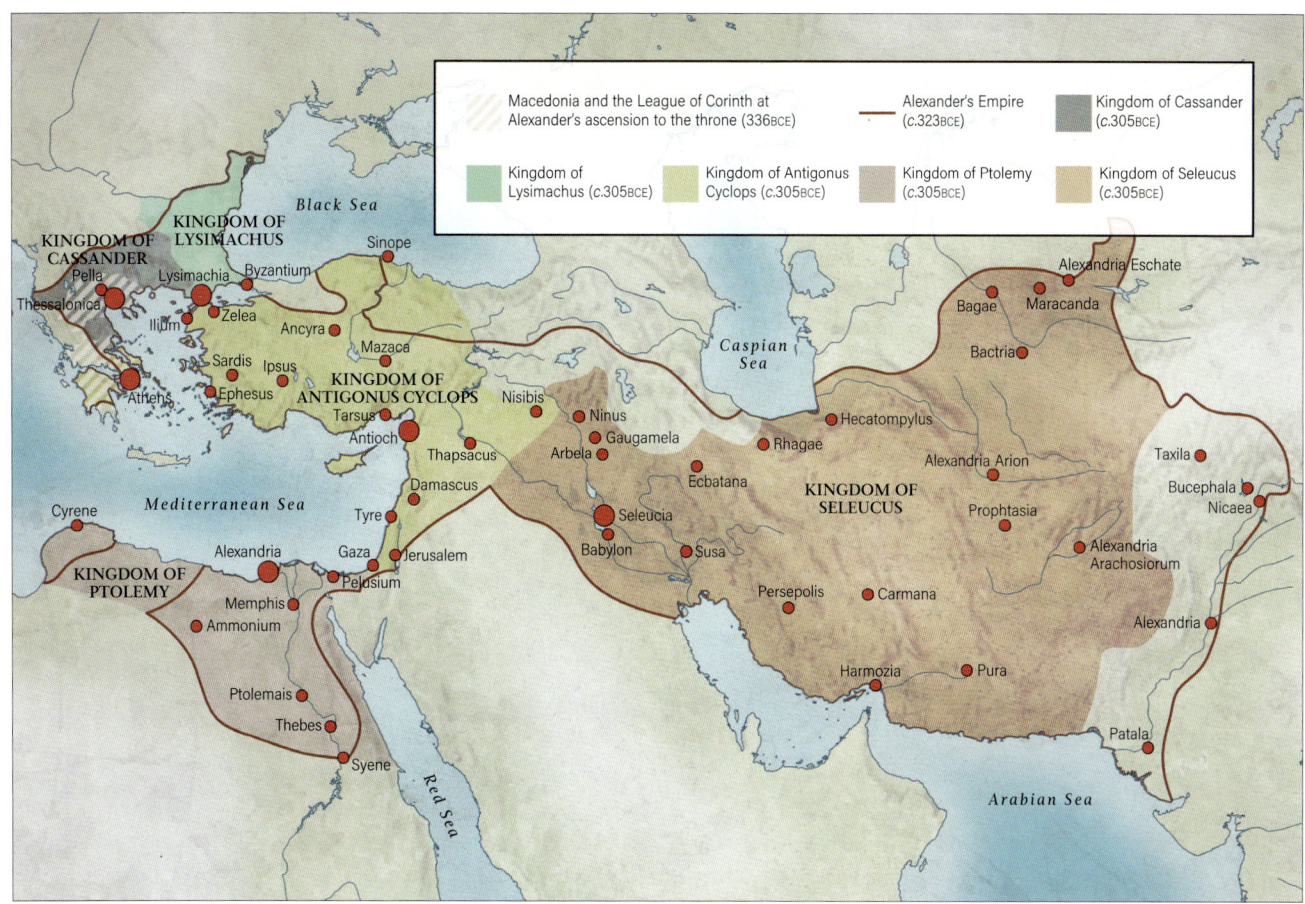

▲ This map shows the approximate extent of the conquests and empire of Alexander the Great. Upon his death the empire was divided among his generals, as indicated.

the hardest seiges ever undertaken. At Gaugamela in 331BCE he showed great bravery and strategic intelligence and again proved the might of his Macedonian army. Alexander personally led his elite Companion cavalry in a powerful drive at the middle of the Persian battle line that threw the Royal Guard into panic and made Darius run for his life.

Alexander and his hard-marching, hard-fighting Macedonians and Greeks won every fight and took every city they besieged. His vast territory eventually ran from Greece right across Asia Minor, Mesopotamia and the Persian territories to the Indian Punjab and from the River Danube down to Egypt, conquering the ancient land of the pharaohs, where he founded the city of Alexandria at the mouth of the Nile.

The only thing that finally stopped this great conqueror was his army itself, as after defeating the Indian potentate Porus, the Macedonian troops refused to go any further. This mutiny brought Alexander to an enforced halt, and he had, reluctantly, to turn back from the Persian eastern marches and head back home. The journey was hard, with many losses, and Alexander also suffered from a lingering wound. He died in Babylon, possibly of typhoid fever, just short of his 33rd birthday, in 323BCE.

Military Legacy

Alexander was one of an exclusive group of soldiers who were heads of state as well as army commanders. The ranks of military history's great captains would include: Julius Caesar, the celebrated Roman politician, general and would-be head of state; Gustavus Adolphus, the Swedish soldier king, known as 'the Lion of the North'; the French Marshal General Turenne; the Duke of Marlborough, the brilliant British general who humbled Louis XIV, the Sun King; Frederick the Great of Prussia; and Napoleon Bonaparte. Alexander's campaigns were avidly studied by Napoleon, a young captain of French artillery who won his general's stars through the skilled employment of artillery at a siege and who went on to become a celebrated French general, then French head of state and finally Emperor of the French.

Napoleon said that Alexander's personality and military genius drove his army to greatness: "It was not the Macedonian phalanx which broke through as far as India, but Alexander himself." He also said he admired the "political sense" of the great Macedonian, shown in the way he settled his conquests.

Alexander's life resembled a great flashing streak across the sky of history like a brilliant comet, only to suddenly burn out as suddenly as it had appeared on history's stage, and finally disappear, just as his hard-won empire would disappear under the leadership of Alexander's ambitious and quarrelling successors.

TIMELINE OF ALEXANDER'S EMPIRE

382BCE: Philip II, father of Alexander the Great, is born.

359BCE: Perdicus III of Macedon is killed in action against the Illyrians and is succeeded by his brother Philip II. Philip instigates the resurrection of the Macedonian army, giving it the organization and training to become a battle-winning force.

358BCE: Philip wins victories over the Illyrians and the Paeonians, gaining territory for Macedon.

357BCE: Philip gains control over the Pangaean gold mines.

356–355BCE: Philip occupies the former Athenian subjects of Pydna and Potidaea, in a series of conquests called The Sacred Wars.

356BCE: Alexander, son of Philip, is born.

353 or 352BCE: After consolidating his place on the throne and defeating invading enemies, Philip leads his army against the Phocians, defeating them in what has been described as the bloodiest battle of Ancient Greece, and becoming the ruler of Thessaly.

346BCE: Philip II forces a Phocian capitulation.

343–342BCE: Aristotle is appointed as Alexander's tutor.

342BCE: Artaxerxes III of Persia reconquers Egypt.

341BCE: Philip is defied by Athens and Persia, who support Byzantium and Perinthus.

340BCE: Leaving Alexander as his regent in Macedon, Philip begins the conquest of Byzantium.

338BCE: Philip invades Greece for the second time, defeating the combined forces of Athens and Thebes at Chaeronea. Alexander commands on the Macedonian left flank, facing the famed Sacred Band of Thebes. After hard fighting, Alexander's troops defeat the Thebans.

337BCE: The League of Corinth is formed. Philip is 'elected' the League's commander. He is declared the 'General of the Greeks' and prepares to invade the Persian empire.

336BCE: Darius III becomes king of Persia.

336BCE: Philip II is assassinated and Alexander ascends the throne of Macedon. He attacks the Thracians to the north of Macedonia and defeats them, along with their allies the Triballians and Illyrians.

335BCE: Alexander leads his army against Thebes to the south. He takes Thebes and then ruthlessly destroys the city, ordering the men to be killed, and their wives and children sold into slavery. After being victorious in Thrace, Alexander campaigns on the Danube.

334BCE: The Macedonian army besieges and takes Miletus and Halicarnassus. Alexander fights and wins the Battle of Granicus against the Persians.

333BCE: Alexander fights Darius III and wins the Battle of Issus, routing the Persians, and conquers Phrygia, Lycia, Caria, and Pamphylia. He cuts the Gordian knot at the tomb of Achilles in Gordium (in present-day Turkey).

332BCE: The Persian fleet is defeated. Alexander besieges and takes Tyre; he besieges and takes Gaza, and turns on Egypt.

331BCE: The army is reorganized and reformed in order to continue Alexander's campaigns. He fights and wins the Battle of Gaugamela against the Persians. Babylon surrenders to Alexander and his army. Sparta is defeated by the Macedonians. Alexander founds what will become the city of Alexandria in Egypt.

330BCE: Alexander fights and wins the Battle of the Persian Gate and takes the Persian capital of Persopolis, and then burns it. The Greek allies of the Persians are sent home. Darius is murdered by his own people.

330BCE: The son of one of Alexander's officers, Philotas, is executed after being accused of conspiracy. The garrison commander of Ecbatana, Parmenio, father of Philotas, is ordered to be murdered.

329BCE: Led by Alexander, the army conducts a march through the mountains of Afghanistan. He conducts offensive operations in the area of Samarkand. He fights and wins the Battle of Jaxartes.

328BCE: Alexander campaigns in Bactria and Sogdia.

327BCE: Alexander marries Roxana. He crosses into India with the army. He kills his friend and trusted companion, Cleitus, in a drunken rage.

326BCE: The Macedonians capture Aornos Rock. Alexander fights and wins the Battle of the Hydaspes and the Punjab against the Indian army of Porus. The Macedonian army then

◀ The late 4th-century BCE tomb in Agios Athanasios, thought to have been of a companion to Alexander, reveal paintings of two mourning soldiers (shown here in montage), wrapped in long chlamyses or mantles, with felt caps and long spears. The pediment illustrations include hoplites with round shields and plumed helmets.

mutinies and refuses to go farther east, causing Alexander to turn westward towards home. He divides his army for the return. The part that he leads goes through the Gedrosian Desert and endures great hardship. The other half of the army, under Nearchus, returns by a better route and suffers less privation and loss.

325BCE: Alexander campaigns against the Mallians and is wounded severely. Alexander's admiral, Nearchus, who had travelled from the Indian Ocean to the Persian Gulf, joins Alexander and the rest of the army close to the strait of Hormuz.

324BCE: Another mutiny among Alexander's veterans occurs. He orders the execution of corrupt satraps.

323BCE Alexander prepares a campaign against Arabia but dies in Babylon aged 33. Alexander Aigos, Alexander's son by Roxana, was born after his death.

323–322BCE: The Lamian War – the Greeks rebel against Macedon. There is an additional rebellion in Bactria.

320–281BCE: Over this period there are six so-called Wars of the Successors.

311–309BCE: The Babylonian War.

The Successor Kings of Macedonia

323–317BCE: Philip III.
323–310BCE: Alexander IV (co-ruler with Philip III).
306–297BCE: Cassander.
297BCE: Philip IV.
297–294BCE: Antipater and Alexander (co-rulers).
306–301BCE: Demetrios I.
306–301BCE: Antigonos I (co-ruler with Demetrios).
283–239BCE: Antigonos II.
239–229BCE: Demetrios II.
229–221BCE: Antigonos III.
221–179BCE: Philip V.
179–168BCE: Perseus.
149–148BCE: Andriscus ('Philip VI').

▲ *The 'Alexander Mosaic' depicts the Battle of Issus, between Alexander and Darius III. Alexander was one of the greatest commanders in military history and was never defeated, although the empire he conquered did not last past his death. Mosaic from a floor at the House of the Faun in Pompeii, itself based on a 4th-century Hellenistic painting.*

301BCE: The battle of Ipsus between the Successors.

283–282BCE: Civil war breaks out in Asia Minor.

279BCE: The Celts invade both Greece and Macedon.

▼ *Silver tetradrachm of Perseus, the last king of Macedon; it came under Roman rule after the Battle of Pydna in 168BCE.*

▼ *The head of Philip II of Macedon on a gold victory medal, 2nd-century BCE.*

THE MACEDONIAN JUGGERNAUT

The architect and developer of the deadly efficient Macedonian army was Alexander's father, Philip II of Macedon. As carefully as he trained his son up to be a great military leader, Philip built the Macedonian army to be the most effective in the known world, establishing a cavalry arm known for its shock value alongside an efficient, well-trained infantry.

Philip also paid attention to the army's artillery and engineer troops, and the Macedonians became master besiegers. They were trained and armed with the most modern weapons and equipment. Philip also developed an officer corps to lead his army and, for an army of the ancient period, it had a remarkably efficient staff to command and lead in the field.

Building his military forces around his excellent cavalry arm, Philip developed a professional army based on the Macedonian peasant, herder and basic citizen. This was in direct contrast to the general system among the Greeks – with the exception of the warlike and military-minded Spartans – of only allowing citizens to become hoplites during emergencies. Philip made the arming of the infantry the responsibility of the state.

The Macedonian peasant made a superb soldier. He was generally armed and armoured similarly to his southern neighbours, but Philip made several major and important improvements to military equipment. He lengthened the basic Greek spear, which was 2.7–3.7m (9–12ft) in length, creating the 5.4–6m (18-20ft) pike, the sarissa, instead. This was made in two parts, making it much easier to carry when marching. The sarissa could be taken apart at the balance of the arm: it screwed together at a brass joint.

By the time of Alexander the chariot was largely obsolete. Cavalry was the primary mounted arm. Both Macedonians and Persians fielded excellent cavalry. The Persians still used chariots and they were proven

▶ **ALEXANDER**
Alexander probably wore this easily distinguishable armour both because he was king, and so that he would be recognized by his own men in the middle of the blood and mess of combat. He is pictured here without a helmet, though he definitely wore one when necessary. The leopardskin shabraque, the saddlecloth on his horse, whom he also considered a Companion, is distinctive.

THE MACEDONIAN JUGGERNAUT

ineffective against Alexander's veteran Macedonian and Greek infantry. After Alexander's campaigns destroyed and conquered the Persian empire, the chariot was no longer employed by any modern army. The combination of the Macedonian cavalry and the reformed and retrained Macedonian infantry, commanded first by Philip and later by Alexander, would become nearly invincible on the battlefields.

Engineering and the Siege of Tyre

Philip created a balanced force of infantry and cavalry, and supported the two with an excellent engineer arm whose skill was more than useful during Alexander's own conquests. In July 332BCE Alexander and the Macedonian army captured the important and strategically vital city-state of Tyre, a port on the Mediterranean coast of Phoenicia (modern Lebanon). This brought a bitterly contested seven-month siege to an end. Alexander led the attack personally from the top of a siege tower and once the walls were breached the city's garrison fell quickly. Earlier in the siege Alexander's engineers had come to the fore. The city consisted both of a coastal settlement and a fortified town on an offshore island. The inhabitants of Tyre took refuge on the island, which was about half a mile offshore, and possessed forbidding defensive walls 60m (200ft) high. Alexander and his engineers built a stone causeway to link the city and the island, and constructed siege towers 50m (160ft) high. These were destroyed by the defenders but later in the siege he used boat-mounted battering rams against the city walls.

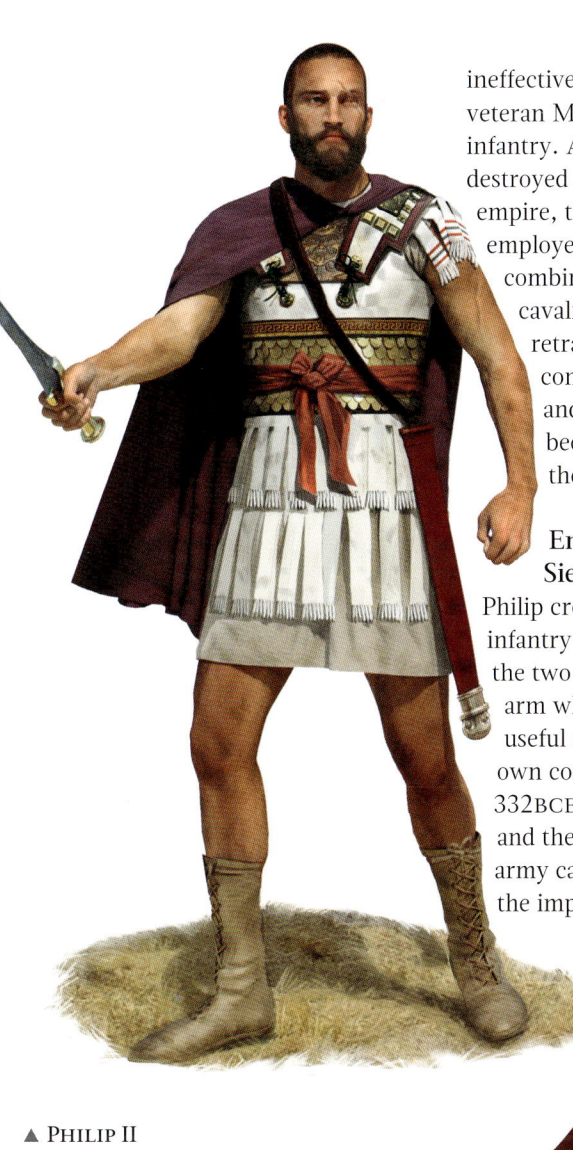

▲ PHILIP II
One-eyed Philip II, King of Macedon, was not only the father of Alexander the Great, but the creator of the outstanding Macedonian army that Alexander would inherit. Philip is wearing typical armour and is armed with a Macedonian short sword.

▶ COMPANION CAVALRYMAN
These elite cavalrymen were well-trained and well-disciplined, and were used as heavy cavalry by Alexander on the battlefield. His helmet is plumed, he wears a muscle cuirass over white clothing, and is armed with sword and lance.

ELITE TROOPS – CAVALRY AND COMPANIONS

The Macedonians were not only skilled horsemen, meaning they were adept in riding and fighting from the horse, but were also knowledgeable and skilful horsemasters, meaning they knew about the care and feeding of horses. Philip and Alexander ensured that there were enough replacement horses for those killed, hurt or hobbled during campaigns. They also gave priority to horse breeding – and improving the existing horse breeds not only in their native Macedon, but in the lands that were conquered by the army.

War Horses

An officer's mount would be identified by a leopard- or tiger-skin shabraque. A mount with such a shabraque could also belong to an elite cavalryman, a member of the Companions. Grooms took care of the cavalryman's horse: their task was to have the animal ready at all times. Horses are tough animals, that can endure hardship along with their master, and will generally carry on until their rider drops. However, horses also require constant care, feeding and water. On campaign, horses will lose weight, and if not properly cared for their rider will become an infantryman. They have to be carefully and regularly fed with healthy food, usually grain or good grass. They also need to be watered carefully, fully and regularly, for too much or too little water can kill. A good cavalryman will always take care of his mount before looking after himself. Horses need to be regularly groomed, especially after

▶ **GREEK CAVALRYMAN**
This cavalryman is well-armoured with a bronze cuirass and helmet, the latter being something of a transitional type between Greek and the later Roman helmets. It is probably a modified Thracian helmet; there is cheek protection and it gives excellent all-round protection to the head. It should be remembered that the term 'uniform' can only loosely be attributed to ancient armies – even the Greeks and Macedonians. Several types of helmet and body armour could be found in the same formations and units.

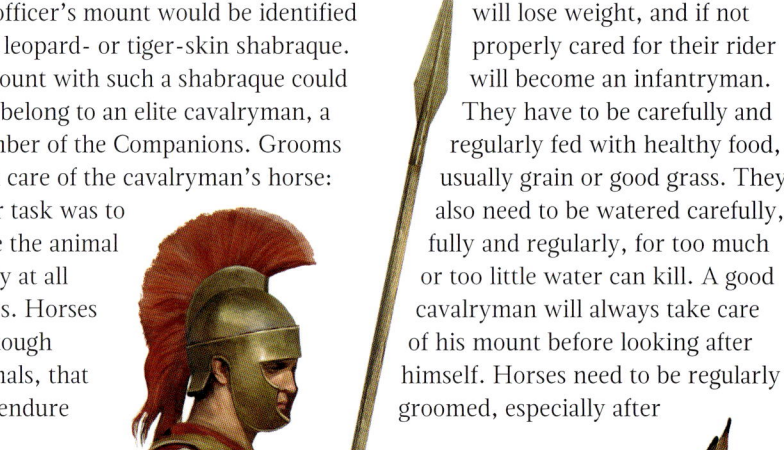

sweaty exertion, and the horse's feet and hooves need constant care. Eyes and nostrils need to be cleaned after a dusty march, usually with a clean, wet cloth or rag. These skills are often lost today, but for any horse-powered army with chariots, cavalry or both, they were essential.

As with later armies, the Macedonians had various orders of dress, such as ceremonial dress, off-duty dress, 'stable' dress, and the garments they usually wore under their armour in combat.

Prodromoi

These cavalrymen were cousins of the light cavalry employed as skirmishers in ancient Greece. The Macedonian version of light cavalry wore a Phrygian helmet with leather or linen armour. Their weapons consisted of a cavalry sword as well as a javelin, of which they carried more than one. A cavalry shield was also carried. They performed the usual light cavalry roles of reconnaissance and screening, but were also capable of effective mounted action in battle along with the heavy Companion cavalry.

Companions

The Companion cavalry, the hetairoi, were the elite of the Macedonian cavalry arm, much as the hypaspists were the elite of the Macedonian infantry. They would follow their king anywhere and under any circumstances. They were the reliable cavalry reserve whom Alexander could trust to ride to the rescue if necessary, and to make a decisive difference on the battlefield at a critical moment.

As could be expected from a kingdom known for its mounted arm, the Companions were excellent horsemen. They were well-mounted, well-trained, and expertly led and commanded. They were armed with a slashing sword (*kopis*) and a cutting and thrusting sword (*xiphos*), together with a lance (*xyston*) 3.5–4.25m (11–14ft) in length. For armour they had a muscle cuirass, additional shoulder protection, and a Macedonian cavalry

▼ **Prodromoi Cavalryman**
The Athenian prodromoi horsemen were javelin men who engaged while mounted and threw their javelins from that position. They may have evolved or been raised during the military reforms of Iphicrates in Athens in the 4th century BCE. His Phrygian helmet would be new for Athenian troops. His leopardskin saddlecloth is noteworthy, especially for an enlisted man.

helmet, topped off with a plume. They wore boots and greaves, as well as the Macedonian military cloak. They did not carry a shield.

The Companion cavalry was the senior cavalry in the Macedonian army, recruited from young noblemen who would be personally loyal to the king. Some sources list the strength of the Companions as 1,800 before the beginning of the Persian expedition, but it is possible that the entire unit did not embark on the campaign and that some remained in Macedonia, probably to provide security there.

The Companions were subdivided into eight subunits (*ile*), the senior or first being the Royal Squadron, the *basilike ile*. This unit was also designated the vanguard of the Companions, the *agema*, and was always positioned on the right of the Companions, the position of honour, when drawn up for battle. The Royal Squadron had a strength of 400, twice that of any other squadron in the regiment. The other seven squadrons were usually identified by their commanders and each was recruited from different regions in the homeland.

Alexander's tactics often relied upon pinning the enemy in position with the infantry and then using the Companions to launch an attack on the flanks or rear of the enemy formation. Alexander usually led the Companions' attack in a wedge formation.

▼ **Companion Cavalryman**
This elite horseman wears a plumed helmet but his cuirass is of stiffened linen. He has drawn his sword, probably for use in a melée if his lance was lost in combat or broken.

▲ **Officer**
This is an officer of an elite battalion in the foot Companions, as indicated by the officer's helmet. The absence of greaves is curious as most Companion officers would wear them, a symbol of rank and status. In combat he would most probably also be armed with a shield. His helmet is noteworthy for the decorative feathers, which might also indicate rank.

Selected members of the Companions formed the king's bodyguard or *somatophylakes* – these were members of the nobility whom Philip or Alexander trusted to fill positions of command. Under Alexander the bodyguard included men such as Hephaestion, Menes of Pella, Ptolemy and Perdiccas. Alexander wore the uniform cloak of the Companions, which was purple with a yellow border (described in some sources as 'golden yellow'). This cloak was worn by the 'personal companions' instead of the cloak worn by the rest of the regiment which could be yellow or white. Some sources also believe that Alexander issued cloaks of Persian style with a purple border after the death of Darius III. Alexander was always personally identified with the Companion cavalry and repeatedly led them in combat as the soldier-king that he was. His leadership and valour in action made the Companions devoted to him as commander.

The Companions at the Battle of Issus

The Companion cavalry was decisive in several battles during Alexander's conquest of Asia Minor. They played a key role in the conquering general's victory over Darius III in the Battle of Issus in November 333BCE. Alexander deployed the Companions on the right wing of the battle formation, the infantry phalanxes in the centre, and an allied group of Thessalian cavalry on the left wing commanded by the Macedonian general Parmenion. The battle was fought near the ancient settlement of Issus (close to modern Iskenderun in Turkey). An initial Persian attack on the Macedonian left wing was

▲ **COMPANION INFANTRYMAN**
Alexander's Companions were also fielded as infantry. They were considered to be an elite group. This infantryman is wearing a nominal cuirass with an interesting lion head motif. His shield and Phrygian helmet are typical of the period.

▶ **COMPANION INFANTRYMAN**
This is an excellent back view of a Companion infantryman, showing details of the shield and greaves, and the back of the soldier's cuirass. The protection on the lower body that is over the 'kilt' is also noteworthy.

successfully blocked by Parmenion. Alexander led the Companions to attack the Persian left wing and then in a direct assault on Darius and his Royal Guard in the centre of the Persian line. The cavalry overwhelmed the Royal Guard, Darius fled and the Persian army broke – handing victory to Alexander.

The Silver Shields

By invading Persia and consistently defeating the Persian armies that were mustered to meet them, the Macedonians gained access to a large amount of wealth in gold and silver that had been accumulated by the Persian kings through their conquests and via the satraps that governed the subordinate satrapies of the Persian kingdom. The gold and silver was allowed to trickle down to the troops in the ranks who embellished their clothing and equipment.

The Macedonian hypaspists, the elite infantry of the army, amassed so much wealth in precious metals, mainly silver, that they began to adorn their shields with it. As a result, they became known as 'the Silver Shields' (the Argyraspides).

▲ OFFICER'S MOUNT AND GROOM
Officers were allowed to have a groom whose sole purpose was to take care of the horse, to ensure that it was always ready for combat or any other duty. Grooms were personal servants and were not soldiers.

◄ COMPANION CAVALRYMAN
This Macedonian Companion cavalryman is more simply dressed than many; this one does not have a plume on his helmet and would usually be armed with a lance as well as short sword. The Companions' saddlecloths were done with fine embroidery which would indicate their status as elite troops.

Alexander's Companions, the elite group of Macedonian infantry, also shared in the spoils of the fantastically wealthy Persian empire. Alexander formed a Persian equivalent to the Companions for his campaign into India, which may have contributed in part to the famous mutiny there, where the worn-out Macedonian veterans of the original army told the king in no uncertain terms that they had gone far enough and wanted to go home.

War Elephants

The only enemy seriously to trouble the Macedonian phalanx was the army of King Porus whom Alexander encountered in the Battle of the Hydaspes during the Macedonian invasion of the Punjab in 327–326BCE. Porus's massed ranks of war elephants disrupted the phalanx and were able to cause major casualties. Alexander won the battle, however, by making the most of the mobility of his Companions cavalry and archers and, by driving back the left wing of the Indian army, causing the elephants to panic. Alexander was impressed by Porus himself, who ruled territory between the Hydaspes (modern Jhelum) and Acesines (modern Chenab) rivers in what is now Pakistan, and subsequently allowed him to remain in power as a subordinate ruler. War elephants could be armoured and were expected to use their tusks in combat, probably out of a sense of self-preservation, and Alexander took them into his own army. The Indian elephant was the species utilized by the Macedonians. There could be a 'howdah' used as a firing platform on top of the elephant, but it was not necessary nor was it always used. The 'crew' of an elephant usually consisted of a driver and two soldiers to fight with either javelins or bows, or both.

◀ WAR ELEPHANT
A Macedonian-style war elephant. The driver is unarmoured while the elephant and two-man crew wear protective armour. The castle tower is a version of the original Indian howdah. This war elephant and crew differs somewhat from the later version employed by the Successor armies.

TRAINED INFANTRY – HYPASPISTS AND PHALANGITES

The Macedonian army of Philip and Alexander developed into the best trained and organized army in history up to that period. Because of the almost endless campaigns these two kings conducted, the army became a professional fighting force composed of hardened marchers and killers who knew no other life. The army became the soldiers' home. This was true for the Macedonian cavalryman, engineer, light infantryman or hypaspist, and the phalangite who stood in ranks in the near-invincible Macedonian phalanx.

The cornerstone of the Macedonian army was its training. A Macedonian recruit's coaching and instruction was rigorous and tough; it began as soon as the recruit stepped into the army from civilian life. Macedonian soldiers were toughly disciplined, having been trained by a veteran cadre who knew their business.

Phalangite and Hypaspist

Of the two types of regular infantry in the Macedonian army, the phalangite was the usual infantryman who formed the mass of the infantry who fought in the phalanx, while the hypaspist was an elite phalangite – generally a selected veteran, hand-picked by his superiors for his skill, long service and loyalty to the king. Hypaspists were sometimes called 'Foot Companions'; the term means 'shield bearer' and their principal weapon was a spear between 2–2.4m (7–8ft) long. They often protected the right wing of the phalangite infantry. In the Battle of Issus Alexander led an attack of the hypaspists on foot before launching the ultimately decisive Companions' cavalry assault.

◄ **Hypaspist**
This smartly armed and accoutered elite infantryman wears an unadorned Thracian helmet, as well as what may be called a standard Macedonian shield, with no painted markings. His spear has an iron-tipped butt and he is otherwise in standard panoply.

▲ **Greek Phalangite**
Part of the allied contingent fighting with Alexander, this phalanx soldier wears a Thracian-style helmet with a tall comb that is in the middle of the helmet ridge. He wears a linen cuirass and his Spartan-style shield marking is either an indicator for his unit, a personal emblem, or a clan identifier.

TRAINED INFANTRY 229

▼ **Recruit in Training**
This simple dress, which now might be referred to as fatigue dress, was worn in camp when performing ordinary duties or by new recruits. Macedonian training was tough and demanding, in order to prepare the recruits for fighting as part of a disciplined unit in the phalanx.

◀ **Officer**
A hypaspist officer, one of the elite infantrymen of the army. While uniformly armed, the hypaspists could be individually accoutered, in as much as it could vary between versions of the same equipment. For example, while this one wears a Phrygian helmet, the men he commands might wear helmets of different design.

▼ **Infantryman in Camp Dress**
The conical hat is noteworthy, as is the fact that he is still armed and ready for any emergency should one arise.

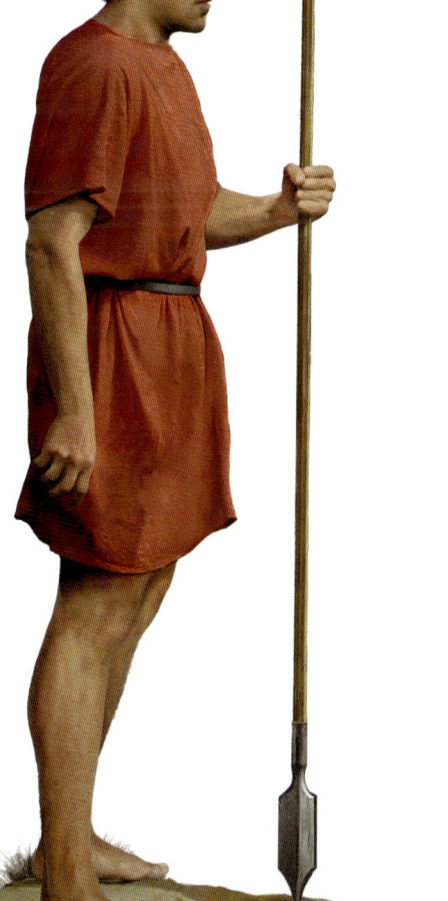

Training Recruits

Recruits' physical training inured them to hardship when campaigning. They were introduced to the long and heavy sarissa, the Macedonian pike that was the main arm of the phalangite. At 5.4–6m (18–20ft) in length, with an iron spear point and an iron butt to counterbalance the weight of the spear point, the sarissa was heavy; awkward for a new man, it took intensive training to be able to handle it, both individually and in formation.

The troops had to be conditioned to handling the sarissa; carrying it for different lengths of time, both in formation and on the march, increased the strength in the recruit's upper body and arms.

THE MACEDONIAN PHALANX

The phalanx reached its peak during this period. Because Philip armed his phalangites with the 5.4–6m (18–20ft) pike, the sarissa, instead of the 2.7–3.7m (9–12ft) Greek spear used by the traditional hoplite, he greatly increased the reach of the Macedonian phalangites. They could out-arm Greek hoplites and any enemy they might encounter. For protection the phalangite wore a bronze cuirass on top of leather armour and on his head had a bronze, Thracian-style helmet.

Phalanx Organization

In the Macedonian army, the basic unit of the phalanx was the *syntagma*, which was commanded by a *syntagmatarch*. The strength of the syntagma was 256 phalangites, formed in a square formation 16 files deep and in ranks of 16 across. Every file was a subordinate unit, led by a *lochagos*, with the file-closer, the *ouragos*, being the second in command. This was a commonsense approach in that if the lochagos were killed in action, the ouragos would take over in the heat of battle.

In the file there was a further division into subordinate units, each with their own leaders. The *hemilochites* commanded half of the file, and two *enomotarchs* were subordinate leaders to the hemilochites. So in a file of 16 phalangites, there were five leaders in the chain of command.

Two files were commanded by a *dilochites*, and a *tetrarch* commanded four files; each tetrarch therefore had two main subordinates through whom to exert command and control. The tetrarch's immediate superior was the *taxiarch*, who commanded two tetrarchs, which consisted of eight files. All of the unit commanders in the syntagmas were ranged across the front of the unit, and led their respective men into combat.

◀ PHALANGITE
This heavy infantryman wears a linen cuirass and a Phrygian helmet. His sarissa is broken down into two parts for carrying on the march. He could quickly assemble it when the order or alarm was sounded for combat in formation. The sarissa put the phalangite at a distinct advantage in a melée with sword-armed opponents at a distance, until the advent of the Roman Legion (see page 240).

▶ PHALANGITE
This heavy infantryman shows one type of armour worn by those who fought in the phalanx. He wears a bronze muscle cuirass, a Thracian helmet, carries the typical round Macedonian shield, and his main weapon, the sarissa, that made an unbroken phalanx nearly unbeatable.

Phalanx Formations

Twelve syntagmas made up the phalanx and they could be formed in combat, depending on the situation, into at least five formations. The line formation was undoubtedly the most common, with the phalanx advancing in a line abreast or standing fast in defence. Commanders sometimes used a crescent formation, with the syntagmas on both flanks being to the front, and the line bowing inwards. A third formation was the wedge, with two syntagmas abreast at the apex of the wedge and five syntagmas ranged at an angle on both sides of the leading two units. This was an effective offensive formation and probably easier to command and manoeuvre in the advance than the line. An oblique formation was also used, ranged either the right or the left behind the lead syntagma. It was employed to protect an exposed flank. Lastly a large square formation, made up of 24 syntagmas (two phalanxes) for all-round defence, could also be employed in an advance.

At the rear were the file closers, usually consisting of five individuals: two officers, one signaler or communicator, one herald and one trumpeter.

As in the original Greek phalanx, the Macedonians had two orders – open and closed – for the phalanx and its subordinate syntagmas. Open order was used for the movement to contact or for any manoeuvring before coming into contact with the enemy. When contact was imminent the phalangites would close up on order, the shouted commands being echoed by the subordinate commanders in the syntagmas. When the units closed up, the phalangites would 'lock shields' and the first five ranks of the phalanx would lower their sarissas towards the enemy. The remaining ranks and files would hold their sarissas up and to the front, keeping them out of the way of the first five ranks. When contact was made and the first casualties incurred, the phalangites in the rear ranks would step forward and take their place.

The superiority of the Macdeonian phalanx was made clear at the devastating Battle of Granicus in 334BCE, when their phalangites advanced against the Greeks, also arrayed in their phalanx prepared to cross spears and shields with the Macedonians. However, as the Macedonian infantry was armed with the sarissa, more pike than spear, they began to inflict casualties on the hoplites without incurring injuries in return. The shock, both physical and mental, of the two lines must have been terrific.

◄ **Hypaspist**
This soldier wears a bronze muscle cuirass, bronze greaves and a Thracian-type helmet with feathers as plumes, which were placed in small tubes soldered to the helmet. His round shield and 2–2.4m (7–8ft) spear are typical of this elite soldier.

► **Infantryman**
This man is a hypaspist but is accoutered quite differently. He wears a modified Thracian helmet with comb and plume, a linen cuirass and bronze greaves, giving a striking appearance.

ALLIES AND ENEMIES – SCYTHIANS, PHRYGIANS AND PARTHIANS

Macedonian neighbours, enemies and occasional comrades in arms included the Phrygians, the Scythians and the Parthians. The Scythians were well armed and armoured and used the horse both for mobility and to fight as cavalry. If necessary they were able to fight dismounted. A warlike, nomadic people who roamed the territory north of Macedon and who either hired themselves out as mercenaries or fought on their own account in search of loot or in self-defence, they were some of the finest mercenary cavalry in the ancient world.

The Scythians wore well-crafted scale armour and round iron helmets and sometimes helmets that resembled those worn by the Assyrians with a large, somewhat awkward horsehair crest. They carried lances and javelins as well as straight, broad-bladed swords. They also fought with daggers and a deadly type of axe – it could be called a war-hammer – that was of a quite modern design and proved extremely useful in melées and hand-to-hand combat. The Scythians also used a short composite bow and had a wide arrow quiver attached to their person. Their shields were small and either rectangular or round, with a crescent-shaped cut-out in the round shield. Sometimes the Scythians wore pointed turbans and multicoloured trousers like those of the Medes and Persians. They were called the Sacae by the Persians.

The Phrygians of Asia Minor wore trouser-like legging along with either a tunic that came to either just above the knee or mid-thigh. They usually wore long-sleeved shirts and sometimes a cap of soft linen. In cold weather they added fur-lined over-garments. They put on shoes or boots when mounted, which was often, if not most of the time. The Phrygians had a distinctive style of soft headgear, the shape of which would be developed into the helmet worn by the Macedonian heavy infantry of Alexander the Great.

The Macedonians believed that the Phrygians had formerly been known as the Briges when they lived close to Macedon and had become known as the Phrygians only when they migrated to Asia Minor. Greek historian Herodotus mentions that the Armenians were dispatched as colonists of the Phrygians, and if that is an accurate assessment, they were related to them; perhaps the Phrygians migrated because they had sent the Armenians across to Asia Minor before them.

▶ **Scythian Cavalryman**
This horseman is well-armoured in leather covered with metal scales. He is well-armed with a small cavalry-type shield, javelins and a cavalry sword. He would also have a composite bow which would be carried in a gorytos, *the Scythian arrow scabbard that was also large enough to carry the bow.*

The Phrygians were very similar in arms and appearance to the Scythians and like them were nomads, originally from Eastern Europe, north of Macedon, but finally drifting eastwards into Asia Minor. The Armenians were cousins to the Phrygians; their arms, equipment and clothing were nearly identical to the Phrygians. The Parthians from ancient Parthia developed the celebrated 'Parthian shot' with their horse archers. The Parthian shot was performed on horseback by a horse archer who, at whatever gait the horse was moving, but usually at the gallop, turned to his left and faced to the rear as he shot. This could be done while moving away from the enemy or after passing the enemy; either advancing or retreating, the horse archer could still fire at his enemy. The Eastern Romans would later adopt this method of firing from horseback with their horse archers and used the technique to deadly effect.

▲ PARTHIAN ARCHER
He is armed only with his composite bow and has no armour. He wears typical nomadic dress and while his cap may protect him from the elements, it would provide almost no protection in combat. He could very well be a horse archer who is dismounted. The Parthians were known, and greatly respected, for their skill with the bow, and were heavily recruited for that purpose.

▶ SCYTHIAN CAVALRYMAN
This is a Scythian nobleman, well-mounted and well-armed, who is wearing a Greek-style Attic helmet as well as scale armour. He is armed with a war-hammer, javelins and a composite bow, and his horse harness and trappings are fitted to his rank and status.

BEYOND PERSIA – THE INDIAN ENEMY

The Indian armies that Alexander faced had two basic threats – elephant-mounted troops and infantry. This was the Macedonian's first encounter with war elephants and it undoubtedly was a tactical and personal shock.

Greek historian Herodotus described the Indian troops who marched with Xerxes in his invasion of mainland Greece in 480BCE as wearing cotton clothing and being armed with bows made of 'reeds' and having arrows also constructed from reeds. The Indian infantrymen wore a wrap-around skirted garment that came down almost to their ankles. They often went bare-chested and barefoot. They carried a long broadsword at the waist; the sword itself was easily the length of an arm of a man of average height, if not longer.

The Indian javelin was constructed with bamboo and this made it both sturdy and light – bamboo being hollow. The Indian bow was 1.8m (6ft) in length and used a 0.9m (3ft) arrow. Probably the most important weapon of the Indian princes and potentates, it was made from bamboo with a string of hemp or animal sinew. Arrows were long, also. These were made from reed or cane with vulture feathers and were tipped with animal horn or iron. Sometimes the Indian archers fired poisoned arrows. Reports vary on the accuracy and effectiveness of the arrows. Some sources suggest they were virtually unstoppable and could pass through any shield or cuirass. Some of Alexander's military leaders said, however, that the bow and arrow were too heavy and the archers were unable to aim it accurately.

Indian swordsmen used a shield constructed with a hide covering that was similar in shape to the early Egyptian shields of the New Kingdom (1539–1075BCE), being generally rectangular, with the top of the shield being rounded.

▶ INDIAN WAR ELEPHANT
The war elephants were well-trained and usually had a 'crew' of three, one of them a driver. The middle man is an archer and the third man is assigned the duty of keeping the sun out of the archer's eyes. There is no howdah with this elephant.

BEYOND PERSIA – THE INDIAN ENEMY

◀ The Defeat of Porus by Alexander the Great (356-323 BC) 327 BC, *painted by Francois Louis Joseph Watteau in 1802, showing the chaos the elephants caused within the Macedonian phalanx.*

▼ INDIAN ARCHER
Indian archers were highly skilled and used the Indian version of what would later be called a longbow. This one is clothed to fit the climate and is armed with a long sword and a sheaf of arrows as well as his powerful bow. The Indian broadsword could be up to 112cm (44in) long and was a very powerful weapon. All of the Indian infantry were armed with it, whether or not they were bowmen. They could also be armed with a javelin with a three-pronged head, along the lines of a short trident.

Indian War Elephants

There was considerable shock among Alexander's veterans when they first faced the war elephants – just as the Romans were to experience later when they encountered them at the Battle of Heraclea in 280 BCE. Initially, troops who had never come across elephants were liable to panic, but they gradually learned how to fight them and render them hobbled or dead on the field.

The Indians used two to four men per elephant, one of them being the driver with an *ankusha*, a wooden stick that was pointed and with a hook that was used to control the elephant. The elephants had brass mountings on their tusks, which made them dangerous to opponents.

One type of armament of the elephant crew was the spear or javelin, thrown into the enemy from above, but the more usual weapon was an Indian bow. Sometimes a standard bearer would also be on the elephant.

Elephants gradually replaced chariots in Indian armies. After encountering them as Alexander went eastward towards India, the Macedonians adopted the formidable war elephant themselves into their own armies. Both the small-eared Indian elephant and the larger-eared African elephant were used by the armies of Alexander and his successors.

The End of the Road

Alexander's continued advance into India, while initially successful, pushed the Macedonian army to its limits. They had been gone from their homeland for years, and although Alexander had led them from victory to victory without losing any battles, they were worn out and wanted to go home. Alexander's increasingly erratic behaviour undoubtedly influenced his lieutenants and that filtered down to the men in the ranks. The resulting mutiny among his veterans finally influenced Alexander to withdraw and return.

The Macedonians had reached what they undoubtedly considered the end of the earth and probably saw no point in continuing. It is noteworthy that Alexander paid attention to them and made the decision to stop his journey of conquest and order the army to return, by land and by sea. In the power vacuum that followed his death, the Macedonian generals took over, dividing the loot and empire among themselves, to rule and fight over.

MACEDONIAN ARMIES AFTER ALEXANDER

The Macedonian generals who inherited Alexander's empire upon his early death not only had to fight to secure and maintain the new realm divided amongst themselves, but they also ended up warring against each other for more power, territory and prestige. The three generals who came out on top in the immediate aftermath of Alexander's death were Antipater, Perdiccas and Craterus. Antipater had been a trusted advisor to Philip II and had been left in Macedonia as regent when Alexander took the bulk of the army eastwards on the road to conquest. Antipater, who by all evidence had served Alexander loyally and ably, fell out of favour and Alexander sent Craterus home to replace him. Before Craterus reached Macedonia, however, Alexander died and the order was not carried out.

When news of Alexander's death was received in Greece and at home in Macedonia, it sparked a Greek revolt against Macedonian rule: the Lamian War. Many city-states joined the rebellion, which was led by Athens; the rebels fielded an army that attacked and then besieged Antipater in his fortress of Lamia, hence the name given to the revolt.

Antipater was besieged at Lamia until he was relieved by Leonnatus, who was killed in action leading the relieving force. Craterus later arrived with a Macedonian fleet and defeated the Athenians at the Battle of

▶ **Heavy Cavalryman**
A mercenary cavalryman from Asia, the equipment of his horse indicates he comes from Bactria or Sogdia. Despite his cuirass, armour on his arms, helmet and carrying a lance, he could be a light cavalryman, because he has no shield.

MACEDONIAN ARMIES AFTER ALEXANDER

◀ **Cavalry Officer**
This horseman is dressed for dismounted duty or is off-duty. He does wear his linen cuirass but with his cloak, and he is not armed. His leggings are probably worn for warmth.

Successor Mounted Troops

The elite Macedonian cavalry under the Successors retained their status and combat reputation. During this period the traditional Macedonian tunic went to short sleeves, probably to acclimatize to the weather in the former Persian empire. Cavalry officers would have a somewhat more elaborate linen cuirass than the enlisted troopers, and could be in more than one colour. Bleached white linen was still used for the cuirass, but sometimes other colours such as sky blue were used – at least for the officers.

Macedonian light cavalry in the period of the Successors were often Thessalonians, who served as mercenaries. They did not wear the traditional Macedonian military cloak, but one of two types – either dark red with a white border piped red, or black with a white border piped black. They adopted a soft cap after the campaigns in Persia: the Macedonian army were happy to take on some useful elements of the clothing worn by the Persian troops, and even took over some kinds of Persian civilian clothing to wear 'under arms'.

The Thessalonians were highly effective light cavalry. They were armed only with simple lances, built without a counterweight opposite the lance head. They did not carry a shield and were not issued any body armour or helmets.

Macedonian heavy cavalry maintained its reputation for excellence during the period of the Successors. They were very well trained and well disciplined, as well as being excellently led and commanded. Off-duty, they adopted

▶ **Guard Cavalryman**
This cavalryman's headdress indicates that he is a Guard on duty, probably at a headquarters or palace, as he is both armoured and armed. White stockings worn with sandals form an interesting feature of his 'uniform'.

Crannon in September 322BCE. The Greek revolt was crushed and another revolt in the eastern empire was suppressed by Peithon. Perdiccas and Eumenes mopped up the resistance in Cappadocia in Asia Minor.

These smaller conflicts evolved into the First War of the Successors (see also page 217), from which Antipater emerged as Regent of the Empire. There were in total no fewer than six wars of the successors over the half-century that followed, between 320 and 281BCE.

the same soft headdress worn by the Thessalonian light cavalry, but in combat they wore a helmet. They favoured white or sky blue tunics along with a traditional Macedonian saffron and purple military cloak, although there is evidence that some wore a red cloak with a sky blue stripe along its bottom. The Macedonian cavalry boot was an open-toed sandal-type shoe, something along the lines of the later *caligae* worn by the Roman army.

The cavalrymen wore a linen cuirass dyed sky blue to match the tunic. Off-duty, they sometimes wore a white tunic with the red and sky blue cloak. They carried a lance similar to the one used by Thessalonian light cavalry, produced without a counterweight at the butt of the spear.

Horse Care

For all that the Macedonian cavalry arm was excellently trained and equipped, a group of cavalry is only as good as its mounts – and the Macedonians took great care in mounting and remounting when necessary their cavalry. As we have seen, there is little doubt that the Macedonian cavalry of Philip II, Alexander and the Successors was the best of the Ancient World. Macedonian skill in horsemanship remained a constant during the period and the resupply of remounts to the army because of killed, lame or old horses was well developed; there does not seem to have been a major deterioration after Alexander's death in the era of the initial break-up and/or division of the empire under the Macedonian commanders.

▶ **Light Cavalryman**
With a Boeotian helmet typically used by mainland Greek cavalry, no armour, and armed with lance or javelin and shield, this is undoubtedly a light cavalryman.

Stable dress was worn when mucking out stables, grooming horses and for general fatigue duties. The dress was simple and functional – often merely the usual cavalryman's dress without weapons, armour and equipment. The Macedonian cavalry did have and use a simple spur, which was not worn with stable dress.

A cavalryman in typical stable dress would wear a long-sleeved Macedonian tunic, together with a cloak – often in the traditional Macedonian military colours of saffron trimmed with a broad purple stripe at the base of the cloak. He would be given a Boeotian helmet, which was popular with the Macedonian cavalry arm. The trooper's horse would be simply accoutered, especially for his head harness.

Guard Units

Guard troops, both infantry and cavalry, wore a mixture of clothing after the campaigns in the east. Infantry tunics went to short sleeves and were of many colours and patterns, both solid colours and stripes. The main kit consisted of tunic, military boots, round shield and helmet – with or without a horsehair crest and often with feathers, usually white, one on either side of the helmet crest. The usual decoration on the shields of the infantry was the traditional Macedonian sunburst, although sometimes it could be different, probably indicating a particular unit. Guard cavalrymen were very well equipped and armed, with a well-made cuirass, bronze or linen, and with an armoured skirt that came down to the knees over the tunic skirt. They carried round shields that were smaller than the ones used by the infantry. Their helmets bore long, flowing horsehair plumes dyed a uniform colour for each unit. Officers wore smaller plumes on either side of the helmet crest instead of feathers, and these were probably white. They wore a saffron and purple

MACEDONIAN ARMIES AFTER ALEXANDER

▶ **Cavalryman in Stable Dress**
Stable dress was worn when caring for the cavalryman's horse. It was comfortable to wear and practical enough so that if it did get dirty working around horses, it could be washed.

▼ **Heavy Cavalryman**
This heavy cavalryman is wearing a linen cuirass, a deep Macedonian-style helmet with plume, and a lance. He would also be armed with a cavalry sword.

military cloak and carried a sword, often with an eagle head, in a scabbard on the left side on a baldric over the right shoulder.

The Roman Legion

Macedon and the remains of Alexander's empire eventually had to face the threat from the west – Rome. The Macedonian army of Philip II and Alexander the Great was the best trained, organized and led in the ancient world – until the coming of the Roman legion. The Macedonian phalanx was defeated by the Roman manipular legion during Rome's three wars with Macedon. These were fought simultaneously with Rome's confrontation with Carthage, and they culminated in the end of Macedon's existence as an independent kingdom and its transformation into a Roman province. It was at the Battle of Pydna in 168 BCE that the Macedonian phalanx finally failed against an enemy, when the Roman manipular legion proved to be more flexible than the phalanx.

The Roman legionary's main weapon was the *gladius*, the short thrusting double-edged weapon that was used in conjunction with the *scutum*, the large, rectangular heavy Roman shield that was not merely for protection but, used with the gladius, was also a weapon. The polearm used by the Romans, the lead-shaft javelin, was mainly a missile weapon that was useful for killing and wounding the enemy infantry, but also for partially disarming him, the javelin penetrating the enemy's shields and then the lead shaft bending under the javelin's own weight, making the shield useless; this caused the enemy infantry to cast aside their shields and fight with either spear, sarissa or sword only. That was a distinct disadvantage against the well-trained Roman legionaries.

In the Battle of Pydna, part of the the Third Macedonian War and fought south of Pydna, the legionaries managed to break into the massed ranks of the phalanx. Fighting at close quarters, the combination of the Romans' short swords and

▲ *Silver tetradrachm of Philip V of Macedon.*

shields were much more effective than the long pikes of the Macedonians. In its aftermath the Macedonian king, Perseus, fled and the Romans annexed Macedonia, dividing it into four republics.

The Last Kings of Macedon

In the reigns of Philip V of Macedon (ruled 221–179 BCE) and his son and successor Perseus (reigned 179–168 BCE), Macedon was in direct confrontation with Rome, which was expanding from Italy. Philip V's panoply, his arms and equipment, were typical of Macedonian kings of the period. His armour was linen reinforced with metal scales; his cloak denoted his royal status. His armament and horse equipment were standard for the Macedonian cavalry.

A cavalryman in the period of Philip V was armed and equipped on the model of the Companion cavalry of Alexander the Great. He wore a

◀ PHILIP V

Philip V (238–179 BCE) was a later Macedonian ruler who was the second-to-last king of an independent Macedon. He fought hard to keep Macedon independent from Rome, and was also able initially to expand his territory. He was active and courageous in action, was a popular king, and finally died of ill-health.

MACEDONIAN ARMIES AFTER ALEXANDER 241

conical, plumed helmet, one central plume with one to either side of it. His cuirass was overlaid with scale armour and he was armed with a spear or lance, along with a sword. He also carried a small shield.

Macedonian infantry in the era of Philip V was armed and equipped in a manner little different to the time of Alexander, although the helmets were more ornate, some having horns on each side of a horsehair crest. The Macedonian peltasts, their light infantry, were unarmoured and wore a skullcap, but they carried the pike or sarissa along with sword and a small shield. The shield had three leather straps attached to the inside of the shield that enabled it to be handled easily in combat. Macedonian peltasts had either shoes or boots, or they would go barefoot.

Rome did not, or could not, completely defeat Macedon as the wars against Macedon were a *de facto* second front and the main Roman effort was against Carthage, but the three wars Macedon fought against Rome for its national existence eventually led to Macedon's permanent defeat and disappearance as an independent kingdom.

In 149BCE there was a Macedonian resurgence led by Andriscus the 'Pseudo-Philip' but the pretender was put to death. These cataclysmic defeats and the destruction of the Macedonian

▲ GUARD CAVALRYMAN
This Guard horseman, carefully selected as were all Macedonian Guard Cavalry, is wearing armour and clothing fit for an elite troop. His bronze cuirass is undecorated, but his shield is definitely Macedonian as identified by the eight-pointed star symbol on the shield's face. The typically deep (tall) Macedonian helmet, decorated with red and white plumes, indicate his Guardsman status.

▶ GUARD INFANTRYMAN
This elite Guardsman is easily identifiable in the red and white striped tunic. He carries the usual 2–2.4m (7–8ft) spear, and shield with the Macedonian identification device. He wears a Phrygian helmet with white feathers.

state effectively marked the end of the Successors of Alexander, and although bits and pieces of Alexander's empire remained under rule by the descendants of the original Successors, the collapse of Macedon and its transformation into a Roman province closed an era: the Hellenistic Period.

Greek culture had been taken and exported to the Indus in the east, and Egypt in the south, as well as Italy and Sicily in the west. While the kingdom of Macedon was erased, the Greek culture of learning, theatre and poetry, architecture and the sciences, especially mathematics, would live on – both admired and emulated by the Romans. It would come full circle when the Eastern Roman empire, which survived the fall of Rome by 1,000 years, gave up the western Roman language of Latin and adopted the language of the Hellenistic Period, Greek. Nonetheless, Alexander's empire was dwarfed in impact, greatness and the length of its existence by the Romans, who achieved a level of power and glory which Alexander and his generals could never have envisioned.

Alexander the Great's hard-won empire did not last long after his early death. His commanders divided the loot among themselves and almost immediately began squabbling among themselves which resulted in a succession of wars, even within the home country of Macedon. The Successor kings did learn from the enemies that they had fought and defeated under Alexander. Asian modes of dress, both for off-duty and in combat were adopted that gave the army/armies an eastern aspect in appearance. Weapons were also borrowed, such as the war elephant, which some commanders found useful. However, wounded elephants would be difficult if not impossible to control, might sow both destruction and panic within the battle array, and could

◀ **LIGHT INFANTRYMAN**
This light infantryman wears a linen cap in the shape of a pilos, and his clothing is light and comfortable. He carries the smaller round shield typical of javelin men and slingers.

▶ **INFANTRYMAN**
This is an older-style infantryman, without armour except for helmet and greaves. He wears a modified Thracian helmet decorated with horns. His regulation spear and shield complete his outfit.

◀ Successor War Elephant
The Macedonians were not too proud to copy innovations from an enemy and it appears that Alexander's Successors used war elephants also. Their howdah was shaped like a fighting tower which held two soldiers armed with javelins and sarissas. The sarissa was long enough to reach enemy soldiers on the ground. The driver sits in front of the fighting tower. Both African and Indian elephants were used by the Macedonian armies.

become a significant factor in changing the outlook of a battle.

What the Successors' wars did accomplish was to ruin the Macedonian empire and lead to disunity and disruption, which Rome would later take full advantage of. One aspect of the army did not change – the phalanx was still employed and it would be overcome by the inherent tactical flexibility of the Roman legion on the battlefield. The end result was that Rome would defeat Macedonia and all the disparate units of Alexander's empire, making them part of the Roman empire.

The Romans responded much more readily to changing tactics. They began with the phalanx, as did the Greeks and Macedonians. However, they developed the manipular legion, which was much more flexible tactically and much easier to manoeuvre, and ended by overcoming the phalanx.

▶ Cavalryman
This heavy cavalryman is fully accoutered and equipped. He wears scale armour, the high or deep Macedonian helmet with red and white plumes, and carries a shield – this one without the usual type of Macedonian markings. Lance and sword complete his panoply.

ARTILLERY AND SIEGE ENGINES

In the ancient world, siege equipment and engines were developed to undermine walls and to launch projectiles into fortified places. Towers were designed to enable assaulting forces to scale and span the defended walls of an enemy fortress. Rams and borers were used to batter down gates. Other machines were built to protect siege engines from enemy countermeasures, such as fire and molten liquids.

Rams were designed to be swung against the gates of a fortress to batter them into giving way. Besieging troops held simple rams in their arms and swung them rhythmically against the enemy gates. Larger rams were suspended from a frame by ropes; after the contraption was wheeled against the fortress gates, it was swung on the suspension ropes to gather momentum in order to crush the wooden gates.

Borers were a type of ram used to bore through the walls or to weaken them so that they would collapse; they could also be used in conjunction with a ram to pierce or weaken the fortress gates. Borers usually had a hardened point on the end, made of iron or other hard metals, that would be effective against the masonry of a fortress.

Mantlets were wooden shields, either on a wheeled carriage or placed upright on the ground and moved when necessary, that were designed to protect the besiegers whenever they were in range of the fortress walls. They could shield archers or cover troops who were trying to get close to the fortress walls in order to undermine them.

▲ *An illustration depicting the siege of Gaza by Alexander's army in 332BCE.*

▶ **MECHANICAL STONE THROWER (LITHOBOLOS)**
These artillery pieces, lithoboloi, were constructed in different sizes to throw stones of different weights. Their overall appearance would be similar if not identical regardless of the weight of the projectile, and they could be unassembled for transport. The smaller ones would be used on the battlefield, with the larger ones usually relegated to sieges. The utility of this piece of artillery is that the ammunition could be picked up in the field.

Gaining Height to Attack
The siege tower, of which there were different designs, was intended to be wheeled up to the enemy's walls: troops would then climb an internal staircase in order to get to a level that was the same height as the enemy's walls and, using some type of ramp or drawbridge, would attempt to attack across the ramp or drawbridge and gain access on to the enemy walls.

Macedonian Catapults
The Macedonian artillery arm was excellent. Three of the machines for which they were particularly known were the *lithobolos*, the

ARTILLERY AND SIEGE ENGINES 245

◀ **DART THROWER (OXYBELES)**
This early type of oxybeles was large enough to require a stand for it to be used. The crossbow was pulled back by levers and a winch and then loaded with a suitable bolt. The bolt was shaped like a large arrow, including stabilizing fins on the tail of the bolt.

onager and the *oxybeles*. The lithobolos was a mechanical stone thrower; the onager, a basic catapult; and the oxybeles a dart-thrower, of which there were two models.

The lithobolos came in a number of sizes. The smallest could throw stones of around 4.5kg (10lb). The largest threw a missile weighing 82kg (180lb). The lithobolos was mounted on a base or stand to give it stability in firing and was a large crossbow. The oxybeles, in both types, was a simple crossbow or a torsion bar arrangement set on a base. Both models fired a bolt capable of going through a man. The onager was either on four wheels or had no wheels at all and was so called (the term onager means 'wild ass') because when the arm of the catapult was loosed, being stopped by the frame extending upward and perpendicular to the basic frame, the catapult would literally jump or buck as the projectile left the catapult arm. Onagers were of different sizes, from a small catapult that could also be used at sea, mounted on galleys, to big onagers with large crews that could loose a projectile of a size intended to demolish solid walls and towers.

There was also a type of catapult that launched spear- or javelin-like projectiles, also of different sizes. These were very effective against troops and could be employed in conjunction with the onager to batter fortress walls and clear them of enemy troops, in order to move other siege engines close to the chosen point of attack. Siege machines would usually be covered with a fire-retardant material, usually animal skin, that would be difficult to ignite by fire or by molten liquid poured against it. Siege engines could be taken apart for transport so that an army intent on conducting a siege would at least have some siege engines on hand with which to begin. Other siege engines too large to transport could or would be constructed on the spot by the engineers and workmen of the besieging force.

▶ **DART THROWER (OXYBELES)**
This artillery piece is a more sophisticated oxybeles that was designed to be powered by torsion, which, simply, was rope twisted into shape that provided the force to fire the crossbow. This piece also fired a large bolt, again shaped like an arrow. This piece was also known as a katapeltes, or 'shield piercer', as the amount of force generated by the torsion mechanism could pierce both shield and armour at ranges over 400 metres or yards. Both this and the smaller oxybeles could be used in the field as well as in sieges.

ARMS AND ARMOUR

The Macedonians were armoured similarly to the Greeks, but in lighter, less decorative armour. This was functional, without the decorative features on metal cuirass and greaves – with the exception of the senior officers and Alexander himself.

Armour

Like the Greeks, the Macedonians usually wore a cuirass of either leather or stiffened linen, which gave fair protection and was much lighter for ease of movement, especially on long marches on the Asian mainland. The cuirass could be a muscle cuirass of bronze, but sometimes a half-cuirass that only covered the chest was worn. While the phalangite could be lightly armoured with a linen cuirass, the elite hypaspists would be armoured and accoutered similarly to a Greek hoplite, including hoplon and thrusting spear.

There was no great innovation with horse equipment in the Macedonian army. The saddle, saddlecloth and horse equipment were simple – as were those of other ancient armies and, of course, there were no stirrups in use yet. The innovation with the Macedonian cavalry, which was decisive to Alexander's successes, was the employment and skill of the Macedonian cavalry arm itself – well-trained, tough and well-led.

Shields

Phalangites' shields were round, as were those used by the Greeks, but they were smaller and handier to use, especially with a longer pike. In contrast to the hoplon, which was 1m (3ft) in diameter, the phalangite shield was only 60cm (2ft) across. Macedonian shields were usually, if not always, decorated with their national symbol, an eight- or later twelve-pointed stylized star. Alexander's elite Companions (the 'Argyraspides') had silver-plated shields.

▲ *Gold stater of Alexander the Great of Macedon. A vast number of coins bearing his head were issued during his reign.*

Helmets

The Macedonians adopted the Phrygian helmet, which was simpler and lighter than the older-style Greek helmet, though the latter was worn by Greeks that joined Alexander, by 'fear or favour' after he conquered Greece. The Phrygian helmet was worn sometimes with a horsehair crest on the comb and with feathers on the side of the helmet, or in any combination of the three 'styles'.

This was not the only helmet worn by the Macedonian infantry. There were at least three other types: the

▼ Shields

The Macedonian shield was smaller than the hoplon because of the length of the sarissa. It was undoubtedly worn slung across the back and had a plain bronze surface with the symbol cast into it. It was still constructed of wood with a bronze layer on the outside, just as the hoplon was.

ARMS AND ARMOUR 247

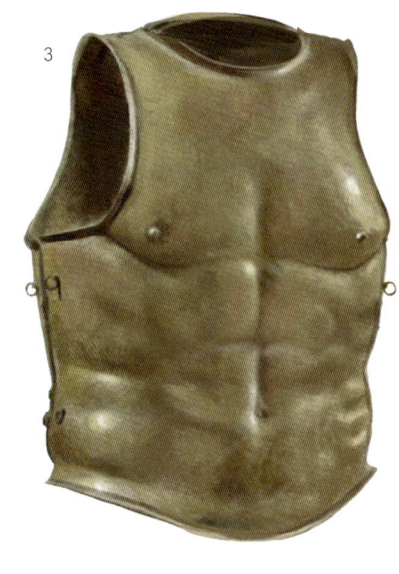

▲ Armour
Leather cuirass with bronze reinforcements (1); the older, more comfortable linen cuirass which could have metal inserts for extra protection (2); bronze muscle cuirass (3).

▲ Helmets
Alexander the Great's famously distinctive helmet (1); Companion cavalry Boeotian helmet with plume (2); Boeotian helmet (3); Attica helmet (4); Phrygian helmet (5) – note the holders for feathers and plumes that were soldered on the helmet; Thracian-style helmet with moveable cheek guards (6); late Corinthian helmet (7); Corinthian helmet with comb (8); Chalcidian helmets (9, 10).

Chalcidian helmet, the pilos, and the Thracian helmet. The Chalcidian helmet was a derivative of the classical Greek helmet and offered good protection for the back of the neck, had fixed cheek pieces, as well as protecting the nose. The ears were left uncovered which greatly helped hearing in combat. The pilos was adopted from the Thebans, and was basically a conical helmet that only offered protection for the skull without any protection for the back of the neck or the nose, and was without cheek pieces. The Thracian helmet provided some protection for the back of the neck and had moveable cheek pieces as well as provisions for a crest and other military 'plumage'.

The hypaspists, who were probably the most uniformly equipped and armed of the Macedonian infantry, wore at least two types of helmets. One was the Vergina helmet, which was similar to the Thracian helmet with the exception that it had a high metal comb along the centre line of the helmet, to which a horsehair crest could be attached.

These crests could have been in different colours to distinguish between hypaspist subunits. The other helmet worn was the Thracian helmet with coloured feathers and plumes attached. While it would make sense that the different subunits would wear the same style of helmet, it is probable that the hypaspists might not have done so.

The Macedonian cavalry helmet, as worn by the Macedonian heavy cavalry, had the appearance of an inverted decorative punch bowl. It was effective: there was no attempt to change it. Usually there was a horsehair plume that hung from the top of the helmet.

Alexander's personal helmet was somewhat ostentatious, decorated with intricate scrollwork and adorned by two white feathers on the side. The Romans would later copy the use of feathers in their helmets, undoubtedly influenced by the Greeks and Macedonians.

Edged and Missile Weapons

Like the Roman army that came after, the Macedonian army generally had two types of swords – a short one for the infantry and a longer for the cavalry. The infantry sword was secondary armament for the Macedonian infantryman. There were probably three types of infantry swords in use by the hypaspists and phalangites.

Their primary weapon was the pike and the solidity of the Macedonian phalanx. The cavalry sword, like the later Roman spatha, was longer, to give the Macedonian cavalryman the necessary reach to cut down opposing infantrymen. However, like his infantry counterpart, the main weapon of the Macedonian cavalryman was the spear or lance, which gave him even more reach against his enemies. For missile weapons, the Macedonian light infantry employed the bow.

▼ **Missile Weapons**
Arrow sheath for both arrows and bow (1); arrowheads (2). On the right are two types of composite bows; 3 and 5 are not strung, while 4 is. The composite bow was a powerful weapon and you can tell by comparing the strung and unstrung bows that it was strung seemingly backwards, which gave it strength and striking power.

▼ **Polearms**
The 5.4–6m (18–20ft) sarissa came in two parts for ease on the march. It is shown assembled and ready for action (1) and unassembled (2, 3) for carrying. Spearpoints are at 4, 5, 6, and 9. The centre piece for assembling the sarissa is at 7. Finally, the iron butt of the sarissa with two types (8, 10).

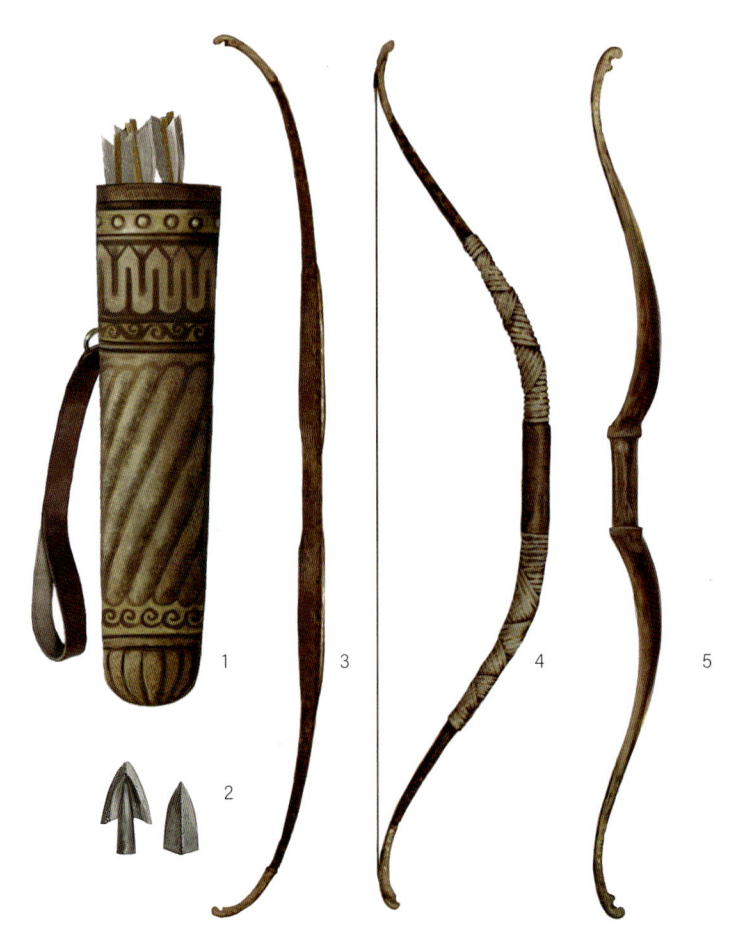

Polearms

The main weapon of the Macedonian phalangite was the sarissa, which was essentially what would today be called a pike. At 5.4–6m (18–20ft) long, the sarissa was around 2.7m (9ft) longer than the older Greek spear and was a formidable weapon when wielded by a trained infantryman. Some sources state that it could be unassembled into two pieces for ease in carrying on the march. The sarissa had to be held with both hands which is why the smaller, more efficient Macedonian shield was worn in combat, as well as on the march, and the phalangites did not 'lock shields' in combat as the Greek hoplites did.

The elite Macedonian infantry, the hypaspists (the 'shield bearers'), did not carry the sarissa but the shorter *dory*, a spear 2–2.4m (7–8ft) in length. In appearance and equipment, the hypaspist was much closer to the traditional Greek hoplite than was the phalangite. Their shield, also called a hoplon, was larger and more concave than the smaller phalangite shield and was carried in combat. These elite infantrymen could form a shield wall in the Greek tradition.

The cavalry spear or lance was much shorter than the sarissa for the use of mounted troops, but was again efficient if used by a trained cavalryman. The main problem with mounted combat during this period is that the stirrup had not yet been invented, and shock action was difficult to achieve in mounted combat because of the absence of a firm 'seat' on the horse. However, the Macedonians, as has already been demonstrated, fielded excellent native cavalrymen and Alexander not only employed them to great advantage on the battlefield, but led them in combat himself, being an outstanding horseman.

The Macedonian cavalry arm was excellent, even without the development of the stirrup at this time, and Alexander's elite cavalrymen contributed mightily to his string of impressive victories. After Alexander's death, the old Macedonian cavalry arm continued to be an important part of the successor armies and the weapons they wielded were the same as during Alexander's time. What arose later was something quite different, with the Sasanians and the resurgent Persians developing the armoured cataphract, the epitome being the Eastern Roman cataphract who did have the use of the stirrup.

▲ A stylized illustration of the Macedonian phalanx. This formation of well-disciplined infantry would be dominant in warfare until defeated by the Roman Legion.

▶ **Edged Weapons**
Swords designed as straight stabbing weapons are at 1 and 7. Slashing swords are at 2 and 6. A dagger is at 5 and two swords in their scabbards with attached baldrics are at 3 and 4. Note the ornate handles of 2, 3, and 4.

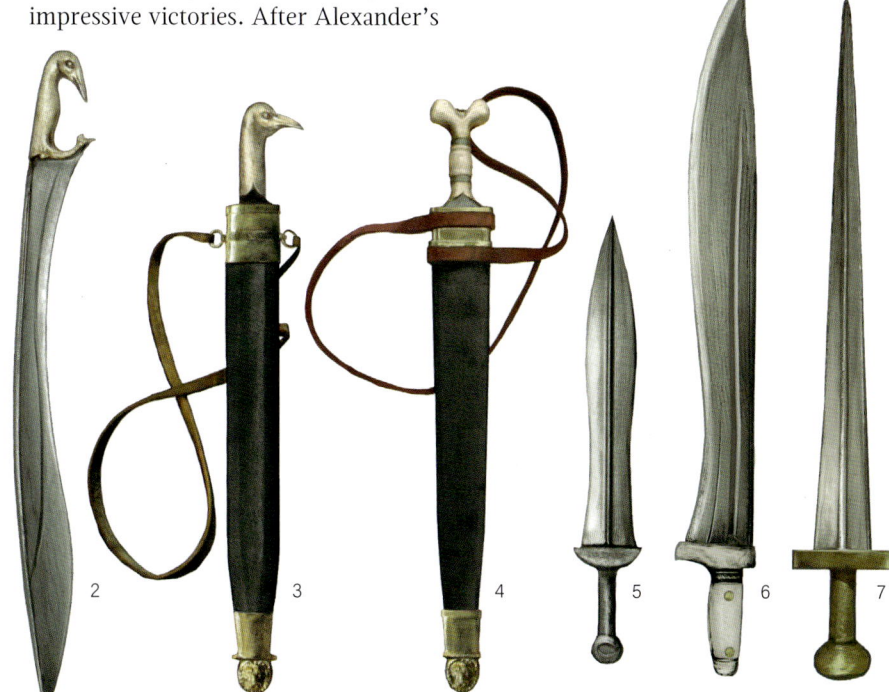

GLOSSARY

Achaemenids: The ruling dynasty of the Persian empire from Cyrus the Great to its conquest by Alexander the Great.
Agema: The vanguard of a Macedonian army.
Amrtaka: the Immortals, the elite infantry regiment of the Persian army.
Anabasis: The march upcountry of Xenophon's Ten Thousand after they were betrayed by the Persians.
Ankusha: A tool used for training elephants.
Antigonids: the Successor dynasty in Macedonia after the death of Alexander.
Argyraspides: An elite Macedonian infantry unit, the 'silver shields'.
Baivarabam: A Persian division, numbering 10,000 men, the most important being the Immortals.
Baivarapatis: A Persian division commander.
Caparison: The decorative covering or ornaments worn by a horse.
Cataphracts: Cavalry troops with both rider and horse heavily armoured.
Chiliarchia: A unit of 1,000 men. A Greek word applied to the Persian and Macedonian armies.
Chiliarch: The commander of a Chiliarchia.
Chlamys: A cloak worn by Greek and Macedonian soldiers.
Composite bow: A bow made of wood, animal sinew and bone or horn, more powerful than a simple bow.
Dathaba: A Persian unit of ten men, a squad.
Diekplus: The Greek naval manoeuvre that would break the enemy line of galleys.
Enomotia: The smallest unit in the Spartan army.
Enomotarch: The commander of an enomotia.
Galley: The typical warship of the period powered by both oars and sails; the masts would be taken down for combat. The most common warship of the Greek period was the trireme, which had three banks of oars on each side.
Gorytos: The case for an archer's bow and quiver of arrows.
Hazarabam: An old Persian term for regiment, meaning 'thousands.'
Hazarapatis: A Persian regimental commander, literally 'commander of thousands'. The hazaparatis of the Spearbearers' regiment became the second most important official in the empire after the king.
Hecatonter: A galley with two banks of 25 oars on each side.
Helots: The subjugated serf or slave class of the Spartan city-state.
Hetairoi: A member of the Macedonian elite cavalry unit, the Companions.
Hoplites: The Greek armoured infantry who carried the round shield, spear and sword.
Hoplon: The Greek round shield that gave hoplites their name.
Hypaspists: Macedonian infantry armed with spear, sword and shield. Roughly comparable to the hoplite and may have had Guard status.
Ile: A Macedonian cavalry squadron.
Irtu: A small bronze disk worn in the centre of the chest by Assyrian infantryman. It was attached to a harness that held it in place.
Katapeltes: The Greek term for a catapult.
Knobkerrie: A stick or club with a large knob at the end; by extension, a hard knob or ball used for striking when part of a combination weapon, such as on a dagger handle or a spear.
Kopis: The curved, slashing sword used by the Macedonian army.
Kyklos: A ring formed by Greek galleys fighting on the defensive.
Lamellar armour: Armour made of rows of small metal plates stitched together.
Lithobolos: A stone-throwing catapult.
Lochos: A Spartan hoplite unit, next down from the mora in size. Also the name of a Macedonian cavalry company within the ile.
Manipular legion: Style of troop organization used by the Romans, based on the maniple, a unit of 120 men.
Maryannu: Chariot-riding military elite of the early Middle East, especially of the Mitanni.
Mora: A large division of the Spartan army, whose commander was a polemarch.
Onager: The most basic design of Macedonian artillery catapult.
Ouragos: In a Greek or Macedonian Army, a file closer, one of the men who brought up the rear.
Oxybeles: A catapult that fired arrows or darts.
Panoply: The complete set of armour worn by a soldier in battle.
Pelta: A small, light shield of wood or wicker carried by Greek or Thracian light infantry.
Peltasts: Light infantry who carried the pelta.
Penteconter: A galley with 50 oars. Also used for the commanding officer of a Spartan pentekostys.
Pentekostys: A unit of the Spartan army between the enomotia and the lochos in size.
Periplus: A naval manoeuvre of extending the line in order to outflank the enemy.
Phalanx: The Greek and Macedonian fighting formation, long and deep, and dominant on the battlefield until defeated by the Roman manipular legion.
Pilos: A simple, roughly conical helmet used by the Greeks and Macedonians..
Polemarch: A Spartan 'war leader'; the commander of a mora.
Sacred Band: Theban elite infantry, comprising 150 pairs of training partners.
Samaina: An early Greek ship with 25 oars on each side, succeeded in design by the galley.
Sarissa: The long Macedonian pike carried by the phalangites in the phalanx. The term was also used for the cavalry lance.
Sataba: Persian company of 100 men.
Satapatis: A Persian company commander.
Satrapy: A province of the Persian empire, governed by a satrap.
Scale armour: Armour made of small, overlapping metal plates stitched to a backing garment.
Shabraque: A saddlecloth.
Sickle: A short sword with curved blade.
Somatophylax: A bodyguard.
Spara: The large, rectangular Persian shield.
Sparabara: A 'shield bearer', a member of an elite Persian infantry unit deployed in the front line to form a shield wall for archers.
Tiara: The cloth Persian headdress.
Ten Thousand: The Greek mercenary forces of Cyrus the Younger in his rebellion against his brother, Artaxerxes II of Persia.
Triaconter: A small, fast galley with 30 oarsmen.
Trireme: The most common type of Greek warship, with three banks of oars and equipped with a ram.
Xiphos: The two-edged, straight-pointed Macedonian sword.
Xyston: The Macedonian cavalry lance.
Zeira: A Thracian cloak.

INDEX

Abdalonymus 203, *203*
Abu Simbel 68, *68, 71*
Achaeans 129
  see also Mycenaeans
Achaemenids 20, 166, 170, 174
  see also Persian empire
Acropolis 115
Ahmose I 72, 83
akinakes 7
Akkadian empire 12, 14, 27, 29, 30, 66, 167
  map *26*
Alexander III (the Great) of Macedon 13, 21, 22–23, 150, 216–17, 218–19
  Battle of the Hydaspes 13, 218, 227
  and the Companions 169, 215, 217, 225, 227, 249
  conquest of Persia 11, 13, 165, 166, 171, 172–73, 213, 216–17 (*see also* Gaugamela, Battle of; Granicus, Battle of; Issus, Battle of; Tyre, siege of)
  death and legacy 13, 23, 169, 217, 219, 236
  depicted *9, 11, 22, 23, 212–13, 216, 219, 220*
  early years 215, 216, 218
  and Egypt 16, 73
  extent of empire 213, 217, *217*
  helmet of *247,* 248
  mutinies and end of campaigning 217, 219, 227, 235
Alexander Sarcophagus *23,* 203, *212–13*
Amenhotep III 72, 91, *91*
Amorites 27, 30
Anabasis (Xenophon) 10, 140, 194–95, 250
animal skin
  cloaks *96,* 96, 196, *204, 205,* 208
  headdresses *23,* 96, 146, 147, 163, *177*
  protective clothing 32, *33,* 34, 60, 76, 77, 146–47
  saddlecloths 45, *220, 223,* 227–8
  on shields 75, *111,* 197, 208
  on siege engines 46, 245
  see also leather armour
Antipater 219, 236, 237

Arabians 196
archers 10, 63
  Assyrian *15, 31, 43,* 44, *44, 47–49, 47, 48, 51,* 51–2, 54
  Egyptian army 74, 76, 77, 80, *80, 85, 85,* 99, *110*
  Egyptian navy *102,* 105, 106, *106*
  Greek navy *160,* 160–61, *209*
  Hittite *38*
  Indian *234, 235*
  Median 191, *193*
  Nubian *74, 76, 85*
  Parthian 233
  Persian *10, 172,* 180, 185, *191,* 191–92, *192, 193,* 196, *197,* 201, *205*
  Scythian 154, *209*
  Thracian 155
  see also bows
Archimedes 145
Argyraspides 226, 246, 250
Argive hoplite *137*
Aristotle 13, 216, 218
Armenia/Armenians 232, 233
armour
  Assyrian 44, 45, 49, 52, 60, 61, *61*
  Babylonian 61
  Canaanite 97
  Celtic 157
  Egyptian 77, *78, 79, 79,* 80, 82, *82,* 84, 90, *90,* 92
  Greek 135, 144, 146, *146,* 147, 148, *149,* 151, *160,* 162, *162,* 195
  of Greek naval troops 160
  Hittite 37, 39, *39,* 60–61
  Macedonian *221,* 223–24, 240, 245
  Minoan 120
  of Mitanni maryannu 71
  Mycenaean 122, *122,* 123, *123,* 124, 125, *125, 126, 127,* 130
  Persian cavalry *182,* 183–84, *184,* 185, 186, *187,* 198
  Persian chariot crews 187
  Persian Immortals 14, 138, 173, 174, 177, *181,* 204, *205*
  Persian infantry 188, 189, 190, 190–91, *193,* 210
  Persian marines 208, *208*
  Persian national contingents 178–79, 181, 183–84, 196, 211

Persian sparabaras *180*
Phrygian 152, *152*
Scythian *152,* 153, 154, 232, *232*
Sherden 98
spread, copying and reuse of 37, 110, 181, 185, 211
Thessalonian mercenaries 237
Thracian 155
see also helmets
arrows 10, 45, 85
  Egyptian *110*
  Indian 234
  Macedonian *248*
  Minoan 121
  Persian troops 188, 189, 208
  Thracian 155
Artaxerxes II 171, 184, 194–95
Artemisia of Halicarnassus 209, *209*
Ashurbanipal 31, 55, 58
Ashurnasirpal II 31, *31,* 42
Assyria/Assyrians 11, 14, 15, 29, 42–59, 102
  archers *15, 31, 43,* 44, *44,* 45, 47, *47,* 48, 48–49, *51,* 51–52, 54
  armour 44, 45, 49, 52, 60–1, 61
  and Babylonians 20, 28, 40, 41
  Battle of Qarqar 44
  cavalry 9, 42, 43, *43,* 45, 48, 48–50, *49, 50,* 53–54, 57, 58, 58–59, *59,* 61
  chariots 42–43, 45, *54,* 54–55, *55*
  infantry 42, 43, 44, *44,* 50, 50–53, *51, 52, 53,* 56, *59, 60,* 61
  map *26*
  overthrow and Persian rule 20
  reforms of Tiglath-Pileser III 44–45
  royalty *42,* 43, 44, 61, 62
  under Sargon II 56–59
  shields *42,* 44, 45, 52, 53, *53,* 62, 63
  siege warfare 15, 29, 46–47
  tactics 42–43, 44, 46–47, 50–51
  in timeline context 12, 13, 30–31
  weapons 45, 60, 63, *63*
  see also Nineveh

Athens/Athenians 13, 19, 117, 118, 119, *148,* 148–49, *149*
  Battle of Crannon 236–37
  and Celts 156–57
  and Macedon 214, 215, *223*
  navy *19,* 21, 145, 158–59, 161, *161*
  and Peloponnesian Wars 13, 116, 117, 119, 145
  and Persian invasions 117, 134, 138, 140, 159
Attic helmet *233,* 247
axes 63, *63*
  Cretan labrys 115
  Egyptian *82, 83, 108,* 108–9
  Hittite *36*
  Mycenaean 127
  Persian army 183, *183,* 190, *191, 204,* 205
  Scythian 232, *233*

Babylon (city) 13, *25,* 28, 30, 31
  Assyrian siege of 47
  death of Alexander 217, 219
  hanging gardens 15, 28, *28*
  Macedonian conquest 169, 218
  Persian conquest 167, 170
Babylonia/Babylonians 11, 14, 15, 28, 30, 40–41, 68
  army and equipment 40, *40, 41,* 61, 62
  capture of Jerusalem 13, 28, 31, 41
  conflict with Assyrians 29, 41, 55, 57
  map *26*
  Persian conquest 13, 15, 20–21, 170
Bactria/Bactrians 166, 172, 184, 189, 197, 198, 199, 201, 236
baggage trains 145, 180, 198, *199*
banners and flags 87, 177
  see also standards
battle-axes *see* axes
biremes *15,* 118, 207
boar tusk helmets (horned) *121,* 129, *130*
boar tusk helmets (plated) *122,* 123, *123,* 124, 125, *126,* 131
boarding spear 208, *208*
Boeotia/Boeotians 116, 151, 156
  helmet style *148,* 238, *238,* 247
  see also Thebes/Thebans (Greece)

bows 9–10, 192
   Assyrian 29, 43, *43*, 49, 54, 63, *63*
   Canaanite 97, *97*
   Egyptian 37, 70, 75, 79, 82, 110, *110*
   Greek 10, 192
   Hittite 37
   Indian 234, *235*
   Macedonian *248*
   Minoan 120–21
   Persian *172*, 177, 189, *191*, 192, *193*, *211*
   Scythian 154, *209*, *232*
   see also oxybeles
broadswords 157
Bronze Age 7, 12, 72, 114, 115, 125

Cambyses I 166
Cambyses II 13, 73, 167, 170, 206, 209
camels 69, 199, 207
   as cavalry mounts *9*, 173, 182, 184, 199
   for transport 177, 199, *199*
Canaanites 67, 68, 83, 97, *97*, *111*
   see also Philistines
caparisons 48, *48*, 49, *50*, 54, 61
   see also saddlecloths
Carchemish, Battle of 15, 31, 41
Caria/Carians 208–9, 216, 218
cataphracts 50, 186, 249
catapults (artillery) *244*, 244–45, *245*
catapults (manual) *see* slings and slingers
cavalry 9
   Assyrian 9, 42, 43, *43*, 45, *48*, 48–50, *49*, *50*, 53–54, 57, *58*, 58–59, *59*, 61
   Babylonian 40, *40*
   Celtic *157*
   Greek *134*, *135*, 144–45, *148*, 149, *150*
   Israelite 101
   Macedonian 9, 186, 220, *222*, 222–23, *223*, *240*, *241*, 237–38, *238*, *239*, 240–41, *243*, 246, 249 (*see also* Companions)
   Mycenaean 123–24, *124*
   Parthian 233
   Persian *10*, 182–86, *187*, 191–92, *197*, *198*, 201, *210*, *211*
   Phrygian 152, *153*
   Scythian 153, *153*, 232, *232*, *233*

Thracian *154*, 155
Celts 13, 118, 155, 156–57, 219
Chaeronea, Battle of 13, 22, 215, 218
chain mail 157
Chalcidian helmets 136, 247, *247*
Chaldea/Chaldeans 15, 28, 31, 40, 41, 57, 58, 114
   see also Babylonia/Babylonians
chariots 8–9
   Assyrian 42–43, 54, *55*, 61
   Canaanite 97, *97*
   Celtic *156*
   Egyptian *8*, 67, 69, 70, 79, 80, *90*, 90–95, *91*, *92*, *93*, *94*
   Hittite *36*, *38*, 38–39, *39*
   Israelite 101
   Mitanni 71
   Mycenaean *8*, *123*, 124–25, *125*, *128*
   obsolescence 9, 220–21
   Persian army 9, 184, 187, *187*, 220–21
   Sumerian war wagon 8, *32*, 32–33, 34
Cilicia/Cilicians 197, 201, 208
commanders *see* officers and commanders
Companions (Macedonian) 169, 186, *221*, 222, 223–26, *224*, *226*
   cavalry helmet *247*
   at Chaeronea 215
   at Gaugamela 202–3, 217
   as infantry *224*, 225, 227
composite bows 10, 37, 192
   Assyrian 45, 49, 54, *63*
   Egyptian 70, 79, *79*, 82, 110, *110*
   Lycian 197
   Macedonian *248*
   Minoan 121
   Persian 192, *193*, *211*
   Scythian 154, *209*, *232*
Corinth/Corinthians 19, *22*, 116
   helmet style *116*, 135, *136*, *137*, 146
Corinthian War 148–49
couriers 89, *89*, 180
Crannon, Battle of 236–37
Craterus 236–37
Crete 18, 99, 114, 208
   see also Lycia/Lycians; Minoans
cuirasses
   Assyrian 51, *57*
   Babylonian *40*
   Egyptian 78, *80*, 84
   Greek 122, 135, 136–37, *143*, 146, *149*, *151*, 162, *162*, *193*
   Macedonian *215*, *221*, 223, *224*, *225*, 230, *230*, *231*, 237, 238, *241*, 246, 247
   Minoan 120, *120*
   Mycenaean *122*, 123, *123*, *124*, 125, *126*, *127*, 130
   Persian 177, 184, 186, 189, *190*, *193*, 211
   Persian navy 208
   Phrygian *152*
   Scythian 153
Cunaxa, Battle of 10, 171, 194–95
Cyprus/Cyprians 18, 118, 119, 170, 208
Cyrus II (the Great) 13, 15, 20, *20*, 28, 166–67, *167*, 174, 184
   cavalry armour 49
   conquest of Babylonia 15, 20–21, 41
   standard of 177, 201
   in timeline context 13, 31, 119, 170
   tomb of *23*, 167
Cyrus the Younger 10, 140, 171, 184, 194

daggers 63, 81
   Assyrian *42*
   Egyptian 108, *109*
   Greek 149, *163*
   Macedonian *249*
   Mycenaean 127
   Persian forces 177, *179*, 183, *193*, 201
   see also short swords
Darius I (the Great) *165*, 167–68, *169*, 171
   invasion of Greece 21, 117, 134, 167–68, 170
   palaces of *13*, *21*, 164–65, *168*, 170, 175
   in timeline context 13, 119, 170
   tomb of *21*
   use of scribe 180
Darius II 21, 171
Darius III 13, 171, 201–3, *202*, 216, 218
   see also Gaugamela, Battle of; Granicus, Battle of; Issus, Battle of
Delian League 117, 119
Delta, Battle of the 65, 102, 106–7
Dendra panoply 125, *126*
Dorians 115
drummers 88, *88*

Eannatum 7, 34, *35*

Early Dynastic Period (Egypt) 26, 27, 65, 66, 73
edged weapons 62–63, 108–9, *109*, *163*
   see also axes; daggers; swords
Egypt/Egyptians 11, 12, 16–17, 27–28, 30, 65, 177
   overview 66–69, 72–73
   chariots *8*, 39, 67, 69, 70, 79, 80, *90*, 90–95, *91*, *92*, *93*, *94*
   footwear 38, 75
   Macedonian conquest 217, 218
   navy 102–3, 105–7, 206
   opponent peoples 70–71, 96–101, 104–5
   in Persian army 175, 196, 208
   Persian conquests and power in 206, 218
   see also Kadesh, Battle of; Middle Kingdom; New Kingdom; Old Kingdom
Elam/Elamites 40, 55, 57, 58
elephants 95, *95*, 227, *227*, 242–43, *243*, *234*, *235*
Epaminondas 150–51, *151*, 214
Ethiopia/Ethiopians 95, 175, 196, 208, 211
   see also Nubia/Nubians

facial hair 36, 52, 96
Fertile Crescent 14–15, 25, 26–31
   see also names of individual civilizations
field dress 176
   see also campaign dress
figure of eight shields
   Hittite *36*, 37
   Minoan 120, *120*, *121*
   Mycenaean *126*, *128*, *129*, *131*
   Persian 176, *178*, *179*, 189, *210*
   Scythian *152*
flags and banners 87, 177
   see also standards
footwear
   Assyrian *48*, 49, *51*, 59
   bare feet 32, 34, 38, 77, 79, 96, *128*, *131*, 208
   Egyptian 38, 75
   Greek hoplites 135, 148
   Macedonian 224, *237*, 241
   Mycenaean 123, 125
   Persian army 188, 196
   Sarangian 196
   Thracian 147
fortifications 26, 28, 74, 117, 157, 221
   see also siege warfare

INDEX

galleys 102, 104, *104*, 107, *107*, 158–60, 161, 206–7, *207*
Gatae 154
Gaugamela, Battle of 13, 171, 202–3, 213, 217, 218
gladius 157, 239
Gordium 152
  Gordian knot *213*, 218
Granicus, Battle of 171, 195, 216, *216*, 231
greaves
  Greek 137, *146*, *150*, 151, *151*, 162, *162*
  Macedonian *224*, 225
  Minoan *120*
  Mycenaean *122*, 123, *123*, 124, 125, *126*, *127*, *130*
  Phrygian *152*
  see also leg armour
Greco-Persian Wars 21, 113, 116–17, 158, 166
  invasion of Darius 134–35, 167–68
  invasion of Xerxes 138–40, 154, 168, 170–71, 173, 182–83 (*see also* Salamis, Battle of)
  Persian national contingents 146–47, 196–98
  in timeline context 13, 119, 170–71
Greece/Greeks 18–19, 132–46, 148–51
  overview 113–19
  arms and armour 10, 135–37, 146, 148–49, 151, 162–63, 192, 195 (*see also* helmets: Greek; hoplon)
  cavalry *134*, *135*, 144–45, *148*, 149, *150*
  Macedonian conquest of 215, 218
  map *114*
  navy 158–61, 206, 209
  opponent peoples 152–57
  in Persian forces 194–95, 202, 208–9
  phalanx warfare 132–33
  uniformity of equipment *138*, 142, 143, 179
  see also Athens; Greco-Persian Wars; Minoans; Mycenaeans; Sparta
grooms *226*, 227
guardsmen
  Assyrian 56
  Babylonian *41*
  Egyptian *81*, 86, *86*
  Hittite 37
  Macedonian *237*, 238–39, *241*

Persian *164–65*, 168, *174*, *175*, *178*, *179* (*see also* Immortals)

hairstyles 36, 52, 96
Halicarnassus 208, 218
Hammurabi 27, 28, 30, 41
Hatshepsut 72, *73*, 102
Hattusa 12, *14*, 27, 30, *30*, 36
Hazarapatis 174, *200*, 201
headgear
  Assyrian *42*, *43*, 52, 61
  Egyptian 76, *78*, *79*, 81, 86, 87
  Greek *146*
  of Hittite nobles *38*, 61
  Libyan 96
  Macedonian *229*, *237*, 241–42
  Median *193*, *210*
  Persian *174*, *175*, *176*, *177*, *181*, 187, *192*, *195*, 205
  Phrygian 152, *153*, 232
  protective cloth or leather 32, 34, *34*, 35, 61
  Scythian 153–54, *169*, 232, *233*
  Thracian *147*
  see also helmets
hecatonter 159, *159*
Hellenic League (Athenian-led) *see* Delian League
Hellenic League (Macedonian-led) *see* League of Corinth
Hellenistic Period 18, 242
helmets
  Assyrian *44*, *45*, *47*, 52, *52*, *53*, 60, 61
  Babylonian 61
  Boeotian *148*, 238, *238*
  Chalcidian *136*, 247, *247*
  Egyptian *82*, 82–83, *105*
  Greek *135*, 135–36, *136*, *137*, 146, 148, 163, *163*, 195, *233*
  Hittite *6*, 36, 37, *37*, 39, 61
  Macedonian (style) 223–24, *239*, *241*, 241, *243*, 248
  of Macedonian army (other types) *221*, *222*, 223, *223*, 224, 226, 229, 238, *238*, 246–48, *247* (*see also* helmets: Phrygian; Thracian)
  of Macedonian kings 240, *247*, 248
  Minoan 121, *121*
  Mycenaean *122*, 123, *123*, 124, 125–26, *126*, *128*, *131*
  Persian army *179*, 182, 186, 189, 196, 197, *210*
  Phrygian *144*, 152, *223*, *225*, *229*, *230*, *241*, 232, 246, *247*
  Scythian *152*, 153, 232

Sherden 99
Sumerian 32, *33*, 34
Thracian 151, *222*, 230, *231*, *243*, 247, *247*, 248
Hephaestion 203, 225
Herodotus 10, *11*, 119
  on Armenians 232
  on Croesus *166*
  on Egypt 17
  on Marathon 134–35
  on north Africans 96
  on Persian army 173, 175, 178, 182, 188, 207, 234
  on Thermopylae 143
hetairoi *see* Companions
Hittites/Hittite empire 11, 14–15, 26, 27–28, 68
  armour *6*, 36, 37, *37*, 39, *39*, 60–61
  Battle of Kadesh 8, 27–28, 37, 38, 65, 70, *71*, *93*, 93, 95
  chariot troops *36*, 38, 38–39, *39*, 61, 93
  infantry *36*, 36–37, 36–38, *37*, 39
  map *26*
  as mercenaries 52–53
  and Mitanni 71
  ships 104, *105*
  in timeline context 12, 30, 31, 73
  weapons *36*, 36–37, 63
Homer 12, 118, 127–28, 128–31, 207
hoplites 7, 113, 115–16, 132–33, *134*, 135–37, *136*, *137*, *139*, 146, *146*, *147*, 151, 162, 163
  combat with Persians 177, 180, *188*, 211
  contemporary depictions *18*, *19*, *113*, *116*, *118*, *142*, *188*, *218*
  under Iphicrates 148, *149*, 195
  as mercenaries *140*, *141*, *194*, 194–95
  naval 160, *160*, 161, 207
  Peloponnesian Wars *144*, 145
  Spartan *136*, *137*, *138*, *142*, 142–43, *143*, *144*, 146
  Theban *150*, 151
hoplon 7, 111, *113*, 132, *133*, *136*, *137*, 137, 145, 146, 163, 249
  Persian adoption 174, *190*, 191, 195, *195*, 210, *210*
  reforms of Iphicrates 148, 195
horn
  in bows 10, 82, 121, 161
  as musical instrument *100*, 100–101
  for weapon tips 85, 234
horned helmets 98, *98*, 99, *122*,

126, 197, 240, 241, *242*
  with boar tusks *121*, *129*, *130*
horse armour 39, 59, 61, *61*, 71, 90–91, 154, *184*, 185
  see also caparisons
horses 8, 12, 39, 61, 89, *89*, 222–23
  see also cavalry; chariots
Hydaspes, Battle of the 13, 218, 227
Hyksos 67, 70, 72, 80, 81, *81*, 83
hypaspists 226–27, 228, *228*, 229, *231*, 247–48, 249

Iliad (Homer) 12, 118, 127–28, 129
Illyria/Illyrians 215, 216, 218
Immortals, the 138, *165*, 173, *174*, *175*, 176–77, *181*, 191, 204
  later development 200, *201*, 204, 204–5, *205*
  standard bearers *173*, 201, *201*
India/Indians 7, 8, 234–35
  and Alexander's empire 217, 218–19, 227, 234, 235
  in Persian army 175, 184, 196, 211
infantry
  Assyrian *42*, *43*, 44, *44*, 50, 50–53, *51*, *52*, *53*, 56, 59, 60, 61
  Canaanite *97*, 97
  Egyptian Old Kingdom 74, *75*, 75
  Egyptian Middle Kingdom 76, *77*, 77, *78*, 78–79, *79*, 80, *81*
  Egyptian New Kingdom 69, *82*, *83*, *84*, 84–85
  Greek 113, *132*, *133* (*see also* hoplites; peltasts)
  Hittite *36*, 36–37, *37*, 39
  Israelite 101, *101*
  Macedonian *224*, *225*, 226–27, 228, 228–31, *229*, *230*, *231*, 241, *242*
  Minoan *120*, 121
  Mycenaean *122*, 122–23, *123*, *127*, *130*
  naval role 160, 206, 207, 208, *208*, 209
  Persian *178*, 178–79, 180, 181, *181*, 188–93, *192*, 195, *196*, *197*, *199*, 201, 202, *210* (*see also* Immortals, the)
  Phoenician *100*, 100
  Phrygian *152*, 152
  Scythian *152*, 153
  Sumerian 32, *33*, 34, *34*, 34–35

Thracian 155, *155*
Iphicrates 148–49, 195
Iron Age 7, 12, 73, 85, 110
irtu *40, 52, 56, 61*
Israel/Israelites 12, 13, 31,
  57–58, 73, *99,* 100–101, *101*
  Babylonian captivity 13,
    20–21, 28, 31, 41, 167
  Battle of Qarqar 44
  and Canaanites 97, 101
  early army 68, 100, 110
  exodus from Egypt 30, 73, 101
  and Philistines 99
  use of chariots 8, 101
Israel Stele *99,* 101
Issus, Battle of 23, 168–69, 171,
  202, *202,* 216, 218, *219*
  Greek mercenaries at *194*
  tactics 202, 225–26, 228

javelins 63, 146, 223, *223, 236*
  Greek *133, 147,* 147
  Indian 234, *235*
  Libyan 96
  Persian *185, 189*
  Roman 240
Jerusalem 13, 21, 31, 41, 47, 58
Jews *see* Israel/Israelites
Joshua 8, *100*

Kadesh 83
  Battle of *8,* 27–28, 30, 37, 38,
    65, 70, *71,* 73, 93, *93,* 95
Kardake 190, 195
Karnak 12, *17,* 83, 99
knobkerries *78, 82,* 85, *109,* 211
Knossos 12, 114, 115, 120
Kurkh monoliths *31,* 44

labrys *115*
Lacedaemon *see* Sparta
lamellar armour 37, 39, 61, 71
  Egyptian 71, 80, 90, 110
  Greek 137
  Persian 179, 186, 187, 188,
    189, 211
  see also scale armour
Lamian War 116, 219, 236
lances 40, 45, 49, 50, 58, 85,
  223, 237, 238
lassos 183, *183*
League of Corinth 22, 215, 218
leather armour 60
  Assyrian *47, 52, 52,* 57
  Egyptian *82, 83, 84,* 85, *86*
  Greek 136–37, 162, 163
  for horses 59, 61
  Macedonian 223, 230, 246,
    247
  Mycenaean *122, 123,* 125

Persian 179, *195,* 211
Philistine *98*
Phrygian 152
Scythian 232
Sherden 98–99
skullcap helmets 26, 32, 34,
  61, *98,* 163
Lechaeum, Battle of 148–49
leg armour 49, 51, *184,* 185
  see also greaves
Leonidas 138, *138,* 139
Leuctra, Battle of 117, 150, 151,
  214
Libya/Libyans 70, *71,* 74, 96,
  96, 99, 118
  in Persian army 175, 184, 196,
    211
linen armour
  Canaanite 97
  Egyptian 78, *78,* 79, 82, *82,*
    84, *84*
  Greek 136, 137, *143,* 146, *149,*
    160, *162, 193*
  Macedonian *223, 224, 230,*
    237, *237,* 238, *239,* 247
  Minoan 120, *121*
  Mycenaean *123,* 127
  Persian 189, 190, *190, 193, 198,*
    205, 208
lithobolos 244, *244*–45
logistics 69, *145,* 177, 180, 207
Luxor (Thebes) 12, *12,* 66–67,
  68, 76
Lycia/Lycians 197, 208, 218
  bow style 197
  swords *189*
Lydia/Lydians 119, *166, 167,*
  170, 196, 197

Macedon/Macedonians 11, 13,
  18, 22, 73, 155, 220–39
  cavalry 9, 186, 220, *222,* 222–
    23, *223, 236, 237,* 237–38,
    238, 239, 240–41, *243, 246,*
    249 (*see also* Companions)
  infantry *224, 225,* 226–27,
    228, 228–31, *229, 230, 231,*
    241, *242*
  opponent peoples 236–39
  Philip II's reforms 22, 213,
    214–15, 220, 221, 230
  siege warfare 220, 221,
    244–45
  Successor armies 236–43
  timeline 218–19
  use of elephants 227, *227,*
    235, 242–43, *243*
  see also Alexander III (the
    Great) of Macedon; Philip II
    of Macedon

maces *63*
Mantinea, Battle of 151, *151*
Marathon, Battle of 13, 21, 117,
  119, 134–35, 170
Mardonios 139–40, 170, 171,
  175
marines 160, *161,* 206, 207, 208
maryannu 71, 97
Media/Medes 28, 165, 188, 191
  absorption into Persian
    empire 20, 166, 167, 170
  clothing style *185, 189,* 191,
    200, 201
  in Persian army 173, 176, 182,
    188
  sack of Nineveh 29, 31
  in timeline context 13, 31, 170
Megiddo, Battle of 68, 73, 83
Mentuhotep II 76, *78*
mercenaries 194–95, 237, 232
  in Egyptian army 74, 75, 76
  Greeks as *140,* 140–41, 168,
    171, *194,* 194–95, 202
  Hittites as 52
  in Persian cavalry *183,* 183–84
  prisoners of war as 99
  Scythian archers as *209*
  Thracians as 154
Merneptah 71, 73, *99,* 101
Merneptah Stele *99,* 101
metallurgy 7, 34, 60, 153, 154,
  157
Methone, siege of 215
Middle Kingdom (Egypt) 12, 16,
  66–67, 72, 73, 76–81
Miltiades 134–35
Minoans 12, 114, 115, 118,
  120–21, 162
  ships 104, *104,* 121
missile weapons 10, 50, 63, 80,
  109, 192
  see also bows; catapults
    (artillery); javelins; slings
Mitanni 12, 27, 30, 37, 40, 67,
  70–71, 72
  Canaanites and 97
  Egyptians and 82, 83, 86, 90
muscle cuirasses
  Greek 122, 136, *151,* 162, *162*
  Macedonian *221,* 223, *230,*
    231, 246, *247*
musicians 88, *88,* 100–101, *131,*
  141, 143, *155*
Muwatallis II 30, 38, 65
Mycenaeans 12, *114,* 115, 118,
  122–31, 162
  arms and armour 125–28
  cavalry 123–24, *124*
  chariots 8, *123,* 124–25, *125,*
    128

as Homer's Achaeans 128–31
infantry *122,* 122–23, *123, 127,*
  130

Nabopolassar 15, 20, 31
naval warfare 65, 69, 117, 121,
  206–9, 245
  Egyptian world 102–7
  Peloponnesian Wars 119, 145
  Phoenicians and 100, 206–7,
    208
  see also Salamis, Battle of
Nebuchadnezzar II 15, 20, 28,
  31, 41, 170
New Kingdom (Egypt) 12, 16,
  67–68, 69, 72, 73, 82–89
  chariots 90, 90–95, *91–94*
  naval warfare 102–7
  war elephants 95, *95*
  see also Ramesses II; Ramesses
    III; Tutankhamun
Nineveh 15, *15,* 20, 24–25, 29,
  29, 31, 40, *62*
Nubia/Nubians 70, *70, 71,* 74,
  74, 76, 76, 77, 77, 85, 91
  in Persian army 175, 196, 211

oarsmen 207, *208*
officers and commanders 7,
  35, 61
  Assyrian 43, 61
  Egyptian Middle Kingdom 78
  Greek 141, *142*
  Macedonian 220, 222, 224,
    224, 230, 237, *237*
  Mycenaean *126*
  Persian 174–75, 179, *179, 181,*
    196, *200, 201, 204, 209,*
    209
  Sumerian 35, *35*
  see also royalty
Old Kingdom (Egypt) 12, 16,
  66, 68, 72, 73, 74–75
onagers 6, 244–45
organization of armies 7, 40–41
  Assyrian 42, 44–45
  Egyptian 65, 68–69
  Greek 133, 141
  Macedonian 22, 213, 214–15,
    218, 220–21, 224, 230
  Persian 173, 174, 175, 180
  Sumerian 34
oxybeles 245, *245,* 250

Pamphylia/Pamphylians 208,
  216, 218
Parmenion 168–69, 215,
  225–26
Parthenon, Athens 13, *13,* 18,
  112–13

galleys 102, 104, *104*, 107, *107*, 158–60, 161, 206–7, *207*
Gatae 154
Gaugamela, Battle of 13, 171, 202–3, 213, 217, 218
gladius 157, 239
Gordium 152
  Gordian knot *213*, 218
Granicus, Battle of 171, 195, 216, *216*, 231
greaves
  Greek 137, *146*, *150*, 151, *151*, 162, *162*
  Macedonian *224*, 225
  Minoan *120*
  Mycenaean *122*, 123, *123*, 124, 125, *126*, *127*, 130
  Phrygian *152*
  see also leg armour
Greco-Persian Wars 21, 113, 116–17, 158, 166
  invasion of Darius 134–35, 167–68
  invasion of Xerxes 138–40, 154, 168, 170–71, 173, 182–83 (*see also* Salamis, Battle of)
  Persian national contingents 146–47, 196–98
  in timeline context 13, 119, 170–71
Greece/Greeks 18–19, 132–46, 148–51
  overview 113–19
  arms and armour 10, 135–37, 146, 148–49, 151, 162–63, 192, 195 (*see also* helmets: Greek; hoplon)
  cavalry *134*, *135*, 144–45, 148, 149, *150*
  Macedonian conquest of 215, 218
  map *114*
  navy 158–61, 206, 209
  opponent peoples 152–57
  in Persian forces 194–95, 202, 208–9
  phalanx warfare 132–33
  uniformity of equipment *138*, *142*, 143, *179*
  see also Athens; Greco-Persian Wars; Minoans; Mycenaeans; Sparta
grooms *226*, 227
guardsmen
  Assyrian 56
  Babylonian *41*
  Egyptian *81*, 86, *86*
  Hittite *37*
  Macedonian *237*, 238–39, *241*

Persian *164–65*, 168, *174*, *175*, *178*, *179* (*see also* Immortals)

hairstyles 36, 52, 96
Halicarnassus 208, 218
Hammurabi 27, 28, 30, 41
Hatshepsut 72, *73*, 102
Hattusa 12, *14*, *27*, 30, *30*, 36
Hazarapatis 174, *200*, 201
headgear
  Assyrian *42*, *43*, 52, 61
  Egyptian *76*, *78*, *79*, 81, 86, *87*
  Greek *146*
  of Hittite nobles *38*, 61
  Libyan 96
  Macedonian *229*, *237*, 241–42
  Median *193*, *210*
  Persian *174*, *175*, *176*, *177*, *181*, 187, *192*, *195*, 205
  Phrygian 152, *153*, 232
  protective cloth or leather 32, 34, *34*, 35, 61
  Scythian 153–54, *169*, 232, *233*
  Thracian 147
  see also helmets
hecatonter 159, *159*
Hellenic League (Athenian-led) *see* Delian League
Hellenic League (Macedonian-led) *see* League of Corinth
Hellenistic Period 18, 242
helmets
  Assyrian *44*, *45*, *47*, 52, *52*, *53*, *60*, 61
  Babylonian 61
  Boeotian *148*, *238*, 238
  Chalcidian 136, *247*, 247
  Egyptian *82*, 82–83, *105*
  Greek *135*, 135–36, *136*, *137*, 146, 148, *163*, *163*, 195, *233*
  Hittite *6*, *36*, *37*, 37, *39*, 61
  Macedonian (style) 223–24, *239*, 241, *241*, *243*, 248
  of Macedonian army (other types) *221*, *222*, *223*, *223*, 224, *226*, *229*, *238*, *238*, 246–48, *247* (*see also* helmets: Phrygian; Thracian)
  of Macedonian kings 240, *247*, 248
  Minoan *121*, *121*
  Mycenaean *122*, 123, *123*, 124, 125–26, *126*, *128*, *131*
  Persian army *179*, 182, 186, 189, 196, 197, *210*
  Phrygian *144*, 152, *223*, *225*, *229*, *230*, *241*, 232, 246, *247*
  Scythian *152*, 153, 232

Sherden 99
Sumerian 32, *33*, 34
Thracian 151, *222*, *230*, *231*, *243*, 247, *247*, 248
Hephaestion 203, 225
Herodotus 10, *11*, 119
  on Armenians 232
  on Croesus *166*
  on Egypt 17
  on Marathon 134–35
  on north Africans 96
  on Persian army 173, 175, 178, 182, 188, 207, 234
  on Thermopylae 143
hetairoi *see* Companions
Hittites/Hittite empire 11, 14–15, 26, 27–28, 68
  armour *6*, *36*, 37, *37*, 39, *39*, 60–61
  Battle of Kadesh *8*, 27–28, 37, *38*, 65, 70, *71*, *93*, 93, 95
  chariot troops *36*, *38*, 38–39, *39*, 61, 93
  infantry *36*, 36–37, 36–38, *37*, 39
  map *26*
  as mercenaries 52–53
  and Mitanni 71
  ships 104, *105*
  in timeline context 12, 30, 31, 73
  weapons *36*, 36–37, 63
Homer 12, 118, 127–28, *128–31*, 207
hoplites 7, 113, 115–16, 132–33, *134*, 135–37, *136*, *137*, *139*, 146, *146*, *147*, *151*, 162, 163
  combat with Persians *177*, 180, *188*, 211
  contemporary depictions *18*, *19*, *113*, *116*, *118*, *142*, *188*, *218*
  under Iphicrates 148, *149*, 195
  as mercenaries 140, 141, *194*, 194–95
  naval 160, *160*, 161, 207
  Peloponnesian Wars 144, *145*
  Spartan *136*, *137*, *138*, *142*, 142–43, *143*, *144*, 146
  Theban *150*, 151
hoplon 7, 111, *113*, 132, *133*, *136*, 137, *137*, *145*, 146, 163, 249
  Persian adoption 174, *190*, 191, 195, *195*, 210, *210*
  reforms of Iphicrates 148, 195
horn
  in bows 10, 82, 121, 161
  as musical instrument *100*, 100–101
  for weapon tips 85, 234
horned helmets 98, *98*, 99, *122*,

126, *197*, 240, 241, *242*
  with boar tusks *121*, *129*, 130
horse armour 39, 59, 61, *61*, 71, 90–91, 154, *184*, 185
  see also caparisons
horses 8, 12, 39, 61, 89, *89*, 222–23
  see also cavalry; chariots
Hydaspes, Battle of the 13, 218, 227
Hyksos 67, 70, 72, 80, 81, *81*, 83
hypaspists 226–27, 228, *228*, 229, *231*, 247–48, 249

Iliad (Homer) 12, 118, 127–28, 129
Illyria/Illyrians 215, 216, 218
Immortals, the 138, *165*, 173, *174*, 175, 176–77, *181*, 191, 204
  later development 200, *201*, 204, 204–5, *205*
  standard bearers *173*, 201, *201*
India/Indians 7, 8, 234–35
  and Alexander's empire 217, 218–19, 227, 234, 235
  in Persian army 175, 184, 196, 211
infantry
  Assyrian *42*, 43, 44, *44*, 50, 50–53, *51*, *52*, *53*, *56*, *59*, *60*, 61
  Canaanite 97, *97*
  Egyptian Old Kingdom 74, *75*, 75
  Egyptian Middle Kingdom 76, *77*, 77, *78*, 78–79, *79*, *80*, *81*
  Egyptian New Kingdom 69, *82*, 83, *84*, 84–85
  Greek 113, *132*, *133* (*see also* hoplites; peltasts)
  Hittite *36*, 36–37, *37*, 39
  Israelite 101, *101*
  Macedonian *224*, 225, 226–27, *228*, 228–31, *229*, *230*, *231*, *241*, *242*
  Minoan *120*, *121*
  Mycenaean *122*, 122–23, *123*, *127*, *130*
  naval role 160, 206, 207, 208, *208*, 209
  Persian *178*, 178–79, 180, *181*, *181*, 188–93, *192*, *195*, *196*, *197*, *199*, 201, 202, *210* (*see also* Immortals, the)
  Phoenician 100, *100*
  Phrygian 152, *152*
  Scythian *152*, 153
  Sumerian 32, *33*, *34*, 34–35

Thracian 155, *155*
Iphicrates 148–49, 195
Iron Age 7, 12, 73, 85, 110
irtu *40, 52, 56, 61*
Israel/Israelites 12, 13, 31,
  57–58, 73, 99, 100–101, *101*
  Babylonian captivity 13,
    20–21, 28, 31, 41, 167
  Battle of Qarqar 44
  and Canaanites 97, 101
  early army 68, 100, 110
  exodus from Egypt 30, 73, 101
  and Philistines 99
  use of chariots 8, 101
Israel Stele *99*, 101
Issus, Battle of *23*, 168–69, 171,
  202, *202*, 216, 218, *219*
  Greek mercenaries at *194*
  tactics 202, 225–26, 228

javelins 63, 146, 223, *223*, 236
  Greek *133*, 147, *147*
  Indian 234, *235*
  Libyan *96*
  Persian *185, 189*
  Roman *240*
Jerusalem 13, 21, 31, 41, 47, 58
Jews *see* Israel/Israelites
Joshua 8, *100*

Kadesh 83
  Battle of *8*, 27–28, 30, 37, 38,
    65, 70, *71*, 73, *93*, *93*, 95
Kardake 190, 195
Karnak 12, *17*, 83, 99
knobkerries *78, 82*, 85, *109*, 211
Knossos 12, 114, 115, 120
Kurkh monoliths *31*, 44

labrys *115*
Lacedaemon *see* Sparta
lamellar armour 37, 39, 61, 71
  Egyptian 71, 80, 90, 110
  Greek 137
  Persian 179, 186, 187, 188,
    189, 211
  see also scale armour
Lamian War 116, 219, 236
lances 40, 45, 49, 50, 58, 85,
  223, 237, 238
lassos *183*, *183*
League of Corinth 22, 215, 218
leather armour 60
  Assyrian *47, 52, 52, 57*
  Egyptian *82, 83, 84*, 85, *86*
  Greek 136–37, 162, 163
  for horses 59, 61
  Macedonian 223, 230, 246,
    247
  Mycenaean *122, 123*, 125

Persian 179, *195*, 211
  Philistine *98*
  Phrygian 152
  Scythian 232
  Sherden 98–99
  skullcap helmets 26, 32, 34,
    61, *98*, 163
Lechaeum, Battle of 148–49
leg armour 49, 51, *184*, 185
  see also greaves
Leonidas 138, *138*, 139
Leuctra, Battle of 117, 150, 151,
  214
Libya/Libyans 70, *71*, 74, 96,
  96, 99, 118
  in Persian army 175, 184, 196,
    211
linen armour
  Canaanite 97
  Egyptian 78, *78*, 79, 82, *82*,
    84, *84*
  Greek 136, 137, *143*, 146, *149*,
    160, *162, 193*
  Macedonian *223, 224, 230,*
    237, 237, 238, *239, 247*
  Minoan 120, *121*
  Mycenaean *123, 127*
  Persian 189, 190, *190, 193, 198,*
    205, 208
lithobolos 244, 244–45
logistics 69, *145*, 177, 180, 207
Luxor (Thebes) 12, *12*, 66–67,
  68, 76
Lycia/Lycians 197, 208, 218
  bow style 197
  swords *189*
Lydia/Lydians 119, *166*, 167,
  170, 196, 197

Macedon/Macedonians 11, 13,
  18, 22, 73, 155, 220–39
  cavalry 9, 186, 220, *222*, 222–
    23, *223, 236, 237*, 237–38,
    238, 239, 240–41, *243*, 246,
    249 (*see also* Companions)
  infantry *224*, 225, 226–27,
    228, 228–31, *229, 230, 231,*
    241, *242*
  opponent peoples 236–39
  Philip II's reforms 22, 213,
    214–15, 220, 221, 230
  siege warfare 220, 221,
    244–45
  Successor armies 236–43
  timeline 218–19
  use of elephants 227, *227*,
    235, 242–43, *243*
  see also Alexander III (the
    Great) of Macedon; Philip II
    of Macedon

maces *63*
Mantinea, Battle of 151, *151*
Marathon, Battle of 13, 21, 117,
  119, 134–35, 170
Mardonios 139–40, 170, *171*,
  175
marines 160, *161*, 206, 207, 208
maryannu 71, 97
Media/Medes 28, 165, 188, 191
  absorption into Persian
    empire 20, 166, 167, 170
  clothing style *185, 189*, 191,
    200, 201
  in Persian army 173, 176, 182,
    188
  sack of Nineveh 29, 31
  in timeline context 13, 31, 170
Megiddo, Battle of 68, 73, 83
Mentuhotep II 76, *78*
mercenaries 194–95, 237, 232
  in Egyptian army 74, 75, 76
  Greeks as *140*, 140–41, 168,
    171, *194*, 194–95, 202
  Hittites as 52
  in Persian cavalry *183*, 183–84
  prisoners of war as 99
  Scythian archers as *209*
  Thracians as 154
Merneptah 71, 73, 99, 101
Merneptah Stele *99*, 101
metallurgy 7, 34, 60, 153, 154,
  157
Methone, siege of 215
Middle Kingdom (Egypt) 12, 16,
  66–67, 72, 73, 76–81
Miltiades 134–35
Minoans 12, 114, 115, 118,
  120–21, 162
  ships 104, *104*, 121
missile weapons 10, 50, 63, 80,
  109, 192
  see also bows; catapults
  (artillery); javelins; slings
Mitanni 12, 27, 30, 37, 40, 67,
  70–71, 72
  Canaanites and 97
  Egyptians and 82, 83, 86, 90
muscle cuirasses
  Greek *122*, 136, *151*, 162, *162*
  Macedonian *221*, 223, *230,*
    231, 246, 247
musicians 88, *88*, 100–101, *131,*
  141, 143, 155
Muwatallis II 30, 38, 65
Mycenaeans 12, *114*, 115, 118,
  122–31, 162
  arms and armour 125–28
  cavalry 123–24, *124*
  chariots 8, *123*, 124–25, *125,*
    128

as Homer's Achaeans 128–31
infantry *122*, 122–23, *123, 127,*
  130

Nabopolassar 15, 20, 31
naval warfare 65, 69, 117, 121,
  206–9, 245
  Egyptian world 102–7
  Peloponnesian Wars 119, 145
  Phoenicians and 100, 206–7,
    208
  see also Salamis, Battle of
Nebuchadnezzar II 15, 20, 28,
  31, 41, 170
New Kingdom (Egypt) 12, 16,
  67–68, 69, 72, 73, 82–89
  chariots *90*, 90–95, *91–94*
  naval warfare 102–7
  war elephants 95, *95*
  see also Ramesses II; Ramesses
    III; Tutankhamun
Nineveh 15, *15*, 20, *24–25*, 29,
  29, 31, 40, *62*
Nubia/Nubians 70, *70*, *71*, 74,
  74, 76, *76*, 77, *77*, 85, 91
  in Persian army 175, 196, 211

oarsmen 207, *208*
officers and commanders 7,
  35, 61
  Assyrian 43, 61
  Egyptian Middle Kingdom 78
  Greek 141, *142*
  Macedonian 220, 222, 224,
    224, 230, 237, *237*
  Mycenaean *126*
  Persian 174–75, 179, *179, 181,*
    196, *200, 201*, 204, 209,
    209
  Sumerian 35, *35*
  see also royalty
Old Kingdom (Egypt) 12, 16,
  66, 68, 72, 73, 74–75
onagers 6, 244–45
organization of armies 7, 40–41
  Assyrian 42, 44–45
  Egyptian 65, 68–69
  Greek 133, 141
  Macedonian 22, 213, 214–15,
    218, 220–21, 224, 230
  Persian 173, 174, 175, 180
  Sumerian 34
oxybeles 245, *245*, 250

Pamphylia/Pamphylians 208,
  216, 218
Parmenion 168–69, 215,
  225–26
Parthenon, Athens 13, *13*, 18,
  112–13

INDEX   253

galleys 102, 104, *104*, 107, *107*, 158–60, 161, 206–7, *207*
Gatae 154
Gaugamela, Battle of 13, 171, 202–3, 213, 217, 218
gladius 157, 239
Gordium 152
  Gordian knot *213*, 218
Granicus, Battle of 171, 195, 216, *216*, 231
greaves
  Greek 137, *146*, *150*, 151, *151*, 162, *162*
  Macedonian *224*, 225
  Minoan *120*
  Mycenaean *122*, 123, *123*, 124, 125, *126*, *127*, *130*
  Phrygian *152*
  see also leg armour
Greco-Persian Wars 21, 113, 116–17, 158, 166
  invasion of Darius 134–35, 167–68
  invasion of Xerxes 138–40, 154, 168, 170–71, 173, 182–83 (*see also* Salamis, Battle of)
  Persian national contingents 146–47, 196–98
  in timeline context 13, 119, 170–71
Greece/Greeks 18–19, 132–46, 148–51
  overview 113–19
  arms and armour 10, 135–37, 146, 148–49, 151, 162–63, 192, 195 (*see also* helmets: Greek; hoplon)
  cavalry *134*, *135*, 144–45, *148*, 149, *150*
  Macedonian conquest of 215, 218
  map *114*
  navy 158–61, 206, 209
  opponent peoples 152–57
  in Persian forces 194–95, 202, 208–9
  phalanx warfare 132–33
  uniformity of equipment *138*, *142*, 143, *179*
  see also Athens; Greco-Persian Wars; Minoans; Mycenaeans; Sparta
grooms *226*, 227
guardsmen
  Assyrian 56
  Babylonian *41*
  Egyptian *81*, 86, *86*
  Hittite *37*
  Macedonian *237*, 238–39, *241*

Persian *164–65*, *168*, *174*, *175*, *178*, *179* (*see also* Immortals)

hairstyles 36, 52, 96
Halicarnassus 208, 218
Hammurabi 27, 28, 30, 41
Hatshepsut 72, *73*, 102
Hattusa 12, *14*, 27, 30, *30*, 36
Hazarapatis 174, *200*, 201
headgear
  Assyrian *42*, *43*, 52, 61
  Egyptian *76*, *78*, *79*, 81, 86, *87*
  Greek *146*
  of Hittite nobles *38*, 61
  Libyan *96*
  Macedonian *229*, *237*, 241–42
  Median *193*, *210*
  Persian *174*, *175*, 176, *177*, *181*, 187, *192*, *195*, *205*
  Phrygian 152, *153*, 232
  protective cloth or leather 32, 34, *34*, 35, 61
  Scythian 153–54, *169*, 232, *233*
  Thracian *147*
  see also helmets
hecatonter 159, *159*
Hellenic League (Athenian-led) *see* Delian League
Hellenic League (Macedonian-led) *see* League of Corinth
Hellenistic Period 18, 242
helmets
  Assyrian *44*, 45, *47*, 52, *52*, *53*, *60*, 61
  Babylonian 61
  Boeotian *148*, 238, *238*
  Chalcidian *136*, 247, *247*
  Egyptian *82*, 82–83, *105*
  Greek *135*, 135–36, *136*, *137*, 146, 148, 163, *163*, 195, *233*
  Hittite *6*, *36*, 37, *37*, 39, 61
  Macedonian (style) 223–24, *239*, 241, *241*, *243*, 248
  of Macedonian army (other types) *221*, *222*, *223*, *223*, 224, *226*, *229*, 238, *238*, 246–48, *247* (*see also* helmets: Phrygian; Thracian)
  of Macedonian kings 240, *247*, 248
  Minoan 121, *121*
  Mycenaean *122*, 123, *123*, 124, 125–26, *126*, *128*, *131*
  Persian army *179*, 182, 186, 189, 196, 197, *210*
  Phrygian *144*, 152, *223*, *225*, *229*, *230*, *241*, 232, 246, *247*
  Scythian *152*, 153, 232

Sherden 99
Sumerian 32, *33*, 34
Thracian 151, *222*, 230, *231*, *243*, 247, *247*, 248
Hephaestion 203, 225
Herodotus 10, *11*, 119
  on Armenians 232
  on Croesus 166
  on Egypt 17
  on Marathon 134–35
  on north Africans 96
  on Persian army 173, 175, 178, 182, 188, 207, 234
  on Thermopylae 143
hetairoi *see* Companions
Hittites/Hittite empire 11, 14–15, 26, 27–28, 68
  armour 6, *36*, 37, *37*, 39, *39*, 60–61
  Battle of Kadesh *8*, 27–28, 37, 38, 65, 70, *71*, 93, *93*, 95
  chariot troops *36*, 38, 38–39, *39*, 61, 93
  infantry *36*, 36–37, 36–38, *37*, 39
  map 26
  as mercenaries 52–53
  and Mitanni 71
  ships 104, *105*
  in timeline context 12, 30, 31, 73
  weapons *36*, 36–37, 63
Homer 12, 118, 127–28, *128*–31, 207
hoplites 7, 113, 115–16, 132–33, *134*, 135–37, *136*, *137*, *139*, 146, *146*, *147*, *151*, 162, 163
  combat with Persians 177, 180, *188*, 211
  contemporary depictions *18*, *19*, *113*, *116*, *118*, *142*, *188*, *218*
  under Iphicrates *148*, *149*, 195
  as mercenaries 140, *141*, *194*, 194–95
  naval 160, *160*, 161, 207
  Peloponnesian Wars 144, *145*
  Spartan *136*, *137*, *138*, *142*, 142–43, *143*, *144*, 146
  Theban *150*, 151
hoplon 7, 111, *113*, 132, *133*, *136*, 137, *137*, 145, 146, 163, 249
  Persian adoption 174, *190*, *191*, 195, *195*, 210, *210*
  reforms of Iphicrates 148, 195
horn
  in bows 10, 82, 121, 161
  as musical instrument *100*, 100–101
  for weapon tips 85, 234
horned helmets 98, *98*, 99, *122*,

126, 197, 240, 241, *242*
  with boar tusks *121*, *129*, *130*
horse armour 39, 59, 61, *61*, 71, 90–91, 154, *184*, *185*
  see also caparisons
horses 8, 12, 39, 61, 89, *89*, 222–23
  see also cavalry; chariots
Hydaspes, Battle of the 13, 218, 227
Hyksos 67, 70, 72, 80, 81, *81*, 83
hypaspists 226–27, 228, *228*, *229*, *231*, 247–48, *249*

Iliad (Homer) 12, 118, 127–28, 129
Illyria/Illyrians 215, 216, 218
Immortals, the 138, *165*, 173, *174*, *175*, 176–77, *181*, 191, 204
  later development 200, *201*, 204, 204–5, *205*
  standard bearers *173*, 201, *201*
India/Indians 7, 8, 234–35
  and Alexander's empire 217, 218–19, 227, 234, 235
  in Persian army 175, 184, 196, 211
infantry
  Assyrian *42*, *43*, 44, *44*, *50*, 50–53, *51*, *52*, *53*, 56, *59*, *60*, 61
  Canaanite 97, *97*
  Egyptian Old Kingdom 74, *75*, 75
  Egyptian Middle Kingdom 76, *77*, 77, *78*, 78–79, *79*, 80, *81*
  Egyptian New Kingdom 69, *82*, *83*, 84, 84–85
  Greek 113, *132*, *133* (*see also* hoplites; peltasts)
  Hittite *36*, 36–37, *37*, 39
  Israelite 101, *101*
  Macedonian *224*, *225*, 226–27, *228*, 228–31, *229*, *230*, *231*, 241, *242*
  Minoan *120*, *121*
  Mycenaean *122*, 122–23, *123*, *127*, *130*
  naval role 160, 206, 207, 208, *208*, 209
  Persian *178*, 178–79, 180, *181*, *181*, 188–93, *192*, *195*, *196*, *197*, 199, 201, 202, *210* (*see also* Immortals, the)
  Phoenician 100, *100*
  Phrygian 152, *152*
  Scythian *152*, 153
  Sumerian 32, *33*, *34*, 34–35

Thracian 155, *155*
Iphicrates 148–49, 195
Iron Age 7, 12, 73, 85, 110
irtu *40, 52, 56, 61*
Israel/Israelites 12, 13, 31, 57–58, 73, 99, 100–101, *101*
  Babylonian captivity 13, 20–21, 28, 31, 41, 167
  Battle of Qarqar 44
  and Canaanites 97, 101
  early army 68, 100, 110
  exodus from Egypt 30, 73, 101
  and Philistines 99
  use of chariots 8, 101
Israel Stele *99*, 101
Issus, Battle of *23*, 168–69, 171, 202, *202*, 216, 218, *219*
  Greek mercenaries at *194*
  tactics 202, 225–26, 228

javelins 63, 146, 223, *223*, 236
  Greek *133, 147*, 147
  Indian 234, *235*
  Libyan *96*
  Persian *185, 189*
  Roman *240*
Jerusalem 13, 21, 31, 41, 47, 58
Jews *see* Israel/Israelites
Joshua 8, *100*

Kadesh 83
  Battle of *8*, 27–28, 30, 37, 38, 65, 70, *71*, 73, *93*, *93*, 95
Kardake 190, 195
Karnak 12, *17*, 83, 99
knobkerries *78, 82*, 85, *109*, 211
Knossos 12, 114, 115, 120
Kurkh monoliths *31*, 44

labrys *115*
Lacedaemon *see* Sparta
lamellar armour 37, 39, 61, 71
  Egyptian 71, 80, 90, 110
  Greek 137
  Persian 179, 186, 187, 188, 189, 211
  see also scale armour
Lamian War 116, 219, 236
lances 40, 45, 49, 50, 58, 85, 223, 237, 238
lassos 183, *183*
League of Corinth 22, 215, 218
leather armour 60
  Assyrian 47, 52, *52*, 57
  Egyptian *82, 83, 84*, 85, *86*
  Greek 136–37, 162, 163
  for horses 59, 61
  Macedonian 223, 230, 246, *247*
  Mycenaean *122, 123*, 125

Persian 179, *195*, 211
Philistine *98*
Phrygian 152
Scythian 232
Sherden 98–99
skullcap helmets 26, 32, 34, 61, *98*, 163
Lechaeum, Battle of 148–49
leg armour 49, 51, *184*, 185
  see also greaves
Leonidas 138, *138*, 139
Leuctra, Battle of 117, 150, 151, 214
Libya/Libyans 70, *71*, 74, *96*, *96*, 99, 118
  in Persian army 175, 184, 196, 211
linen armour
  Canaanite 97
  Egyptian 78, *78*, 79, 82, *82*, 84, *84*
  Greek 136, 137, *143*, 146, 149, 160, *162*, 193
  Macedonian *223, 224*, 230, 237, *237*, 238, *239*, 247
  Minoan 120, *121*
  Mycenaean *123*, 127
  Persian 189, 190, *190*, 193, *198*, 205, 208
lithobolos *244*, 244–45
logistics 69, *145*, 177, 180, 207
Luxor (Thebes) *12*, *12*, 66–67, 68, 76
Lycia/Lycians 197, 208, 218
  bow style 197
  swords *189*
Lydia/Lydians 119, 166, 167, 170, 196, 197

Macedon/Macedonians 11, 13, 18, 22, 73, 155, 220–39
  cavalry 9, 186, 220, *222*, 222–23, *223*, 236, *237*, 237–38, *238*, *239*, 240–41, *243*, 246, 249 (*see also* Companions)
  infantry *224*, 225, 226–27, *228*, 228–31, *229*, *230*, *231*, 241, *242*
  opponent peoples 236–39
  Philip II's reforms 22, 213, 214–15, 220, 221, 230
  siege warfare 220, 221, 244–45
  Successor armies 236–43
  timeline 218–19
  use of elephants 227, *227*, 235, 242–43, *243*
  see also Alexander III (the Great) of Macedon; Philip II of Macedon

maces *63*
Mantinea, Battle of 151, *151*
Marathon, Battle of 13, 21, 117, 119, 134–35, 170
Mardonios 139–40, 170, *171*, 175
marines 160, *161*, 206, 207, 208
maryannu 71, 97
Media/Medes 28, 165, 188, 191
  absorption into Persian empire 20, 166, 167, 170
  clothing style *185, 189*, 191, *200, 201*
  in Persian army 173, 176, 182, 188
  sack of Nineveh 29, 31
  in timeline context 13, 31, 170
Megiddo, Battle of 68, 73, 83
Mentuhotep II 76, *78*
mercenaries 194–95, 237, 232
  in Egyptian army 74, 75, 76
  Greeks as *140*, 140–41, 168, 171, *194*, 194–95, 202
  Hittites as 52
  in Persian cavalry *183*, 183–84
  prisoners of war as 99
  Scythian archers as *209*
  Thracians as 154
Merneptah 71, 73, 99, 101
Merneptah Stele *99*, 101
metallurgy 7, 34, 60, 153, 154, 157
Methone, siege of 215
Middle Kingdom (Egypt) 12, 16, 66–67, 72, 73, 76–81
Miltiades 134–35
Minoans 12, 114, 115, 118, 120–21, 162
  ships 104, *104*, 121
missile weapons 10, 50, 63, 80, 109, 192
  see also bows; catapults (artillery); javelins; slings
Mitanni 12, 27, 30, 37, 40, 67, 70–71, 72
  Canaanites and 97
  Egyptians and 82, 83, 86, 90
muscle cuirasses
  Greek 122, 136, *151*, 162, *162*
  Macedonian *221*, 223, 230, *231*, 246, *247*
musicians 88, *88*, 100–101, *131*, *141*, 143, *155*
Muwatallis II 30, 38, 65
Mycenaeans 12, *114*, 115, 118, 122–31, 162
  arms and armour 125–28
  cavalry 123–24, *124*
  chariots 8, *123*, 124–25, *125*, *128*

as Homer's Achaeans 128–31
  infantry 122, 122–23, *123*, *127*, *130*

Nabopolassar 15, 20, 31
naval warfare 65, 69, 117, 121, 206–9, 245
  Egyptian world 102–7
  Peloponnesian Wars 119, 145
  Phoenicians and 100, 206–7, 208
  see also Salamis, Battle of
Nebuchadnezzar II 15, 20, 28, 31, 41, 170
New Kingdom (Egypt) 12, 16, 67–68, 69, 72, 73, 82–89
  chariots 90, 90–95, *91–94*
  naval warfare 102–7
  war elephants 95, *95*
  see also Ramesses II; Ramesses III; Tutankhamun
Nineveh 15, *15*, 20, 24–25, 29, *29*, 31, 40, *62*
Nubia/Nubians 70, *70*, *71*, 74, *74*, 76, *76*, 77, *77*, 85, 91
  in Persian army 175, 196, 211

oarsmen 207, *208*
officers and commanders 7, 35, 61
  Assyrian 43, 61
  Egyptian Middle Kingdom 78
  Greek 141, *142*
  Macedonian 220, 222, 224, *224*, 230, 237, *237*
  Mycenaean *126*
  Persian 174–75, 179, *179*, *181*, 196, 200, 201, 204, 209, *209*
  Sumerian 35, *35*
  see also royalty
Old Kingdom (Egypt) 12, 16, 66, 68, 72, 73, 74–75
onagers 6, 244–45
organization of armies 7, 40–41
  Assyrian 42, 44–45
  Egyptian 65, 68–69
  Greek 133, 141
  Macedonian 22, 213, 214–15, 218, 220–21, 224, 230
  Persian 173, 174, 175, 180
  Sumerian 34
oxybeles 245, *245*, 250

Pamphylia/Pamphylians 208, 216, 218
Parmenion 168–69, 215, 225–26
Parthenon, Athens 13, *13*, 18, *112–13*

Parthia/Parthians 233
Parthian shot 192, 193, 233
Pasargadae 167, *167*
Peloponnesian Wars 18, 19, 116, 117, *117*, 147, 214
   siege of Syracuse 144–45
   in timeline context 13, 119, 171
peltasts 147, 148–49, 155, *155*, 241
penteconter 158, *158*
pentekostys 140
Perdiccas 225, 236, 237
Persepolis *13*, *21*, 165, 168, 176, *179*, 218
Perseus of Macedon *219*, 240
Persian empire 11, 16, 20–21, 28, 165–211
   overview 166–71
   archers *10*, *172*, 180, 185, *191*, 191–92, *192*, *193*, 196, *197*, 201, *205*
   arms and armour (summary) 210–11
   camel troops 199, *199*
   cavalry *10*, 49, 182–86, *187*, 191–92, *197*, *198*, 201, *210*, 211
   chariots 9, 184, 187, *187*, 220–21
   conquest by Macedonians 168–69, 186, 195, 201–3, 213, 216–17, 218, 225–27, 231 (*see also* Tyre, siege of)
   conquest of Babylonians 15, 20–21, 31
   extent and organisation *166*, 167, 172–73, *174*
   Greek mercenaries in *140*, 140–41, *194*, 194–95
   infantry (non-elite) *188*, 188–92, *189*, *190*, *191*, *192*, *193*, 196, *197*, 201, 210
   military training 178, 191, 210
   national contingents 146–47, 181, 182, 183–84, *186*, 188–89, 196–99, 208–9, 211
   navy 206, 208–9
   officers and commanders 174–75, 179, *179*, *181*, 196, *200*, 201, 204, 209, *209*
   rebellion of Cyrus the Younger 140–41, 184–85, 194–95
   sparabaras 180, *180*, *200*, 201
   Spearbearers 174, 201, 205, 210
   standards *173*, 174, *176*, 177, 180, 201
   in timeline context 13, 31, 73, 119, 170–71, 218
   see also Greco-Persian Wars; Immortals; Salamis, Battle
Persian Wars (with Greece) *see* Greco-Persian Wars
phalanx/phalangites 128, *129*, 132–33, *129*, 139, *142*, 163
   Macedonian 214, 228, *228*, *230*, 230–31, 243, 249, *249*
   Spartan 140, 143
   Sumerian 34, *35*
   Theban 150
Philip II of Macedon 22, 23, 133, 214–15, *215*, 216, *219*, *221*
   army reforms 22, 213, 214–15, 220, 221, 230
   assassination 202, 214, *215*
   Battle of Chaeronea 13, 22, 215, 218
   influence of Epaminondas 150, 214
   in timeline context 13, 171, 218
Philip V of Macedon 240, *240*
Philistines 8, 31, *98*, 99
Phoenicia/Phoenicians 100, *100*, 158, 208, *208*
   ships *15*, *107*, 107, 206
   see also Tyre/Tyrians
Phrygia/Phrygians 152, *152*, *153*, 190, 198, 218, 232–33
   cap style *179*, 187, 191, *192*, 195
   helmet style *144*, 152, *223*, *225*, *229*, 230, *232*, *241*, *246*, *247*
pikes *see* sarissa
pilos *135*, 136, *242*, *247*
Plataea 134
   Battle of 13, 21, 140, 166, 168, 171
polearms 32, *60*, 63, *82*, 85, *163*, *211*, *232*, *248*, 249
   see also lances; sarissa; spears
Porus 13, 217, 218, 227, 235
prisoners of war
   after Siege of Syracuse 145
   ancient depictions *24–25*, *32*, *45*, *70*, *71*, *78*, *169*
   of Assyrians 44–45, 47, 55
   of Egyptians 75, 83, 99
   Jewish Babylonian captivity 13, 20–21, 28, 31, 41, 167
prodromoi 223, *223*
professionalisation 44, 69, 78, 82, 214, 220, 228
Pydna, Battle of 133, 239, 240

Qarqar, Battle of 44
quadriga 54–55, *55*, 187
quivers and arrow sheaths
   Assyrian *42*, *45*, 49, *51*
   Egyptian 70, *85*, *92*, *94*, *102*, 105, *110*
   Macedonian *248*
   Mitanni 71
   Persian *164–65*, 188, 191, *192*, *193*, 211
   Scythian *209*, 232

Ramesses II 37, *64*, 68, 70, 71, 73, *85*, *92*, 92–93
   and Battle of Kadesh 8, 27–28, 65, 70, 71, *71*, *93*, *93*, 95
Ramesses III 65, 73, 99, 102, 106
   Temple of (Thebes) 71, 106, *107*, *110*
rams 46, *46*, 221, 244
   naval 102, *104*, *105*, *107*, 159, *159*, *161*, 206, *207*
Rome/Romans 11, 13, 16, 23, 73, 157
   defeat of Macedonians 23, 133, 239–40, 241–42, 243
   Eastern empire 21, 169, 186, 242, 233
royalty as warriors
   Assyrian *42*, 43, *54*, 54–55, 61, 62
   Egyptian *91*, *92*, 92–93
   Hittite *38*, 61
   Macedonian 168–69
   Minoan *121*
   Persian 167, 168, 169, 174, *184*, 202, 203, *203*
   Spartan *138*

Sacae 209, 230
   see also Scythians
Sacred Band of Thebes 151
saddlecloths 48, 59, 61, *124*, *220*, *226*
   animal skins as *45*, *220*, *223*, *227*, *228*
   of Persian army 185, *186*
Sagartians 183, *183*
Salamis, Battle of *19*, 21, 117, 139, 161, *169*, 209
   ships involved 158, 159–60, 161, *207*
   in timeline context 13, 119, 171
   Xerxes at 174, 209
Sarangians 196, *197*
Sardis 119, 167, 170, 197
Sargon of Akkad 14, 27, 30, 56
Sargon II 31, *31*, 56–57
sarissa 6, 137, 150, 194, 214, 220, 229, *230*, 231, *243*, *248*, 249

vs. hoplite spear 195, 230, 231
satrapies of Persia 167, 172–73
scabbards 63, 120, 122–23, *124*, *126*, 127, 137, *151*, *163*, 249
   for bows and arrows *211*, *232* (*see also* quivers and arrow sheaths)
scale armour 71
   Assyrian *44*, *47*, 51, *53*, 60, 61, *61*
   Egyptian 71, 82, *90*
   Greek 137, *137*, *149*
   Macedonian 241
   Persian 177, 179, *184*, 185, 186, 188, 189, *190*, 190–91, 211
   Scythian *152*, 153, *153*, 232, *232*, 233
   see also lamellar armour
Scythians *152*, 152–54, *153*, 155, 215, 232, *232*, 233
   campaign of Darius against 167–68, 170
   cap style *169*
   as mercenaries *209*, *209*, 232
   in timeline context 13, 170
Sea Peoples 8, 70, 71, *98*, 98–99, 115, 126
   and Egypt 65, 68, 71, 102, 106–7
   and Hittites 28, 37, 71
   and Mycenaeans 115, 126
   and rise of Assyrians 29
   ships 104, *107*
   in timeline context 12, 31, 73
Sennacherib 31, 57–58, *62*
shabraques *see* saddlecloths
Shalmaneser III *15*, 31, 44
Sherden 70, 98, 99
shield bearers *42*, 43, *53*, *90*
   see also hypaspists; sparabara
shield walls 133, 139, 180, 201, 205, 249
shields 62, *62*, 111, *111*
   Assyrian *42*, *44*, 45, 52, 53, *53*, 62, *63*
   Babylonian 40, *40*, *41*
   Canaanite 97, *97*, *111*
   Egyptian 77, 78, 79, *79*, *80*, 82, *82*, *83*, 84, 86
   Greek 135 (*see also* hoplon)
   Hittite 36, 37, *38*, 62
   Indian 234
   Libyan 96
   Macedonian 225, 226–27, *228*, 238, 241, *241*, *242*
   Minoan 120, *121*
   Mitannian 71
   Mycenaean *122*, 123, 125, *126*, 127, *127*, 128
   Persian later styles 174, 186,

190, 191, *198*, *204*, 205, *205*, 210, *210*
Persian national and mercenary troops 190, *195*, 196, 197, 208, *208*, 211
Persian spara 180, *180*, *200*, 201, *210*
Persian traditional styles *111*, 176–77, *178*, 179, *179*, 181, 188, *188*, *189*, *210*, 211
Philistine *111*
Phrygian 152, *152*
Scythian *152*, 154, 232
Sherden 98
Spartan *136*
Sumerian 32, *33*, *34*, 62
Thracian 148
ships and boats
Assyrian *15*
Egyptian *17*, 65, 69, *102*, 102–3, *103*
Greek *19*, 158–60, 206
Hittite 104, *105*
Minoan *104*, 121
Phoenician *107*, 206–7, *207*
Sea Peoples *106*
Tyrian *104*
short swords 50, 81, 86, *109*, 120, *120*, 122–23, 163, *178*, 185
see also daggers
Sicily 18, 118, 145
Sidon 100, 203
Alexander Sarcophagus *23*, 203, *212–13*
siege warfare 46–48, 55, 83, 145, 220, 221, 244–45
Silver Shields 226–27
slings and slingers *50*, 50–51, *62*, 63, 101, *149*, *149*, 180
Snefru 74–75
sparabaras 180, *180*, *200*, 201
Sparta/Spartans 13, 19, 113, 116, 118, 119, *141*, 141–43, 214
Battle of Lechaeum 148–49
Battle of Leuctra 150, 151, 214
hoplites *136*, *137*, *138*, 140, *142*, 142–43, *143*, *144*, 146
and Persian Wars 21, 113, 134, 138–39, 168, 171–72, 176
resistance to Macedonia 22, 215, 218
see also Peloponnesian Wars
spatha 157
Spearbearers (Persian regiment) 174, 201, 205, 210
spears 63
Assyrian *44*, *53*, *60*
Egyptian *78*, 78–79, 84, *84*
Greek *137*, *138*, *149*, 150, 151, 163, *163*, 195
Hittite *36*, 37, *37*, 39, *39*
Macedonian 228, 249
Mycenaean 126–27, *127*, *128*
Persian 177, 188, *211*
Sarangian 196
see also javelins; lances; sarissa
Standard of Ur 32, 33–34
standards and standard bearers 235
Celtic 157
Egyptian 75, *75*, *77*, *81*, *86*, 86–87, *87*
Persian *173*, 174, *176*, 177, *177*, 180, 201, *201*
Sumerian 34, *35* (*see also* Standard of Ur)
stave bows *85*, *96*, *102*, 106, 110, *110*
Stele of Vultures *7*, 34, *35*
stirrups 186, 249
Strabo 178
Successors of Alexander 23, 169
see also Wars of the Successors
Sumer/Sumerians 11, 14, 26–27, 30, 32–35, 68
clothing and equipment *32*, *33*, 34, *34*, *35*, 60, 62, 63
map *26*
Stele of Vultures reliefs *7*, 34, *35*
vehicles 8, 26, *32*, 32–33, 34
writing 12, 14, 26
Ziggurat of Ur *27*
supply trains *see* logistics
Susa *21*, 40, 55
swords 63, 81, *109*
Assyrian *42*, *43*, *45*, *50*, *52*, *59*, *60*, 63, *63*
Babylonian 40
Celtic 157
Egyptian 78, 86, 108, *109*
Greek *136*, *137*, 148, 149, 151, 163, *163*, 195
Hittite *36*, *36*, 63
Indian *235*
Libyan 96
Macedonian 248, *249*
Minoan 120
Mycenaean 122–23, *124*, *126*, 127
Persian forces 177, *178*, *179*, 185, *189*, 201, 208, *208*, 211
Phrygian 152
Roman 157, 239
Scythian *153*, 232
Sherden 98
Sumerian 7
Thracian 155, *155*
see also daggers
Syracuse, siege of 145
Syria/Syrians 14, 27, 30, 47, 57, 73, 196
see also Canaanites; Carchemish; Kadesh; Qarqar; Ugarit

tactics
of Alexander 168–69, 202–3, 224–25, 225–26, 227, 228
Assyrian 42–43, 44, 46–47, 50–51
at Chaeronea 215
Egyptian Middle Kingdom 80
at Leuctra 150, *151*
at Marathon 134–35
naval 106, 161
Persian 180
phalanx formations 231
Takabara 196
terrain 6–7, 55, 133
Egyptian 17
Greek 7, 18, 116, 124, 125, *134*, 144
Thebes (Luxor, Egypt) *12*, *12*, 66–67, 68, 76
Thebes/Thebans (Greece) 19, 115, 116, *150*, 214, 215
Battle of Leuctra 117, 150, 151, 214
Themistocles 139, 158–59, 161
Thermopylae, Battle of (279 BCE) 157
Thermopylae, Battle of (480 BCE) 113, 117, 138–39, 140, 168, 176
in timeline context 13, 119, 171
Thessalonians 237
Thessaly/Thessalians 116, 150, 157, 215, 218, 225–26
Thrace/Thracians 119, 146–47, 152, *154*, 154–55, *155*, 170, 214, 218
helmet style 151, *222*, *230*, *231*, *243*, *247*, *247*, 248
throwing sticks 109, *109*
Thucydides 10, 118, 140
Thutmose III *17*, 67–68, 72, 83–84, *91*
tiara *175*, 176, *178*, *181*, 185, 188, 189
Tiglath-Pileser III 9, 31, 44–45, 47, 54–55, *55*, 56
training
Egyptian 68, 69, 78
importance of writing 38–39
Macedonian 216, 228, 229
of musicians 88
Persian 178, 191, 210
Spartan 118, 141, 142

and warrior–soldier distinction 7
triaconter 158, *159*
triremes 158–60, 161, *161*, 206–7, *207*
Troy/Trojan War 12, 118, 127–31
trumpets 88, *88*, *141*, 155
turbans 189
Tutankhamun *17*, 67, 72
Tyre/Tyrians 31, 55, 100
ships *104*, 105
siege of 105, 216–17, 218, 221

Ugarit 104, *105*
Ur *27*
Standard of *32*, 33–34

Vergina helmet 248

war-hammers 190, *197*, *233*, 240
war wagons 8, *32*, 32–33, 34
Wars of the Successors 13, 219, 227, 236–37, 242–43
wheel blades 55, 187
wheel technology 8, 9
Assyrian 54
Egyptian 39, 90
Hittite 39
Mycenaean 124, 125
Sumerian 8, 26, 32
written records
Egyptian 74, 76, 83, 95, 99
Fertile Crescent 14, 26, 27, 38–39, 54, 55, 56–57, 95
Greek historians 10
Persian 167, 169, 180

Xenophon 10, *140*, 140–41, 178, 194, 195
Xerxes I *20*, 21, 117, 138–40, 168, *168*, 174, 180
and Battle of Salamis 117, 158, 161, 168, 174, 209
Indian troops 234
naval logistics 207
size of army 173, 182
standard of 177, 20
in timeline context 13, 31, 119, 170–71